ANCIENT INDIAN TRADITION & MYTHOLOGY

Translated by

A BOARD OF SCHOLARS

Edited by

G.P. Bhatt

VOLUME 31

ANCIENT INDIAN TRADITION AND MYTHOLOGY

Mahāpurāṇas *Translated into English*

Gen. Ed. Dr. G.C. Tripathi

Founder Eds. Late J.L. Shastri and Late G.P. Bhatt

PUBLISHED VOLUMES

Vols. 1-4	ŚIVA PURĀṆA *Tr.* J.L. Shastri
Vols. 5-6	LIṄGA PURĀṆA *Tr.* J.L. Shastri
Vols. 7-11	BHĀGAVATA PURĀṆA *Tr.* G.V. Tagare
Vols. 12-14	GARUḌA PURĀṆA *Tr.* J.L. Shastri
Vols. 15-19	NĀRADA PURĀṆA *Tr.* G.V. Tagare
Vols. 20-21	KŪRMA PURĀṆA *Tr.* G.V. Tagare
Vols. 22-26	BRAHMĀṆḌA PURĀṆA *Tr.* G.V. Tagare
Vols. 27-30	AGNI PURĀṆA *Tr.* N. Gangadharan
Vols. 31-32	VARĀHA PURĀṆA *Tr.* S. Venkitasubramonia Iyer
Vols. 33-36	BRAHMA PURĀṆA *Tr.* J.L. Shastri
Vols. 37-38	VĀYU PURĀṆA *Tr.* G.V. Tagare
Vols. 39-48	PADMA PURĀṆA *Tr.* N.A. Deshpande
Vols. 49-71	SKANDA PURĀṆA *Ed.* G.P. Bhatt, *Tr. & Annot.* Shridhar Balooni & Pratosh Panda
Vols. 72-73	VĀMANA PURĀṆA *Tr. & Annot.* R.S. Shiva Ganesha Murthy
Vols. 74-76	GAṆEŚA PURĀṆA *Tr. & Annot.* Greg Bailey
Vols. 77-82	BRAHMAVAIVARTA PURĀṆA *Tr. & Annot.* G.P. Bhatt

PURĀṆAS UNDER PREPARATION

Viṣṇu Purāṇa • Harivaṃśa Purāṇa • Bhaviṣya Purāṇa • Matsya Purāṇa • Devī Bhāgavata Purāṇa • Kālika Purāṇa • Mārkaṇḍeya Purāṇa • Viṣṇudharmottara Purāṇa

THE VARĀHA PURĀṆA

Part- I

Translated and annotated by

S. VENKITASUBRAMONIA IYER

MOTILAL BANARSIDASS PUBLISHERS
PRIVATE LIMITED • DELHI

2nd Reprint : Delhi, 2017
First Edition: Delhi, 1985

ISBN: 978-81-208-0361-9

MOTILAL BANARSIDASS
41 U.A. Bungalow Road, Jawahar Nagar, Delhi 110 007
8 Mahalaxmi Chamber, 22 Bhulabhai Desai Road, Mumbai 400 026
120 Royapettah High Road, Mylapore, Chennai 600 004
236, 9th Main III Block, Jayanagar, Bengaluru 560 011
8 Camac Street, Kolkata 700 017
Ashok Rajpath, Patna 800 004
Chowk, Varanasi 221 001

UNESCO COLLECTION OF REPRESENTATIVE WORKS—*Indian Series*
This book has been accepted in the Indian Translation Series of the UNESCO Collection of Representative Works, jointly sponsored by the United Nations Educational, Scientific and Cultural Organization (UNESCO) and the Government of India

MLBD Cataloging-in-Publication Data
The Varaha Purana (Part I)
Translation and Annotated by
S. Venkitasubramonia Iyer
Includes Notes
ISBN: 978-81-208-0361-9
I. Hinduism II. Purana III. Varaha
IV. Iyer, S. Venkitasubramonia

Printed in India

by RP Jain at NAB Printing Unit,
A-44, Naraina Industrial Area, Phase I, New Delhi–110028
and published by JP Jain for Motilal Banarsidass Publishers (P) Ltd,
41 U.A. Bungalow Road, Jawahar Nagar, Delhi-110007

PUBLISHER'S NOTE

The Purest gems lie hidden in the bottom of the ocean or in the depth of rocks. One has to dive into the ocean or delve into the rocks to find them out. Similarly, truth lies concealed in the language which with the passage of time has become obsolete. Man has to learn that language before he discovers that truth.

But he has neither the means nor the leisure to embark on that course. We have, therefore, planned to help him acquire knowledge by an easier course. We have started the series of Ancient Indian Tradition and Mythology in English Translation. Our goal is to universalize knowledge through the most popular international medium of expression. The publication of the Purāṇas in English Translation is a step towards that goal.

PREFACE

The present Volume contains the *Varāha Purāṇa* Part I (Chapters 1-136) *in English Translation.* This is the thirtyfirst volume in the Series on *Ancient Indian Tradition and Mythology.*

The project of the series was planned in 1970 by Lala Sundar Lal Jain of Messrs Motilal Banarsidass, with the purpose to universalize knowledge through the most popular international medium, viz. English. Hitherto, the English translations of eight Purāṇas, namely Śiva, Liṅga, Bhāgavata, Garuḍa, Nārada, Kūrma, Brahmāṇḍa and Agni have been published and released for sale.

In this scheme, the Old Sanskrit Texts of the Purāṇas as printed by the *Veṅkaṭeśvara Press and published by Khemarāja Śrikṛṣṇadass* have been rendered into English. Translation is neither too literal nor too free. Care has been taken to maintain balance between the two extremes. The spirit of the Original Sanskrit text has been preserved in translation without violating the idiom of English language.

The Purāṇas are classified as Vaiṣṇava, Brāhma, or Śaiva according to the degree of quality, sattva, rajas or tamas which they possess in prominence. Judged by this standard the present Purāṇa belongs to the Viṣṇuite class. Majority of the verses relate to Viṣṇuite rituals, stotras or anecdotes. The Purāṇa eulogizes the ten incarnations of Viṣṇu and proclaims that a devotee attains identity with the lord by reciting and listening to his praise. A number of chapters describe the initiation of devotees to Viṣṇuite order. The Purāṇa prescribes initiation not only for the Brāhmaṇas but also for the Kṣatriyas, Vaiśyas and Śūdras.

The Purāṇa records a number of religious vows which a devotee should observe at certain holy places for attaining his desire. Mention may be made in this context of Dvādaśī Vrata observed on the twelfth day of the bright fortnight of each month of the year, the ritual being related to the ten incarnations of Viṣṇu, Padmanābha being the eleventh and Dharaṇi (Earth) the twelfth. The Purāṇa contains a number of hymns in praise of Viṣṇu, addressed to his specific forms, under particular names such as Matsya, Varāha and Kūrma. There is a hymn in prose called Brahmapāramaya stotra which was uttered by the Aśvins in praise of Viṣṇu.

Though predominantly Viṣṇuite in character, the Purāṇa talks highly of lord Śiva, discribing his origin, exploits, the destruction of Dakṣa's sacrifice in particular. The Purāṇa is emphatic about the identity of Trinity, a single entity assuming manifold forms such as Viṣṇu, Brahmā, Śiva and others.

Beside the worship of Trinity we find the cult of Mother Goddesses as the distinct feature of this work. These Mothers are allied to Śiva and their origin is traced to the fury of Śiva, the purpose being the destruction of asuras.

In the miscellany of topics we can include the glory and greatness of holy centres, gifts of cows, enumration of sins and their expiation, causes of sufferings in hell and of enjoyment in heaven. Finally this Part describes Śrāddhakalpa (the institution of obsequial rites and rituals).

ACKNOWLEDGEMENT OF OBLIGATIONS

It is our pleasant duty to put on record our sincere thanks to Dr. R. N. Dandekar and the UNESCO authorities for their kind encouragement and valuable help which render this work more useful than it would otherwise have been. We are extremely grateful to Dr. S. Venkitasubramonia Iyer, Professor of Sanskrit (Retired), University of Kerala, for his critical Introduction, lucid translation and useful notes. We also thank those persons who have offered suggestions for improving the same.

—*Editor*

CONTENTS

PART I

ABBREVIATIONS

Common and self-evident abbreviations such as Ch(s)-Chapter(s), p—page, pp—pages, V—Verse, VV—Verses, Ftn—footnote, Hist. Ind. Philo—History of Indian Philosophy are not included in this list.

ABORI	*Annals of the Bhandarkar Oriental Research Institute*, Poona
AGP	S. M. Ali's *The Geography of Purāṇas*, PPH, New Delhi, 1973
AIHT	*Ancient Indian Historical Tradition*, F. E. Pargiter, Motilal Banarsidass (MLBD), Delhi
AITM	*Ancient Indian Tradition and Mythology* Series MLBD, Delhi
AP	*Agni Purāṇa*, Guru Mandal Edition (GM), Calcutta, 1957
Arch.S.Rep.	Archaeological Survey Report
AV	*Atharva Veda*, Svādhyāya Mandal, Aundh
Bd. P.	*Brahmāṇḍa Purāṇa*, (MLBD), Delhi 1973
BG	*Bhagavadgītā*
Bh. P.	*Bhāgavata Purāṇa*, Bhagavat Vidyapeeth, Ahmedabad
Br.	*Brāhmaṇa* (preceded by name such as Śatapatha
BS. P.	*Bhaviṣya Purāṇa*, Vishnu Shastri Bapat, Wai
BV. P.	*Brahma Vaivarta Purāṇa*, GM, 1955-57
CC.	*Caturvarga Cintāmaṇi* by Hemādri
CVS	*Caraṇa Vyūha Sūtra* by Śaunaka; Com. by Mahidāsa
DB	*Devī Bhāgavata*, GM, 1960-61
De or GDAMI.	*The Geographical Dictionary of Ancient and Mediaeval India*, N. L. De, Orienta Reprint, Delhi, 1971
Dh. S.	*Dharma Sūtra* (preceded by the author's name such as Gautama)
ERE	*Encyclopaedia of Religion and Ethics*—Hastings.
GP	*Garuḍa Purāṇa* Ed. R. S. Bhattacharya Chowkhamba, Varanasi, 1964

GS	*Gṛhya Sūtra* (preceded by the name of the author such as Āpastamba)
HD	*History of Dharma Śāstra*, P. V. Kane, G. O. S.
IA	*The Indian Antiquary*
IHQ	*The Indian Historical Quarterly*
JP	*Purāṇa* (Journal of the Kashiraj Trust) Varanasi
KA	*Kauṭilya Arthaśāstra*
KP	*Kūrma Purāṇa*, Veṅkaṭeśvara Press Edt. Bombay, also Kashiraj Trust Edt., Varanasi 1971
LP	*Liṅga Purāṇa*, GM, 1960; also MLBD, Delhi, 1981
Manu.	*Manusmṛti*
Mbh.	*Mahābhārata*, Gītā Press, Gorakhpur, VS 2014
MkP	*Mārkaṇḍeya Purāṇa*
MN	*Mahābhārata Nāmānukramaṇī*, Gītā Press Gorakhpur, VS 2016
MtP.	*Matsya Purāṇa*, GM, 1954
MW	*Monier Williams Sk. English Dictionary* MLBD, Delhi, 1976
NP.	*Nāradīya or Nārada Purāṇa*, Veṅkaṭeśvar Press, Bombay
PCK	*Bhāratavarṣīya Prācīna Caritrakośa*, Siddheshwar Shastri, Poona, 1968
Pd. P.	*Padma Purāṇa*, GM, 1957-59
PE	*Puranic Encyclopaedia*, V. Mani, English, MLBD, Delhi, 1975
PR or PRHRC	*Puranic Records on Hindu Rites and Customs* R. C. Hazra, Calcutta, 1948
ṚV	*Ṛg-Veda*, Svādhyāya Mandal, Aundh
Śat. Br.	*Śatapatha Brāhmaṇa*
SC or SMC	*Smṛti Candrikā*—Devanna Bhaṭṭa
SEP	*Studies in Epics and Purāṇas*, A.D. Pusalkar Bharatiya Vidya Bhavan (BVB), Bombay

INTRODUCTION

The *Varāhapurāṇa* is an old Purāṇa considered as a major Purāṇa (*mahāpurāṇa*) in the accounts given in the Purāṇas themselves. But although it states in an early chapter the five general characteristics of a Purāṇa (*pañcalakṣaṇa*), it itself does not contain all these, a feature which it shares with several other Purāṇas. It, of course, contains an account of the first two, namely primary creation and secondary creation (*sarga* and *pratisarga*), but contains very little of the others (*vaṁśa*, *manvantara* and *vaṁśānucarita*). It is full of religious and theological matters and glorification of the gods, mainly Viṣṇu, and of the holy tīrthas and rules for the observance of various vows. Nevertheless, it is an old Purāṇa in its essential parts, though, as in most other works of a like nature, there are many portions added to it from time to time as is evident from the repetitions, inconsistencies and what would normally appear to be irrelevant matter in some contexts. Its date must be early and Wilson's assigning it to the 12th centuary A.D., is arbitrary and unjustified. The earlier parts may not be later than 1oth century as pointed out by P. V. Kane and accepted by scholars like R. C. Hazra, who, however, considers some interpolations to be possibly as late as the 15th century. The work is presented here in an English translation, which is neither too literal nor too free, of the text published by the Venkateswar Press, Bombay, with the most essential corrections. It may be noted that although the work is traditionally believed to contain 24,000 ślokas, the text available now contains only a little over 10,000 ślokas.

The Purāṇa is in the form of a conversation between Varāha, the Boar-incarnation of Lord Viṣṇu, and Dharaṇī, the Earth held up by him in his tusk, as given by Sūta, the mythological narrator. The whole discourse is in reply to Earth's questions to the Lord seeking enlightenment as to the creation, sustenance and destruction of the world and what would constitute righteous conduct and virtuous actions for happiness in life and ultimate liberation from worldly existence.

We may make a rapid survey of the Purāṇa dividing it into convenient sections and noting the most essential things in each.

1. *Chs.* 1-8. This is of a preliminary nature. Earth puts her questions to the Lord who reveals to her his universal form. We find the account of primary creation from Vyoma through the Pradhāna and the three guṇas, Sattva, Rajas and Tamas, to Brahmā, the origin of Rudra, Prajāpati and Svāyambhuvamanu, Rudra's form constituted of man in one half and woman in the other, the division of the male part into eleven and further development of creation from Svāyambhuvamanu. Nārada's narration to Priyavrata, son of Svāyambhuvamanu, of his previous life and his meeting goddess Sāvitrī is interposed. The story of king Aśvaśiras whom the sages Kapila and Jaigīṣavya convince of the omniscience and omnipresence of Viṣṇu and the need to do one's duty for spiritual knowledge and liberation and the king finally getting dissolved in the Lord, follows. We may note that although the chief emphasis of this Purāṇa is on devotion, here we find the stress on *jñāna* as the ultimate means for *mukti*.

King Vasu practising penance and obtaining liberation by reciting the Puṇḍarīkākṣapāra hymn, sage Raibhya performing penance at Gayā and getting liberation by uttering the Gadādhara stotra, the ghost of a Brahmin unwittingly killed by king Vasu becoming a hunter by name Dharmavyādha merging in the lord by his praise of him, are narrated to illustrate the efficacy of penance and prayer. The Dharmavyādha, it is stated begot daughter and gave her in marriage to the son of the Brahmin, sage Mataṅga, but afterwards she was illtreated by her mother-in-law particularly referring to her father being a meat-eating hunter, and, indignant at this, the Vyādha made Mataṅga admit that while he, as a hunter, was killing only one animal a day for food, the sage who prides at his being a vegetarian, is actually destroying numerous potential forms of life contained in the grains he cooks and eats. We may note two things in this story, one, the free and formal intermarriage between a Brahmin and a lower caste and the other a defence of non-vegetarianism.

2. *Chs.* 9-17. This continues the account of creation. Lord Nārāyaṇa creates Umā and the syllable 'Om' identified with Śiva, out of which latter arise the seven worlds Bhū etc, the sun, the moon, fire, people of the four castes, Yakṣas, Rākṣasas and Devas and day and night. The Vedas hide themselves in water, but the Lord, assuming the form of a huge fish, recovers them from the water when extolled.

Durjaya, son of Supratīka, conquers all the worlds including Indra's, but on the way chances to enter the hermitage of sage Gauramukha who offers him and his army great hospitality with the help of a miraculous gem given by Viṣṇu. Wishing to get possession of the gem for himself but unable to do it, Durjaya enters into a fight but his army is defeated by the army that arises from the gem, and Viṣṇu appears there and kills the king and his men by his disc. Distressed at the death of the son, Supratīka extols Viṣṇu as Rāma (the delighter) and attains merger in him.

In answer to a further question about Gauramukha by Earth, Varāha narrates a conversation between that sage and Mārkaṇḍeya in the course of which details relating to śrāddha (propitiation of manes by libation) are given, such as the kinds of manes, the different ways of performing the ceremony according to means, the nature of those who are fit to be invited for it and of those who are unfit, the occasions for its performance, the number of persons to be invited and the form of the different rituals. Gauramukha utters a hymn of Viṣṇu extolling the ten incarnations as a result of which the Lord appears before him and he becomes merged in him.

Sage Mahātapas tells king Prajāpāla how worship of Viṣṇu leads to liberation and narrates the story of the different Devatās residing in the body of the cosmic egg, Hiraṇyagarbha, like Agni, Aśvins, Gaurī and others each feeling that without itself the body will not function and leaving it one after another, but finding Hiraṇyagarbha unaffected being protected by the Supreme Person in his form as the moon (Soma), praise him seeking his favour and the Lord allots them their positions and names and gives them each a form in the world of gods and a formless state in the beings on earth.

3. *Chs.* 18-38. Here the circumstances under which the subtle Kṣetradevatās (the deities in the body) assumed concrete forms are given in the order Agni, Aśvins, Gaurī, Vināyaka, Nāgas, Skanda, Āditya, Durgā, Diks, Kubera, Viṣṇu, Dharma, Rudra, Pitṛs and Soma, as also the significance of the different names and the day in each fortnight important for their worship, starting with Prathamā for Agni and ending with Amāvāsyā for Pitṛs and Paurṇamī for Soma. Much that is seen in chapter 12 is repeated in chapter 33 which is introduced as 'another account of the first appearance of Rudra'. There are variations

in some of the popular stories here. For example, Śiva appears before Pārvatī not as a Brahmacārin but as an old man who creates an illusory shark to catch hold of him and requests Pārvatī to save him by lifting him up by holding his hand. In the praise of Skanda by the gods, many terms are with reference to what he was yet to accomplish, but this is explained as due to their knowing already what he would do later. Vināyaka was created by Rudra out of his laughter and in his own form, but changed into a being with elephant-face and protruding belly at the passionate look of Umā on him. Viṣṇu is a form of Lord Nārāyaṇa created by himself for the protection of the world.

Mahātapas gives the names of the fifteen kings born out of the gem of Gauramukha when they would be born in Tretāyuga, pointing out to Prajāpāla that he himself is one of them, Suprabha, reborn. Then, Prajāpāla praises Viṣṇu as Kṛṣṇa and merges in him. King Dīrghabāhu, cursed to become a tiger for his disrespect to Brahmins, gets redemption by accidentally hearing the name of the Lord. This illustrates the efficacy of the Lord's name even when unintentionally uttered and reminds us of the more familiar story of Ajāmila narrated in the Śrīmadbhāgavata. A hunter pleases sage Durvāsas by the wonderful hospitality he extends to him as a result of his devotion to his preceptor, and gets renamed as Satyatapas and the Vedas and Śāstras dawn upon him, thereby showing that it is devotion not birth, that makes one eligible for spiritual elevation.

4. *Chs*. 39-50. This is devoted to the details of the Dvādaśīvrata with the variations and the benefits accruing therefrom, one in each month starting from Mārgaśīrṣa and ending in Āśvayuja, respectively for the ten avatāras of Viṣṇu beginning with Matsya, the ninth being Buddha and the last one being Padmanābha. For the month of Kārttika the Dvādaśīvrata is called dharaṇīvrata, since Viṣṇu was worshipped on that day by Earth for raising her from the water.

5. *Chs*. 51-67. An account is given of various Vratas for attaining various things like health, wealth, progeny, peace, regaining lost possessions etc, and the Pāñcarātra system of the Vaiṣṇavas is claimed as equal to the Vaidika. The first two chapters in the section, given as Agastyagītā is an allegory on liberation and evolution on the basis of Sāṅkhya philosophy and the

last chapter is another allegory on day and night, months, seasons and year.

6. *Chs*. 68-73. Illicit sexual association and the atonement therefor are discussed in the first chapter in this section and a wonderful experience of sage Nārada in the next. The following three chapters speak of the identity of Viṣṇu, Śiva and Brahmā as given by Rudra, and a hymn on Viṣṇu uttered by him occurs in the last.

7. *Chs*. 74-89. This deals with cosmology with the earth as the central point and the seven islands, Jambū, Śaka, Kuśa, Krauñca, Śālmalī, Gomeda and Puṣkara with their mountains, rivers, valleys, lakes, trees, gods and denizens. Mount Meru and the continent Bhārata are given special importance.

8. *Chs*. 90-98. The subject of this section is the Triple Power, the goddess unifying in herself the energies of Viṣṇu, Brahmā and Śiva, born at their looks at one another, and this goddess triplicating herself as the white Brāhmī, the red Vaiṣṇavī and the black Raudrī and performing their respective functions in the universe. We get here the concept of the triple energy of the later Tāntric system though not in its details. We also find that, against the popular story, it is Vaiṣṇavī who kills Mahiṣāsura after assuming a fierce form with twenty hands, and not Raudrī. Raudrī gets the name Cāmuṇḍā for killing Ruru, and not for killing Caṇḍa and Muṇḍa.

Then is given an account of a Vrata for Rudra as Kapālin, and the mokṣa of Satyatapas by his unflinching truth and dharma.

9. *Chs*. 99-113. We get here the glorification of the gift of images of cows with gold and gems, together with special objects like sesamum water, sugarcane juice, sugarcandy, honey, milk, curd, butter, salt, cloth, grain etc, each separately and on separate occasions to worthy Brahmins. The deity propitiated by these is not Viṣṇu in all; it is Rudra in some and Pārvatī in one. The special value of the gift of parturient cow is stated, as also the importance of the Kapilā variety.

The last chapter is a hymn on Viṣṇu by Earth praying for lifting her up from sinking in the ocean.

10. *Chs*. 114-121. This constitutes a series of questions by Earth to Varāha on the nature of ritualistic worship and the merits accruing therefrom and the reply stating the rules of obser-

vance, lists of meritorious and unmeritorious actions, the well known thirtytwo major offences in worship, the rituals of idol worship and of the quarters during morning, noon and evening. It comprises numerous moral precepts for a virtuous and pious life. Purity, sincerity, piety and generosity are stressed. Many of the Smṛtis are mentioned here and every one is advised to follow whichever suits his faith.

11. *Chs.* 122-126. The first and last chapters here are in glorification of two tīrthas Kokāmukha and Kubjāmra where death of even minor creatures on Dvādaśī day is declared to be giving them birth as human beings and illustrated by stories. In the intervening chapters the materials for worship and the variations in this matter in the different seasons are given. There is also an account of the *māyā* of Viṣṇu and how everything in the world is carried on by its power.

12. *Chs.* 127-136. Initiation of the devotee and the expiations for offences form the subject of this section. The initiation into Bhāgavatadharma of the devotees with the variations in the details of the rituals for the four different castes and the objects to be offered are described. The importance of the Guru is stressed, who alone can do the initiation. The role of the rosary in meditation is given, as also the desirability of copper vessels in worship. The mode of ritualistic worship is further elaborated in the last chapter.

13. *Chs.* 137-151. The glorification of Tīrthas is continued here. We get an account of great tīrthas, the various holy spots in them, the merit associated with each, the wonders perceptible in many of them and several stories in illustration of their efficacy. The greatness of Saukara, particularly its Somatīrtha, where a jackal became a princess, a vulture a prince and a wagtail an opulent trader, all by mere death there is pointed out. The holy spots in Kokāmukha are recounted, followed by those in Badarī. Tīrthas like Mandāra, Someśvara, Muktikṣetra, Triveṇī in the river Gaṇḍakī, and holy places like Sālagrāmakṣetra, Rurukṣetra, Harikṣetra, Goniṣkramaṇa, Stutasvāmi, Dvārakā, Sānandūra and Lohārgala are then described with emphasis on the Dvādaśīvrata in many of them and connected incidents.

Two intervening chapters are on the value of Lord's service. The importance of service through music keeping awake on

Dvādaśī day is highlighted by the story of an outcaste being able to liberate the ghost of a Brahmin by transferring to him a bit of his merit so acquired. The rules relating to women devotees during the menstrual period are also incidentally given.

We are told of Viṣṇu seeking boon from Śiva at Muktikṣetra, Śiva incurring a curse from Prajāpati Aurva for destroying his hermitage and sage Sālaṅkāyana getting as his son Nandikeśvara, a form of Śiva. We find two brothers quarrelling over a share turned into an elephant and a crocodile and getting redemption by Viṣṇu's disc, which reminds us of the more popular story of king Indradyumna and his curse. Lohārgala, about which information elsewhere is practically absent, is stated to be situated in a place difficult of access amidst settlements of Mlecchas.

14. *Chs.* 152-180. This is the longest section in the Purāṇa and is on the glory of the city of Mathurā and the numerous tīrthas in and around it, the various gardens, deities and so on with the wonders in each, the benefits they confer, the days particularly sacred in each etc. Mathurā is declared as superior to all other holy spots including Prayāga and Vārāṇasī and the people there to be Viṣṇu himself unstained by the faults they may be having and the sins they may be comitting and as deserving of the respect of all and gifts from them, a statement which seems to be indicative of the possible origin of this Purāṇa or, at least, this bulky part of it, in this region. Its association with the deeds of Kṛṣṇa is naturally highlighted. The efficacy of pleasing the Lord by fast and dance on Ekādaśī day is brought out by the story of a dancing devotee redeeming a Brahmarākṣasa narrated in terms identical with the one stated earlier of an outcaste doing a similar deed by the transfer of the merit of his service by song. The significance of social service by planting trees, digging wells, laying gardens and renovating ruins is brought out in the long story of the merchant Gokarṇa. The list of offences in worship is repeated with the means of atonement, only to say that for all this, fasting and bathing in Mathurā is a good substitute. We also get the story of a servant maid made to release her manes by śrāddha, and also what actions lead to ghosthood and what protection from it.

15. *Chs.* 181-186. This deals with the consecration, and rules of worship of idols made of wood, stone, clay, copper, bronze, silver and gold and also about the worship of Sālagrāma

stones. Worship of idols is sanctioned for all castes but not of Sālagrāma.

16. *Chs*. 187-192. The details of śrāddha constitute the subject of this section. The origin of śrāddha, its significance, the place and time of performance, persons eligible as well as those ineligible to be fed in śrāddha, the various rituals etc, are all elaborately given. There is emphatic prohibition against a bestard being fed in this ceremony even unknowingly. The nature of *madhuparka* preparation and its administration are also given in two chapters.

17. *Chs*. 193-212. This is a separate section quite unconnected with the rest narrated by Vaiśampāyana about the world of Yama as seen by Naciketas who goes there at an angry uttarance of his father Uddālaka, but returns to give a description of it. The Naciketas here is not one whom we are familiar with in the Upaniṣad discoursing with Yama on the nature of the soul and ultimately gaining from him *ātmavidyā*. According to his account, Yama's is a splendid world full of enjoyment for the good souls that go there, but also having numerous fearful hells full of torment for the bad. It contains a hall of justice with the well known lawgivers like Manu, Bṛhaspati, Āpastamba and Aṅgiras as the jury. The supremely virtuous souls bypass Yama but the sinners are never spared and his lieutenant Citragupta is asked to deal with them as they deserve. In the course of a discussion of Yama with Nārada, righteous and unrighteous deeds are enumerated, generosity is praised and the power of chastity illustrated. It is interesting to note that this section contains an incident of Citragupta's men getting fed up with their duty of executing punishments, their fight with the demons called Mandehas who are sent to subdue them by Citragupta and finally a settlement being reached by the intervention of Śiva in the form of a Jvara. This has some similarity with the demands of modern workmen, their strike and settlement and reconciliation.

18. *Chs*. 213-218. This, the last section, deals with the greatness of Śiva as Gokarṇeśvara, Śṛṅgeśvara and Śaileśvara where his single horn in the form of a deer was taken out into three pieces and installed respectively by Indra, Viṣṇu and Brahmā. It is noteworthy here that this Purāṇa which is predominantly Vaiṣṇavite in nature concludes with an account of the greatness of Śiva.

The penultimate chapter states the benefits of the recitation of this Purāṇa and the last one gives its contents from beginning to end as it is available now, and is, in all probability, a later addition.

In addition to what we have incidentally seen as worthy of special notice in the brief survey made above, there are certain other matters in this Purāṇa which deserve attention and we may now look into some of them.

We come across the tīrtha Lohārgala which it is hazardous to reach although powerful to remove sins. There is another one mentioned, Stutasvāmi, which also we do not come across in other Purāṇas. The identity of these two is not known now. Both these relate to Viṣṇu and occur in the portions of the work which are considered as its early and original parts.

Numerous Vratas are mentioned mainly meant to propitiate Viṣṇu but not infrequently to propitiate Śiva, Pārvatī and others with fasting, prayer, worship and gifts, and each is taken as capable of dissolving sins, sometimes of many generations in his family and many of them also confer special benefits like health, wealth, wife and progeny. But performance of Vratas without any desire is also recommended:

niṣkāma evaṁ vratam asya kṛtvā
naśyanti pāpāni ca tasya puṁsaḥ (45.10)

what we get more emphatically propounded in the Bhagavadgītā.

Many mantras are prescribed for ritualistic worship in several Vratas, but all are Purāṇic and not drawn from the Vedas and, in some cases, they are not fully intelligible.

Although this Purāṇa is primarily meant to extol Viṣṇu, glorifying his achievements and inculcating steadfast devotion for him, it is not biased that way. Devotion for Viṣṇu is only preferential and not exclusive to that of others like Śiva and Śakti. It aims at harmony and cordiality among worshippers of different gods. True that a fighting between Viṣṇu and Śiva stopped by Brahmā is mentioned in one place (21.53) and people devoted to gods other than Viṣṇu are spoken of as doing so under delusion in another (117.45), but passages proclaiming the identity between Viṣṇu and Śiva are numerous, as for instance:

-yeyam mūrtirbhagavataḥ
śaṅkaraḥ sa svayaṁ hariḥ / (9.7),

yo hariḥ sa trilocanaḥ / (58.4), and
na bhedaścāvayordeva ekabhāvāvubhāvapi/ (73.40)

and anyone who draws a distinction between the two, it is stated, goes to ruin.

māṁ viṣṇorvyatiriktaṁ ye brahmaṇaśca dvijottama /
bhajante pāpakarmāṇaste yānti narakaṁ narāḥ // (70.40)
Rudra declares Nārāyaṇa to be supreme god,
nārāyaṇaḥ paro devaḥ sarvarūpo janārdanaḥ (70.14)

and Viṣṇu observes that he and Śiva remain together and worship of the one is the worship of the other too.

ahaṁ yatra Śivastatra Śivo yatra vasundhare /
tatrāham api tiṣṭhāmi āvayornāntaraṁ kvacit //
Śivaṁ yo vandate bhūme sa hi māṁ eva vandate /
labhate puṣkalāṁ siddhim evaṁ yo vetti tattvataḥ // (145. 108-9)

However, a Śaiva becoming a Vaiṣṇava is instanced by Rāvaṇa who does so when Varāha tells him that, being a Rākṣasa he cannot have the sort of devotion required for achieving his aim. (163. 29-47.)

Śakti is spoken of as the triple power, representing the energies of Viṣṇu, Śiva and Brahmā and is extolled in a series of chapters (90-96). In Śauryavrata the devatā to be worshipped is Durgā. We also get worship of Yantras or mystic diagrams, as in Dharaṇīvrata in which Viṣṇu is to be invoked in a sixteen-petalled lotus and as Yogīśvara.

kuryācca vaiṣṇavaṁ yajñaṁ yajed yogiśvaraṁ harim /
ṣoḍaśāre tathā cakre yogibhir bahubhiḥ kṛte // (50.14)

The Pāñçarātra system of Vaiṣṇava theology is eulogised and its follower is spoken of as superior to all others, a statement which bears testimony to its wide popularity. In the Dharaṇivrata the gift of the image to a Pāñcarātra Ācārya is pronounced to be a thousand times more meritorious than to others.

ācārye pāñcarātrāṇām sahasraguṇitam bhavet. (50.18)

Although the food offered in worship is generally grains, vegetables and fruit, the flesh of some animals like the deer, goat and hare and some birds like lāvaka, vārttika and kapiñjala is permitted, probably indicating a primitive practice.

mārgamāṁsaṁ varaṁ chāgaṁ cāṣaṁ samanuyujyate |
etā hi prāpaṇe dadyānmama caitat priyāvaham ||
pakṣiṇām ca pravakṣyāmi ye prayojyā vasundhare |
ye caiva mama kṣetreṣu upayuñjanti nityaśaḥ ||
lāvakaṁ vārttikaṁ caiva praśastaṁ ca kapiñjalam| (119.12,16-17)

In the preparation of offering Madhuparka also, flesh is used (114.27).

Social service is laid down as an important function of the devotee. The value of planting trees, digging wells etc, is stressed. *Iṣṭāpūrta* is important for dharma. Heaven is acquired by *iṣṭa* or sacrifices and liberation by *pūrta* or service to humanity. The provision of trees, gardens etc, and renovation of wells, ponds, parks and temples gain the benefit of pūrta.

iṣṭāpūrtaṁ dvijātīnām prathamaṁ dharmasādhanam |
iṣṭena labhate svargam pūrte mokṣaṁ ca vindati ||
vāpīkūpataṭākāni devatāyatanāni ca |
patitānyuddhared yastu sa pūrtaphalam aśnute ||

bhūmidānena ye lokā godānena ca kīrtitāḥ |
te lokā prāpyate pumbhiḥ pādapānām prarohaṇe ||

aśvattham ekam picumandamekaṁ
nyagrodham ekaṁ daśapuṣpajātiḥ |
dve dve tathā dāḍimamātuluṅge
pañcāmraropī narakaṁ na yāti || (172. 36-38)

The Purāṇa abounds in stotra in praise of various deities. Naturally there is a larger number for Viṣṇu than for others. Among the hymns of Viṣṇu are those uttered by Dharaṇī (1.20-28) the last four verses being a *kavaca*, another by her (113. 18-68), praising him in his universal form, by Nārada (3.11-20), known as the Brahmapārastotra, by Aśvaśiras (5.49-57) known as Yajñamūrtistava, extolling Viṣṇu as the lord of sacrifice and as combining in himself the Trinity, by Vasu (6. 10-16) known as Puṇḍarīkākṣapārastotra, identifying Viṣṇu with the universe, by Raibhya (7. 21-40), known as Gadādharastotra, by Dharmavyādha (8.43-49), by (Waters) (9.28-33), by Gauramukha (11. 11-21) and another by the same sage (15.9-21) known as Daśāvatārastotra, by Supratīka (12. 5-16) praising Viṣṇu as Rāma (the delighter), by Kṣetradevatās (17. 59-63), by Prajāpāla (36. 12-122) praising Viṣṇu as Kṛṣṇa, the lord supreme, by Dṛḍhavrata (55. 33-43), by Rudra (73. 18-38) and by Rāvaṇa (163. 34-37). Among the hymns to Śiva are those by Devas (21. 68-75; 25. 17-28; 33. 16-24, the last being practically a repetition of the first), by Soma (114. 20-28) and by Nandin (213. 43-49). There is a stotra each for several others, like the one for Brahmā by the Aśvins (20. 27-30), for Vināyaka by Devas (23. 33-34), for Skanda by Devas (25. 40-42), for Āditya by Devas (26. 10-14), for Durgā by Śiva (28. 29-35), for Sarasvatī by Brahmā (91. 9-16), for Vaiṣṇavī in the form as Mahiṣāsuramardinī by Devas (95. 58-66), for Yama by Naciketas (198. 9-20) and for the Dharmadevatā by Devas (32. 20-25).

Buddha is given as an avatāra of Visṇu even in an early chapter (3.2) and more explicitly later:

nṛsiṁha vāmana namo jamadagni nāma
daśāsyagotrāntaka vāsudeva /
namo'stu te buddha kalkin vareśa
Śambho namaste vibudhārināśana // (54.37)

As stated earlier, one Dvādaśī day in the year is in his propitiation and the acquisition of personal charm is its special benefit.

rūpakāmo bhajed buddham (48.22).

The importance of the preceptor in formal initiation into devotion and ritualistic worship is stressed, but strangely it is carried to the indulgent extent of permitting him to be not learned or good-natured.

avidyo vā savidyo vā gurureva janārdanaḥ /
mārgastho vāpyamārgastho gurureva parā gatiḥ // (50.20)

A devotee seeking initiation should be tested for one year as to his way of life and true eligibility.

brāhmaṇakṣatriyaviśām bhaktānāṁ tu parīkṣaṇam /
saṁvatsaraṁ guruḥ kuryāt jātiśaucakriyādibhiḥ // (99.15)

The performance of Śrāddha is given great importance and the right mental disposition, necessary money, the purity of the persons invited, the proper time, the prescribed rituals and, above all, deep devotion are laid down as the conditions for its fulfilment (13.48), but for one who has not got the means for this, though he has the mind, a mere prayer to the manes in the open with outstretched hands is a substitute and this declaration is put in the mouth of the manes themselves in what is given the title 'Pitṛgītā.'

sarvābhāve vanaṁ gatvā kakṣamūlapradarśakaḥ /
sūryādilokapālānām idam uccaiḥ paṭhiṣyati //
na me'sti vittaṁ na dhanaṁ ca nānyat
śrāddhasya yogyaṁ svapitṝn nato'smi /
tṛpyantu bhaktyā pitarau mamaitau
bhujau tatau vartmani mārutasya // (13. 56-57)

Various occasions for the Śrāddha are mentioned, including the anniversary in the tithi of the month of the death of the pitṛ, which is the most important in present day practice. Another thing not common in current practice in general, is the feeding during Śrāddha of uninvited Brahmins and particularly saints. Not only is this permitted:

prathamehni dvijaḥ kuryād viprāgryāṇāṁ nimantraṇam /
animantrya dvijān paścād āgatān bhojayed yatīn // (14.8)

but the warning is given that if a guest arriving when śrāddha is being performed is not honoured, the very ceremony may go in vain.

tasmād abhyarcayet prāptaṁ śrāddhakāle'tithiṁ budhaḥ /
śrāddhakrityāphalaṁ hanti dvijendrāpūjito'tithiḥ // (14.20)

The same liberal spirit is perceptible in social relations to some extent. We have seen a hunter approaching a saintly Brahmin requesting that his daughter's hand may be accepted by his learned son and the offer being readily accepted. We have also seen how an outcaste liberates the ghost of a Brahmin and himself attains absolute merger in the supreme. The Lord says that a pious Śūdra devoted to him and performing his duties in right earnest is more dear to him than even the sages.

śraddadhāno'tipūtātmā lobhamohavivarjitaḥ /
namaskārapriyo nityam mama cintāvyasthitaḥ sadā //
śūdraḥ karmaṇi me devi ya evam samamācaret /
tyaktvā ṛṣisahasrāṇi śūdram eva bhajāmyaham // (115. 38-39)

We have noticed in the story of Aśvaśiras the emphasis on knowledge as the means for liberation. Māyā is referred to in many places but it is more in the sense of power, at times magical power, not generally in the sense of illusion. It denotes, in the main, the potency of Viṣṇu, the miraculous power that activates the world and carries it on. Of the four kinds of mukti, namely *sālokya, sāmīpya, sārūpya* and *sāyujya*, however, the last standing for absolute merger (*laya*) in the Lord is frequently referred to (5.58; 7.41; 8.52; 12.16; 15.22; 36.10; 98.37; 105.18 etc), and in one place, in the case of Dharmavyādha, the Lord gives him a boon by which he gets merger in Brahman, the absolute.

varo visṛṣṭaśca kulasya te mayā
layastathā brahmaṇi śāśvate tava | (8.52).

Sālokya or residence in the world of the deity worshipped is guaranteed for the performers of various vratas and visitors of various tīrthas, and *sārūpya* or attainment of the form of Viṣṇu is the benefit accruing from some (see 126.233, 137.17, 147.33, 169.18 etc.), a privilege extended even to animals, birds and worms dying in Mathurā (169.34), but *sāmīpya* or nearness to the Lord is not separately mentioned, probably since it can be taken as implied in *sālokya*.

In a pertinent passage the Purāṇa observes that the mythological stories should be viewed as pertaining to two different planes, the concrete and the abstract, the concrete exemplified by the characters figuring in the stories and the abstract by the qualities in them. In the story of the Goddess vanquishing the demon Mahiṣa, she represents true knowledge and he ignorance, and it is the triumph of the right over the wrong and that is its aim.

athavā jñānaśaktiḥ sā mahiṣo'jñānamūrtimān |
ajñānaṁ jñānasādhyaṁ tu bhavatīti na saṁśayaḥ ||
mūrtipakṣe cetihāsam amūrte caikavaddhṛdi |
khyāpyate vedavākyaiśca iha sā vedavādibhiḥ || (99.6-7)

In a work like this, the aim of which is the propagation of religious ethics and illustrative stories to establish it, one need not normally expect any poetry. Still we do get a few instances of passages of poetic value, as in the description of night and the lustre of planets, couched in Vaṁśastha metre, in the hermitage of Gauramukha (11.51-61), in the description of Śiva's chariot and equipment with abstract forces and personifications (21.

33-36) and in the description of the rainy and autumn seasons (138. 65-72).

Lastly, we may see what the *Varāha purāṇa* speaks of itself. It is one of the eighteen Mahāpurāṇas and the twelfth among them as known to Vyāsa.

> *aṣṭādaśapurāṇāni veda dvaipāyano guruḥ /*
> *vārāhaṁ dvādaśam proktam.* (112. 74, 76)

It is the cream of all Śāstras.

> *Yathā ca mathyamānād vai dadhnaścoddhriyate ghṛtam /*
> *evaṁ sarveṣu śāstreṣu vārāhaṁ ghṛtasammitam //* (148.21)

The recitation of this Purāṇa in all seriousness is equivalent to the recitation of the entire lot of scripture comprising the Vedas, Purāṇas and other works.

> *dikṣitātmā punarbhūtvā vārāhaṁ śṛṇuyād yadi /*
> *tena vedapurāṇāni sarve mantrāḥ sasaṅgrahāḥ //*
> *japtāḥ syuḥ /* (99.50)

A king who worships this with his subjects for one year gets merger in Viṣṇu.

> *yathāśaktyā nṛpo grāmaiḥ pūjayed vatsaraṁ dhare /*
> *sarvapāpavinirmukto viṣṇusāyujyamāpnuyāt //*

CHAPTER ONE

Earth's Enquiry about Creation
Benedictory Prayer

1. Bowing to Nārāyaṇa, Nara the greatest Man, and goddess Sarasvatī, may Jaya be narrated.

2. Adoration to the Varāha (incarnation of God Viṣṇu) who lifts up the Earth with ease and under whose hoofs the mount Meru (the golden mountain) tinkles.

3. May the foremost God, Varāha, dispel my foes; who is Kṛṣṇa, Viṣṇu and the lord of gods; who is the enemy of the demon Kaṁsa; who killed (the demons) Mura, Naraka and Rāvaṇa (in his different incarnations); who, in his huge and extensive form, raised, like a clod of clay, by the tip of his tusk, the Earth encircled by oceans and full of mountains and rivers.

Sūta (*the Purāṇa-narrator*) said:

4. The Earth asked the Supreme god (Viṣṇu) as to when, in yore, was she lifted up with force by the mighty god in the form of the boar.

Earth said:

5. In each Kalpa (cosmic age) O Lord, it is you that raise me up. And I do not know, O Keśava (Viṣṇu), your form in the first creation.

6. Again, when the Vedas were stolen (by the demon Hayagrīva), you, in the form of a fish, entering Rasātala (the nether region) took them out and gave them to Brahmā.

7. Again, O destroyer of the demon Madhu, on the occasion of churning the milky ocean jointly by gods and demons (for obtaining the divine nectar), you, taking the form of a tortoise, raised up the mountain Mandara (which formed the central churning rod).

8. O illustrious lord of the worlds, you, again, with one of your tusks lifted up me, the Earth, from the deep ocean when I was sinking down to the nether regions.

9. Still again, by you (in your incarnation as Nṛsiṁha ('man-lion') was destroyed (the demon) Hiraṇyakaśipu who was haughty on account of the boon (bestowed on him by God Brahmā) and who was tormenting the world.

10. Then, O God, you, (in another of your incarnations) assuming the form of (Paraśurāma, the son of (the Brāhmaṇa sage) Jamadagni, made the Earth once devoid of Kṣatriya rulers.

11. And, then, (in another of your incarnations as Rāma, son of king Daśaratha), through your kingly strength, the demon Rāvaṇa was killed by you. O illustrious God, in still another incarnation of yours in the form of Vāmana (dwarf), the demon Bali was bound by you.

12. I do not know, O God, even a small portion of your multifarious actions. (Now), after lifting (me up how do you create and why?

13. By whom is the creation destroyed, and by whom is it protected? By whom, O all-pervading one, are you attainable?

14. How does creation originate and how does it end? How are the aeons (Yugas—Kṛta, Tretā, Dvāpara and Kali) reckoned and why are there four Yugas?

15. Of them, what is the speciality of the present aeon? And, O great god, what is the desire? Who are the sacrificers? Who are the kings? Who have attained final emancipation?

16. Be pleased to tell me all this briefly. Being asked thus, the great God in the form of the boar laughed.

17-18. In the belly of that laughing lord, the Mother World saw the (eleven forms of God) Rudra, the several gods (Devas), the (deities called) Vasus, the groups of (semi-divine beings) Siddhas, the great sages, the seven worlds, the sun, the moon and planets and the inhabitants therein performing their duties. All this, the Earth beheld with her entire body shivering.

19. Soon after the great God was seen with his mouth opened wide, He was seen by the Earth in His four-armed form sleeping in the great (milky) ocean.

20. While seeing the God Janārdana (Viṣṇu) sleeping on the serpent-bed in the ocean, she also saw God Brahmā (seated) in the lotus-flower (that sprouted) from His navel. The goddess Earth, with folded hands, extolled Him as follows:

Earth said:

21. Obeisance to you whose eyes resemble lotus-petals, you wearing the yellow garment; obeisance to you, the supreme soul who destroys the enemies of Gods.

22. Obeisance to you sleeping on the bed of (the thousand-hooded serpent) Śeṣa and bearing (your consort, goddess) Lakṣmī on your chest; obeisance to you, O God of gods, the giver of the final liberation.

23. Obeisance to you bearing the bow, sword and disc; you without birth and death; obeisance to you, from whose navel-lotus Brahmā has taken birth.

24. Obeisance to you with tender hands and rosy lips. I surrender myself to you: protect me, this innocent woman.

25. Seeing you as a boar dark like collyrium all over, O Janārdana (Viṣṇu), I was fear-stricken; and seeing the whole world in your body, I am afraid again. O preserver, now, bestow your benevolence upon me and, O great lord, protect me.

26-27. (May the twelve forms of Viṣṇu protect me. (Thus) may Keśava protect my feet, Nārāyaṇa my shanks; may Mādhava protect my hip, Govinda the genitals; may Viṣṇu protect my navel, Madhusūdana the belly; may Trivikrama protect the breast, Vāmana the heart; may Śrīdhara protect my neck, Hṛṣīkeśa my face, Padmanābha the eyes, and Dāmodara the head.

28. Thus having covered herself (as above) with the (twelve) names (of Viṣṇu), the Earth uttered, "O illustrious Viṣṇu, I bow to you", and stopped.

CHAPTER TWO

Primary Creation

Sūta (the narrator) said:

1. Then pleased by the devotion of the Earth resting in his body, Viṣṇu manifested Māyā (the power of illusion) and stood therein the same form of Varāha.

2. And he said: O lovely damsel, why this strange question ?

I shall tell you the subject of the Purāṇa from all the Śāstras (disciplines of knowledge).

3. This verse applies to all the Purāṇas. Therefore, O Earth, listen to it intently.

Varāha said:

4. Primary creation, secondary creation, genealogy, reigns of the Manus (the lords of the aeons) and history (of the solar and lunar) races—these are the five characteristic topics in a Purāṇa.

5. Now, I shall speak of the primary creation from which begins the history of gods and kings.

6. The eternal supreme soul is said to be consisting of four parts.

7. First, I was endless Vyoma (indiscrete in space). Then the principal atomic intellect came out of me. The Intellect was threefold, consisting of *Sattva*, *Rajas* and *Tamas*, each of which being added separately with the form of *Sattva*.[1]

8. As *Tamas* predominated in this trinity, there appeared what is called the Pradhāna (the originator or source Prakṛti of the material world). And out of that *Pradhāna*, the powerful Kṣetrajña (the Supreme Soul) arose. From that came out the intellect.

9. From these, next manifested the sense-organs of the world, the causes of hearing etc., with latent elements, O auspicious lady, the cosmic matter was created by me.

10. In the beginning there was only void. Then sound and ether, then air and after that fire and water, and next, O goddess, you, the mother of all beings were created by me.

11. As a result of the union of these,in the earth, appeared an egg with frothing generative fluid in the water. When the egg expanded, I assumed the form of water myself.

12. Having created water and resting therein, I (Viṣṇu) came to be called 'Nārāyaṇa'. In each Kalpa (grand aeon), I, again and again, lie on the water. And while sleeping there, a lotus flower came out of the navel, as now.

13. Then, from the navel-lotus, the four-faced (God Brahmā) came out. I ordained him to create men.

1. The verses 7 and 8 seem to be corrupt. The idea is not clear.

14. Then, I disappeared. And as he (Brahmā) stood brooding over (what I had said), he did not know what to do.

15. Then this mysteriously-born Brahmā became very angry and from that anger arose a boy.

16. The boy was crying but he was stopped by Brahmā. Then the boy demanded: 'Give me a name', and Brahmā gave him the name 'Rudra' ('the crying one').

17. O auspicious lady, he was then ordered by Brahmā: "create this world". Being unable to do that, then, he plunged into water and decided to perform penance.

13. As he sank into the water, Brahmā created another Prajāpati (Creator) out of his own right thumb.

19. And from his left thumb, he created also a wife (for the Prajāpati).

20. In her, the Prajāpati procreated Svāyambhuva Manu. Thus was given the idea of progeny by Brahmā.

Earth said:

21. Tell me in detail, O God of gods, the primary creation, and how this Brahmā (in the form of) Nārāyaṇa, came into existence at the beginning of Kalpa.

The Lord said:

22. Goddess Earth, listen to my detailed description how, as Nārāyaṇa, I created all the beings.

23. At the end of the previous Kalpa, while he was sleeping at night, O auspicious lady, as the quality of *Sattva* predominated in him, Brahmā saw the world empty.

24. Nārāyaṇa is the supreme, incomprehensible, elder even to the old, in the form of *Brahman* (the supreme soul), the great god, beginningless and present in all beings.

25. The following verse is said about Nārāyaṇa, the supreme Brahma, the source of the world and imperishable.

26. "Water is said to be *Nāra*, since it is verily the progeny of *nara* (man). As water is the repose of the Lord, He is called Nārāyaṇa."

27. While, he, in yore, in the beginning of the *Kalpas*, pondered over creation, there arose a creation beginning with ignorance and consisting of darkness.

28. From that great being, came out the five-fold ignorance consisting of *Tamas* (obscurity), *Moha* (illusion), *Mahāmoha* (extreme illusion), *Tāmisra* (gloom) and *Andhatāmisra* (utter darkness).

29. On meditating, he knew the five-fold creation. This should be understood as the *Mukhya-sarga* (principal creation) by the learned.

30. On meditating again, creation of a high character occurred, as a result of which the animal world came into being and it is known as *Tiryakasrotas* (in which the stream of life of the created beings is horizontal).

31. Cattle and other animals of that kind were straying on wrong paths. Brahmā thought that this creation, *Tiryaksrotas*, was imperfect.

32. There took place, therefore the three-fold *Ūrdhvasrotas* (in which the stream of life of the created beings tends upwards) which was of a Sāttvika type and based on virtue. From that, all the gods living in the upper world were created.

33. After making this creation, the creator found that the productions of the principal creation etc., were not competent and he continued his meditation.

34. Then the Lord meditated on the creation *Arvāksrotas* (in which the stream of life of the created beings moves downwards). In the *Arvāksrotas* the human beings were created who were quite competent.

35. They have Prakāśa (abundant light of clear knowledge, internal and external) but (the qualities of) darkness (*Tamas*) and passion (*Rajas*) predominate in them. Hence they have a lot of sorrow and are continuously engaged in action.

36-37. O beautiful lady, I have thus told you six creations. Of these, the first creation was of *Mahat* (intellect); the second was of *Tanmātrās* (subtle elements), the third was of *Vikāras* (being products evolved from the basic *Prakṛti*) which is also called *Aindriyaka*. These three creations were known as *Prākṛta* creations preceded by *Buddhi* (intellect).

38-39. The fourth one was called the *Mukhya-sarga* (principal creation). Immovable beings are principal. The fifth was called *Tiryaksrotas* wherein the animal world was created. Then the sixth one, *Ūrdhvasrotas*, creation of gods, and it was the best. The seventh was the creation of mankind (*Arvāksrotas*) and the eighth creation was *Anugraha*. That was characterised by *Sattva* (good) and *Tamas* (darkness).

40. These last five creations were called *Vaikṛta*, the first three being *Prākṛtas*. There was also a ninth creation called *Kaumāra* which was *Prākṛta* as well as *Vaikṛta*.

41. These are the nine creations of Prajāpati. *Prākṛtas* and *Vaikṛtas* are the root causes of the world. Thus the creations have been told. What else, then, do you want to know?

Earth said:

42. Out of the mysteriously-born Brahmā, nine types of creation came out. How did they multiply? Tell me this, O imperishable god!

Varāha said:

43. First Rudra and other sages were created by Brahmā. Then Sanaka and the rest and afterwards (sage) Marīci and the rest:

44. (Namely, the sages) Marīci, Atri, Aṅgiras, Pulaha, Kratu, Pulastya, great-prowessed Pracetas, Bhṛgu, Nārada and as the tenth Vasiṣṭha, performer of great penance.

45. By him (Brahmā), (sage) Sanaka and others were appointed for the functions of renunciation, and Marīci and others excepting sage Nārada, for those of action.

46. In the race of the first Prajāpati who was born from the right thumb of Brahmā, this world with all the animate and inanimate beings appeared first.

47. Gods, demons, Gandharvas, snakes and birds—all these most virtuous beings were born from Dakṣa's (Prajāpati's) daughters.

48-49. Rudra who came out of the forehead of Brahmā with his eyebrows knit in anger, was in one half of his body a man and in the other half a woman. Asking the fierce Rudra to divide himself, Brahmā disappeared.

50. When said thus, he divided himself into a man and a woman. Then the masculine part divided itself into eleven parts.

51. Then onwards the eleven Rudras became famous as originated from Brahmā.

52. I have thus told you, O sinless lady, the creation of Rud-

ras in brief. I shall now tell you briefly the greatness of the Yugas (aeons).

53. There are four Yugas, namely, *Kṛta*, *Tretā*, *Dvāpara* and *Kali*.

54. Hear from me of the noble and generous kings, gods, demons and others who performed righteous deeds in these yugas.

55-56. Long ago, in the first *Kalpa*, there lived Svāyambhuva Manu. He got two virtuous sons of super-human capacity by name Priyavrata and Uttānapāda. Among these two, king Priyavrata was a great performer of sacrifices and spiritually eminent.

57. After performing many sacrifices munificently, and placing his sons Bharata and the rest in the seven islands (namely, *Jambū*, *Plakṣa*, *Śālmali*, *Kuśa*, *Krauñca*, *Śāka* and *Puṣkara*), he went to the grand Viśālā and performed great penance.

58. While the virtuous emperor was thus doing penance, (sage) Nārada came there to see him.

59. Seeing Nārada descending from the sky like the lustrous sun, the king was delighted and stood up in respect.

60. After giving him seat and the water for washing his feet, both of them began to speak with introductory words of welcome.

61. At the end of these formalities, the king asked the seer Nārada:

Priyavrata said:

62. O illustrious Nārada, tell me a little of the wonders you have seen or heard in this Kṛtayuga.

Nārada said:

63. Listen to a wonder, O Priyavrata, seen by me. Yesterday, O King, I went to (the island of) Śvetadvīpa.

64. There was a lake with an array of full-blown lotuses and on its bank was a girl having large eyes.

65. At the sight of that lovely sweet-tongued girl, O king, I was wonder-struck and I asked her:

66. "O auspicious lady, who are you ? How are you here ? What do you want ? Tell me, O charming lady, what is to be done ?"

67-68. When asked by me thus, she looked at me intently

and stood thinking and silent. Just then I forgot all my great knowledge, all the Vedas (*Ṛk*, *Yajus* and *Sāma*), all the Śāstras (*Śikṣā*, *Kalpa*, *Nirukta*, *Chandas*, *Vyākaraṇa* and *Jyotiṣa*), Yogas (psychic disciplines) Śikṣā (physical discipline) Smṛtis (codes of conduct) and all the rest.

69-70. By merely looking at me, O king, all this was taken away by the girl within a moment. Struck with wonder and full of anxiety and sorrow, then, I went near her and begged for her kindness. As I was beholding her, O king, a divine person appeared on her body.

71. And, in the heart of that person another one appeared, and on the breast of the latter appeared another with reddish eyes and lustrous like the twelve suns.

72. Thus three men were seen on the body of that lady. At the next moment, O righteous king, only the girl was seen, and not the men.

73. Then I asked that illustrious girl: "How are my Vedas lost? Tell me, O auspicious lady, the reason for this."

The girl said:

74. "I am Sāvitrī, the mother of all the Vedas. Since you did not know me, you lost the Vedas."

75. When thus told, I asked her in wonder: "O beautiful lady, tell me who are these men".

The girl said:

76. "This beautiful one, residing in my body, with all his (six) *aṅgas*, is known as *Ṛgveda*. This Veda is Nārāyaṇa himself. Soon after its utterance, it becomes verily a fire to burn all sins.

77. He, whom you saw in his heart, is the mighty Brahmā in the form of *Yajurveda*.

78-79. He who was seen in his heart, resplendent and pure, is called *Sāmaveda*, manifested in the form of Rudra. This Veda, when recited, destroys sins like the sun.

80. These three great Vedas are, O sage, the three great gods. These are the letters beginning with 'a'. It is here, O Dvija (twice-born), all the sacrifices dwell.

81. O best of the Brahmins, I have told you all this in brief.

Now take back, O Nārada, your Vedas, Śāstras and your omniscience.

82. In this lake of the Vedas, O great Brahmin, take your bath. After this bath, O good sage, you will recollect all the things of the other births."

83. Saying this, O king, the girl disappeared. Having taken bath in that lake, I have come here to see you.

CHAPTER THREE

Birth of Nārada

Priyavrata said:

1. Tell me, O divine sage, all your doings in the other birth. I am deeply interested to know them.

Nārada said:

2. When I bathed in the lake of Vedas at the behest of Sāvitrī (the mother of Vedas), O great king, I got memory of my doings in numerous previous lives. Listen to the happenings in my past life.

3-4. In the *Kṛtayuga*, in the country named Avanti, I was born as a Brahmin by name Sārasvata, very intelligent, well-versed in the Vedas and Vedāṅgas, served by many attendants and possessing a lot of wealth.

5. Then, in solitude, I thought: "What shall I do with (material) things that are (mainly) pairs of opposites (like good and evil, cold and heat, etc.) ? So, giving all this to my sons, I shall go to the lake Sārasvata with determination to perform penance."

6. Having thought thus, I propitiated Viṣṇu with rituals, the manes with *Śrāddhas*, and the gods and men with sacrifices.

7. Then, I went to the lake Sārasvata with full resolve to perform penance.

8. Reaching there, I worshipped Viṣṇu, auspicious and primordial spirit, uttering (the sacred name) 'Nārāyaṇa' with great devotion.

9. When I recited the great hymn (by name) *Brahmapāra*, O king, the Lord was pleased and he appeared before me.

Priyavrata asked:

10. I wish to hear, O excellent sage, the nature of the (hymn) *Brahmapāra*. Be pleased to tell me this clearly, O divine sage.

Nārada replied:

11. I bow to Viṣṇu, who is higher than the highest, farther than the farthest, the most powerful, the eternal and the refuge of all.

12. I bow to the illustrious Lord Viṣṇu, the eternal, the incomparable, the ancient, the farthest, the most effulgent, the foremost among the most intelligent.

13. With pure mind I extol Nārāyaṇa, the highest, the Supreme, the important, the great refuge, pure and extensive, and the Almighty.

14. May the stainless and ancient Nārāyaṇa protect me. He who, in yore, created this *Pura* (body) namely *Prakṛti* and residing therein, has become known as *Puruṣa* (spirit).

15. I always extol Viṣṇu, the great and auspicious, of endless form, the most ancient, the foremost among the just, possessing fortitude and peace and the lord of earth.

16. I extol the great immortal god Nārāyaṇa, possessing thousand heads and numerous feet and hands, having the sun and the moon as his eyes, and sleeping in the milky ocean.

17. I bow to the immeasurable Nārāyaṇa, *Triyuga* (the creator, protector and destroyer), who can be attained by three Vedas (*Ṛk*, *Yajus* and *Sāma*), who has twentyeight forms, who stands firmly in *Triśukla* (the sacred combination of three days, namely *Uttarāyaṇa*, the day of gods; the bright-half of the moon, the day of the manes; and the day-time), who is divided into three sacred fires (*Dakṣiṇa*, *Gārhapatya* and *Āhavanīya*), who can be seen by the three qualities (*Sattva*, *Rajas* and *Tamas* and who has three eyes.

18. I bow to Viṣṇu, the ancient one, who is white in *Kṛtayuga*, red in *Tretāyuga*, yellow in *Dvāparayuga* and black in *Kaliyuga*.

19. I bow to Him who has the world as his body and who created Brahmins (the caste of priests) from his mouth, Kṣatriyas (the caste of kings) from his breast, Vaiśyas (the caste of merchants etc.) from his thighs and Śūdras (the caste of servants) from his feet.

20. I bow to the immeasurable Nārāyaṇa, the supreme entity, the highest of the highest, the lord of fighters, who took the form of Kṛṣṇa with a purpose, and who holds in the hands mace, sword and nectar".

21. Thus extolled by me the god was pleased and several times asked me in a voice majestic like the rumbling of clouds, to seek a boon. I sought the union with Him.

22. Having heard this the eternal god told me: "O Brahmin, attain the original nature. That will lead to the aim.

23. Water is *Nāra*. You give it to the manes. Therefore your name will be 'Nārada'.'

24. Saying thus, the god immediately disappeared. Then after doing penance for a long time I gave up my body and got dissolved into the *Brahmaloka* (the world of the creator) and rose there, O king.

25-26. Then the day was created along with ten sons. It is the beginning of the day of the mysteriously-born god Brahmā, no doubt, with the creation of all the gods and others. This is the creation of all the worlds by the prowess of the lord.

27. This is my previous birth, O King, about which you asked me.

28. Since by meditating on Nārāyaṇa, I attained greatness, you also, O best of kings, be a devotee of Viṣṇu.

CHAPTER FOUR

Greatness of Nārāyaṇa

Earth said:

1. Tell me whether this illustrious Nārāyaṇa, the supreme soul and the eternal, is God in all respects or not.

Varāha replied:

2-3. Matsya (fish), Kūrma (tortoise), Varāha (boar), Narasiṁha (man-lion), Vāmana (dwarf), Paraśurāma, Rām. (son of Daśaratha), Kṛṣṇa (dark-one), Buddha (enlightened) and Kalki—these ten are told as His forms, O beautiful one bearing all the beings. These are the steps for those who wish to attain the vision (of Viṣṇu).

4. Even the gods do not see His real form. Hence they satisfy themselves with the forms like mine.

5. Brahmā, the Rājasa and Tāmasa forms establish and sustain the universe.

6. O Earth, you are the first form of that God. The second is water and the third fire.

7. The fourth form is air and the fifth ether. These are His forms. With the controller of these in three aspects, the total forms are eight.

8. All this world is pervaded by Nārāyaṇa. Thus, I have told you this. What else, O goddess, do you wish to hear ?

Earth asked:

9. Be pleased to tell me, O great lord, what king Priyavrata did after having been told thus by Nārada.

Varāha replied:

10. After hearing the wonder from Nārada, Priyavrata, giving his sons you (the earth, i.e., his kingdom), divided into seven, performed penance.

11. Uttering the great *Nārāyaṇa-mantra* and his mind absorbed in it, he attained liberation.

12. Hear, O beautiful lady, again, the deeds of the great Lord for the worship by kings in olden days.

13-14. There was a righteous king named Aśvaśiras. When the saintly king performed munificently the Aśvamedha sacrifice and accompanied by Brāhmaṇas finished it with the Avabhṛtha bath, there came the great sages Kapila and Jaigīṣavya.

15. Then the king quickly stood up in great delight and welcomed them.

16. Offering them seats and showing hospitality the great king asked them who had keen intelligence and knowledge of Yoga and who had come there of their own accord.

17. "O great Brahmins, be pleased to tell me how we should worship the eternal god Viṣṇu—Nārāyaṇa ?"

The Brahmins replied:

18. O king, who is this Nārāyaṇa about whom you ask ? We two, standing before you, are Nārāyaṇas.

Aśvaśiras said:

19. "Both of you are Brahmins who are cleansed of sins due to penance and attained great spiritual power. But how do you say that you are Nārāyaṇas ?

20. The great God Janārdana (Nārāyaṇa) has in his hands the conch, disc and mace, and is clad in yellow garment. He sits on Garuḍa (the king of birds). Who can be like Him in this world ?"

21. Hearing the words of the King, the two ascetic Brahmins laughed aloud and said: 'O king, see Viṣṇu (in us)'.

22. Then Kapila transformed himself into Viṣṇu and at the same time Jaigīṣavya became Garuḍa.

23. Suddenly, there arose an uproar of wonder in the assembly of the king.

24-25. Then the great king, having seen the eternal God Nārāyaṇa sitting on Garuḍa, told them with folded hands: "Forbear, O Brahmins, Viṣṇu is not like this. He is the great god, from the lotus in whose navel Brahmā arose, and from that Brahmā arose Rudra !"

26. Then those great sages made a miracle by their Yogic power.

27. (Thus) Kapila became Padmanābha (one having a lotus-flower in his navel) and Jaigīṣavya Brahmā. Brahmā shone on that lotus-flower and the resplendant Rudra thereon.

28-31. The King saw Him who had reddish eyes and who was emanating the lustre like the enveloping fire at the end of the world. And he said: "The lord of the world cannot be seen. This is the illusion created by you, sages. The illustrious Viṣṇu is all-pervading."

As soon as he uttered this, O Earth, there appeared in the assembly of the king, bugs, mosquitoes, lice, beetles, birds, snakes, horses, cows, elephants, lions, tigers, jackals, deer and other beasts, domestic and wild, in crores.

32-33. Dismayed at the sight of this multitude of beings, the king thought: "What may be this !" Realising the greatness of Jaigīṣavya and the intelligent Kapila, king Aśvaśiras asked those (two) sages with hands folded in respect: "O excellent Brahmins what is this ?".

The Brahmins said:

34 O king you asked us how Viṣṇu should be worshipped and how he could be attained. Therefore, O great king, we have shown this to you.

35. The powers of omniscience are, O king, shown before you. The god Nārāyaṇa is omniscient and has the power to take any form.

36. This benign being can be attained by men everywhere. Worship (in any particular form alone) will not be the ultimate.

37-38. But the lord of world, the Supreme Soul, is omnipresent. As he is present everywhere, he can be seen in one's own body through devotion. That was why the form of the illustrious Supreme Soul was shown to you in our body so that you may be convinced.

39. Likewise, O king, the omnipresent Viṣṇu is there in your own body. So too in your ministers and servants.

40. O king, the divine beings as well as the multitude of animals and germs are all Viṣṇu himself. Meditate upon Viṣṇu as present in all beings.

41. Worship Him with the conviction that there is no being like Him. It is the attainment of knowledge, O king, that is revealed to you.

42. Remember the great Nārāyaṇa with full dedication, with oblations, offerings, incense and by propitiating Brahmins. The supreme lord can easily be attained by firm meditation.

CHAPTER FIVE

Attainment of Liberation Through Duty

Aśvaśiras said:

1. Kindly clear my doubt as a result of which I may be able to get release from the bondage of worldly life.

2. Asked thus, the great sage told the king who was the best among the performers of sacrifice.

Kapila said:

3. O righteous king, tell me your doubt so that I may clear it.

The king asked:

4. O sage, be pleased to clear my doubt whether liberation is attained by one who does righteous duties or by one who acquires spiritual knowledge.

Kapila replied:

5. O great king, this very question was formerly put to Bṛhaspati by Raibhya, son of Brahmā, as well as by king Vasu.

6. Long ago, in Cākṣuṣa Manvantara, there lived a great king Vasu, who was a scholar and liberal donor and descendant of Brahmā.

7. One day, Vasu went to the abode of Brahmā to see Him. On the way he saw Caitraratha, the Vidyādharachief, and asked him about the convenience of Brahmā.

8. He said that a meeting of the gods was going on in Brahmā's house. Hearing this, Vasu stood at the gate.

9. Just then, the great sage Raibhya came there and king Vasu was very much pleased at this.

10. He saluted him and asked him where he was going.

Raibhya replied:

11. "I am returning from Bṛhaspati to whom I had gone on some business".

12. At that time the assembly of Brahmā was dissolved and the hosts of gods returned to their homes.

13 Then Bṛhaspati went to his home with Raibhya, followed by Vasu who worshipped them both.

14-15. Raibhya, Bṛhaspati and king Vasu sat down and then Bṛhaspati told Raibhya: "O great sage proficient in the Vedas and Vedāṅgas, what shall I do for you?".

Raibhya said:

16. O Bṛhaspati, please clear my doubt whether liberation is attained by one who performs righteous duties or by one who acquires spiritual knowledge.

Bṛhaspati said:

17. If a man does any work, be it good or bad, dedicating it to Lord Nārāyaṇa, he becomes not attached to it.

18-19. O best of Brahmins, there is the well known conversation between a Brahmin and a hunter.

There lived a descendant of sage Atri learning the Vedas intently, performing penance, bathing early in the morning, and worshipping Sandhyā all the three times. His name was Saṁyamana. One day he went to Dharmāraṇya to bathe in the auspicious river Ganges.

20. A big herd of deer was taking rest there. A clever hunter by name Niṣṭhuraka came running there with bow and arrow, like Yama, to kill the deer.

21. Noting the aim of the hunter, sage Saṁyamana forbade him saying: 'O friend, don't kill them'.

22. Hearing this, the hunter said with a smile: "O excellent Brahmin, I am not killing the individual souls.

23. The Supreme God plays himself by the beings. Like illusion created by mantras He works thus.

24. O Brahmin, those who wish liberation should never have ego. Everything in the world is for the sustenance and progress of life. The word 'I' is not good there."

25. On hearing this, the great Brahmin Saṁyamana was struck with wonder and he asked the hunter Niṣṭhuraka thus:

26. "What you say, O friend, is apparently reasonable."

27-28. Then the hunter, who knew Dharma, made an iron-net and placed fire underneath. He then asked the Brahmin to blow into the fuel to blaze the fire. He did so.

29. When the fire was thus blazing, the iron-net, with flames spreading through its holes, shone like a globe of arrows.

30. Though the fire was only on a single spot, thousands of its tongues spread through the holes of the iron-net.

31. Then the hunter told the Brahmin: "O great sage! please take a single flame within these so that I may destroy all the remaining ones".

32. Saying this, he poured a pot of water on it and the entire fire subsided.

33. Then the hunter told the saintly Brahmin: "O lord; please give me the flame which you have just taken from the fire, so that I may roast the flesh for my food."

34. Being told thus, the Brahmin went there and looked at the iron-net. But there was no flame since its base was fully extinguished.

35. Then, as the Brahmin stood perplexed and silent, the hunter told him.

36. "The fire when flamed up, had numerous tongues, but all of them disappeared when the fire was extinguished. Similar is the case here.

37. The soul (Ātman) in its primordial form is the repository of all beings. When it transforms itself, the world evolves.

38. No one falls who performs the duties enjoined in accordance with the embodied nature of his soul".

39. When the hunter told the Brahmin thus, O king, flowers were showered on him from the sky.

40. The excellent Brahmin saw many an aerial car that were divine, great and jewelled, and capable of going everywhere.

41. The Brahmin saw in all of them the hunter Niṣṭhuraka.

42. With the yogic power to multiply himself, he had obtained the fruit of the instinct of non-duality. Pleased at this sight, the Brahmin returned to his hermitage.

43. O Raibhya, best of Brahmins, O king Vasu, he who does his duties according to his caste, will acquire spiritual knowledge and attain liberation.

44. Thus Raibhya and Vasu who had got their doubt cleared left Bṛhaspati's home and went to their hermitage.

45. Therefore, O great king, you also worship the great God Nārāyaṇa and see Him, identical with yourself in your own body.

46-47. Hearing these words of Kapila, King Aśvaśiras called his son, Sthūlaśiras, and placed him on the throne. Then he went to the Naimiṣa forest, O beautiful lady, and there he pleased Viṣṇu, the sacrificial Man, with penance and the hymn in his praise (*Yajñamūrtistava*).

Earth asked:

48. How did the king present the hymn of Nārāyaṇa, the sacrificial Man ? Be pleased to tell me.

Varāha replied:

49. "I bow to Viṣṇu, the embodiment of sacrifice, who takes many forms like Indra, Śiva, sun, moon, fire, king and Maruts.

50. I bow to the everlasting and extremely strong sacrificial Man possessing terrific canines, having the sun and the moon as his eyes, having year and the two *ayanas* as his belly and having the kuśa-grass as his hairs.

51. I always prostrate before that Janārdana (Viṣṇu) who pervades the sky and earth and all the directions, who is worthy to be extolled, who rules over the world, and from whom the world arose.

52. I always prostrate before that Parameśvara (Supreme God), the embodiment of sacrifice, who, though birthless and beginningless, takes birth himself first in each yuga for victory, though invincible by the gods and demons.

53. I always prostrate before the great prowessed Viṣṇu, the embodiment of sacrifice, who bears pure and white disc (*Sudarśana*), the Śārṅga-bow and conch in his hands to achieve victory, and the abode of Māyā.

54. I bow to the sacrificial Man, sometimes having thousand heads, sometimes having the body like a huge mountain and at other times like an atom.

55. I always prostrate before that sacrificial God, who takes birth as Brahmā, the four-faced, to create all the worlds, as Viṣṇu, the disc-bearer, to preserve it, and as Śiva resembling the fire in deluge to destroy the same.

56. I always prostrate before that immeasurable sacrificial God, who is meditated upon by sages, who is primordial and all-

pervading, and who performs sacrifices for the systematic operation of the wheel of worldly life.

57. When in my mind I place well your 'principle' which is well manifest in my own body, I am of the firm view that nothing other than this is existent, then my mind attains purity."

58. There appeared before the king who finished his prayer thus, a lustre resembling the flaming fire. With firm determination the king entered into that sacrificial God and dissolved himself in Him.

CHAPTER SIX

Attainment of Liberation Uttering The Puṇḍarikākṣapāra hymn

Earth asked:

1. Having cleared their doubt by the words of Bṛhaspati, what did Vasu and Raibhya do?

Varāha replied:

2. The virtuous king Vasu ruled over his country and performed munificently many sacrifices.

3. Meditating solely on Viṣṇu and doing righteous actions, the great king pleased the Lord.

4. As time went on, the king who crossed the ocean of Dvandvas (opposite things like pain and pleasure, cold and heat etc.) developed in his mind complete detachment from royal pleasures.

5. Then he entrusted his kingdom to Vivasvat, the eldest of his hundred sons, and went to the forest.

6. There was the sacred lake named Puṣkara where Viṣṇu is worshipped by His devotees in the name of Puṇḍarīkākṣa.

7. The saintly sage Vasu, ruler of Kashmir, went there and doing extremely severe penance emaciated his body.

8. Reciting the Puṇḍarīkākṣapāra hymn in devotion, the wise king worshipped the sinless God Nārāyaṇa, and at the end of it, the excellent king became dissolved in Him.

Earth asked:

9. O Great God ! tell me clearly what the Puṇḍarīkākṣapāra hymn is.

Varāha replied:

10. "Bow to you, O Puṇḍarīkākṣa (one having eyes resembling white lotuses) ! Bow to you, O Madhusūdana (one who killed the demon Madhu) ! Bow to you, O lord of all worlds ! Bow to you having a scorching disc (in the hand) !

11. Obeisance to Puṇḍarīkākṣa, the embodiment of all worlds, the long-handed, the giver of boons, the great-prowessed, the omnipresent, and the one having the form of both Vidyā (knowledge) and Avidyā (ignorance).

12. Salutation to the primordial great God, who crossed the ocean of the Vedas and Vedāṅgas, profound of all gods and having eyes like lotus-petals.

13. Salutation to the supreme God who has thousand heads, thousand eyes, long hands, and who stands pervading the whole world.

14. Salutation to God Viṣṇu, the victorious, the primordial, the repose to all devotees, one resembling the dark cloud, and having a disc in hand.

15. Salutation to the pure, eternal and all-pervading Viṣṇu who has the form of sky and is freed from both Bhāva (existence) and Abhāva (non-existence).

16. O Acyuta (imperishable) ! I can see nothing other than you. I see all these movable and immovable beings identical with you !"

17-18. As he finished this prayer, out of his body arose a person with a small body in blue complexion, extremely terrible, having reddish eyes, and resembling a burning pillar. With folded hands, he asked the king: 'O great king ! What is to be done by me?'

The king said:

19. Who are you ? What do you want? Where do you come from ? Tell me, O hunter.

The Hunter said:

20. "O king ! in Kaliyuga, formerly, you were the king of

Dakṣiṇāpatha (South India), quite righteous and skilful, reigning at Janasthāna.

21. One day, O brave king ! You with your horses went to a forest for hunting.

22. There a sage in the form of a deer was thrown down on the earth with two sticks by you, although unwittingly.

23. Immediately the sage breathed his last. You were, O king, very happy thinking that the deer was dead.

But when you went forward, on the Prasravaṇa mountain, you found dead the Brahmin in the form of deer.

24. Seeing him, O great king, you went to your palace with a mind extremely distressed and told some one about this incident.

25. As some more days passed, at one night, O king, you got struck with the fear for the sin of killing a Brahmin and you thought: "I will do something by which I will be freed from the sin".

26. Then, meditating on Lord Nārāyaṇa, you performed the sacred Dvādaśī fast.

27. Saying 'Nārāyaṇa is pleased with me', on a sacred day, a cow was offered by you according to religious rules. Then and there, you fell down dead due to stomach-ache.

28-29. I shall tell you why your Dvādaśī fast did not result in good. Your wife, Nārāyaṇī, was an auspicious lady. You called her by her name when your life breath was leaving your neck (and not the name of the Lord).

30. For a Kalpa, O great king, you were in Viṣṇu region. I was living in your body and I know all that occurred.

31-32. I felt, being the terrible ghost of the dead Brahmin, I could harass you. But then I was driven out by Viṣṇu's servants by their clubs and I came out of the pores of your skin. And I remain my own even in heaven.

33-34. After this, when the day-kalpa was followed by the night-kalpa, O best of kings, in the first creation, you were born in the palace of king Sumanas who ruled over Kashmir. I was then in your hairs. During that occasion, you performed many sacrifices munificently.

35-36. I was not released from your hairs by those sacrifices which were lacking in the remembrance of Viṣṇu. But, now, when you uttered the Puṇḍarīkākṣapāra hymn, by its power, I was released from your hairs and I have attained the form of a hunter.

37. Just sometime before, I heard the hymn to the God with my sinful body. Hence my liberation. Now, O lord, I am changed into a completely righteous-minded man."

38. Having heard this, the great king was struck with wonder and pleased the hunter giving a boon to him.

The king said:

39. As you have reminded me of my previous birth, O hunter, you will be famous by the name 'Dharmavyādha' (a righteous hunter).

40. One who hears this Puṇḍarīkākṣapāra hymn will get the same result as that of bathing in the sacred lake Puṣkara.

Varāha said:

41. After saying this, the king entered into the aerial car. O Earth, then he attained union with the Supreme light.

CHAPTER SEVEN

Attainment of Liberation Uttering Gadādhara Hymn

Earth asked:

1. Having heard that Vasu had attained liberation, what did the great sage Raibhya himself do ? O God, I wish to know this.

Varāha replied:

2. Having heard that Vasu had attained liberation, the great sage Raibhya went to Gayā, the sacred lake of the manes.

3. There he propitiated the manes offering Piṇḍa (the lump of rice offered in obsequial ceremonies) in devotion and performed extremely severe penance.

4. Before sage Raibhya performing great penance, there appeared in an aerial car an exceedingly effulgent Yogin.

5. In the aerial car which was small like a particle of dust, resembling the sun, shone forth a man like an atom.

6. He asked Raibhya: "O sage, with what end in view are you doing penance ?' Asking this, that man swelled himself into a huge figure touching the sky and earth.

7. He found the aerial car which was resembling the sun, also becoming very big and pervading the abode of Viṣṇu (sky).

8. Then, possessed with great wonder, Raibhya prostrated before him and asked 'O great yogin, please tell me who you are'.

The Man said:

9. "I am Rudra's younger brother and I am Brahmā's mind-born child. My name is Sanatkumāra and I am living in Janaloka.

10. I have come before you, O sage, out of love for you. O child, you are blessed all times since you increase the race of Brahmā.

Raibhya said:

11. Bow to you, O great yogin, Be pleased with me. Please shower on me your benevolence, O Yogin, with the body consisting of all the worlds. O great yogin, please tell me what I should do now. Why do you call me the blessed.

Sanatkumāra said:

12. O great Brahmin, you are blessed because you, interested in discussions on the Vedas, pleased the manes by hymns, vows, sacrifices and all kinds of Piṇḍas at this Gayā.

13-14. And hear me, O sage ! There lived in the city Viśālā another king by name Viśāla, gratified and courageous, ruling over the whole country Viśālā. He, who had destroyed all his enemies, asked the great Brahmins what was to be done to get a son for him. Those benign Brahmins told him: 'O king, please go to Gayā and propitiate the manes there by giving munificent offerings of rice for getting a son.

15. No doubt, then, you will get a son, O great king, who will be the lord of the earth and a munificent donor.

16-17. When the Brahmins said this, the king of Viśālā was very glad and he went to the sacred lake and in great devotion offered Piṇḍas to the manes in Maghās (tenth lunar asterism). At that time, he saw before him three persons in white, red and black complexions. He asked them: Why do you look at me intently? I am anxious to know everything. Please tell me".

The White man said:

18. O Child, I am your father Sita (the white) by name, conduct, race and actions. This is my father, the Red, cruel and prone to do sinful deeds like killing of Brahmins.

19. The other is his father, the Black, and the lord of all who are black of conduct and character. It is by this Black one that a good number of ancient sages were killed.

20. Both these my father, the lord Red, and his father, the Black, died and, O child, went to the hells named Raudra and Avīci and lived there for a long time.

21. As a result of my chaste actions I was led to the seat of Indra (the heaven), one that is rare to be attained. It is by you, well-versed in Mantras, I am united with these, who were in hell, by the power of offering Piṇḍas in this sacred lake.

22. O destroyer of enemies, you have offered water saying: "I shall propitiate my father, grandfathers and great-grandfathers.

23. By that word, we are united now, O good child, I can undoubtedly go to the world of manes by the power of this sacred water.

24. By offering Piṇḍas here, both these your grandfathers got liberation in spite of their misfortunes and sinful deeds.

25. The power of this sacred water is so great that even a killer of Brahmins can be liberated by his son through the offering of Piṇḍas in this lake.

26. That is why, I, accompanied by both these, have come here to see you. Now I am going.

27-28. For the same reason, O Raibhya, I am saying that you are blessed. It is very rare to go to Gayā even once and offer Piṇḍas there. You have been always here. What else is to be said, O lord; this is your good luck.

29. Since Nārāyaṇa himself was seen here as Gadādhara (holding the mace in his hand), He is installed in this temple in the same form. O best of Brahmins ! this sacred lake, therefore, is the most famous.

Varāha said:

30. After saying this, the great yogin (Sanatkumāra) disappeared. Raibhya extolled Nārāyaṇa in the form of Gadādhara as follows:

Raibhya said:

31. Bow to Gadādhara, who is extolled by gods, who is forebearing and auspicious, who destroys demons in Viśālā and who destroys, on mere remembrance, the sorrow of the poor and all inauspicious things.

32. Bow to Gadādhara, the primordial Man who is extolled again and again, the ancient, the purified, the great prowessed, the shelter to all, Trivikrama (one having three footsteps in the Vāmana incarnation) and who killed demon Keśin and protected the world.

33. One who prostrates before Gadādhara lives happily—Gadādhara who is wedded to Lakṣmī (goddess of wealth) and thus amply rich, who is extolled by sinless kings, who is devoid of sin and has purified feelings and is skilful.

34. One who prostrates before Gadādhara lives happily—Gadādhara who has the feet like lotuses and is worshipped by gods and demons, who wears a bracelet, necklace of pearls, armlet and crown, and has a disc in his hand, and who sleeps in the sea.

35. One who prostrates before Gadādhara lives happily—Gadādhara, the all-pervading, the imperishable, and the great lord who is white in Kṛta age, red in Tretā, blue in Dvāpara and black like a bee in Kali age.

36. May Gadādhara be victorious—Gadādhara having three forms at a time, who as one born from a seed creates the four-faced Brahmā, who in the form of Nārāyaṇa creates and protects the world, and who in the form of Rudra destroys it.

37. It is well known that all beings are formed of three qualities, Sattva, Rajas and Tamas. May Gadādhara possessing all these three in himself provide me with courage in discharging my righteous and spiritual duties.

38. It is the raft of Gadādhara that has protected me who was drowning deep in the ocean of worldly life, terrible with snares of sorrows, and crocodiles of separation (from my relatives).

39. I prostrate before God (Gadādhara) preserving the earth, who being himself the trio of Gods created this world out of his power as in the case of sky, i.e., in Ātman by Ātman, who created fire and water in it and seated himself in the water.

40. May Gadādhara Viṣṇu provide me with liberation—he who attained the form of fish and the like to protect gods and others and who is present in all beings in the form of sacrifice.

Varāha said:

41. When the intelligent Raibhya thus extolled Viṣṇu in great devotion, He clad in yellow-garment, appeared before him in the sky.

42. Then He having a conch, disc and a mace in his hands, sitting on Garuḍa, said in words lofty like the sound of a cloud.

43. "O great Brahmin-sage Raibhya ! I am pleased with your devotion, hymn and by your oblution in this sacred lake. Tell me what you want".

Raibhya said:

44. Be pleased, O great lord Janārdana, to give me the beatitude by which I shall live where Sanaka and others dwell.

God said:

45-46. 'Let it be so, O Brahmin !' Saying this, the Lord disappeared. By the grace of God Viṣṇu, Raibhya became possessed of divine knowledge within a moment. And he attained the world where the great sage Sanaka and others live.

47. One who goes to Gayā and recites this hymn, uttered by Raibhya to Gadādhara Viṣṇu, achieves better fruits than those by offering Piṇḍa.

CHAPTER EIGHT

The Life of Dharmavyādha

Varāha said:

1. He who was in the body of king Vasu became a hunter and he lived some four thousand years doing his traditional work (hunting).

2. For his family he killed one beast each day and with it propitiated his servants, guests and the fire (installed in his hut).

3. In Mithilā, O beautiful lady, he used to perform obsequial ceremonies for the manes on every new moon day in accordance with practice.

4. Doing daily worship of fire and uttering truth and sweet and appropriate words he lived a modest life.

5. As he was living thus, a son was born to him by name Arjunaka. He was righteous in mind; performed penance and controlled his passions like a sage.

6. In course of time this intelligent and chaste hunter got a charming daughter also by name Arjunakā.

7. As she came of age, the righteous hunter thought about her marriage: To whom is she to be given in marriage? Who is a suitable man for her?

8. While he was thinking about this, Mataṅga's son, Prasanna, came to the hunter's mind.

9. Having tentatively fixed him (as a bridegroom to his daughter), he asked Mataṅga: "O great sage! please receive Arjunī, my daughter, whom I am giving on my own accord to the great-souled Prasaṇna, your son".

Mataṅga said:

10. My son Prasanna is well versed in all Śāstras. O great hunter, I shall receive your daughter Arjunakā for him.

11. Then the righteous hunter, performer of great penance, gave his daughter in marriage to the intelligent Prasanna, son of Mataṅga.

12. After this, the righteous hunter went to his hut. His daughter began to attend on her husband and parents-in-law.

13. As time went on, the auspicious girl's mother-in-law told her. "You are a hunter's daughter. That is why you are like this. You don't know how to perform penance and how to attend on a husband."

14. The timid lady, scolded by her mother-in-law for such a silly offence, went to her father's house weeping again and again.

15. The father asked her. "O my daughter, why are you crying like this?" The beautiful girl told him in detail all that happened.

16. "O my father, my mother-in-law scolded me loosing her temper that I was a hunter's daughter and my father had killed so many living beings".

17. Hearing this, the righteous-souled hunter got angry and went to Mataṅga's house which was surrounded by a village.

18-19. The victorious Mataṅga, his relative, welcomed him giving water for washing his feet and provided him with a seat. Then he asked the guest: "Please tell me for what purpose you have come here. What shall I do for you ?".

The hunter said:

20. I want some food bereft of life. I came to your house eagerly for this very purpose.

Mataṅga said:

21. There is a lot of cooked wheat and rice in my house. O best of righteous men and great sage, you can eat these as much as you wish.

The hunter said:

22. May I see the wheat, rice and barley. I have to check whether these are the same as I know them.

Varāha said:

23. When he said this, Mataṅga showed the righteous hunter a winnowing basket full of wheat, and another full of rice.

24. Seeing the wheat and rice, the righteous hunter stood up from his seat and started to go but Mataṅga prevented him, saying as follows.

25. "Please tell me, O great soul, why are you going so hastily even without taking food. There is still excellent food here in my house. You may cook it yourself if you like, and eat it. Why not you eat this ?"

The hunter said:

26. "Each day you kill thousands and crores of lives. Which virtuous man can eat food given by such a sinner like you ?

27. If there is well-cooked food free from living organisms in your house, then I shall eat it since you are my relative.

28. I kill for my family only one animal each day. And even that, after cooking I offer first to the manes and then only I eat it with my family members.

29. You, on the other hand, kill many living organisms everyday and eat them with your family. I think, therefore, this food is not eatable to me.

30. Brahmā, in yore, created all plants and creepers for the purpose of sacrifice. It is sanctioned by the Vedas, that these are eatable to all beings.

31. Long ago, Brahmā created five great sacrifices: Divya (divine), Bhauma (of earth), Paitra (of the manes), Mānuṣa (of man) and Brāhma (of Brahmā).

32. These sacrifices are intended for the good of Brahmins and other castes. For other castes they are fruitful if got performed by Brahmins.

33. A man should eat food only after doing this. Only through this, the food becomes purified. Otherwise the rice and the like are considered to be birds and animals for both the guests and hosts. These are called 'great meat'.

34. I have given you my beautiful daughter as your daughter-in-law. Your wife scolded her that she is the daughter of a hunter who kills animals. So I have come here to test you also.

35. Traditional rites, worshipping gods, receiving guests—nothing of these can be seen here.

36. Therefore I wish to go to my own house to perform obsequial rites for the manes. Unless these are done, I do not take my food even in my house.

37. When my daughter was married by your son, she attained some of his eminence as a result, and that is sufficient expiation for her birth in my family.

38. When your son married my daughter, this decency had not come to you. Now, O sage, it is time for doing expiatory rites."

39-40. With these few words, he rose up and pronounced a curse on women. "Never shall the mothers-in-law have confidence in their daughters-in-law ! And never shall a daughter-in-law wish her mother-in-law live !" Cursing thus, O lady, the hunter went to his hut.

41-42. Then having worshipped gods and manes with devotion, and having entrusted his son Arjunaka with looking after the family, the righteous hunter, performer of great penance, went to the world-famous sacred lake named Puruṣottama. There, O Earth, he performed penance in accordance with rules with a concentrated mind reciting the following hymn :

43. "Bow to Viṣṇu, who destroyed the enemies of gods, who has Lakṣmī on his broad chest, who rules over the world well, who is a shelter to the virtuous, who placed three steps (in his dwarf incarnation), and who uplifted the mount Mandara (in his tortoise incarnation).

44. Bow to Viṣṇu, Dāmodara (one who had been bound by rope by his foster mother Yaśodā), who has seized the earth with his intellect, who is white with his fame, who is black like a bee, who is the enemy of demons, who is extolled by everyone time and again and who protects his devotees.

45. Bow to Viṣṇu, Puruṣottama (best of men) who is seen in three forms, who has a lustrous disc in his hand, who stands on the part of justice, who has excellent qualities, who has the name Beatitude, who is imperishable and who is the preceptor of all.

46. May Viṣṇu protect me praying for shelter, who is the great boar, who receives the sacrificial offerings, who destroys the mischievous, who fulfils my wishes, who has four faces, and who is a mountain for me in crossing the ocean of worldly life.

47. May Viṣṇu, the Lord of the world, protect me who created the three worlds covered by illusion, and who, like the fire, pervades himself all over the animate and inanimate beings.

48. In each yuga, Viṣṇu creates Brahmā from whom arose this world consisting of animates and inanimates and in whom in the form of Rudra all this is dissolved; so He is called Hari and Hara.

49. May the eternal Lord Viṣṇu, provide me with good whose different forms are the sun, moon, earth, air and water and whose form is unthinkable and indescribable."

50. When the hunter uttered this, the eternal God appeared himself before him in a wondrous form. The eternal Lord having

innumerable feet, bellies, hands and faces asked him to choose a boon.

51. When the Lord told him this, the great hunter said: "This very boon may kindly be given to my sons also. Through righteous duties and spiritual knowledge may my successive generations of descendants also be your devotees.

52. My race may ever be given spiritual knowledge and I may, O eternal God, attain union with the Supreme Soul".

53. Pleased with this request, the God told him: "May it be so. I have given you and your race this boon. You have now been provided with union with the Supreme Soul".

54. As soon as the God said this, he saw a light rising out of his own body and he was absorbed into it.

55-56. One who utters this excellent hymn and listens to it always worshipping Viṣṇu and performing fast, especially on the day of Viṣṇu, would get His world and live there a happy life for seventy Manvantaras.

CHAPTER NINE

Description of the Fish-Incarnation

Earth said:

1. O Lord, I wish to know precisely what was done in the beginning of Kṛta Age by Nārāyaṇa who has the entire world as His form.

Varāha said:

2. In yore, O Earth, there was nothing other than Nārāyaṇa. Being single and doing everything on his own accord, He was not happy.

3. As he longed for another one also with Him, within a moment there arose a form of Intellect by name Abhāva (non-being) resembling the sun.

4. This knower of Brahman wanted this to be divided into two. One having the name Umā was placed in mortal beings.

5. The other one, the single syllable, namely 'Om', created this earth. The worlds Bhūḥ, Bhuvaḥ, svar and Mahar were then created.[1]

6. Then was created Jana (loka). Ātman dissolves in it. It is woven with this just like jewels in a thread.

7. The world that was evolved out of the Praṇava (oṁkāra) was then completely void. This form of the Lord was Śaṅkara (Śiva) which is the form of Hari (Viṣṇu).

8. After creating this world, He, with a view to creating the best form, stirred the seat of His mind and sat there in His own form. When thus stirred, there arose the Brahmāṇḍa (universe).

9. When this was divided into pieces, there came to existence the Bhūloka (the earth). Another world also arose there resembling the sun.

10-11. In yore, there was the lotus on Navṛka. That was God Nārāyaṇa resplendent with creative lustre. From Him there arose the vowels beginning with 'a' and also the consonants. Then He uttered Śāstras for creating abstract beings.

12. After the creation, the immeasurable Lord thought about the preservation of the created things. While He was thinking, a brilliant lustre arose from His eye.

13. The right part of it was like fire and the left like frost. Seeing this, the Creator called them the sun and the moon.

14. Then the life-breath came out from the Creator. It is the very air, the all-pervading God, that is now in our heart.

15. Fire arose from it; great water arose from the fire. The same fire is the lustre of Brahmins.

16. The lustrous God produced the lustre of Kṣatriya out of His arms. He created Vaiśyas from His thighs and Śūdras from His feet.

17-18. Then the Lord created Yakṣas and Rākṣasas. He filled up the Bhūloka with the four kinds (Brahmins, Kṣatriyas etc) and the Bhuvarloka with aerial beings; Svarloka with other types of celestial beings who followed his path. Likewise Maharloka with sages like Sanaka.

19. Then he filled Janaloka with Vairājas and Tapoloka with the gods performing penance.

---

1. A half verse relating to Mahar and Satya seem to be lost here.

20. Similarly, he filled Satyaloka with the gods freed from re-birth.

After having this creation, the benevolent God gave it the meaningful name Kalpa, the whole thing being his creation.

21. In that cosmos, the three worlds Bhūr Bhuvaḥ and Suvaḥ arise, no doubt.

22. The time when the God sleeps at the end of a Kalpa is called night. Then all these three worlds are subject to turmoils.

23. Night being over, the lotus-eyed God got up and thought about the four Vedas and in them the Goddess of the Vedas.

24. Despite this thinking, he did not get the Vedas because He was illusioned by the sense of sleep. He was in utter confusion.

25. Then seeing them hidden in his own form called water, he thought of entering into it taking the form of a fish.

26. So after meditating for sometime He took the form of a great fish and entered into the water agitating it all around.

27. When the excellent God in the form of the huge fish resembling a big mountain, suddenly entered the ocean, He who had uplifted the earth before was extolled.

28. "Obeisance to you, O God, who is difficult to be attained even by Vedānta ! Obeisance to Nārāyaṇa in the form of fish. Obeisance to you, the embodiment of all the worlds and the lord of gods; Obeisance to you taking the form of the two kinds of knowledge (spiritual and worldly).

29. Obeisance to you having manifold forms like the sun and the moon and having beautiful eyes, and now in the ocean; Obeisance to you, O Viṣṇu. We seek shelter in you ! Giving up this form of fish, please protect us.

30. O God having endless body, this world is pervaded by you. O God, there is nothing here except you. There is nothing other than yourself in this world. We seek protection in you.

31. O God having eyes resembling lotus petals, ether, soul, moon, fire, mind and form—all these are your primordial body itself. It is by you that this cosmos is illumined. Please forgive me if I am devoid of proper devotion to you.

32. O God, this form of yours is contradictory in itself. It is pleasant-speaking and pleasant-voiced and at the same time it is like a mountain. O the ancient and imperishable great God who is the repose of all the worlds, please turn this scorching form into one that is benign.

33. We all seek shelter in you. We prostrate before you terrified by this huge form. There is nothing in this world outside yourself."

34. Extolled thus, the God caught the Vedas with Upaniṣads and Śāstras out of the water and then took his own form.

35. As long as the God bears his own form, this world exists. When the God assumes his primordial form this world is dissolved. When He takes his manifested forms, this world also evolves.

CHAPTER TEN

The Creation and The Life of Durjaya

Varāha said:

1. After creating all the worlds thus, the benevolent Lord, stopped the endeavour. Then the creation, O Earth, is increased itself.

2-3. When the creation was developed, the gods pleased the venerable Viṣṇu by performing devoutly many sacrifices in all the Dvīpas (islands or continents) and countries.

4. As thousands of years passed, the God became pleased and appeared before them.

5. The God having many hands, bellies, faces and eyes and resembling the peak of a big mountain, asked them. "What shall I do for you ? Please seek a boon from me, O gods !"

The gods said:

6-7. Be victorious, O great Viṣṇu ! We seek this boon from you. Even in the world of men, you alone are worshipped by all and none of us is worshipped by any. The moon, the sun, Vasus, Sādhyas, Viśvedevas, Aśvins, Maruts, fire—all these have sought shelter in you. O embodiment of all beings, please make us venerable for men.

8. Hearing this, the great lord Viṣṇu told them: "I shall make all of you venerable". Saying this, He disappeared.

9. The eternal gods also went home uttering hymns in his praise. The great Lord assumed three aspects.

10. Becoming threefold thus the great Lord worshipped the gods, with Sāttvika, Rājasa and Tāmasa forms.

11. Viṣṇu recited the Vedas in Sāttvika mood and performed sacrifices to the gods.

12. He worshipped with great devotion Rudra in the form of Kāla (time) having a trident in his hand, in the Rājasa form.

13. And he attained his Tāmasa form in Asuras.

14. Thus the great Lord of the world taking three kinds of forms worshipped the gods. Then the world also became varied.

15. In this manner Viṣṇu established the names of great gods. In Kṛtayuga He is Nārāyaṇa.

16. In Tretāyuga He is Rudra and in Dvāparayuga Yajña-mūrti, the form of sacrifice. In Kaliyuga the God Nārāyaṇa attains many forms.

17. Hear from me, O fair damsel, the story of the great God, the first creation.

18. In Kṛtayuga there lived a powerful king by name Supratīka. He had two beautiful queens.

19. Their names were Vidyutprabhā and Kāntimatī. Though he was very healthy, he did not get a son by either of these wives.

20. So, he offered worship in the prescribed manner to the great sinless sage Ātreya in the famous mountain Citrakūṭa.

21. Pleased at his long and steady worship, the sage Ātreya spoke to him with the intention of giving him a boon.

22. At that time the mighty Indra seated on his elephant accompanied by an army of gods, passed by him without showing him respect.

23. Seeing this the sage got offended and he cursed Indra.

24. "Since you have shown disrespect to me, O stupid lord of heaven, you will lose your kingdom and you will have to live in another world."

25-27. Having uttered this, the sage told king Supratīka: "O king, you will get a son valiant like Indra. He will be endowed with wealth, prowess, and spiritual knowledge and he will be a performer of brave deeds. He will have great strength and will have the name Durjaya". Saying this, the sage went away.

28. The righteous king Supratīka got his queen Vidyutprabhā pregnant. In due course, she gave birth to a child who was very strong and was given the name Durjaya.

29. The sage himself performed the ceremonies in connection with his birth.

30. As a result of the sage's rites, the child became gentle, righteous and proficient in the Vedas and Śāstras.

31. Kāntimatī, the second queen of the great king Supratīka also gave birth to a child by name Sudyumna who also became well versed in the Vedas and Vedāṅgas.

32-33. As time went on, Supratīka, the mighty king of Vārāṇasī, seeing his son Durjaya becoming mature and himself old, O Earth, thought that Durjaya was to be crowned king.

34. Thinking thus, the righteous king bestowed on his son the kingdom and he himself went to the mountain Citrakūṭa.

35. Adding to his great kingdom more elephants, horses and chariots, king Durjaya thought about the widening of its boundaries.

36. Thinking thus the intelligent king assembled an army consisting of elephants, horses, chariots and soldiers and went to the northern quarters.

37-38. All the countries in the northern quarters were captured by the great king. Then he won over this country, Bhārata. Subsequently the countries Kimpuruṣa, and Harivarṣa were seized by him.

39. Then he captured all the countries around mount Meru like Romāvata, Kuru, Bhadrāśva and Ilāvṛta.

40. After having seized this Jambūdvīpa, the king went to conquer Indra with all the gods.

41. Sage Nārada, son of Brahmā, climbing on the mount Meru told Indra the gods, demons, Gandharvas, Guhyakas, Kinnaras about the victorious advance of Durjaya (over the whole Jambūdvīpa).

42-43. As soon as he heard this, Indra along with the lords of the quarters set out to kill Durjaya. Climbing the mountain Meru, he came to the earth, the abode of mortals.

44. Lord Indra accompanied by the lords of quarters stood in the east. It was then that the wonderful exploits of Durjaya occurred.

45. After conquering the gods, Durjaya made his camp in the table-lands of the mount Gandhamādana.

At that time two ascetics came there to see Durjaya.

46. They told him: "O king Durjaya, all the lords of quarters have been driven away by you. Without them the world cannot get on. So please give us their exalted position."

47-48. Requested thus, the righteous king Durjaya asked them: "Who are you ?" They replied: "We are Asuras by name Vidyut and Suvidyut. We wish the righteousness well set by you among the good.

49. O Durjaya, we shall do all the duties of the protectors of the quarters."

50. On hearing their words, Durjaya appointed them in heaven as the protectors of directions. Then both of them disappeared. O Earth, they did their work well.

51. On the mount Mandara the great king Durjaya found the celestial garden (Citraratha) of Kubera which was like the Nandana garden (of Indra).

52. While he was on a stroll in that beautiful garden he saw there under a golden tree two girls.

53-54. They were wonderfully charming and he stood there for a moment wondering who they could be. Just then he saw two sages.

55. Seeing them the king with great joy got down from his elephant quickly and prostrated at their feet.

56. He sat down and gave them two seats of Kuśa grass. They asked him: "Who are you ? Wherefrom have you come here and what for.".

57. With a smiling face the king replied: "A famous king by name Supratīka was ruling. I am his son named Durjaya.

58. With a desire to defeat all the kings in the world, I came here.

59. O excellent sages, who are you ? Be pleased to tell me your names."

The sages said:

60. We are Hetṛ and Prahetṛ, sons of Svāyambhuva Manu. To destroy gods we went to the mountain Meru.

61. There we won many times the huge army of gods consisting of elephants, horses and chariots.

62-63. Seeing their army destroyed by the demons, the gods, seeking shelter, went to the bank of the Milky ocean where the great lord Viṣṇu was sleeping. Saluting the Lord, the gods requested Him:

64. "O God Viṣṇu, please protect our frightened army defeated by the demons.

65. It is you, O Keśava (destroyer of the demon Keśin) who, long ago, in the war between the gods and demons, protected us from the attack of the eternal thousand-armed Kālanemi.

66. Here also, O great Lord, there are two demons by name Hetṛ and Prahetṛ being accompanied by a huge army and they are oppressing us all. Killing both these, O great God, the protector of the worlds, please save us."

67. Hearing this, Viṣṇu, the great Lord of the worlds told them: "I shall go to kill them".

68. Being told by Him thus, the gods waited there by the mountain Meru meditating on Him Who was the destroyer of the mischievous people.

69-70. Soon the mighty God having a mace in His hand entered into our army multiplying himself into one, ten, hundred, thousand, lakh and crore by his miraculous power.

71. As the mighty God stood in the middle of our army in this manner, every soldier in our army began to fall down dead.

72-73. Thus within a few minutes, our fourfold army having flesh and blood and full of soldiers and flagstaffs was destroyed by the magical power of the God, the embodiment of all beings. Then seeing us only remaining, the God with a disc in his arm, disappeared.

74. We saw this wonderful act of the God having the Śārṅga-bow in his hand. Then we sought shelter in him and worshipped him.

75-76. You are the son of our friend king Supratīka. These two are our daughters. Please accept both these, O great king. Hetṛ's daughter is Sukeśī and Prahetṛ's Miśrakeśī.

77. When Hetṛ said thus, king Durjaya received those two girls as his queens for the sake of righteousness.

78. Marrying them the joyful king returned to his own kingdom accompanied by his army.

79. In course of time, he got two sons by his two wives Prabhava by Sukeśi, and Sudarśana by Miśrakeśī.

80. Having got the two auspicious sons, the wealthy king Durjaya, as he became old, went to the forest.

81-82. As he was living in the forest driving away wild beasts, he found a sinless and auspicious sage by name Gauramukha performing penance who was the protector of hermits as well as the sinful men.

83. The sage's penance-grove with ponds full of pure water and with big trees imparting fragrance to the breeze shone like a cloud descended from the sky to the earth.

84. There was in his hermitage fire blazing with flames upwards brightening the sky, a grinder covered by pure white cloths; Sāma-hymns sung by his disciples, lovely hermitage girls, and all the trees with full-blown flowers.

CHAPTER ELEVEN

Fight Between Durjaya and Gauramukha

Varāha said:

1-2. Seeing the hermitage of Gauramukha, Durjaya thought: "I shall enter this beautiful hermitage and see the virtuous sages". He then entered the hermitage.

3. Delighted to see the king, Gauramukha welcomed him.

4. Then the great Brahmin sage told him, "O great king, I wish to give you and your retinue food according to my capacity. So release your horses."

5. Saying this, the virtuous sage remained quiet. Seeing his devotion the king also stood there with his followers.

6. "Five batallions of the army are with me here. What food can this sage give us all?" he thought.

7. After inviting king Durjaya for food, sage Gauramukha also thought: "what shall I give the king now?".

8. The sage who was thinking thus had the great Lord Viṣṇu in his heart then.

9. Then the great sage went to the Ganges and meditated on Viṣṇu and propitiated him.

Earth asked:

10. I am anxious to know, O Lord, how Gauramukha propitiated Viṣṇu. Tell me this clearly.

Varāha replied:

11. "I bow to you (Viṣṇu) always. Bow to you, clad in yellow garment. Bow to you, the primordial Man. Bow to you in the form of water.

12. I bow to you the Omni-present. Bow to you lying on the water. Bow to you in the form of the earth. Bow to you in the form of light.

13. Bow to you in the form of air. Bow to you in the form of sky. You are the God of all beings. You are the Lord reposing in the heart of all.

14. You are the syllable 'Om', the word 'vaṣaṭ'. You are present everywhere. You are the beginning of all gods; but you have no beginning.

15. You are (the world) Bhūḥ. You are (the world) Bhuvaḥ. You are (the worlds) Janas and Mahar. You are (the world) Tapas. You are (the world) Satya. O God, all the animate and inanimate dwell in you.

16. All this world came out of you. The Ṛk etc. came out of you. The Śāstras were born from you. It is in you that the sacrifices are installed.

17. All the trees, creepers, plants in the woods, animals, birds and serpents—O Janārdana, all these are born from you.

18. O God of gods, king Durjaya has come to my hermitage. I wish to treat him as my guest.

19. O Lord of all the worlds, I am very poor and all the same, an obedient devotee of yours. Give me rice and the like (to feed the king).

20. Whatever I touch with my hands, whatever I look at with my eyes—may it be a log of wood or a blade of grass, let all that turn into the fourfold food.

21. Also whatever my mind calls for, let all that appear before me. Bow to you, O great God."

Varāha said:

22. By this hymn, the great God of all the worlds was pleased very much. He appeared before the sage and showed him his real Form.

23. Then the God told him with great pleasure. "O Brahmin, please ask for a boon". Hearing this the sage opened his eyes.

24-26. Then he saw Viṣṇu clad in yellow-garment and bearing a conch and mace in his hands. Sitting on Garuḍa, he shone forth with the lustre similar to that of the twelve suns, why, the lustre of a thousand suns rising together in the sky. The sage, O beautiful lady, saw him with his eyes wide open with wonder.

27-28. He prostrated before the God with folded hands and told Him. "O God, if you are pleased with me, your devotee, and intend to give me a boon, then, please make arrangements in order that this king with his company can stay in my hermitage and take food and then return to his palace."

29. Hearing this, the great God gave him a boon according to which his desire would be fulfilled. He also gave him a shining jewel.

30. The God then disappeared. Sage Gauramukha also went to his holy hermitage with many sages.

31. Then the great sage contemplated on a hundred-storied mansion looking like the peak of mount Himālaya and high up like the huge cloud, and pleasing like the beams of the moon.

32. Then, by the power of the boon attained from Viṣṇu, the Brahmin created lakhs of mansions like this.

33-34. Then he got huge walls around them. Also there came into existence beautiful gardens, pleasant with the charming songs of cuckoos, and full of many other kinds of birds; and trees like Campaka, Aśoka, Punnāga, Nāga and Kesara appeared in the gardens in these homes everywhere.

35. Stalls for elephants and stables for horses appeared there. Many varieties of food were provided everywhere.

36. All kinds of food—to be chewed, bitten, licked and sucked—made of rice and the like and golden utensils for them were seen everywhere.

37. Then the sage told the great king: "Let the entire army enter into these houses".

38. When told thus, the king went to a mountain-like mansion. His servants also went into it.

39. Seeing all of them in the mansion, sage Gauramukha, with the divine jewel in his hand, said to the king.

40. When you want to bathe and have your food, O king, I shall send charming damsels and obedient servants to attend on you.

41. After saying this, the great Brahmin put the Viṣṇuite jewel in a solitary place. The king was watching all this.

42. As soon as the sage put the shining jewel there, thousands of celestial damsels appeared on the spot.

43. Smeared with cosmetics, the lovely ladies attracted everyone with their beautiful cheeks, hairs, eyes etc.

44-45. Some of them taking golden pots in their hands started to go. Thus, men and women followed the king and his servants to attend on them.

46. Those ladies found all the servants taking bath following the king. The elephants were seen walking gently and beautifully.

47-48. When the king was bathing, many kinds of tabors were played everywhere and some ladies danced beautifully and some others sang songs as at the time when Indra was taking his bath.

49. Thus the great king finished his bath with divine accompaniments. Struck with wonder, he thought: "How is all this done ? Is it by the power of the sage or by his penance or by this jewel ?"

50. Then, after bathing and wearing fine clothes, the great king took his food consisting of numerous items.

51. The great sage showed his hospitality to the king's servants also as he did to the king.

52. As the king and his servants took their meals, the rosy sun went to the setting mountain.

53. Then came the night, decorated by the grand mark of the autumnal moon. Even though having only soft qualities Rohiṇī's spouse (moon) showed his passion (also reddish colour) proper to the context.

54. The planet Venus (Śukra) rose with strong rays. Jupiter (Bṛhaspati) also rose at the time, but with lustre

suppressed (by that of Venus). The position of all beings is in accordance with their association.

55. The planet Mars gave up its reddish colour and Rāhu its sharpness. The moon's beams were white. The nature of all beings is influenced by its association according to whether it is with the good or with the bad. Nature is the chief factor that imparts strength and valour.

56. Although within the influence of Saturn, Ketu did not spread his dense darkness in that brightness, pure like the sun. If the master is great, then even the bad behave well.

57. The planet Budha, the intelligent son of the moon, shone forth with his actions and smiling at the good.

58. Ketu standing in the path of the moon (also king) and the gods made the sky tawny. In an assembly of good men the bad do not exhibit their tricks in full.

59. The moonlight increased the passion of even highborn wives. The contact of the great rouses the great.

60. The results of the Vedic rites performed were evident.[1]

61. By virtue of the remembrance of Viṣṇu, Dhruva, who in yore, worshipped him, brightened the king's seat by wealth and intellect.

62. Thus, the auspicious night came to the auspicious hermitage of Gauramukha in keeping with the grand reception accorded with sumptuous meals, clothes and ornaments to king Durjaya and his servants and to his elephants and horses.

63. There were beautiful couches in the mansions lustrous with precious jewels and covered by the best silks, and lovely damsels were standing nearby.

64. The king sent his chieftains and servants to other buildings and slept in his mansion in the company of charming ladies, like Indra in the heaven.

65. Thus, by the sage's power, the king with his retinue slept well during the whole night.

66-67. As the night was over, the king found that the ladies had disappeared; so too those huge mansions and their grand seats. Seeing this, the king was struck with wonder and he felt unhappy.

68-69. King Durjaya thought: "How can I get a jewel

1. The idea in this stanza is not clear.

like this ? I will steal this jewel which fulfils all the wishes of him who possesses it." Thinking thus, the king did not feel inclined to leave the hermitage.

70-71. Going somewhere not far away from the hermitage, the king with his horses sent his minister Virocana to sage Gauramukha to request him for the gift of the jewel. He went there and requested the sage for it.

72. He told the sage: "It is the king who deserves to keep jewels. So this jewel may be given to him."

When the minister said thus, Gauramukha got angry and replied to him.

73. "The Brahmin is the recipient; the king, on the other hand, is the donor. Being a king how do you request for this, like a poor man ?

74. What you are telling me amounts to saying that king Durjaya himself is an ill-conducted man. Soon go to that ill-conducted king. May not the people disobey him."

75. Hearing this, the messenger went to the king and conveyed to him all that was told by the Brahmin.

76. Hearing the Brahmin's words Durjaya got angry and called one of his chieftains, Nīla, and told him:

77. "Do not wait for a minute. Snatching the Brahmin's jewel come here quickly."

78. Receiving this order, Nīla, with a huge army, went to the Brahmin's hermitage in the forest.

79. There, seeing the jewel placed in the Agnihotraśālā (the house where the sacred fire is worshipped everyday), Nīla got down from the chariot and stood on the ground.

80-81. While the most cruel Nīla got down from the chariot, numerous valiant soldiers holding weapons, came out of the jewel with chariots, flag-staffs, horses, swords, bows and quivers.

82. From among the powerful soldiers that came out of the jewel, fifteen were particularly valorous and were capable of accomplishing anything in battle.

83-84. O auspicious lady, I shall tell you their names. Suprabha, Dīpratejas, Suraśmi, Śubhadarśana, Sukānti, Sundara, Sunda, Sudyumna, Sumanas, Śubha, Suśīla, Sukhada, Śambhu, Sudānta, Soma—these were the fifteen chiefs that arose from the jewel.

85. Seeing the vast army and its brilliant leader they closely fought with various weapons in their arms.

86. Their bows glittered like gold and arrows were bound with gold in their feathered parts. Their sharp swords, powerful missiles and lances fell (on the enemies).

87. Chariot encountered chariot; so also elephant, horse and foot-soldier of high valour attacked their counterparts.

88. Likewise, abusing each other, the mighty soldiers in the two armies entered the array. Thus the war became horrible producing a flood of blood and deviated from the path of the righteous.

89. In the tumultuous war, the king's minister fell in a swoon and soon embraced death with his army.

90. When the minister died, king Durjaya himself rushed to the spot along with horses, chariots and soldiers and continued the battle with those who arose from the jewel.

91. In the fight the king also faced very many reverses.

92. Then, hearing that their son-in-law was in the warfield, Hetṛ and Prahetṛ brought an army there.

93-95. In that army, O Earth, the leading demons were Praghasa, Vighasa, Saṅghasa, Aśanisaprabha, Vidyutprabha, Sughoṣa, Unmattākṣa, Agnidatta (Agnidaṁṣṭra), Agnitejas, Bāhu, Śakra, Pratardana, Virādha, Bhīmakarman and Vipracitti; these fifteen having strong weapons with them were the chiefs of the demons.

96. Each of them had a large army. These chiefs with miraculous power fought with the jewel-born soldiers.

97. Satejas (Dīpratejas) pierced Vighasa with three arrows. Likewise, Suraśmi struck Saṅghasa with ten arrows.

98. Śubhadarśana shot five arrows at Aśaniprabha. So did Sukānti and Sundara on Vidyutprabha and Sughoṣa respectively.

99. Sunda pierced Unmattākṣa with five arrows and cut his bow with a pointed shaft.

100. Sumanas fought with Agnidaṃṣṭra and Suveda (Sukhada) with Agnitejas. Similarly, Sunala (Śubha) with Bāhu (Vāyu) and Śakra and Sudanta with Pratardana.

101. After a terrible fight in which weapons were hurled on each other incessantly, the demons were killed by the jewel-born soldiers.

102-103. As the fight became extremely terrible, sage Gauramukha came there collecting the Samit and Kuśa grass (for his daily rituals). Seeing the wonderful and horrible war in which huge aımies were fighting and seeing Durjaya standing by, the sage stood near the gate in deep thought.

104. Finding that his jewel was the cause of that huge battle, sage Gauramukha meditated on God Viṣṇu.

105. Suddenly, there appeared before him the God, clad in yellow garment and seated on Garuḍa and asking him what he might do.

106. With folded hands the sage replied to Him: "Please kill this sinful Durjaya and his army."

107-108. Then he threw his fire-like disc (Sudarśana) towards them. Within a moment the king and his army and the demons were reduced to ashes completely.

109-110. After this, the God told sage Gauramukha. "This race of demons is killed within a minute (*nimiṣa*) and so this forest will be called significantly Naimiṣāraṇya. This will be an abode of Brahmins.

111. In this forest, I will be known as Yajñapuruṣa (Sacrificial Man) and sacrifice is to be offered here always.

112. In Kṛtayuga these fifteen jewel-born leaders will be born as kings."

113. After saying this, the God disappeared. The sage also went to his hermitage in great joy.

CHAPTER TWELVE

Nārāyaṇa Offers a Boon to Supratīka

Varāha said:

1. Hearing that so many men were reduced to ashes in the fire of (Viṣṇu's Sudarśana) disc, king (Supratīka) became most unhappy and he thought of what he might do.

2. Then an idea came into his mind: "Viṣṇu in the form of Śrī Rāma is here on mount Citrakūṭa.

3-4. I will extol Viṣṇu, the Lord of all the world, uttering

His names." Thinking thus, the king went up the sacred mountain Citrakūṭa and recited a hymn.

Supratīka said:

5. "Obeisance to the great God Rāma the lord of the people, the imperishable, the ancient, having the form of Śiva (auspicious), the origin of all beings, the destroyer of the enemies of gods, the dispeller of all sorrows of his devotees and the bearer of Lakṣmī (goddess of wealth, on his chest).

6-7. O God, it is you bearing the forms of all beings that always bestow lustre to all lustrous things. In earth you (appear) with five qualities (colour, taste, touch, sound and odour); in water with four (omitting odour); in light with three (omitting taste also); in air with two (omitting colour also); and in ether you are present as the person of sound. You are the moon, sun and fire. It is said that in you this world lies in a latent form.

8-9. As the world rejoices being installed in you, you are well known as Rāma (the delighter). The man who has the raft in the form of meditation on you is not drowned in the ocean of the worldly life which is full of waves of pains and terrible with the fish and crocodiles in the form of senses. Therefore, you are contemplated on as Rāma in hermitages. O Viṣṇu, when the Vedas are lost, you take the form of a fish (and recover them).

10. In the end of Yugas, O all-pervading God, you in the form of Fire, take many shapes and cover all directions. Similarly, on the eve of churning the ocean, O Mādhava, you take the form of a tortoise.

11. There is nothing like you anywhere. All the best things are born from you, Janārdana. O great God, you pervade the whole universe, and all worlds, and all directions are your creations.

12. You are the primordial and ultimate lustre, where else can I seek shelter? First, only you were there (in the vast cosmos). Then, out of you, Mahat (Intellect), Ahaṅkāra, (Ego), water, fire, air, ether, mind, intellect and three qualities were born. Everything originates from you.

13. All this world is pervaded by you. I take you as the primordial Man. Be victorious, O great God having thousand

hands, having the forms of all the worlds and the Lord of all. I bow to you, O great Rāma."

14. Pleased by this hymn, the great God appeared before king Supratīka and asked him to choose a boon.

15. Then the king hurriedly prostrated before the great God and requested him: "O God of gods, please give me union with yourself."

16. As soon as he said this, the great king attained union with the God. Meditating on the supreme soul, the king got liberation from his bondage of enormous actions and attained identity with the supreme soul.

Varāha said:

17. Thus I have told you a part of what occurred in the age of Svāyambhuva (Manu). No one can tell easily all that occurred then, even if he has thousands of tongues.

18. O auspicious lady, I have told you this ancient story from mere memory. Drops of water from the ocean which fall in many places form valuable later on.

19. What was narrated by Brahmā and Nārāyaṇa cannot be easily narrated by us. It is difficult to picture in the mind his primordial form.

20. In sea there are numerous grains of sand, and in earth numerous particles of dust. Even if they can be counted, it is impossible to count the doings of God.

21. O lovely damsel, I have told you a part of the story of Nārāyaṇa in Kṛtayuga. What else do you want to know?

CHAPTER THIRTEEN

Rules for Śrāddha

Earth said:

1. It is wonderful to learn that those soldiers arose from the jewel to help sage Gauramukha. What is the further fruit of the boon?

2. Who is this great righteous sage Gauramukha? Seeing the actions of God what did the great sage do?

Varāha said:

3. Seeing what was done by the God, the sage with a view to worshipping him went to the same forest.

4. There is an important Tīrtha Prabhāsa by name, sacred to Soma, wherein the God (Viṣṇu) who destroyed demons is meditated on by pious men.

5. There the sage worshipped Viṣṇu in the name of Daityasūdana (destroyer of demons). The great sage Mārkaṇḍeya came to him who worshipped Lord Viṣṇu Nārāyaṇa.

6. Seeing Mārkaṇḍeya coming towards him, sage Gauramukha welcomed him in great joy with venerable offerings and the water for washing his feet.

7. When sage Mārkaṇḍeya sat on the seat of Kuśa grass sage Gauramukha asked him: "Tell me, O great sage, what shall I do ?"

8. Hearing this, the great saintly Brahmin Mārkaṇḍeya told sage Gauramukha in gentle and soft words.

Mārkaṇḍeya said:

9. The first preceptor of all gods is Nārāyaṇa. Brahmā was born from him and he (Brahmā) created seven sages.

10. Brahmā asked them (the seven sages) to sacrifice for him, and it is known that each of them sacrificed himself before him (Brahmā).

11. Then Brahmā cursed them, although born from himself, for their rushing to rash actions just out of emotion. Since you committed this serious mistake, all of you will, no doubt, be devoid of knowledge.

12. Thus cursed by Brahmā, those seven sages created sons and then went to heaven.

13. And those sages, the knowers of Brahman, went to heaven; their sons offered them oblations without any delay.

14. All the seven sages, the mind-born sons of Brahmā, appeared in the sky in aerial cars seeing the oblations offered to them with mantras.

Gauramukha asked:

15. O Brahmin, who are those Pitṛs (the manes) ? Which is the time (for those offerings) ? How many groups of manes are there in that world ?

Mārkaṇḍeya replied:

16. There are some good personages who increase the Soma-juice for the gods. Those seven gods, Marīci and others, are called the manes in heaven.

17. Of these, four have form; the remaining three are formless. I shall tell you their worlds and creations.

18. There are worlds by name Santānaka wherein live the luminous manes of the gods. The gods perform sacrifice there for those manes.

19. These who get out of this world, attaining eternal worlds, after a thousand years, again, take birth as knowers of spiritual wisdom.

20. With the memory of the past, they practice yoga, and as a result, attain liberation with little chance of rebirth.

21. These were the manes in obsequial ceremonies who increased the yogic powers of yogins. All of them were full of yogic powers.

22. Therefore, O excellent yogin, obsequial rites have to be offered to yogins. This is the first and great creation of the gods (who drink Soma-juice).

23. These great Brahmins (manes) live in heaven with a single body. They have to be offered sacrifices by the inhabitants of the earth.

24. Marīci and others are sons of Brahmā. They should perform sacrifice for Maruts. The Maruts who are respected by people are to be pleased with sacrifices by those who are called Kalpavāsikas.

25. Then there are Sanaka and others. They were born out of Virāṭ, and they performed penance. There are seven groups of them. This is the line of the manes.

26. These are also to be pleased with sacrifice separately by castes other than Śūdra. With the sanction of the remaining three castes, Śūdra should also sacrifice for the manes.

27. For Śūdras there are separate manes belonging to the same caste. We do not get among the manes, the liberated yet living.

28-29. By the knowledge of special Śāstras and the Purāṇas, of the Ṛṣis, and knowing those that arose from him as worthy to accept sacrificial offerings, Brahmā at creation, recalled his sons, and they attained liberation due to their spiritual knowledge itself.

30. Kāśyapa and others among Vasu and the like, Vāsava and others among caste-holders and the whole class of Gandharvas and the like (are also the manes).

31. O great sage, I have told you the creation of the manes in a general manner. By even a crore of years this cannot be told in full.

32. Now I shall tell you the time of the Śrāddha rites. O great Brahmin, please listen to this.

33-34. After procuring the required money for the Śrāddha ceremonies and choosing a Brahmin of particular qualities for the purpose, the rites are to be done on the occasions of Vyatīpāta (the day of full-moon when it falls on a Monday), Ayana (the solstices) Viṣuva (the equinoxes) eclipses of the sun and the moon, and of all signs of zodiac (Rāśi) at the time each is entered into by the sun.

35. And at those times also when calamities occur due to stars and planets, when one has an inauspicious dream, and when new vegetation appears, Śrāddhas may be performed, if desired.

36. When Amāvāsyā (the new-moon day) occurs in conjunction with the asterisms Ārdrā, Svāti and Viśākhā the manes get pleased with offerings for eight years.

37. When Amāvāsyā occurs in conjunction with the asterisms Puṣya, Raudra (Ardrā) and Punarvasu, the manes, if worshipped, get pleased for twelve years.

38. Those who wish the manes to be gratified should perform obsequial rites when Amāvāsyā occurs in the asterisms Dhaniṣṭhā, Pūrvā bhādrapadā and Śatabhiṣak. This is a rare occasion even for the gods.

39. Those who wish to have an unending result should perform obsequial rites when Amāvāsyā occurs in the above nine asterisms. Then their merit does not come to an end even after crores of years.

40-41. There are yet other sacred times proper to the Śrāddha ceremonies. They are—the third day of the month Vaiśākha, the ninth day of the bright fortnight in the month Kārttika, the thirteenth day of the dark fortnight in the month Bhādra pada, the fifteenth day of the month Māgha, the eclipses of the sun and the moon and all the four Aṣṭakas (the eighth day of each quarter of the year) and at the commencement of the two Ayanas or solstices (Uttarāyaṇa and Dakṣiṇāyana).

42. A man, purified by austerities, should offer the manes the water mixed with sesamum. Then, it is deemed that he has done the Śrāddha rites for a thousand years.

43. On rare occasions the Amāvāsyā in the month Māgha joins with the asterism Śatabhiṣak. This is the most happy day of the manes. But, O Brahmin, this is not for a man of inferior worth.

44. O great Brahmin, if this occurs in the asterism Dhaniṣṭhā, then the relatives should give offerings to their manes on that day. That will give them great satisfaction for thousands of years.

45. If oblations are offered to the manes when this occurs in Pūrvā Bhādrapadā, they will be highly gratified and for a full yuga they will get deep sleep.

46. By offering cows and the like on the banks of the Ganges, Śatadru, Vipāśā, Sarasvatī, or Gomatī the dissatisfaction of the manes, if any, can be removed.

47. The manes would wish: When at the end of the dark fortnight of the rainy season the thirteenth day coincides with the asterism Maghā, we may be gratified with sacred waters in the pilgrim centres by our sons and other relatives.

48. Purified heart and wealth, auspicious time enjoined by the rules, the nature of the performance and ardent devotion—these in the performance of Śrāddhas fulfil men's wishes.

49. Listen to the verses sung by the manes on this and then act in accordance with them.

50. "May that kind of man take birth in our family who is intelligent and contented and who without any consideration of monetary benefit offers us oblations with Piṇḍa rice.

51. Who, if he is rich, munificently offers jewels, garments, vehicles, all the wealth, well and pond to Brahmins for our sake;

52. Who if not well-to-do gives meals to Brahmins at the appropriate time in great devotion according to his means;

53. Who, being unable to give meals, gives venerable Brahmins wild Śāka-leaves and a little money;

54. Who, being unable to give even this, offers to a great Brahmin in devotion a handful of dark sesamum;

55. Who offers us a handful of water with seven or eight seeds of sesamum in great devotion;

56. Who gives with devotion to cows a daily measure of food obtained from somewhere, and in the absence of it, pleases them caressing and so on;

57. Who, if he is not in a position of doing any of these, goes to the forest and with palms joined in reverence utters aloud this hymn to the protectors of the quarters like the sun, namely;

58. "I have no money, wealth and the like to offer in the Śrāddha rites; I prostrate before the manes. May they be contented with the respect I offer in devotion."

59. This is sung by the manes, and shows the results of performing Śrāddha and not doing so. The Brahmin who does according to this, does rightly the rites for manes.

CHAPTER FOURTEEN

Rules for Śrāddha

Mārkaṇḍeya said:

1. O Brahmin sage, this was said to me by the intelligent Brahmin, younger brother of Sanaka, son of Brahmā. Listen to me now:

2-4. One who knows all the six Vedāṅgas, who worships the three sacred fires at three sandhyās (morning, noon, and evening) and who offers libations with the three madhus (sugar, honey and ghee), the priest (of the family), nephew, daughter's son, father-in-law, son-in-law, maternal uncle, saintly Brahmin, particularly one who worships the five sacred fires, disciple, matrimonial relative and one who respects his parents—these are fit to be invited in Śrāddha.

5-7. One who troubles his friend, one having bad nails, a brown-toothed Brahmin, an outrager of virgins, one who donates his sacred fire, one who sells Soma-juice, one who is cursed, a thief, a slanderer, a priest who conducts the religious ceremonies for all castes, a hired teacher, a charioteer's teacher, one who has married another's wife, one who does not look after his parents, one who is born of or looked after by a Śūdra woman, the husband of a Śūdra girl, and one who performs worship to an idol for the sake of others—none of these deserves to be invited for Śrāddha rites.

8. The invitation should be made on the day previous to the Śrāddha. They should be fed first (on the day of the Śrāddha) and afterwards the sannyāsin and others who come uninvited.

9. The feet of the Brahmins who come to the house should be washed, and then with *pavitra* (the ring of Kuśagrass in hand) they should be seated.

10. The performer of Śrāddha should offer oblations to the manes in odd numbers and to the gods in even numbers or to both these each in single.

11. Likewise, he should perform Śrāddha rites for his maternal grandfather with great devotion, along with Vaiśvadeva (an offering to all deities made by presenting oblations to fire before meals) or may perform Vaiśvadevika rites alone.

12. The Brahmin representing (Viśvedevas should be seated to face the east and the Brahmin representing the father and paternal grandfather should be seated to face north.

13. Some sages say that a Brahmin should perform both these (for the gods and the manes) separately whereas others hold that both should be done together.

14. Giving Kuśa-grass as the seat and receiving with *arghya* (oblation consisting of rice, Dūrvā-grass etc.) the performer should invoke the gods with their permission.

15. He should offer oblations to the gods with barley water.

16. After worshipping the manes with incense and sacred lamps according to rules, he should do so to the Pitṛs with *apasavya* (the sacred thread in the left position).

17. Then getting Anujñā (the permission of the priests) offering Kuśa grass divided into two with Mantras he should invoke the manes. Then he should give *arghya* and the like with sesamum and water with *apasavya*.

18. With the permission of Brahmins, one should honour also the Brahmin traveller who comes there for food at that time.

19. Yogins with a view to helping others, roam about everywhere in this earth in various forms without disclosing their identity.

20. Therefore, a discerning man should worship the guest

coming on the occasion of obsequial ceremonies. O great Brahmin, a guest who is not honoured destroys the fruits of the Śrāddha.

21. With the permission of those Brahmins, one should put rice devoid of salt and the like thrice into the fire.

22. The first invocation is—'this is to the fire who bears the oblation of food'. Next—'this is to be conveyed to Soma having the manes.'

23. The third invocation is to Vaivasvata. The remnants of offerings should be put a little in the plates of Brahmins.

24. Then he should give sumptuous food to them and request them in pleasant words to eat well and to their heart's content.

25. He should feed them in all sincerity, and they should eat silently, pleasantly and steadfastly.

26. The Rakṣoghna mantra (meant to drive away the demons) should be recited. Then spreading sesamum as seat on the earth he should say—"these Brahmins are verily the manes to whom we have offered ghee (in fire).

27. May my father, grandfather and great grandfather invoked in this home, feel fully satisfied.

28. May my father, grandfather and great grandfather invoked by these Brahmins feel fully satisfied.

29. May my father, grandfather and great grandfather feel fully satisfied with the Piṇḍas (balls of rice) offered by me on this floor.

30. May my father, grandfather and great grandfather feel fully satisfied with the devotion shown by me.

31. May my maternal grandfather feel satisfied. May all other manes feel satisfied. May Viśvedevas (all gods) attain great satisfaction. May the demons perish.

32. Here is God Viṣṇu, the god of sacrifice, the leader of all sacrifices, the enjoyer, the eternal soul. By his presence, may all demons get away quickly."

33. When these Brahmins are thus made satisfied, some rice should be scattered on the floor, and then each of them should be given in the hand water separately for *ācamana* (sipping).

34-35. With the permission of these who are thus fully fed to satisfaction, he should take all balls of rice from the floor with water and offer them with the sacred water of the manes in a sacred *tīrtha* (pond or river) for the maternal grandfathers.

36. Then he should offer the piṇḍas sanctified by flowers

and incense, on darbha grass placed with tip facing South near the remnants. The first piṇḍa is to be for the departed father.

37. The next one is for the grandfather and the third to the great grandfather. At the root of the darbha, the piṇḍa should be smeared with *añjana* paste.

38. Likewise, for the maternal manes also, one should offer balls of rice along with incense, flower and the like, and give water for *ācamana* to the Brahmins who are fed.

39. He should with devotion utter Svastimantras (words of propitiation) and then give *dakṣiṇā* (money).

40. After giving them this, he should make them recite Vaiśvadevika (mantras of blessings). He should say: "May Viśvedevas (all gods) be pleased".

41. When those Brahmins say "let it be so", he should request them for their benedictions. Then he should send off Viśvedevas first and then the manes.

42. Similarly, in the case of maternal manes also along with Viśvedevas in the matter of feeding, giving money and sending off, from *Pādya* onwards.

43. In the rites for maternal manes the Brahmin having spiritual knowledge should be sent off first and then the others.

44. The performer should accompany them upto the outer door and then, with their permission, return. After the Śrāddha ceremonies he should offer oblations to all deities.

45. Then he should take his food with revered men, servants and relatives.

Thus should the wise perform Śrāddha for the paternal and maternal manes. Propitiated at the Śrāddha, the manes will grant all desires.

46. These three are sacred in Śrāddha, namely grandson, *Kutapa* (the afternoon time suitable for the performance of sacrifices to the manes) and sesamum; so also the *dakṣiṇā* of silver and proper reception and the like.

47. The performer of Śrāddha should avoid three things towards the Brahmin who is to be fed on the occasion—anger, going to the street, and hurry.

48. O Brahmin, all the deities, fathers, maternal grandfather, and the family are purified by the performer of Śrāddha.

49. The manes depend upon the moon and the moon on

yoga. Therefore, O Brahmin, Śrāddha joined with yoga (concentration of mind) is considered superior.

50. A (single) yogin amidst even a thousand Brahmins, liberates all these that are fed in the Śrāddhas as well as the performer.

51. These are the rules of Śrāddha generally described in all Purāṇas. One should free oneself from bondage of worldly life with the knowledge of duties like this.

52. Knowing this from Gauramukha, the sages performing penance got liberation. You also attain the same.

53. I have told you this, O great Brahmin, since you asked me this. What else should be attained by him who meditates on Viṣṇu after performing Śrāddha for the manes." Nothing else is there, no doubt, more than the Śrāddha for the manes.

CHAPTER FIFTEEN

Sage Gauramukha's Liberation after Uttering the Hymn of Ten Incarnations of Viṣṇu

Earth asked:

1. After hearing the rules for Śrāddha ceremonies from Mārkaṇḍeya, what did sage Gauramukha do?

Varāha replied:

2. After hearing this science pertaining to the manes, Gauramukha was reminded of a hundred births by the intelligent Mārkaṇḍeya.

Earth asked:

3. Who is this Gauramukha? Who was he in the previous births? How did he remember all this? What did he do recollecting this?

Varāha replied:

4. He was Bhṛgu himself in the other birth of Brahmā. This great sage Mārkaṇḍeya was also born in his race.

5. Brahmā told him before: "Taught by your sons you will attain supreme bliss." Therefore, he was taught by Mārkaṇḍeya.

6. He recollected his previous births. I shall tell you briefly, O lovely girl, what he did after remembering all that.

7. He saw his manes after performing Śrāddha for twelve years and then, O Earth, he began to utter a hymn.

8. Near Prabhāsa, the sacred lake famous in the three worlds, Gauramukha stood to extol the God, who destroyed demons.

Gauramukha said:

9. "I extol lord Hari who is Mahendra, Śiva, the dispeller of haughtiness of enemies, Nārāyaṇa, the best among the knowers of the spiritual wisdom, the ancient being who permeates the sun, moon, Aśvins and destroys demons.

10. I extol him, destroyer of the enemies of gods who took the form of the primordial fish when the Vedas were lost— the fish that bore the Earth on its body and whose fin was like fire.

11. May the Lord of gods and the destroyer of demons protect me, who being the primordial Man took the form of tortoise on his own accord and uplifted the mount Mandara in churning ocean.

12. May the destroyer of demons, who is called yajñāṅga (with sacrifice as limbs)) by the multitude of gods and Siddhas and who entered the Talātala (one of the nether worlds) taking the form of a boar, protect me.

13. May the great destroyer of demons the great yogin who took the form of the fierce Man-lion (Nṛsiṁha) with a frightful face and golden hue, protect us.

14. May the short Brahmacārin with staff and deer-skin who changed into a measureless huge body with yogic power, transcended the earth and made the sacrifice of Bali ineffective, purify us.

15. May Hiraṇyagarbha, the destroyer of demons, who as the son of Jamadagni and the protector of Brahmins, conquered the whole world twentyone times and gave it to Kāśyapa, protect me.

16. May the destroyer of demons protect us, whose primordial Hiraṇyagarbha-form attained a fourfold division into Rāma and others (Lakṣmaṇa, Bharata and Śatrughna).

17. (May the God protect me) who in each yuga took the wonderful form of Vāsudeva (Śrī Kṛṣṇa—son of Vasudeva) to look after gods who were frightened by the haughty demons like Cāṇūra and Kaṁsa.

18-19. May the great God, the supreme soul, who takes the form of Kalki in every yuga to uphold the caste system whose form cannot be known by the gods, demons and Siddhas without the spiritual knowledge and who is worshipped in his assumed form like the fish, protect us.

20. Obeisance to the exalted Man; obeisance to you again and again. Kindly lead me to the state of liberation. I bow to you."

21. Extolled thus by the sage with great devotion, the God appeared before him holding the disc and mace.

22. Seeing Him, the soul in the form of steady knowledge (Vijñāna) issued out of his body and got merged in the eternal and attained the state called *apunarbhava* (without rebirth).

CHAPTER SIXTEEN

The Story of Saramā

Earth said :

1-4. When Indra, the king of Gods, was cursed by sage Durvāsas to live among mortals, being defeated by the son of Supratīka, what did he and other gods do in the mortal world ? What did Vidyut and Suvidyut with high yogic power do in heaven after the fall of Durjaya ? Be pleased to tell me.

Varāha said :

5. Defeated by Durjaya, O Earth, Indra with all the gods and Yakṣas and Nāgas, first lived in Vārāṇasī in the Bhārata country.

6-7. At that time Vidyut and Suvidyut, O lovely lady, by the power of yoga generated intensive fever in the lords of quarters.

8. Hearing that Durjaya was dead, they brought the submarine fire and rushed to the gods.

9. These two demons went to mount Himavat with the army and stood there.

10. The gods also collected a huge army and discussed about regaining the position of Indra.

11-12. Then the preceptor sage Āṅgirasa told the gods; "First you perform the Gomedha sacrifice and then all other sacrifices. That is the practice. This is my advice. Do follow it."

13. When he said this, the gods left the cattle to graze and entrusted Saramā (the bitch of gods) to look after them.

14. Those cows being looked after by Saramā, the dog of gods, O Earth, went to the place of demons.

15. Seeing those cows, the demons told their priest Śukra: "See, those cows, O Brahmin, grazing, being looked after by Saramā, the bitch of the gods. Tell us what we should do now"

16. When they asked him thus, Śukra said: "Steal these cows quickly; don't delay".

17. Accordingly the demons took away the cows.

18. When the cows were stolen, Saramā searched for them; and found out that they were carried away by demons. The demons realised that Saramā had traced the path of cows.

19. Seeing her they told her in a soft manner: "O auspicious Saramā, please drink the milk of these cows." Then they gave the milk to her.

20-21. Then the leaders of demons told her: "O auspicious, bitch, don't say about these cows of Indra." Then the demons left her in the forest. She, then, went quickly to the gods shivering.

22. Saramā prostrated before Indra, the lord of gods.

23. Indra told the gods Maruts: "O mighty gods, you please go secretly along with this bitch to find out the cattle." Thus they went quickly taking subtle forms.

24. They came back and, O Earth, prostrated before Indra.

25. The king of gods asked: "Saramā, where are the cows?" Saramā replied: "I don't know".

26. Full of anger, then, Indra asked Maruts: "O Maruts, where are the cows intended for sacrifice? Why does Saramā say so?"

27. Then unperturbed, the Maruts reported to him what Saramā had done.

28. Then the great Indra kicked the bitch in great anger.

29. Saying, "O you fool you have drunk the milk ! The cows are stolen by the demons.", he kicked her again.

30. As a result of that kick by Indra, Saramā vomited the milk she had drunk and ran to the place where the cows were held. Indra followed her accompanied by his army.

31. He saw the cows stolen by demons. But the demons who looked after the cows were very strong.

32. Still they were crushed by Indra's army and so they gave up their bodies along with the cows. Regaining the lost cows the king of gods along with his chieftains became delighted.

33. Thus recovering the cows, Lord Indra with great joy performed a thousand different sacrifices.

34. As he performed these sacrifices, his power also got increased. Then Indra told the army of gods.

35. "O Gods, prepare quickly, to kill demons." Hearing this, gods got themselves ready in a moment.

36. Then they marched with Indra and in the battle they defeated the army of Asuras.

37. O Earth, the few demons that survived the battle, plunged into the sea struck with fear and completely perplexed.

38. And the great lord Indra followed by gods and protectors of the quarters reigned in heaven as before.

39. The man who hears daily this excellent story of Saramā attains the fruit of Gomedha sacrifice.

40. If a king who lost his kingdom listens to this story intently, he will be able to recover his kingdom like Indra the heaven.

CHAPTER SEVENTEEN

The Story of Mahātapas

Earth said :

1. Those great men who were born of the gem were given a boon indeed by the God in Tretāyuga.

2. How was the birth of those kings to be ? What were their deeds ? Tell me this for each.

Varāha said:

3. O Earth, listen to the origin of the great king Suprabha who rose from the gem.

4. In Kṛtayuga there lived a powerful and noble king named Śrutakīrti.

5. Suprabha was born as his son, and was named Prajāpāla.

6. One day he went to the forest infested with wild beasts, and saw there the great hermitage of a sage.

7. In it an exceedingly virtuous sage by name Mahātapas was performing penance giving up food and meditating on the Supreme Soul.

8. King Prajāpāla felt desirous of entering the hermitage, and he quickly went into it.

9. In the grand hermitage, there were pleasant bowers beautiful like the moon with attractive creepers surrounded by hovering bees. The very pathway was fine with big trees on the sides.

10.* The ponds with full-blown red lotuses looked like celestial women with rosy feet, who had left Indraloka and come there.

11. In the protruding branches of trees which looked very symmetrical, were blossoms of flowers with honeyfed blackbees and a variety of birds reposing as if fully satiated.

12. There were many kinds of trees like Kadamba, Nīpa Arjuna and Sāla, nourished by the householders and served by sweet-voiced birds.

13. The hermitage was surrounded by Brahmins with families and by sacred smokes coming up from the sacrificial fire. The elephant of vice there was killed by the lions of virtue.

14. Seeing there different objects like these, the king entered the hermitage. In it he saw the great sage Mahātapas, the champion of duty and seeker of Brahman, sitting on a seat of kuśa-grass, and resplendent like the sun.

15. Seeing the sage, the king forgot his hunt. The sight of the sage diverted his good mind to righteous action.

1. The stanza is very corrupt.

16. The sage received Prajāpāla with words of welcome and offered him a seat.

17. Then the king prostrated before the great sage and sat on his seat. O Earth, then he asked him:

18. "Tell me, O Great sage, what should be done by those plunged into woes of worldly life, but wish to overcome it."

Mahātapas said:

19. Those men who are plunged into the ocean of worldly life have to obtain a firm raft to cross it. They have to make the lord of all the three worlds this raft with proper worship, homas, gifts and prescribed sacrifices and meditations and fixed to the liberated souls by the strong strings of their vital airs.

20. One who bows to Nārāyaṇa, the destroyer of hell and the Lord of gods in devotion, attains the imperishable abode of Viṣṇu, free from all sorrows.

Prajāpāla asked:

21. O sage, the knower of all that is righteous, tell me precisely how the eternal Viṣṇu is worshipped by those men who wish to get final emancipation.

Mahātapas replied :

22. Hear from me, O intelligent king, how Viṣṇu, the lord of all the yogins, is pleased at men and women.

23. The Vedas say that Brahmā and all other gods and the manes all of whom were in the cosmic egg were born from Viṣṇu.

24-25. Agni, Aśvins, Gaurī, Gaṇapati, Nāgas, Kārttikeya, Ādityas, Mātṛs, Durgā, Diks, Kubera, Viṣṇu, Yama, Rudra, Candra, Pitṛs—all these were born of the lord of the worlds, according to their importance.

26. All these beings were in Hiraṇyagarbha's body. But each became highly egoistic.

27. Their loud claims, 'I am competent', 'I have to be propitiated by sacrifices', were heard in the assembly of the gods like the roar of agitated ocean.

28-29. Among them, O king, Agni (fire)stood up and said: "Sacrifice for me; meditate on me. This body created by Brahmā will perish without me. Hence I am great".

30. So saying Fire left the body; but even when he disappeared, the body did not perish.

31. Then Aśvins, the personified forms of Prāṇa and Apāna airs said: "We are important and so we have to be pleased with sacrifices".

32. Saying this they stood apart leaving the body. The body was a bit emaciated, but it did not perish.

33. Then Gaurī, the speech, said : "Importance is in me". So saying she also left the body.

34. Even without her, the body remained, though without speech. Then Gaṇapati, the space, said:

35-36. "Without me no body stands for long in course of time." So saying he also left the body. Without him too, the body did not perish.

37. Finding the body devoid of holes, all the *dhātus* of the body said thus:

38. "In our absence the body cannot bear itself"—saying this, all of them left the body.

39. Even without them the body was looked after by Puruṣa (the Supreme Soul). Seeing that, Skanda who is the embodiment of Ahaṁkāra (ego) said:

40. "Without me the body cannot exist". So saying he left the body and stood away.

41. Without him too, the body stood intact and as if emancipated. Seeing this, Sun, the Āditya, got angry.

42. "How can this body stand without me even for a moment ?" Uttering thus, he left the body. Even then the body was not destroyed.

43. Then the group of passion and the like called as Mothers said: "The body cannot bear itself if we leave this." They left the body. Then also the body was unaffected.

44. Then Durgā well known as Māyā (illusion) said angrily: "without me there is no life (Bhūti)". Saying this Durgā disappeared from the body. Even then the body was not destroyed.

45. Then the quarters stood up and said, "No doubt, without us, nothing could be done".

46-47. Within a moment they went away. Then Kubera, the air occurring in the middle of the body, also left the body and went upwards.

48. Then Viṣṇu, the mind, said: "Without me this body cannot stand even for a moment. Saying this, he also disappeared.

49. After this Yama said: "I protect all this. When I leave this body nothing should be there."

Saying this, Yama went away. Even then the body was not affected.

50. Then said Mahādeva, the subtle cause of beings: "I am great and without me the body will not be there."

51. Saying this Śiva (Mahat) left the body. Then also it was not destroyed.

52. Seeing this the Pitṛs (sense organs) said: "As long as we along with other life-airs live in this, this body stands; otherwise it will be destroyed." So saying they left the body and disappeared.

53-54. Saying this, Agni, Prāṇa, Apāna, Ākāśa Dhātus, Ahaṁkāra, sun, desire, Māyā quarters, Vāyu, Viṣṇu, Dharma, Śambhu and the sense-organs left the body.

55. Still the body stood as if liberated, being protected by Puruṣa in the form of Soma, the moon.

56. When the imperishable Soma consisting of sixteen digits stood thus, the body with its qualities stood up and began its work as before.

57. Seeing the body protected by Sarvajña (Puruṣa) as before, all those deities of the body got ashamed and extolled that great god.

58. O king, all those entered into the body and took their own positions and extolled Him: "You are the Fire, you are Prāṇa, Apāna and Sarasvatī (word).

59. You are Ākāśa, Kubera and Dhātus of the body. You are Ahaṁkāra; you are the Sun, and the Mātṛgaṇa.

60. You are the Māyā and the earth, you are Durgā, quarters and Indra; you are Viṣṇu and Dharma. You are the victor and the vanquished.

61. You are called Parameśvara (Supreme lord) in its liberal sense. Otherwise how could this happen (the body remaining unaffected) when we left it.

62. When we gave up the body, O God, there was none else but you. So please protect us.

63. O Creator, having created yourself in our forms, don't change positions."

Thus extolled by them, the God was pleased very much.

64. He told them: "I have created you for my sport. I have only one purpose to be gained by you.

65. If you don't like your form, then you divide it into two and stand formless in the beings on earth and with form in the world of gods. In due course attain dissolution (in the Supreme soul) yourselves.

66. Do not be egoistic any more with regard to yourselves in the body. I shall assign you your names now.

67. Agni will be Vaiśvānara; Prāṇa and Apāna, Aśvins; Gaurī-Himavat's daughter.

68. The qualities like those of the earth will be Gaṇapati. These various other beings are the dhātus (the essential elements) of the body.

69. Skanda Kārttikeya will be the ego. At the end Durgā will be the last of the causes for the body and will be Māyā (the power of illusion).

70. These ten virgins will be ten quarters. Kubera will be the air.

71. This mind will be called Viṣṇu, no doubt; so also Dharma (righteousness) will be Yama.

72. The 'great principle' (Mahattattva) will be Mahādeva. The sense organs will be the manes, no doubt.

73. This moon will be always in the Jāmitra, no doubt.[1]

Thus I have described the Vedānta-puruṣa (Vedāntic Man) in the form of Nārāyaṇa." All the gods sat on their respective seats. And the God thus finished the account.

74. I have told you, O king, about God Viṣṇu who is of such prowess and who can be known only through the Vedas. What else do you want to know?

---

1. Jāmitra is the seventh house in horoscopy. This is taken as the house concerned with matrimony. The passage indicates that moon will govern marital relations.

CHAPTER EIGHTEEN

(The Origin of Fire)

Prajāpāla said:

1-3. O great sage, how did Agni, Aśvins, Gaurī, Gaṇapati, Nāgas, Skanda, Āditya, Candra, Mātṛs, Durgā, Diks, Kubera, Viṣṇu, Dharma, Śiva, Pitṛs and Candra take birth ? How did all these deities of the body attain concrete forms ?

4. Also tell me, O sage, for each of these the food, name, and the sacred day of the month, on which each gives to the people the result of their worship. I wish to know all this secret.

Mahātapas said:

5. When the omniscient soul in the form of Nārāyaṇa played himself with the form attained by the yogic power, he willed in himself the desire to enjoy.

6. Then the great cosmos (Mahābhūta) was stirred, the wonderful basis of all existence (water) arose.

7. Pleased at this, he willed its transformation, and during this transformation, there arose the great fire.

8. This fire was burning with countless flames and with noise. The effulgent fire underwent transformation and then arose from it the terrific wind.

9. By the transformation of air, Ether (space) came into existence with sound as its distinctive quality.

10. The space, air, heat and water interacted among themselves.

11. The water was dried by the heat and wafted by the wind, and the sky was made distinct.

12. The whole mass thus solidified and hardened. Thus came into being this earth and later the trees and the rest in it.

13. By the harmonious combination of these four (water, fire, air and space) as well as by the preponderance of each, the earth attained five qualities established in it. Getting hard thus, it became the Brahmāṇḍa (the universe).

14. In it, God Nārāyaṇa having four hands and a fourfold form wished to create different beings taking the form of the creator.

15. Thinking about it as he did, he could not properly conceive it. Then he became extremely angry.

16. From that anger arose fire with a thousand flames and it came to burn the Creator himself. It was then told by him as follows.

17-18. "You bear (*vaha*) the offerings *havya* (for the gods) and *kavya* (for the manes)". Thus Fire became *Havyavāhana*. But fire was itself hungry and asked Brahmā (the creator): what it might do. Brahmā replied. "You will be gratified in three ways.[1]

19. Propitiated by dakṣiṇās (offerings of money) first, you carry the dakṣiṇās to the gods. So you be *Dakṣiṇāgni*.

20. You take what is offered to the gods in sacrifices all over the three worlds. So, O fire, you are *Havyavāhana*.

21. The body is said to be Gṛha (a home). Since you are its Lord, you be *Gārhapatya* everywhere.

22. When propitiated by offerings you lead all men to final liberation. Therefore you be *Vaiśvānara*.

23. *Draviṇa* (money) is power and it is wealth. Since you give this, you are *Draviṇodāḥ* (giver of money).

24. Sins disappear always. The word *nis* stands for certainty. Therefore and also since you are everywhere, O Agni, you will get (the name) *Tejas* (splendour).[2]

25. Since you blaze when *Idhma* (the bundle of sacred sticks) is placed in you and air blows, you are yourself *Idhma*.

26. O my son, surely people who sacrifice will propitiate you with offerings in these names in great sacrifices."

CHAPTER NINETEEN

The Greatness of Fire

Mahātapas said:

1. I have told you incidentally the greatness of Viṣṇu's

---

1. This refers to the three sacred fires—Gārhapatya, Dākṣiṇātya and Āhavanīya.

2. This verse is highly corrupt and does not yield any cogent sense. Some matter seems to be missing between the two lines.

manifestations. Now I shall tell you about the importance of *tithis* (dates). Listen to me.

2. The great fire born from Brahmā's anger asked Brahmā: "O lord, please give me a day in which I shall get the praise of the whole world".

Brahmā said:

3. O fire, the foremost among the gods, Yakṣas and Gandharvas, you were born on *Pratipad*, the first day (in the fortnight).

4. On account of this that day will be honoured by all gods. Thus the day *Pratipad* is yours.

5. On that day the gods and manes will be gratified by the offerings given in *Prājāpatya* form.

6. Four kinds of beings, men, beasts, demons and gods, together with Gandharvas, will be pleased if you are gratified.

7. Your devotee who on the Pratipad day, fully fasts or takes milk alone, gets the great result of beng worshipped in heaven for twentysix aeons.

8. And he will be the powerful, beautiful and wealthy in this life and after his death he will be respected in heaven as a king.

9. The fire went to the hermitage given by Brahmā and kept quiet.

10. The man who hears this story of the birth of fire getting up early morning, no doubt, will be free from all sins.

CHAPTER TWENTY

The Origin of Aśvins

Prajāpāla said:

1. The fire was thus born from the great Brahmā. How did Prāṇa and Apāna in the form of twin gods Áśvins take birth ?

Mahātapas said:

2. Marīci was Brahmā's son, the foremost among the fourteen forms assumed by him.

3. His son was the great sage by name Kaśyapa. Being himself a creator, he became the father of gods.

4. He got as his sons twelve suns, (ādityas) all endowed with the spirit of Lord Nārāyaṇa.

5. These suns (ādityas) are the twelve months while Viṣṇu himself is the year. Mārtaṇḍa is the most lustrous among those twelve suns (ādityas).

6. Tvaṣṭā gave him his gracious daughter named Saṃjñā in marriage. He got two children by her, Yama and Yamunā.

7. But unable to bear his virility she became a steed fast as the mind and leaving her shadow (Chāyā) there, went to the Northern Kurus.

8. The Sun had union with Chāyā who was in form and complexion similar to her and got two chidren—Śani (Saturn) and Tapatī.

9. Chāyā did not treat all these children equally and so Mārtaṇḍa became angry and told her: "O dear, don't show partiality among your children."

10. Yet, she did not change her attitude. Then Yama said to his father with great sorrow:

11. "O my father, she is not my mother. She always behaves towards us as an enemy. In a stepmotherly manner, she behaves cruelly towards us, but kindly towards her own children."

12. Hearing Yama's words, Chāyā lost her temper and cursed him: "You will shortly be the king of the dead".

13. Hearing this, Mārtaṇḍa consoled him saying: "You will be the judge in deciding merit and demerit. And you will have the position in heaven as a guardian deity".[1]

14. Then, agitated by Chāyā's anger, he cursed Śani (Saturn). "O my son, you will be of cruel eye on account of your mother's fault".

15. Then, the Sun rose up and went to Northern Kurus to see Saṃjñā and saw her there in the form of a mare.

16. Then he too took the form of a steed and united himself with her.

---

1. Yama is the *dikpāla* guarding the southern direction.

17. In that daughter of Tvaṣṭā in the form a mare, he, in the form of the horse, laid the glowing seed, but that came out split into two.

18. These in the uterus were Prāṇa and Apāna but attained embodied forms due to boon.

19. Since they were born from Tvaṣṭā's daughter who was in the form of a mare (*Aśva*), these sons of the Sun by her are praised as the Aśvins.

20. The Sun himself was the Creator, the daughter of Tvaṣṭā the power (Śakti) by name *parāpara*. These two were in her body first formless and then they attained their form.

21. Then the gods Aśvins approached the Sun and asked him: "What shall we do ?"

The Sun said:

22. "O my sons, worship the Creator Nārāyaṇa with devotion and get from Him a boon".

23. Advised by the great Sun thus they, performed severe penance reciting the Brahmapāra hymn.

24. After so many years, Brahmā, the manifestation of Nārāyaṇa, was pleased by their penance and he gave them a boon with extreme joy.

Prajāpāla said:

25. O great sage, I wish to know the hymn recited by the Aśvins on Brahmā.

Mahātapas said:

26. Hear from me, O sinless king, the hymn to Brahmā recited by the Aśvins and the fruit that they obtained by the recitation of that hymn.

27. "I bow to you, the being free from action, free from the world, one without any base or dependence, devoid of qualities and beyond vision, and one free from the feeling 'I' and 'mine'.

28. O Brahman, great Brahman, dear to Brahmins, O man, Supreme Man, excellent Man; O god, great god, excellent god; O immovable, one who preserves harmony.

29. O being, great being, lord of beings; O Yakṣa, great Yakṣa, lord of Yakṣas; O Guhya, great Guhya and Lord of

Guhyas: O soft, very soft, and lord of all that is soft.

30. O bird, lord of great birds, O demon, lord of great demons; O Rudra, lord of great Rudras; O Viṣṇu, lord of great Viṣṇu; O Supreme lord Nārāyaṇa; I bow to you, O Prajāpati (creator)."

31. Extolled by those twin gods, the Aśvins, the Creator was pleased very much and said thus:

32. "Please woo a boon which is rare even to the gods and by which you can go everywhere in heaven."

Aśvins said:

33. "O great Creator, please give us our share among gods. Please give us the position of gods who drink Soma-juice and an eternal place in the generality of gods."

Brahmā said:

34. You will attain all these—beauty, lustre, uniqueness, the position of physicians for all beings, and a place among gods entitled to drink Soma-juice in the worlds.

Mahātapas said:

35. All this was given by Brahmā to Aśvins on the second day. Therefore, the second (*Dvitīyā*) is the best day among all days.

36. The man who wishes to attain beauty should eat flowers only on this day. And if he does this for a year in all purity, he will attain great beauty of form.

37. One who hears this account of the origin of Aśvins daily, attains all those qualities of Aśvins and will be freed from all sins and blessed with sons.

CHAPTER TWENTYONE

The Origin of Gaurī

Prajāpāla said:

1. O wise sage, how was Gaurī extolled on account of the boon, and how did she become part of the body of the great god (Rudra) ?

Mahātapas said:

2. Formerly, the virtuous god Brahmā, in order to create different beings, entered into deep thought, but could not gain the end.

3. He then became angry, and from the anger arose the valiant Rudra (lit. 'roarer'), so-called because he was crying loudly at birth.

4. To him Brahmā gave as wife the auspicious virgin his daughter, the goddess of speech, named Gaurī.

5-7. He was extremely happy at getting this beautiful damsel, but when Brahmā persuaded him repeatedly to create, he found himself incapable of it and entered into water (to perform penance) feeling that what could be done through penance alone could not be accomplished without it.

8-9. When he thus remained within water, Brahmā lodged the beautiful Gaurī within his own body, and then, desirous of creation, produced seven beings[1] from his mind and also Dakṣa, and progeny was thus increased.

10. The children of Dākṣāyaṇī (lit. Dakṣa's daughter[2]) are the gods and (their king) Indra, eight Vasus, Rudras,[3] Ādityas and Maruts.

11-12. The beautiful Gaurī, formerly married by the great Rudra was then given by Brahmā as daughter to Dakṣa. She thus became Dākṣāyaṇī.

13. Dakṣa was pleased with his daughter's children and in

---

1. These are the seven sages Marīci, Atri and others.
2. Presumably identical with Aditi.
3. This group of gods should be taken as different from the Rudra created by Brahmā earlier.

order to make them prosperous, he started a sacrifice to propitiate Brahmā.

14. In that the functions of the priests were taken upon themselves by the sons of Brahmā, namely Marīci and others, in a specific manner.

15-17. Marīci became Brahman (priest), Atri the supervisor, Aṅgiras the Āgnīdhra (priest to kindle fire), Pulastya the Hotā (to recite Ṛgvedic hymns), Pulaha the Udgātā (to recite Sāman hymns), Kratu the Prastotā (to assist the Udgātā), Pracetas the Pratihartā (also to assist the Udgātā) and Vāsiṣṭha the Subrahmaṇya (priest). The Sabhā (assembly) was constituted of Sanaka and others.

18. The person to be propitiated by the sacrifice was Brahmā himself and the sacrifice was for the world. The persons to be honoured were the sons of Dakṣa's daughter, Rudras, Ādityas, Aṅgiras and others because they are the visible Pitṛs, and once they are pleased, the whole world is pleased.

19-20. The sacrificial offerings were meant for the Devas, Ādityas, Vasus, Viśvedevas, Pitṛs, Gandharvas and Maruts, and they received fully all that was offered in the sacrificial fire.

21. At that time, suddenly arose Rudra, the anger-born son of Brahmā, from the water into which he had formerly entered.

22. He came out of the water completely pure, full of knowledge and resplendant like a thousand suns.

23. He shone with his penance which enabled him to visualise the whole universe. Then took place the creation of five things, the celestrials and the four kinds of mortals.

24. The creation by Rudra occurred quickly. O great king, now listen to the account of that creation.

25-26. When Rudra came out after performing penance in the water for ten thousand years, he saw the earth full of fine vegetation and big forests and peopled by human beings and beasts.

27. He then heard the recitations of the priests in Dakṣa's house and the words of praise in the hermitage.

28. At that the omniscient and resplendent god (Rudra) became extremely angry and said:

29. "Formerly I was created by Brahmā to be fully potent

to create beings and I was asked to start the process. Who has done that action now".

30-31. So saying he roared aloud in high rage and from his ears issued forth huge flames and from them came out with weapons ghosts and goblins in crores.

32. After creating such an army equipped with numerous weapons he produced a chariot of Veda and Vidyā (knowledge).

33-34. In it two deer were the drawing horses, the triple principle[1] was the central pole, the three sandhyās (morning, noon and evening) the three shafts (wheels), dharma the axle, air the sound, day and night the two flags, merit and demerit the flagstaffs all the Vidyās together with Kalās the seat and Brahmā the charioteer.

35. Gāyatrī was the bow, the syllable Om the bowstring, the seven notes of music the arrows for that great god.

36. With all this array and equipment the valiant god flew to Dakṣa's sacrifice.

37. As Rudra was descending from the sky, there was a loud noise at which the mantras of the priests were lost.

38. Seeing this portent the priests said in fear; "A great danger has befallen us; let the gods get ready for battle".

39. A big demon created by Brahmā is coming here to partake of the special offering in this sacrifice".

40. Then the gods addressed their maternal grand-father Dakṣa: "O Sire, please tell us what you think we should do".

Dakṣa said:

41. "Take up your weapons immediately and wage a war".

42. Told thus, A big battle was then fought by the gods with the army of Rudra, carrying various weapons.

43. The vampires, goblins and imps holding different weapons fought with the guardian deities.

44. The Bhūtagaṇas came out of heaven and entering Yama's abode showered arrows, fierce swords and axes.

45. They attacked Devas with firebrands and bows and arrows in fury before Rudra.

46. Then in that fierce battle Rudra pierced with an arrow

1. Signifies God, Soul and matter.

both the eyes of Bhaga.

47. Seeing Bhaga thus made eyeless, Pūṣā got angry and engaged Rudra in fight.

48. Seeing Pūṣā aiming an array of arrows, Rudra caught him and pulled out his teeth.

49. At the sight of these fallen teeth the army of gods took to their heels.

50. Seeing the army scattering away Viṣṇu, the younger brother of Āditya, addressed it.

51. "Where do you run away giving up your valour, pride and position. Why don't you remember your calling, family and responsibility ?

52. Since you get your life from Brahmā, you prostrate before that great god."

53. Saying thus, Viṣṇu wearing yellow garment and bearing conch, disc and mace, seated himself on Garuḍa.

54. Then occurred the thrilling battle between Viṣṇu and Rudra.

55. Rudra hit Hari with the Pāśupata weapon. Infuriated at this Hari hit Rudra with the Nārāyaṇa weapon.

56. These two weapons fought each other in the sky intensively, each to gain victory over the other. The fight continued for a thousand divine years.

57. One was having a crown on his head, and the other tresses of matted hair. One blew the conch, the other sounded the drum.

58. One was holding a sword and the other a staff. One was glowing with the Kaustubha gem, the other was shining with ashes all over the body.

59. One was whirling the mace, the other the pole. One shone with gems round the neck and the other with a string of skulls.

60. One was wearing the yellow garment, the other a girdle of serpents. Thus were the two opposing weapons, one Viṣṇu's and the other Śiva's in essence.

61. Seeing them combating each other, Brahmā appealed to them to calm down.

62. They did so and Brahmā told Viṣṇu and Rudra.

63. "Both Viṣṇu and Rudra will attain prominence in the world. This sacrifice which was smashed, also will be completed.

64. Dakṣa will attain fame in the world because of the progeny".

65. Telling thus to Viṣṇu and Rudra, Brahmā, the grandfather of the world, asked the people to give Rudra a share in the sacrifice.

66. (He said): "The portion to Rudra is declared to be the foremost in the Vedas. So you Devas, praise this great god Rudra the destroyer of the eye of Bhaga and the teeth of Pūṣā.

67. Quickly sing his praise with all his names, and he will be pleased to grant you boons.

68. Thus asked, Devas bowed to Śambhu and sang his praise in great reverence.

The gods said:

69-70. "Bow to the uneven-eyed, bow to the three-eyed, bow to the hundred-eyed, bow to the bearer of trident, bow to the bearer of Khaṭvāṅga,[1] bow to the holder of staff.

71. You are resplendent like the shooting flame as well as like a crore of suns. We were foolish before seeing you, we are enlightened now at your sight.

72. Bow to the three-eyed Śambhu, the remover of all distress, holder of the trident, with mouth fierce, lord of all gods, the essence of purity, immanent, omnipresent, O Rudra, be pleased.

73. O lord of the worlds pervading the universe, O fierce destroyer of the teeth of Pūṣā, with neck full of hanging serpents with expansive body and bluish neck, be pleased.

74. O great lord endowed with all virtues, the crusher of Bhaga's eye, be pleased to receive the main share of the sacrificial offering and save us all.

75. O lord that arose from Brahmā, O lord of Umā, O destroyer of Tripura, O holder of the bowl, with ash smeared in body, save us from all fear.

76. We find in your person, O Lord of gods, the entire

1. A mace with a skull at the head.

creation, the Vedas with their Pada, Krama etc.,[1] and the Vedāṅgas and all branches of knowledge.

77. "O Bhava, O Śarva, O Mahādeva, O Pinākin, O Rudra, O Hara, we all bow to you, protect us all".

78. Praised by the gods in this way, Maheśvara was much pleased, and he spoke thus to them all:

Rudra said:

79. "Let Bhaga get back his eye and Pūṣā his teeth. Let the sacrifice of Dakṣa also attain completion.

80. At my sight, O Devas, you have all become animals to me and I take you all to me. I thus become your master.

81-82. I am also the prime master of all knowledge. Being thus the master of all you animals, I will attain the name Paśupati (lord of all beasts) in the world.

83. Those who sacrifice for me will have the observance called 'Paśupati' ".

84. When Rudra spoke thus, Brahmā told him affectionately with a smile:

"Certainly you will be hailed as 'Paśupati' in the world, and the world will gain renown by your name.

85. The entire world will surely worship you.

86. The clever Brahmā then spoke to Dakṣa: "As already decided, give Gaurī in marriage to Rudra".

87. Saying so he gave the highly auspicious Gaurī to Rudra in the presence of Dakṣa, thus showing him a great favour.

88. When Dakṣa's daughter was thus married, Brahmā gave to Rudra an abode on mount Kailāsa before all gods.

89. Rudra with his attendant Bhūtas then went to Kailāsa.

90. Devas in great joy returned to their places and Brahmā with Dakṣa went to his abode.

---

1. Pada, Krama, Jaṭā, Ratha and Ghana are methods of rendering the Veda, each word being differently combined with the preceding and following words.

CHAPTER TWENTYTWO

The Marriage of Gauri

Mahātapas said:

1. While they were thus living there, Gaurī got angry towards Rudra, thinking of the enmity between him and her father.

2. She thought of the place[1] taken away by him and his smashing the sacrifice and decided to give up her body.

3. She thought: "Being born in his house,[2] I shall attain the lord by penance. How can I go to my father Dakṣa who has nothing with him now?

4. Thinking thus, the beautiful wife of Rudra, went for penance in the great mountain Himālaya.

5. Then she allowed her body to gradually emaciate and finally burnt it by the fire from within, and then she became the daughter of Himavān by name Umā, also called Kṛṣṇā.

6. Thus born with a beautiful and auspicious body in the house of Himavān, she again performed penance meditating on the three-eyed Rudra.

7. She remained in penance for a long time with the resolve: "This (Rudra) is my husband".

8. When she was thus performing severe penance in the great mountain Himavān, god Maheśvara felt propitiated and appeared in her hermitage in the form of a Brahmin.

9. The Brahmin was very old with crippled limbs and was faltering at every step. He came near her with difficulty and told her: "O gracious lady, I am extremely hungry, please give me some food".

10. Asked thus, Umā, the daughter of the mountain told him: "O Brahmin, I shall give you fruits to eat. Please take your bath and then eat well".

11. At this, the Brahmin got down for bath in the river Gaṅgā which was flowing close by.

12. While bathing there, he created in it an illusory shark, big and fierce, and that caught him.

13. He then told Umā showing her the shark that had caught him.

---

1. Kailāsa.
2. In the house of Himavān.

14. "O girl, a great mishap has happened. Save me from this shark before I am mutilated by it".

15. Hearing this Pārvatī thought: "I touch Himavān as my father and Śiva as my husband. In this state of mind, purified by penance, how can I touch this Brahmin?

16. If I don't hold him by the hand and drag him out of the water, no doubt the sin of being responsible for the death of a Brahmin will befall me.

17. Any other transgression of righteousness can be atoned for, but never being the cause of a Brahmin's death". So saying she hastened towards him.

18. Going there quickly she held the Brahmin by the hand and dragged him out of the water. He then assumed his real form.

19. The same lord Rudra to please whom Pārvatī was performing penance was now holding her hand.

20. Seeing him she was bashful, and remembering her act of giving up her body, did not speak.

21. Seeing Gaurī silent, Rudra said with a smile: "Having held me by the hand, how can you give me up?

22. If you are going to make this vain for wedlock, then I ask you, the daughter of Brahmā, to give me food (for which I came).

23. O lady, I am not joking; I have told you what I should".
She then said with a smile:

24. "O great lord of the three worlds, all my endeavour has been to attain you. I worshipped you as my husband in my previous life.

25. Now too you are my husband, and none else can be so. But my master is now my father, the lord of mountains. I shall go to him.

26. Duly getting his consent. you will marry me".

27. So saying, she went to her father Himavān and with palms joined in reverence she told him thus.

28. "Rudra, the smasher of Dakṣa's sacrifice, who was my husband in my former life, has now become, as a result of my penance, full of love for me.

29. He came to me in my hermitage in the guise of an old Brahmin and asked me food.

30. I asked him to have his bath (before the meal), and accordingly he descended into the Ganges for the purpose. He was then caught by a shark and he cried for help.

31. Being afraid of incurring the sin of killing a Brahmin (if I did not help him), I pulled him out by the hand, and then he showed me his real form.

32. He then told me that our hands have been mutually held together (and thus the marriage has been effected), and that I should not have any hesitation.

33. Being thus told by the great Śaṅkara, I have now come to tell you.

34. Whatever is proper now, you may kindly do quickly".

35. Hearing these words, the king of mountains was much pleased, and he told his daughter:

36. "O daughter, I am indeed blessed in this world in that Rudra has by himself chosen to become my son-in-law. I have become the father of a worthy daughter.

37. I have now been placed at the head of Devas by you, my daughter. Please wait for a while till I return".

38. So saying, the king of the mountains went to Brahmā, the grandfather of all Devas.

39. Bowing to him in reverence, he said that he proposed to give his daughter Umā in marriage to Rudra.

40. Brahmā, the grandfather of Devas and progenitor of the world, gave his consent.

41. Then the king of mountains rushed back to his home. He then invited Tumburu, Nārada, Hāhā, Hūhū, Kinnaras, Asuras and Rākṣasas.

42. The mountains, rivers, hills, trees and plants all came in their personal forms to see Himavān's daughter and her marriage with Śaṅkara.

43. The earth became the altar for the marriage, the seven seas the ritual pots, the sun and the moon the lamps, and the rivers the carriers of water.

44. Making thus the materials for the marriage, the king of mountains sent mount Mandara to Rudra.

45. Called by Mandara, Śaṅkara came quickly and he took the hand of Umā in marriage according to the rites.

46. In that ceremony Parvata and Nārada sang, the Sid-

dhas danced, the trees showered flowers and celestial damsels danced in joy.

47. In that marriage wherein holy water was flowing, Brahmā, in consideration of the world, told Umā, "O daughter, you will be a model for other women in the world", and told Rudra "you will be a model for other men".

48. So saying to Umā and Rudra, Brahmā went to his abode.

49. Thus said sage Mahātapas to Prajāpāla who asked him. (He continued).

50. "The origin of Gaurī as well as the account of her marriage has been thus said to you."

51. All this happened on Tṛtīyā tithi. Therefore on Tṛtīyā tithi day give up salt in your food.

52. A man or a woman who fasts on that day gets prosperity.

53-54. A man or woman in utter misery, if he or she gives up salt and listens to this, attains all desires, acquires great wealth and gains health, brilliance and opulence.

CHAPTER TWENTYTHREE

The Origin of Vināyaka

Prajāpāla said:

1. O good sage, I am eager to know how Gaṇapati was born. Be pleased to tell me.

Mahātapas said:

2. Formerly, the hosts of Devas and all the sages and saints began to do things to gain the result.

3. It was seen that the actions of the righteous faced numerous impediments to success while the actions of the unrighteous were unimpeded.

4. Then the gods and manes seriously deliberated on the matter and thought of ways for creating obstacles in the actions of the bad.

5. It occurred to Devas then that they may very well consult

the highly intelligent Rudra.

6. They, therefore, went to him in Kailāsa and, bowing to him, said in great respect.

The gods said:

7. "O great god with three eyes and trident in hand, it behoves you to create (a being) for obstructing the actions of the bad".

8. Thus requested by Devas, Rudra with great pleasure looked at Umā for a moment.

9. When he was looking at Umā in the presence of gods, he was worried why no form of his was seen in the sky.

10. "There is the body in earth, there is one in water; so also in fire and air.

11-15. How is it not there in sky?" So thinking he laughed. By the power of knowledge, by what was seen by Rudra in the sky, by what was said by Brahmā formerly as the body of all beings, by the laughter of Rudra, by all these four in the four elements Earth and the rest, there arose a boy effulgent with glowing face, looking like Rudra himself and stupefying Devas with the charm of his dazzling brilliance.

16. Seeing the person of this great boy, Umā remained with eyes stuck on him.

17. Looking at the beautiful form of the boy and thinking of the fickleness of women's minds Rudra got angry and cursed him.

18. "O boy, you will attain an elephant's face, protruding belly and yajñopavīta of serpents".

19. He cursed him thus in great anger, and then rose up shaking his body.

20. With each shake of the body, water fell on the earth and from it arose numerous Vināyakas, elephant-faced and dark-coloured, holding various weapons.

21-22. The Lord (Rudra) then got annoyed and wondered when even one of them could do extraordinary things, how much more will the multitude do?

23. When Devas were thus thinking, the earth became agitated by Vināyakas. Brahmā then rose up in the sky in his vehicle and said:

24. "O gods, you are lucky. You have been blessed by the wonderful Parameśvara (Rudra). The actions of demons will be surely hampered".

25. After telling them thus, he turned to the holder of fire in the palm (Rudra): "O Lord, let him who was born out of your mouth (i.e., laughter), Gaṇapati, be the chief of these Vināyakas, and let the rest be his followers.

26. Occupying the sky as well, let him be in the other four elements with you. And let the sky with all its parts be for him.

27. You be the master to give him great weapons."

When Brahmā departed after saying thus, the three-eyed (Rudra) told his son:

28-29. "May you have the names Vināyaka, Vighnakara, Gaṇeśa and Bhavaputra, and may all these (other) Vināyakas with fierce eyes and prowess be your servants, and let them with their flowing ichor and massive body, bring about success in all undertakings.

30. In sacrifices and ceremonies to propitiate the gods, and in other deeds, you will bestow success if you are worshipped in the beginning, and hamper the whole thing if not done so".

31. Then Rudra as well as Devas poured holy water on him in golden pitchers and declared him king of the Vināyakas.

32. The Devas then praised him in the presence of Rudra.

Devas said:

33. "Bow to the elephant-faced, bow to the leader of gaṇas (group of Vināyakas), bow to Vināyaka (the chief), bow to the valiant.

34. Bow to the creator of obstacles, bow to the serpent-girdled, bow to him who rose from the mouth of Rudra, bow to the pot-bellied. O lord of all, we prostrate before you to remove all obstacles".

35. The great Gaṇeśa thus praised by the gods, and anointed by Rudra, became the son of Umā.

36. All this occurred in the tithi Caturthī. Hence Caturthī is the most important of all tithis.

37. O king, on this day if one eats only sesamum and worships Gaṇeśa, the lord will certainly be pleased.

38. He who recites this stotra and he who listens to it never encounter any obstacles.

CHAPTER TWENTYFOUR

The Origin of Serpents

Earth said:

1. O Varāha, be pleased to tell me how the mighty serpents arose by contact with your body.

Varāha said:

2. After hearing about the origin of Gaṇapati, king Prajāpāla asked the sage (Mahātapas) in a soft voice.

Prajāpāla said:

3. O sage, be pleased to tell me how the crooked serpents were born and how they got the enmity of Garuḍa.

Mahātapas said:

4. When Brahmā was creating, he first conceived in his mind his son Kaśyapa to beget Marīci.

5. Dakṣa's beautiful daughter Kadrū became his wife. In her be begot many valiant sons.

6-7. Ananta, Vāsuki, Kambala, Karkoṭaka, Padma, Mahāpadma, Śaṅkha and Kulika were the chief among them.

8. The earth was filled by the progeny of these.

9. They were all crooked, heinous and violent, and with their fangs stung people and reduced them to ashes.

10. Their contact was reducing human population day by day severally.

11. Finding their kind thus becoming steadily reduced, men went to the great god Brahmā, the refuge of all.

12. They flocked to him who was seated on the lotus, and told him.

13. "Protect us, O god, from these venomous serpents. Please realise that (otherwise) all men and beasts will be soon reduced to ashes.

14. What was created by you is being annihilated by the serpents. Please do what is fit to avert this danger".

Brahmā said:

15. Doubtless I shall give you protection. You may all go to your homes in confidence.

16. When they were all gone, Brahmā called the serpents Vāsuki and others, and cursed them in great anger.

Brahmā said:

17. Since you are annihilating my progeny, the men, in another age, in the Svāyambhuva manvantara, by a curse of the mother, you will face a serious decline.

18. Said thus by Brahmā shivering with anger, they fell at his feet and implored:

The serpents said:

19. O god, we were made crooked by nature by you. Our venom, cruelty, and the use of eye as weapon were all given by you. The intensity of all that was given may be reduced.

Brahmā said:

20. Granting that I have created you crooked, what right have you to eat away men every day ?

The serpents said:

21. O god, prescribe us a limit and allot us separate regions.

22. Hearing the words of the serpents, Brahmā said: "I shall make for you an agreement with men.

23. Listen with attention my verdict.

24. Pātāla, Vitala and Sutala are the regions allotted to you. You may all have your abode there.

25. I ordain that you shall enjoy all pleasures there and remain there till the seventh manvantara.

26. At the beginning of Vaivasvata manvantara you will become the relations of Devas as well as of Garuḍa the wise.

27. Then all your progeny will be consumed by fire but for your own selves there will be no danger.

28. The end of such serpents as are fierce and insolent will certainly occur, but not of others. You may eat and bite a person if he is so destined, and also to retaliate when somebody injures you.

29. You should move away in fear from persons who recite the mantras, or take in the medicine or wear the garuḍamaṇḍala (yantra) (all these being precautions against snake bite). O Earth, otherwise you will bring about your own disaster".

30. Thus said by Brahmā, the serpents went to the netherworld allotted to them.

31. And gaining in the end, Brahmā's relenting mood, they remained in Pātāla with satisfaction.

32. All this happened on the Pañcamī tithi. So this tithi is auspicious and capable of removing all sins.

33. If one remains austere on that day, gives up all that is sour in food and bathes the (images of) Nāgas in milk, they become friendly towards him.

CHAPTER TWENTYFIVE

Origin of Skanda

Prajāpāla said:

1. O great sage, how was Skanda born out of Ahaṁkāra (Ego) ? Please clear my doubt in this matter.

Mahātapas said:

2. From Puruṣa, considered as the highest of all Tattvas, arose Avyakta which is of three kinds.

3. Between Puruṣa and Avyakta, there arose Mahat which is also known as Ahaṅkāra.

4. Puruṣa is called Viṣṇu, and is also known by the name Śiva. Avyakta is Umā or Śri (Lakṣī).

5. By the union of these two (Puruṣa and Avyakta) arose Ahaṅkāra, also known as Senāpati and Guha. Listen O king, I shall narrate to you his origin.

6. The first is Nārāyaṇa. Out of him arose Brahmā, and then Svāyambhuva, and others like Marīci from the sun.

7. Thereafter came creation consisting of gods, demons, Gandharvas, men, birds, beasts and all other beings.

8. When the creation was thus progressing, the powers of gods and demons began to fight each other in order to gain victory.

9. Among the demons there were strong leaders of warlike Hiraṇyakaśipu, Hiraṇyākṣa, Vipracitti, Vicitra, Bhīmākṣa and Krauñca.

10. These mighty warriors were gaining victory over the gods in the battle every day.

11. Seeing the defeat of gods, Bṛhaspati said: "O gods, your army is without a proper leader.

12. It is not possible for a single Indra to manage the whole army. So quickly search for a commander."

13. Thus told, the gods went to Brahmā and prayed to him to give them a commander.

14. Brahmā then entered into serious thought to find out what he could do in this predicament of Devas, and his mind then fell upon Rudra.

15. Then led by Brahmā, Devas, Gandharvas. Ṛṣis, Siddhas and Cāraṇas went to mount Kailāsa.

16. Seeing there the great god Śiva, the lord of all beings, Indra and the other gods praised him.

The gods said:

17. O Maheśvara, the three-eyed god, lord of all beings, we supplicants bow to you. O lord of Umā, lord of the worlds, lord of Maruts, protect us all.

18. O god everlasting and holding the trident in hand, and illumining the whole world with the rays of the moon on the locks of matted hair, protect us who have come to you out of the fear of demons.

19. You are the first of gods, the best of men, Hari, Bhava, Maheśa, the destroyer of Tripuras, all-pervading, the enemy of demons, the most ancient, the bull-bannered. O great god, protect us.

20. You are the husband of Pārvatī, and the great lord worshipped by all gods. You are Gaṇeśa and the lord of all beings. For averting danger to us, protect us from the fierce demons.

21. You are established in Tattvas like the Earth; parti-

cularly you are of the nature of sound in the sky. You are hidden two-fold in fire, threefold in water, fourfold in earth and five-fold in qualities.

22. In the tree you are of the nature of fire, in stone you are of the nature of truth, in sesamum you are of the nature of oil. O Maheśvara, protect us who are oppressed by demons.

23. O three-eyed god, when there was no stem of the universe, and there was no sun, moon or Indra, then you alone remained beyond the purview of any reasoning.

24. O lord of gods, wearer of the garland of skulls, bearer of the crescent moon on the head, resorter to the cremation ground, smearer of ashes all over the body and encircled by serpents, you are capable of protecting us.

25. You are the Male and the beautiful daughter of the mountain is your Energy. You are fierce to the whole world with your trident, but the three sacrificial fires (Gārhapatya, Āhavanīya and Dakṣiṇa) remain in your three eyes.

26. In the form of your matted hair remain all oceans, all great mountains and all rivers. The whole universe is your body, though men without proper inner vision see only the physical aspect.

27. You are Nārāyaṇa, the source of the universe. Similarly, you are the great Brahmā. By the difference in the Guṇas and difference in the fires and by the difference in the yugas you remain threefold.

28. O lord, all these chieftains of the gods now seek your favour. O you Rudra, who shine with ashes, we bow to you again, be pleased to save us all.

Mahātapas said:

29. Thus praised by Devas, Rudra asked them as to what he was to do.

The gods said:

30. O great god, give us a commander. That is the desire of Brahmā and others.

Rudra said:

31. O Gods, be free from anxiety. I shall give you a com-

mander. Good time will befall the people.

32. Saying thus, he sent away Devas and then excited the Śakti (Energy) in him for producing a son.

33. By this excitement there arose Kumāra glowing like fire, holding Śakti (lance), the embodiment of knowledge.

34. O king, the origin of Kumāra is different in different manvantaras.

35. What remains in the body as Ahaṅkāra, the same appeared as Senāpati for a purpose.

36. When he was born, Brahmā together with Devas worshipped him and Śiva.

37. The Senāpati was thus propitiated by all the gods, sages and Siddhas. He then asked gods to give him a plaything and a pair of companions.

38. Hearing this, the great Śiva said: "I shall give a cock as your plaything and Śākha and Viśākha as your followers. You are the leader of all beings and you become the commander of the army (of Devas)".

39. Then Rudra and other gods all praised profusely Skanda the commander.

The gods said:

40. "O lord, Maheśvara's son, six-faced, cock-bannered, the issue of fire, Skanda, may you be the commander of the army of gods.

41. O Kumāra, a terror to the enemies, the smasher of the Krauñca mountain, son of Kṛttikā, son of Śiva.

42. O the foremost of all beings, giver of joy to fire, son of the lord of all beings, three-eyed god, we bow to you."

43. Thus extolled by Devas, the son of Śiva grew up and became resplendent like the dozen suns and of matchless valour.

44. O king, he illumined the whole world by his effulgence.

Prajāpāla said:

45. How is it that you referred to him as the son of Kṛttikā, son of fire, and the son of six mothers ?

Mahātapas said:

46. What I narrated relates to the first birth of Skanda.

But the gods, by their omniscience knew about the future also and extolled him accordingly.

47. In the second birth of Skanda, Kṛttikā, Fire, Mothers and Pārvatī were the causes of his origin.

48. O great king, I have told you the secret of the birth of Ahaṅkāra (as Skanda) and this is a secret which pertains to self-knowledge.

49. Skanda is a great god and he dispels all sins. During his anointment, Brahmā allotted to him the Ṣaṣṭhī tithi.

50. On that (Ṣaṣṭhī) day, if one worships him with concentration of mind, and eating only fruit, he becomes blessed with child if he is childless, and attains wealth if he is poor.

51. Whatever man desires, he attains (by worshipping him on that day).

52. He who recites the stotra of Kārttikeya (Skanda), in his house the children get health and prosperity.

CHAPTER TWENTYSIX

The Origin of Sun

Prajāpāla said:

1. O Brahmin, how did light attain embodiment? Please clear my doubt in this matter.

Mahātapas said:

2. When this eternal soul, the power of knowledge, desired to form a second, there arose light.

3. This was known as Sūrya (Sun) and Bhāsvān and all the radiance contained in it, illumined the three worlds.

4. In it were seen all gods, Siddhas and sages. Since it was self-born, the appellation *Sūrya* came into vogue.

5. From it the latent lustre assumed a body. This is called *Ravi* by the Vedic seers.

6. Since it illumines all the worlds from the high sky, it is called *Bhāskara* (from *bhās* to illumine).

7. Since it produces the day (*divasa*), it is known as *Divākara*. Since it is the beginning (*ādi*) of the universe, it is called *Āditya*.

8. From its lustre arose twelve suns, and the principal one among these now revolves round the world.

9. Seeing it pervade the entire universe, the gods came out and praised it.

The gods said:

10. "You are the first-born in the world. You protect the world and also destroy it at the time of deluge. When you rise, you enliven the whole universe. We always bow to you.

11. You spread light everywhere. You are the heat in sacrifices. You ride in a chariot pulled by seven steeds, fast and never tardy.

12. You are Prabhākara, Ravi and Ādideva, and the soul of all that is moving and stationary. You are Brahmā, Varuṇa and Yama. You are also the past and the future, so say the Siddhas.

13. You are the Veda, you are effulgence, you destroy all enemies. Protect us all who have sought refuge in you. You are to be known through Vedānta. In sacrifices you are known as Viṣṇu.

14. Be pleased at our prayer, and protect us all, O God."

15. When thus extolled by Devas, the Sun assumed a gentle form and shed lustre on them.

16. The fierceness thus became reduced for Devas. It was in the tithi Saptamī that the sun became embodied.

17. He who worships Sūrya on that day, gets all desires fulfilled.

18. This ancient story of the sun has been thus narrated to you, O king. Now, hear the story of Mothers in the first manvantara.

CHAPTER TWENTYSEVEN

The Origin of Mātṛgaṇa

Mahātapas said:

1. There was a powerful demon named Andhaka who had made all gods subservient to him by a boon got from Brahmā.

2. Being made his servants and driven out of mount Meru, they were very much afraid of Andhaka and sought refuge in Brahmā.

3. Seeing the gods, Brahmā asked them the cause of their arrival there.

The gods said:

4. O grandfather, four-faced, we bow to you and seek your protection from Andhaka who is harassing us.

Brahmā said:

5. "O gods, I am helpless to protect you from Andhaka. So we will seek the help of Śiva the great god.

6. But I have already given him a boon the effect of which cannot be nullified and his body will not touch the earth.

7. The one person who can kill him is Rudra. So we will all go to Kailāsa and see him".

8. So saying, Brahmā along with the other gods, went to Śiva. Śiva rose up and received them and then asked Brahmā.

Śambhu said:

9. With what purpose have all of you gods come to me. Command me soon.

The gods said:

10. "Save us from the wicked and powerful Andhaka".

11. When the gods were thus reporting to Śiva, Andhaka came there with a big army.

12. His aim was to kill Śiva in battle with all the four divisions of the army, as also to kill his consort Pārvatī.

13. When the demon thus suddenly appeared ready with all weapons, the gods ranged themselves with Rudra.

14. Rudra then called mentally Vāsuki, Takṣaka and Dhanañjaya, and made for himself a waist girdle of them.

15. The big demon called Nala then assumed the guise of an elephant and quickly began to attack Śiva.

16. Nandin (the vehicle of Rudra) indicated the demon by a sign to Vīrabhadra (the army chief), who thereupon assumed the form of a lion and quickly killed him.

17. He then peeled off the skin of that elephant dark like collyrium and presented it to Śiva who wore it.

18. From then on Śiva became the wearer of elephant's skin.

19. Wearing this skin, and ornamented with the serpents, Śiva with his trident in hand and accompanied by his Gaṇas, rushed towards Andhaka.

20. Then started a fierce battle between gods and demons. the guardians of quarters like Indra, Skanda the commander and the gods fought in the battle.

21. Seeing this Nārada quickly went to Viṣṇu and informed him of the severe fighting between gods and demons in Kailāsa.

22. Hearing this, Viṣṇu took his disc and rode on Garuḍa to that place and fought against demons.

23. Although much relieved at the intervention of Viṣṇu, the gods were full of despair and were taking to their heels.

24. When the gods thus became dispirited, Rudra himself darted towards Andhaka and engaged him in a terrible fight.

25. He pierced Andhaka with his trident, but from the blood that fell from his body, arose numerous other Andhakas.

26. At this wonder, Rudra caught up the original Andhaka in the trident and began to dance.

27. The other (secondary) Andhakas that came were all annihilated by Viṣṇu with his disc.

28. With blood and ice in the trident, Rudra rose up in anger.

29. By this anger, there arose from his mouth a fierce flame. The goddess in this form is known as Yogeśvarī.

30-32. Then Viṣṇu produced another goddess having his own form: so did Brahmā, Kārttikeya, Indra and Yama. Viṣṇu then created another having his form at the time of raising up the earth. These together with Māheśvarī and Māhendrī are the eight Mothers.

33. I have thus told you about the cause as well as the form of these goddesses.

34. The eight goddesses have as their aspects love, anger, greed, pride, stupefaction, rivalry, malignity and tolerance respectively.

35-37. Know love to be Yogeśvarī, anger as Māheśvarī, greed Vaiṣṇavī, pride Brahmāṇī, stupefaction Kaumārī, rivalry Indrajā, malignity Yamadaṇḍadharā and tolerance Vārāhī.

38. The group love etc., constitute their bodies. They assumed the forms as I have told you now.

39. When the blood of Andhaka was completely drawn by these goddesses, his Māyā (magical power) became extinct and he became a Siddha.

40. I have now told you all this which is the nectar of self-knowledge.

41. O king, he who listens to this account of the origin of Mothers, can get protection everywhere.

42. He who recites this, becomes blessed in the world and finally attains the world of Śiva.

43. To these Mothers the tithi Aṣṭamī was ordained by Brahmā. By worshipping them (on that day) with devotion eating only Bilva, one attains their favour, wealth and health.

CHAPTER TWENTYEIGHT

Origin of the Goddess Durgā

Prajāpāla said:

1. How was the auspicious Durgā, who is Kātyāyanī and Māyā, born with a separate body out of the primordial subtle state.

Mahātapas said:

2. Once there was a valiant king named Sindhudvīpa, a manifestation of Varuṇa. He was performing severe penance in the forest with a view to begetting a son who would kill Indra.

3. With this determination he stood fast in constant penance emaciating his body.

Prajāpāla said:

4. How was he offended by Indra that he wished to get a son to kill him?

Mahātapas said :

5. In his former birth, he was the son of Tvaṣṭā, and being immune against the attack of any weapon, he was killed with foam.

6-7. Killed by foam, he was dissolved in it. Then he was born in Brahmā's line as the valiant Sindhudvīpa, and he performed penance always thinking of his enmity to Indra.

8. After a long time, the auspicious river Vetravatī assumed a beautiful human form and went to the place where the king was engaged in his austerities.

9. Seeing her in that beautiful form the king's mind was disturbed and he asked her who she was.

The river said:

10. "I am the wife of Varuṇa, the lord of waters and my name is Vetravatī. I came here loving you.

11. He who rejects a woman who approaches him with intense desire, although she belongs to another, brings upon himself a sin like the one on killing a Brahmin. Knowing this, accept me".

12. Said thus, the king enjoyed her heartily.

13. In Vetravatī was born immediately a son named Vetrāsura who was resplendent like the dozen suns, mighty and brilliant, and he became the king of Prāgjyotiṣa.

14-15. In due course he became a powerful and courageous youth, much lucky, and he conquered the whole world consisting of seven islands and then, going up the Meru mountain, conquered Indra, then Agni and then Yama.

16. Indra, when vanquished, went to Agni, Agni when vanquished went to Yama, Yama when vanquished went to Nirṛti, and Nirṛti when vanquished went to Varuṇa.

17. Varuṇa with Indra and others went to Vāyu, and Vāyu went to Kubera with them.

18. Kubera went to his friend Śiva. The Asura was chasing them all with his club, and so he too came to Śivaloka.

19. Śiva, knowing that he could not be easily killed, took the gods to Brahmā worshipped by Siddhas and others.

20-21. There Brahmā, having created the world, was engaged in meditating on Gāyatrī, the Māyā of the Supreme Being, within the water which was flowing from Viṣṇu's feet.

At this Devas cried aloud:

22. "O Brahmā, protect all of us Devas and sages, who have now come to you being harassed by the demon (Vṛtra)".

23. Prayed thus, Brahmā looked at Devas and contemplated on Māyā by whose prowess there will be no Asuras or Rākṣasas (left to harass them).

24-26. Then appeared there out of the water the great Goddess, a maiden wearing garlands and crown, clad in white cloth, with eight hands each holding a divine weapon, disc, conch, mace, rope, sword, bell, bow (and arrow) and with a quiver, riding on a lion.

27. She fought with the Asuras with great agility for a thousand divine years and with various divine weapons.

28. Finally the demon Vetrāsura was killed by her in battle and there was then a great shout of joy in the ranks of Devas.

29. When the Vetrāsura was thus killed, the gods bowed in reverence. Śiva uttered praise.

Maheśvara said:

30. "Hail goddess Gāyatrī, Mahāmāyā, the great Devī, the highly auspicious.

31. I bow to you O Maheśvarī, mother of Vedas, with celestial sandal smeared over the body adorned with celestial garlands and necklace, and remaining in letters.

32. (I bow to) you who remain in all the three worlds, in the three Tattvas, in the three fires, hold the trident, have three eyes and are fierce in face and eyes.

33-34. I bow to you Sarasvatī, the daughter of Brahmā, Mahāmāyā, lotus-eyed, shedding ambrosia, omnipresent, the lord of all beings, Svāhā, Svadhā,[1] O Mother.

35. (I bow to you) who arose from Bhava, the Perfect, resembling the moon in lustre, with resplendent body, the great knowledge, capable of being known only by the great, the destroyer of mighty demons.

36. O you goddess who rose from the great Intellect, free from sorrow, the goddess of the hunters, you are justice, you are fortune, you are speech, you are the cow, you are the everlasting.

37. I bow to you, O great goddess; you are intelligence, you are opulence, you are the Praṇava, you are the Tattvas. You do good to all beings."

38-39. When she was thus extolled by the great Rudra and hailed by the gods, Brahmā came out of the water and saw her fully gratified.

40. Seeing her and knowing that the purpose of Devas had been accomplished, he spoke to them thinking of the future.

Brahmā said:

41. "Let this beautiful goddess go to the mountain Himavān and all of you go there and offer her worship.

42. She should be worshipped with all concentration of mind on Navamī tithi. She will then certainly give boons to the whole world.

43. On the Navamī day if a man or woman fasts taking only some flour, he or she gets all desires accomplished.

44. He who recites the above stotra by you every morning, will get all boons from you and the goddess, and will also surmount all calamities.

45. Having said thus to Śiva, Brahmā spoke to the goddess:

46. "O goddess, you have to render us another great service in future by killing the demon Mahiṣāsura".

47. Then, O king, Devas left the place and installed her in the Himālayas and paid her homage. Since she was thus honoured (*nandita*) she came to be known as *Nandā*.

48. He who listens to this account of the origin of the goddess and recites it himself, gets freed of all sins and attains salvation.

1. 'Śvāhā' and 'Svadhā' are expressions uttered when offering oblations in fire respectively to Devas and Pitṛs.

CHAPTER TWENTYNINE

Origin of Diks

Mahātapas said:

1. "O king Prajāpāla, listen intently to the story of the origin of diks (quarters) from the ears (of Brahmā).

2. When the first creation was in progress, Brahmā became anxious as to who would hold all that he created.

3. As he was thinking thus, there arose from his ears ten radiant girls.

4. Among them six were more important, namely Pūrvā (East), Dakṣiṇā (South), Pratīcī (West), Uttarā (North), Ūrdhvā (the upward direction) and Adharā (the downward direction).

5. Then amidst them arose four, particularly attractive, auspicious and endowed with great dignity.

6-7. They asked the sinless Brahmā earnestly to give them their quarters as well as husbands to live with there.

Brahmā said:

8. "O lovely girls, this universe is ten crore broad and in this vast expanse you can choose to your liking and tell me soon.

9. I shall also create sinless and beautiful husbands for you. Go you each to the place you like.

10. Thus told, they went to the regions they liked. And Brahmā soon created the powerful guardian deities of the quarters.

11. Then Brahmā arranged their marriage.

12-13. One he gave to Indra, another to Agni, the third to Yama, the fourth to Nirṛti, the fifth to Varuṇa, and one each to Vāyu, Kubera and Īśāna. Ūrdhvā he himself took and gave Adharā to Śeṣa.

14. Then Brahmā allotted the tithi Daśamī to them. Daśamī became their favourite.

15. He who observes vow on that day taking in only curd, becomes cleansed of his sins by their favour.

16. He who listens to the account of the origin of Diks, undoubtedly gets a secure place in the world of Brahmā.

CHAPTER THIRTY

Origin of Kubera

Mahātapas said:

1. Listen to the holy story of the origin of the lord of wealth from the body of Vāyu.

2. Vāyu was originally within the primordial body, but was later on given a concrete body with a purpose.

3. That was how Vāyu came to possess a concrete shape. Listen to me for details.

4. When Brahmā was creating, there arose from his mouth this air (Vāyu). It was coming out showering stones. Brahmā, therefore, stopped it and gave it a concrete shape saying "Assume a finite shape and become calm".

5. When that form was obtained, Brahmā ordained that the new being may be the keeper of the wealth of Devas. Thus came into being Dhanapati (Kubera).

6. Then being pleased, Brahmā allotted to him the tithi Ekādaśī. On that day, if one remains pure and takes in only uncooked food, Dhanada becomes pleased and gives him everything.

7-8. Such is the body of Dhanapatī capable of clearing one of all one's sins. He who listens to (the story of) his origin or recites it, accomplishes all desires and attains heaven.

CHAPTER THIRTYONE

The Origin of Viṣṇu

Mahātapas said:

1. Manu about whom we learn now, is only a manifestation in specific form of the great Viṣṇu.

2. O king, to the Supreme Being, Nārāyaṇa, an anxiety arose, as he was bringing about creation.

3. "I have now brought into being this creation and I have

to protect it myself. It is not possible to establish the performance of duties without a body. Therefore, I shall create a body for the protection of the world".

4. O king, while the great Being was thinking thus, the whole creation appeared embodied before him.

5. Lord Nārāyaṇa then saw himself entering into it and all the three worlds constituted his person.

6. Then the Lord remembered the assurance he had to fulfil and gave boons.

7. "You are omniscient and omnipotent and you are worshipped by the entire world. You be the eternal Viṣṇu governing the three worlds.

8. You should always look after Devas and do whatever Brahmā wants. Doubtless you will be knowing everything."

9. The Lord then withdrew to his original form. And Viṣṇu evoked his own intellect.

10. The great Lord then mentally summoned Yoganidrā (cosmic slumber) and lodging therein all the creatures that arose out of the senses, entered into slumber.

11. While thus sleeping, there arose from his belly a big lotus.

12-13. It was spreading over all the seven islands of the earth and all the waters and forests and extended upto the nether world. In its interior was Meru and at its top Brahmā.

14. Seeing the new being come out of his body, Vāyu (air within) was delighted and produced the atmosphere (and said):

15. "Hold victory over illusion in the form of a conch and a sword to cut off ignorance.

16. Bear this disc which represents Kālacakra (the course of the world) and a mace to crush unrighteousness.

17. Let there be round your neck this garland which represents the string of beings, and the sun and the moon in the form of Śrīvatsa and Kaustubha.

18. For quick travel you have Garuḍa. Let the great goddess Lakṣmī be always with you.

19. Dvādaśī shall be your tithi. Any person who takes in only clarified butter on that day and meditates on you, attains heaven, be the person man or woman."

20. He is Viṣṇu and his body is constituted of Devas and Asuras. From his own self he creates, protects and destroys.

21. In every yuga he pervades everything. He is verily the Vedāntapuruṣa. No one should take him as an ordinary man.

22. He who listens to this holy account of Viṣṇu, acquires great fame and attains heaven.

CHAPTER THIRTYTWO

The Origin of Dharma

Mahātapas said:

1. Now listen, O king, I shall tell you about the origin of Dharma, its greatness and the tithi associated with it.

2. Formerly, the eternal and pure Brahmā, who is inferior only to the Supreme, thought of creation as well as the protection of the created.

3. Then from the right side of his body came out a person with body smeared with white unguent and wearing white garland and white earrings.

4. Seeing him who was four-footed and bull-shaped, he said: "You be the foremost of my creation and protect all these beings".

5. Thus ordained, he protects the world with all the four feet in Kṛtayuga, three feet in Tretāyuga, two feet in Dvāparayuga and a single foot in Kaliyuga.

6. Dharma was established with six divisions in Brahmins, three in Kṣatriyas, two in Vaiśyas and one in Śūdras. This lord (Dharma) is prevalent everywhere in all the islands in the earth.

7. His four feet are acclaimed as Guṇa (quality) Dravya (substance), Kriyā (action) and Jāti (genus).

8. In the Veda he is considered as having three horns, Saṁhitā, Pada and Krama.[1] He is Oṁkāra and has two heads and seven hands.

---

1. *Saṁhitā* is the Veda with the words conjoined, *Pada* with the words separated, and *Krama* with each word joined with its succeeding word.

9. He was bound by the three svaras, Udātta, Anudātta and Svarita.[1] Such was Dharma.

10-11. Dharma was persecuted by Soma (moon) desirous of (getting for himself) Tārā, the wife of his own brother Āṅgirasa, and somehow escaping from him, he resorted to the expansive forest.

12-13. When Dharma was gone, the groups of gods began to wander about desiorus of killing Asuras, being bereft of dharma. The Asuras too similarly wandered about in the abodes of gods.

14. As a result of Soma's sin based on the woman, Devas and Asuras fought each other with numerous weapons.

15. Seeing them at war with each other Nārada came to his father Brahmā and spoke about it.

16. Brahmā then mounted his swan and forbade them from fighting, and asked them about the cause of fight.

17. They all said Soma to be the cause, and then he was able to see that his son Dharma had resorted to the forest because of persecution.

18. Then Brahmā went there quickly with Devas and Asuras and saw him there four-footed, bull-like and white like the moon.

Brahmā said:

19. This is my first son, the sage by name Dharma, harassed by the moon desirous of the wife of his own brother.

20. O Devas and Asuras, propitiate him so that your former position may be established.

21. Thus knowing his identity through Brahmā, Devas and Asuras extolled him.

Devas said:

22. "Bow to you, O lord of worlds, moon-like in complexion, bow to you with divine form, the guide to heaven's path.

23. Bow to you of the form of Karmamārga (the path of action) and omnipresent. The earth is governed by you, in fact all the three worlds.

24. The other worlds like Jana, Tapas and Satya are also

---

1. *Udātta* is the high tone, *Anudātta* the low tone and *Svarita* a combination of the two.

governed by you. Without you there is nothing, moving or stationary.

25-26. Without you the world perishes in a moment. You are (the qualities) Sattva, Rajas and Tamas respectively manifesting in the good, the common and the bad people.

27. Bow to you the bull-shaped one with four feet, four horns, three eyes, seven hands and three joints.

28. O lord, without you, we all go astray. So give us the right path as we are ignorant. You are our great refuge."

29. Thus praised by gods, the lord of beings in bull's form, became pleased and spoke with benignity.

30. By the very look of Dharma Devas became freed from ignorance and attached to righteousness. So too Asuras.

31-32. Then Brahmā said: "O Dharma, from today onwards let your tithi be Trayodaśī. He who fasts on that day and worships you will attain you and become freed of sins.

33. This forest where you have been wandering long will be known by the name 'Dharmāraṇya'.

34. The world will see you four-footed, three-footed, two-footed and single-footed respectively in the yugas Kṛta, Tretā, Dvāpara and Kali, and extending over earth and heaven, protecting the whole universe".

35. Saying this Brahmā disappeared while Devas and Asuras were looking on. They too went to their homes fearlessly.

36. He who recites to others this story of Dharma and he who propitiates his Pitṛs with milky food on Trayodaśī, goes to heaven and remains with gods.

CHAPTER THIRTYTHREE

The Origin of Rudra

Mahātapas said:

1. "Now you listen to another account of the first appearance of Rudra," so said the great sage Mahātapas who had cut down the tree of Adharma (evil) and whose weapon was forbearance.

2. The creator with great prowess came into being and realising knowledge to be the greatest principle, was desirous of performing creation. But seeing that creation did not proceed forth, he got highly agitated in mind.

3. He was then performing penance, but there came out of himself a person reddish blue in colour with tawny eyes, valiant and free from Rajas and Tamas.

4. The person was crying (*rudan*) and Brahmā asked him not to cry (*mā ruda*). He thus became Rudra (one who cries). He then said to him that he was competent to carry on extensive creation.

5. Told thus, he plunged himself in water. And Brahmā then produced mentally his son Dakṣa who carried on the process of creation.

6. As it was proceeding, Indra performed a sacrifice to Brahmā and then Rudra came out of the water to create the world and gods.

7. He stopped the sacrifice and was very angry to see Devas, Siddhas and Yakṣas, and discarding even the beautiful damsel (Dakṣa's daughter), asked who created the world without him.

8. 'Hā, hā' he said and there issued forth from his red face flames of fire and there appeared multitudes of ghosts, goblins and vampires.

9. When the sky, earth and quarters were densely covered by them, out of his omniscience he made a bow twentyfour cubits long.

10. He then made the bowstring three-fold and took up quiver and divine arrows. He then pulled down the teeth of Pūṣā, the eyes of Bhaga and the testicles of Kratu.

11. Stripped thus of his testicles, Kratu ran away through the north-western part of the sacrificial altar. Devas became like beasts and prostrated before him.

12. Brahmā then came there and embraced gods who were thus prostrating before him, although they were offended by him.

13. Seeing Rudra he said, "O Rudra, enough of your anger, the sacrifice is obstructed". Hearing the words of Brahmā, Rudra spoke in anger.

Rudra said:

14. I was formerly created by you. These are also yours.

Then why do they not give me a share in the sacrificial offering."
This form of mine which arose out of the sacrifice, made these bereft of knowledge.

Brahmā said:

15. O Devas, for regaining your (lost) knowledge may you all propitiate Rudra by prayers. Let Asuras also do the same. Rudra will thus become pleased and will give you back your knowledge.

Thus instructed, Devas praised the great Rudra.

Devas said:

16. "Bow to the great god, three-eyed and red-eyed, wearing matted hair and crown.

17. Bow to him who is served by ghosts and goblins, who has the snake as his sacred thread (yajñopavīta), who is sthāṇu (the permanent one) and whose mouth is with terrific laughter.

18. Bow to him who uprooted the teeth of Pūṣā and the eyes of Bhaga and who will have the bull as his emblem.

19. Bow to Bhairava whose matted hair is tied upwards, who wears the elephant's skin and who resides in Kailāsa and who will kill Tripuras and Andhaka.

20. Bow to him who is fierce with tongues of fire and who bears the moon on the head.

21. Bow to him the great Lord bearing the sharp trident who will undertake Kāpālivrata and destroy Dāruvana.

22. Who is blue-necked, holds trident, has serpents as bracelets, gives blows with his mighty hands and has a fiery face.

23. Who is the creator of the three worlds, who is the embodiment of sacrifice but destroyed Dakṣa's sacrifice and who is known through Vedānta.

24. Bow to Mahādeva, Śiva, Śambhu, Bhava, Kapardin, Karāla, Viśveśvara."

25. Praised thus by Devas, Rudra the eternal, holding a fearful bow, told them that he was the god of gods and asked them to say what he could do for them.

Devas said:

26. Give us, O god, the knowledge of the Vedas and Śāstras

and also of the sacrifice and its secret, if you are pleased with us.

Mahādeva said:

27. "May you all be *paśus* (beasts) and I shall be the lord of beasts. Thereby you will attain mokṣa".

28. The gods agreed and Rudra became *Paśupati* (lord of beasts).

Brahmā then spoke o Paśupati with great pleasure.

29-30. "O Rudra, let Caturdaśī be the tithi for you. On that day those who worship you fasting, and later take in only wheat food, will get your pleasure and this will lead to their liberation".

31. When thus said by Brahmā, Rudra restored to Bhaga, Pūṣā and Kratu the teeth, eyes and testicles respectively.

32. He gave to Devas all knowledge.

33. Thus occurred the emergence of Rudra from Brahmā. On account of what was detailed above, he came to be called the lord of gods.

34. The person who listens to this account early in the morning, becomes free from all sins and attains the world of Rudra.

CHAPTER THIRTYFOUR

The Origin of Pitṛs

Mahātapas said:

1. O king, listen to the origin of Pitṛs I am going to tell you now.

2. Formerly Brahmā, the lord of all beings, desirous of performing creation in all its variety, thought of keeping all Tanmātrās out of his mind and engaged himself in deep meditation.

3. When he was thus in meditation, there came out of his body the Tanmātrās tawny in colour.

4. They were all horizontal in form, moving upwards and telling gods that they would drink the soma juice.

5. Seeing them who were remaining in a horizontal position

and moving upwards, Brahmā told them, "May you be the Pitṛs (manes) for all householders.

6. Those among you whose faces are upwards are named 'Nāndīmukhas'." So saying Brahmā defined their path.

7. He created for them the Dakṣiṇāyana (the southward movement of the sun), and continued the other creations silently. They then asked Brahmā to give them their means of sustenance so that they could remain happy.

Brahmā said:

8. Amāvāsī (New moon day) be your day. You will derive great satisfaction by the water given to you with the Kuśa (darbha) grass and sesamum seeds by the people.

9. On that day if people give gifts of sesamum, fasting and with devotion to the Pitṛs, they will get boons from them early.

CHAPTER THIRTYFIVE

The Origin of Soma

Mahātapas said:

1. There was the famous mind-born son of Brahmā by name Atri. His son was Soma (Moon) who became Dakṣa's son-in-law.

2. Twentyseven renowned and honourable daughters of Dakṣa became his wives and Rohiṇī was the chief among them.

3. He was giving his love only to Rohiṇī and not to others. So they went to their father and told him about this difference in the treatment accorded to them.

4. Dakṣa asked him several times to give equal treatment to all wives, but he cared little. Thereupon Dakṣa cursed him to disappear, and as a result, he waned and vanished.

5. When Soma was thus lost, gods, men, beasts and plants began to wither, particularly the plants.

6. When the plants were thus shrivelling up, gods were worried and said that the moon is the source of all plants.

7. They seriously thought about the matter and resorted to Viṣṇu, and lord Viṣṇu asked them what he might do for them.

8. They told him that Soma was lost because of a curse of Dakṣa and then Viṣṇu suggested that they may churn ocean putting the plants into it.

9. After telling Devas thus, Viṣṇu mentally called Rudra and Brahmā and also the serpent Vāsuki for the churning rope.

10. They all churned the ocean and Soma reappeared.

11. He who is soul within the body and is called Kṣetrajña, is this Soma who is the Jīva (life).

12-13. He attained an invisible form which sustains gods and men and these sixteen deities, as also the trees and plants. His visible form Rudra bore on his head.

14. Water also is his form and hence he is considered universal. Brahmā then gave him Paurṇamāsī (Full moon day) as the tithi.

15. O king, if one fasts and gives him offerings on that day, he bestows on him food, knowledge, effulgence, health and wealth.

CHAPTER THIRTYSIX

The Former Story

Mahātapas said:

1. O king, I shall tell you about kings known as Maṇijas (born of the gem[1]) in the first Tretāyuga, in whose line you are born.

2. You were known as Suprabha in Kṛtayuga and you are now born as the famous Prajāpāla.

3. Others will be born as mighty kings in Tretāyuga. Dīptatejas will be born as Śānta.

4. King Suraśmi will become Śaśakarṇa, Śubhadarśana will become Pāñcāla.

5. Suśānti[2] will be born in the line of Aṅgas; so too Sundara,

1. See chapter XI verses 83, 84.
2. Earlier the name is given as Sukānti.

Sunda as Mucukunda and Sudyumna[1] as Turu.

6. Sumanas will be born as Somadatta, Śubha as Saṁvaraṇa, Suśīla as Vasudāna and Sukhada as Āśupati.

7. Śambhu will be born as Senāpati, Kānta[2] as Daśaratha and Soma as Janaka. All these about kings in Tretāyuga.

8. These kings will rule the world well, perform various sacrifices and will finally attain heaven.

Varāha said:

9. The King, after listening to this account which pertains to the nectarine Brahmavidyā, was extremely pleased and went to the forest to perform penance.

10. And attaining high spiritual potency, he gave up his body, became one with Brahman and was merged in Hari.

11. (Earlier) the king had gone to Vṛndāvana and praised there Hari called Govinda.[3]

The king said:

12. I bow to the great god with the whole universe as body, the chief of the cowherds, brother of Indra, of immeasurable greatness, clever in regulating the movements in worldly existence, and bearer of the earth.

13. I bow to you, O Kṛṣṇa the great lord of cows, the sole source of happiness in the ocean of worldly existence, terrible with the numerous waves of sorrow and whirlpools of advancing age.

14. I bow to you Janārdana, the friend of all, (who give solace to me) who are always battling with diseases, ill-disposed persons and hostile planets.

15. O holder of glowing disc, you are the highest of the omniscient gods. The whole world is pervaded by you. O leader of the Gopas, save me from the fears of mundane life.

16. You are the most exalted of gods. You are the most ancient. You shine like the moon. O imperishable God with

1. In the earlier enumeration name is Pradyumna.
2. The name given earlier is Sudānta
3. This should be presumed to be a praise of the future Kṛṣṇāvatāra of Viṣṇu. It is also possible that this part of the chapter is a later addition.

fire in the mouth, save me from falling a prey to worldly allurement.

17. In the wheel of worldly life revolve men deluded by your Māyā. O great lord, who is able to cross this enveloping Māyā ?

18. O lord of Gopas, those courageous souls that meditate on you who are free from a descent, freefrom touch, colour and smell and without a name, but the greatest of all, get liberated from worldly bondages and attain salvation.

19. I always bow to him who is spoken of in Purāṇas as bearing the disc and lotus, but is really beyond sound, in the form of the sky, without a finite body, without action, but full of auspiciousness.

20. I bow to Viṣṇu the eternal, Trivikrama who occupied the three worlds, who has four forms,[1] the lord of the whole universe, who is Śiva as well as Indra.

21. O lord, you create everything moving and stationary and you dissolve the entire creation. Lead me as I am desirous of salvation, to that place soon from where the yogins do not return.

22. Hail great Govinda, hail Viṣṇu Padmanābha, hail the omniscient, hail the unbounded, hail the lord of the worlds.

Varāha said:

23. Thus praising the lord, the king gave up his body and became permanently merged in the Supreme soul, Govinda.

CHAPTER THIRTYSEVEN

The Story of Dīrghabāhu

Earth said:

1. O great lord, be pleased to tell me how you are to be worshipped by men and women with devotion.

---

1. The four *vyūhas* namely Vāsudeva, Saṅkarṣaṇa, Pradyumna and Aniruddha.

Varāha said:

2. I am to be attained by meditation, not by money or incantation. Still, I shall tell you about the physical restraints to be observed by devotees.

3. Listen to the observances to be adopted by a person who is dedicated to me in mind, action and word.

4. The mental observances are non-violence, truthfulness, faith and celibacy.

5. The bodily observances are taking food only once a day and fasting at night.

6. The oral observances are learning the Veda, reciting the glories of Viṣṇu, speaking truth and not speaking ill of others.

7. Here a story is known: There was a highly spiritual sage named Āruṇi, son of Brahmā.

8-9. He went to the forest on the bank of river Devikā to perform severe penance. Once he went to the river for a bath.

10. While performing japa after bath, he saw a fierce hunter with (bow and) arrow in hand rushing towards him.

11. He came there to kill the sage and snatch away the bark garment he was wearing.

12. The sage became extremely perturbed understanding his criminal intention, but remained there meditating on Nārāyaṇa.

13. Seeing the sage whose mind was thus immersed in meditation on Viṣṇu, the hunter became afraid, and dropping down his bow and arrow, said:

The hunter said:

14. "O Brahmin, I came here with the intention of killing you. But now on seeing you, that intention has left me.

15. I have been killing thousands of Brahmins and even more good women.

16. Will any good befall me after killing so many Brahmins? I now wish to perform penance near you. Be pleased to give me the necessary advice".

17. But the sage did not say anything in reply, thinking that the man who is guilty of killing Brahmins is a high sinner.

18. Still, desirous of acquiring religious merit, the hunter remained there. The sage took his bath and resorted to the foot of the tree.

19. After some time, a famished tiger came to the river, and attempted to kill the serene sage.

20. The sage plunged himself into the water, but the tiger was trying to drag him out. The hunter then quickly killed it.

21. A person came out of the tiger's body then. Hearing the noise (of the hunter killing the tiger) from within the water, the sage exclaimed 'Bow to Nārāyaṇa'.

22. That mantra was heard by the tiger which was about to die, and it then became transformed into a man.

23. He said, "O Brahmin, being freed from my sins and ills, I now go to that perpetual abode of Viṣṇu".

24. Told thus, the sage asked him who he was. He then told him about his former life.

25-26. "I was (a king) known as Dīrghabāhu. I was well versed in Dharma and had mastered the Vedas and known about everything good and bad. I had nothing to do with the Brahmins and was asking "what is this thing called the Brahmin".

27. At this attitude of mine, the Brahmins became angry and they cursed me to become a tiger.

28. They also said that because of my insult to the Brahmins I would lose my memory but would hear the name of the lord at the time of my death.

29. The curse pronounced by the great Vaidik Brahmins took effect on me.

30. I then prostrated before them and sought their pardon. They then said:

31. "You should take food only once in six days, and then whatever comes near you will be your food.

32. When you will be about to die, being hit by an arrow, you will hear a Brahmin uttering 'Bow to Nārāyaṇa'. Then you will attain liberation."

33. Although through another's mouth, I have now heard the name of Viṣṇu and the god is now before me although an offender of Brahmins (and thus a sinner).

34. He who adores Brahmins and himself utters the name of Viṣṇu at the time of death, becomes freed from all sins.

35. With outstretched arms I proclaim again and again the truth that the Brahmins are the gods moving in this earth and the lord is the Supreme Man."

36. So saying the king went to heaven, being freed of sins. The sage, who was thus saved, spoke to the hunter.

The sage said:

37. Since I have been saved by you from the tiger, I am pleased with you. I shall give you the boon you choose.

The hunter said:

38. The fact that you speak to me is itself a boon for me. What else have I to seek ? Please advise me.

The sage said:

39. Formerly, you requested me to instruct you to perform penance. Then you were full of sins and fierce in appearance.

40-41. Now all your sins have disappeared by your holy bath in this river Devikā, by my sight and by hearing the name of Viṣṇu, and you have become pure in body.

42. So now you can ask me a boon. You may perform penance as long as you like.

The hunter said:

43. The one boon that I wish to seek is to know how Viṣṇu, about whom you said, could be attained by mortals.

The sage said:

44. The man who with intense devotion, performs vows in respect of lord Viṣṇu, doubtless attains him.

45. Knowing this, perform austerities. Do not take common food (be contented with whatever food that is available in the forest). Never utter falsehood.

46. This is the instruction and the boon to you. You may remain here practising penance as long as you like.

Varāha said:

47. The sage thus gave the boon to him who was desirous of securing salvation, and went away.

CHAPTER THIRTYEIGHT

The Story of Satyatapas

Varāha said:

1. The eminent hunter followed the auspicious path and began to do penance giving up regular food and meditating on the preceptor (sage Āruṇi).

2. Formerly, when he was hungry, he used to eat the fallen leaves.

3-4. But once when he was hungry and went to the foot of a tree to eat the leaves shed there, he heard a loud aerial voice prohibiting him from eating them.

5. Leaving that tree he went to another. There also he heard the same thing. The same thing happened when he went to other trees also.

6. So he stopped eating anything and began to do penance fully fasting.

7. When he was doing penance in this way, once sage Durvāsas came there and was surprised to find the hunter not only alive (in spite of his fasting) but effulgent like the blazing fire because of the penance.

8-9. The hunter bowed to the great sage and told him: "O sage, I am extremely gratified to see you. By my good fortune you have come here at a time when I have to perform śrāddha. I shall propitiate you with the fallen leaves (which alone I take)'.

10. Durvāsas, with a view to knowing the spiritual powers of this hermit who had fully subdued his sense organs and become fully purified, told him:

11. "Give me, who have come here with the intention of seeing you, well prepared food of barley, wheat and rice".

12. Told thus, the hunter began to seriously think as to how he could meet this demand.

13. When he was thus engrossed, a golden vessel with miraculous powers fell into his hand from the sky.

14. Taking it, he told Durvāsas in great reverence, "O great Brahmin, please remain here till I return after begging food and bless me".

15. The noble hunter then went out to beg alms in the not-too-distant city through forests and hamlets.

16-17. As he was going along, from tree after tree came out nymphs with golden vessels full of food of various varieties and they filled with them his begging bowl.

18. When his aim was thus achieved, he delightfully returned to the sage.

19. He placed the bowl in a tidy place, bowed to him, and said:

20. "O sage, if you are pleased to bless me, kindly take this seat and wash your feet".

21. But the sage, with a view to testing how far his penance was powerful, told him: "I am unable to go to the river, nor have I any vessel with me; how can I wash my feet ?"

22. Hearing this, the hunter again began thinking as to what he could do to enable the sage to take food.

23. Meditating on his preceptor, he sought recourse to the river Devikā.

The hunter said:

24. "O excellent river, goddess, I am a hunter and thereby a sinner. Still when I pray to you, be pleased to give me help.

25. I know not a deity, I know not a mantra, I know not worship. All that I know is to meditate on the feet of preceptor and derive benefit therefrom.

26. I being such a one, have mercy on me. Please flow to the place where the sage is seated so that he may wash his feet".

27. Requested thus by the hunter, the holy Devikā moved to the place where Durvāsas was resting.

28-29. Seeing that wonder, Durvāsas was much surprised, and after washing his hands and feet, ate the food reverentially given.

30. He then blessed the emaciated hunter: "Let the Vedas and Vedāṅgas and Upaniṣads, Pada and Krama recitations of all these (Vedas), Purāṇas and Brahmavidyā dawn on you".

31. After giving this boon, Durvāsas told him that he would become a famous sage by name Satyatapas.

32. When he was thus given the boon, the hunter asked the sage: "O sage, being a hunter how can I learn the Vedas ?"

The sage said:

33. As a result of your fasting, your old body has disappeared

and the present body you are having is born of penance.

34-35. Your former knowledge has perished, and a pure one has come upon the imperishable body you have now acquired. This is the truth. Therefore, O sage, the Vedas and Śāstras will always appear in your mind.

CHAPTER THIRTYNINE

Matsyadvādaśīvrata

Satyatapas said:

1. O sage, the foremost among the learned, be pleased to enlighten me on the two kinds of bodies about which you spoke.[1]

Durvāsas said:

2. Actually there are three bodies, not two, including the one for the operation of the effects of one's good and bad deeds.

3. The first body is called Adhārmic (of demerit) which is without (true) knowledge. The second resulting from proper observances is called Dhārmic (of merit).

4. The third, which is beyond senses, is for the action of the results of one's merits and demerits. It is declared so by those who have attained knowledge of Brahman.

5. And thus, including the body for the manifestation of the result of one's own good and bad deeds, there are three.

6. Your former body (body in the former aspect) was named Sin, because you were doing the sinful deed of killing living beings.

7. Now by doing good deeds and performing penance, you have acquired a Dharmic body. Thereby you have become eligible to know the Vedas and Purāṇas.

8. Upto eight years of age man is, of course, guided by others, but after that he becomes different and does things on his own.

1. The reference is to verse 33 in the previous chapter.

9. It is declared by people with Supreme knowledge that it is one and the same body that is considered as three because of different aspects. The difference between them is as between the clay and the pot.

10. The path of action laid down for the Brahmins and others (Kṣatriyas, Vaiśyas and Śūdras) is of four kinds.[1]

11. There the first three always perform the rites prescribed by the Vedas. The fourth attends on these three.

12. He who performs penance knowing well the Vedic injunctions, certainly gains salvation.

Satyatapas said:

13. O great sage, the form of what you said as the Supreme Soul, cannot be known by even great yogins.

14. It is beyond the scope of name and form, and, as such, how can it be known ? So kindly tell me the sign by which I may know it.

Durvāsas said:

15. That which is spoken of as the Supreme Brahman in Vedas and Śāstras is the (essence of) Veda itself, the lotus-eyed Nārāyaṇa-Hari.

16. This Supreme god, Nārāyaṇa, is attained through the different sacrifices and gifts.

Satyatapas said:

17. O sage, lord Nārāyaṇa is attained by spending a lot of money and by the meritorious persons who have mastered the Vedas. Please tell me how he can be attained by those who have no money (for sacrifices.)

18. Without money it is not possible to give gifts. Those who are tied to the family will not have the mind to spend even if they have the means.

19. To such people, it appears to me, Nārāyaṇa will always be far away.

20. Tell me in particular as to by what efforts he can be reached by people of all castes.

---

1. This refers to the four stages of life namely Brahmacarya, Gārhasthya, Vānaprastha and Sannyāsa.

Durvāsas said:

21. I shall tell you the great secret, what was done by Mother Earth when she was merging into water and moving down to the nether world.

22. The solid part of Earth was engulfed by water, and as a result, she was sinking into the lower world, Rasātala.

23. This mother of all beings, when she reached Rasātala, worshipped the great god Nārāyaṇa.

24. By the fastings and vows and other observances of Earth, Nārāyaṇa became pleased. He raised her up and restored her to her original place.

Satyatapas said:

25. O sage, please tell me what was the sort of fasting undertaken by her and what were the vratas performed.

Durvāsas said:

26-28. In the month of Mārgaśīrṣa (Dhanus), on Daśamī day the devotee should, with great control of mind, perform the prescribed rituals in fire and worship of gods, and with clean dress and pure mind eat the remains of the food offered to gods. He should then walk five steps, wash the feet and clean the teeth by chewing eight inches of the twig of a sappy tree and sip water.

29-31. He should then touch the nine outlets in the body (eyes, ears, nose etc.) and meditate on the great lord Janārdana (Viṣṇu), the wearer of yellow garment and bearer of conch, disc and mace and endowed with all auspiciousness. He should then take water in his hand and reverentially offer it to Him uttering His name.

32. He should then say, "O lord, remaining without food on Ekādaśī day, I shall take food on the next day; O lord, be my refuge".

33. Then in the night he should sleep near (the idol of) the Lord reciting 'Namo Nārāyaṇāya'.

34-37. Then early in the morning, he should go to a river which preferably flows into the sea, or a tank or pond in the house (in the order of preference), and taking the mud from it utter the words, "O goddess, the existence and sustenance of all beings lie in you. Be pleased to cleanse me of all my sins. All the holy

Tirthas (places for holy bath) are made by you, so I take this mud from you and stand here, O Earth. O Varuṇa, all rasas (essences) remain in you. By bestowing them all in this mud make it fully purified". Then the mud with water should be smeared all over the body three times.

38. He may then take bath uttering Varuṇa mantra. After bath, he should observe the essentials prescribed and then go to the temple.

39-43. There he should offer worship to Nārāyaṇa saying, 'I worship the feet as Keśava, the waist as Dāmodara, thighs as Nṛsiṁha, chest as the bearer of Śrīvatsa, the stomach as the wearer of Kaustubha, the breast as Lakṣmī's Lord, the hands as the victor of three worlds, the head as the all-pervading, the disc as the bearer of disc, the lotus as the doer of all good, the mace as the valiant, and the lotus as the serene.

44. After saluting Lord Nārāyaṇa thus, he should arrange four pots of water before Him and put into them sesamum and gold and decorate them with garlands.

45. The four pots should be considered as containing water from the four oceans. In the middle a seat covered with cloth should be placed.

46. A vessel made of gold, silver or copper, or, if they are not available, one made of the leaves of Palāśa tree, should be placed on it.

47-49. This vessel should be filled with water and in it should be placed a golden image of Viṣṇu in his form as the fish with all the limbs and ornaments and worshipped with sandal, Dhūpa and different kinds of food and fruit as prescribed.

50. Then saying "O god, just as you raised up the Vedas from the nether world, raise me up (from worldly life)". He should keep awake (throughout the night).

51-54. In the morning, he should give away the four pots to Brahmins, the one on the east to a Ṛgvedin, the one on the South to a Sāmavedin, the one on the West to a Yajurvedin and the one on the north to an Atharvavedin, uttering respectively 'let Ṛgveda be pleased by this', 'let Yajurveda be pleased by this', 'let Sāmaveda be pleased by this', and 'let Atharvaveda be pleased by this'.

55. The golden image of the fish should be given to the priest

after giving him, according to the prescribed rituals, sandal, Dhūpa and cloth.

56. If the priest is one well versed in the Vedas and Upaniṣads then the result of the gift will be many times more than when given to an ordinary person.

57-58. If one shows any disregard to such a priest, he falls into hell for several lives, because one who guides the worship should be considered as a preceptor.

59. After the worship of Viṣṇu and gifts to Brahmins, they should be fed and given dakṣiṇā according to one's means on the Dvādaśī day.

60. The copper vessel with sesamum on which the image was placed should be given to a Brahmin having a family.

61. After feeding the Brahmins, the worshipper may eat along with children, silently and fully controlling the senses.

62. Now listen to the benefits that befall the performer of this Dharaṇīvrata.

63-64. If only I have a thousand mouths and life as long as Brahmā's will I be able to state in full the results of this Vrata. Still I shall say this in brief.

65-66. Seventeen million, ten million, eight million and four million years respectively constituting the four yugas together constitute a caturyuga. Seventyone such Caturyugas constitute a Manvantara.

67. Fourteen days and nights (form a pakṣa, fortnight). Thirty days make a month, and twelve months make a year.

68. Hundred years is the life of a Brahmā.

69. Even if one performs Dvādaśīvrata but once as detailed above one would reach the world of Brahmā and be there as long as Brahmā himself remains.

70. When Brahmā merges in the Supreme, he too will merge likewise, and at the time of creation again, will be born as a saintly and divine king.

71. Even sins like killing a Brahmin, committed knowingly or unknowingly, disappear from him in a moment.

72. Even a person in utter poverty or a dethroned king, will be born as a king by fasting in the prescribed manner.

73. A barren woman, following this course of worship, begets

a good son.

74. The sin of sharing a prohibited bed disappears by the observance of this vow.

75. By this fasting one who has long neglected the Brahmanic duties, gets restored to the Vaidik position.

76. Why say much, this brings about even what is unattainable in the ordinary course. Hence this should be observed by all people.

77. This was done by Earth herself when she was submerged in water. There is no need, therefore, to deliberate on this.

78. This should not be told to any one who is not righteous or has no faith; nor to any one who denounces gods and Brahmins. If it is imparted to one who is devoted to his teacher, it results in the dissolution of all sins.

79. He who undertakes this fast, gets all splendour, wealth, foodgrain and beautiful women.

80. He who recites to others the important rituals pertaining to Dvādaśī worship, or listens to such narration, gets freed from all sins.

CHAPTER FORTY

Kūrmadvādaśīvrata

Durvāsas said:

1. Similarly in the month of Pauṣa (Makara) amṛta was churned from the ocean, and then lord Viṣṇu, on his own accord, became a Kūrma (tortoise).

2. The tithi Daśamī on the bright half of this month is assigned to Viṣṇu in the Kūrma form.

3. On that day, as before, one should do saṅkalpa (stating the aim), and on the following (Ekādaśī) day take ritualistic bath and worship Viṣṇu with all devotion.

4-5. Adoring His feet as Kūrma, waist as Nārāyaṇa, belly as Saṅkarṣaṇa, neck as Purobhava (the first born), the hands as Subāhu (fine-armed) and head as Viśāla (broad-bodied), and uttering mantras containing the names of the lord, offer sandal, flowers, dhūpa and naivedya of a variety of fruits.

6-7. After worshipping, a pot of water with a gem within it should be placed in front and decorated with flowers and white cloth. On it should be placed a copper vessel containing s ghee and in it should be placed an image of the lord with Mandara (resting on him) made of gold, and it should then be gifted to a Brahmin in reverence.

8. The next day (on Dvādaśī), the lord Kūrma-Nārāyaṇa should be propitiated by giving gifts to Brahmins with dakṣiṇā, and food should be taken afterwards.

9. If done in this way, all sins will disappear. You need not have any doubt about this. And it leads one out of the perils of the world, to the abode of Viṣṇu.

10. All sins disappear instantaneously and he is then born as a righteous man. The sins accumulated over several lives are eradicated by devotion.

11. The benefits stated before accrue to him and Lord Nārāyaṇa becomes very much pleased.

CHAPTER FORTYONE

Varāhadvādaśīvrata

Durvāsas said:

1. Similarly, listen, O sage, to the worship of Viṣṇu as Varāha on Dvādaśī day in the bright half of the month of Māgha (Kumbha).

2-3. Performing Saṅkalpa and pūjā, as stated earlier, on the Ekādaśī day with sandal paste, incense and dry fruits, the pot filled with water should be placed in front.

4-5. Then (the devotee should utter): "I worship the feet of the lord as Varāha, waist as Mādhava, belly as Kṣetrajña, chest as Viśvarūpa, neck as Sarvajña, head as Prajāpati, hands as Pradyumna, Sudarśana (disc) as Divyāstra (divine weapon), and Śaṅkha (conch) as Amṛtodbhava".

6-9. Then he should place on the pot a vessel made of gold, silver or copper, fill it with valuable materials according to his capacity, and place on it a golden image of Viṣṇu as Varāha in the form holding the earth with all its mountains and forests. Thus should be placed the golden image in the vessel filled with grain.

10. The image should be covered by a pair of white clothes and worshipped by offering sandal, flowers and dry fruits of various kinds.

11. Heaping flowers all round, he should keep awake and read the story of the appearance of the lord as Varāha.

12-13. After doing this, the next morning at sunrise, taking bath and performing worship he should give the image together with the pot to a pious Brahmin with family, who is learned in Vedas and devoted to Viṣṇu.

14. Now hear the results that accrue to a person who thus gifts the image of Viṣṇu in his form as Varāha.

15. In this life he gets happiness, prosperity, effulgence and gratification. If he is poor, he becomes rich and if without a son, gets one.

16. Everything inauspicious disappears, and auspiciousness sets in immediately as if by force. In the life beyond he gets eternal happiness. Listen to a story in this connection.

17. In the place called Pratiṣṭhāna there was a famous king named Vīradhanvā.

18. He once went to the forest for hunting, and there near the hermitage of a sage he killed numerous deer.

19-20. There, quite unknowingly, he happened to kill five[1] sons of sage Saṁvarta, who were all devoted to learning the Vedas and who had the appearance of deer.

Satyatapas said:

21. O Sage, be pleased to tell me how they looked like deer.

Durvāsas said:

22. Once they saw in the forest several young deer, just born

1. According to the reading it is fifty, but this seems to be a mistake.

but without their mother near by.

23. They took one of them each and put them in a cave, but they soon died. Sad at this they went to their father and told him about it.

The sage's sons said:

24. O father, we have been the cause of the death of five young deer, though not deliberately. So be pleased to tell as what atonement we should do.

Saṁvarta said:

25. "My father used to injure and I too. And you my sons, also have developed a tendency to commit injury.

26. You put on deer skin and perform penance for five years. You will then become purified."

27. They then put on deer skin and began meditating on the Supreme in the forest.

28. At the close of one year, King Vīradhanvā came to the place where these in deer-skin were sitting.

29-30. Seeing them at the foot of a tree, the king mistook them to be real deer and killed them.

31. But when he realised that he had killed not the deer but some Brahmins doing penance, he was struck with fear and went to the hermitage of sage Devarāta.

32. He told the sage how he happened to kill Brahmins and stood there shedding penitent tears.

33-35. Devarāta consoled him saying that he would be freed from the sin thus committed. He said that the (story of the) earth sinking into Pātāla and Viṣṇu assuming the form of a boar lifting it up, would bring about the king's purification by the lord himself.

36-37. Then the king became glad and asked him as to how the lord would become pleased that he would rid him of all his sins.

Durvāsas said:

38-39. Thus asked, sage Devarāta told him about this Vrata (detailed above).The king performed it, and as a result, enjoyed all pleasures in the world and, at the end of his life, was taken to the world of Indra in a golden aerial vehicle.

40. Indra honoured him by rising from his seat and offering *arghya.*

Seeing Indra thus going towards him, the servants of Viṣṇu said:

41. "O Indra, you are not entitled to see him, because you are inferior to him in penance". All other Dikpālas also were similarly turned away by the servants of Viṣṇu, all of them being eclipsed by his superior lustre.

42-43. He then proceeded to Satyaloka which is unaffected by deluge and the heat which follows it and remains there now applauded by others. When Yajñapuruṣa(Viṣṇu) is pleased, what wonder is there that this happened so.

44. Worshipped in proper form, even once one attains effulgence, long life, sound health and abundant wealth and finally gets immortality.

45. When the worship is in all detail, lord Nārāyaṇa, who has the fourfold form, gives his own abode.

46-48. Just as he restored the Vedas by taking the form of the fish, and held the Mandara mountain in position by assuming the form of a tortoise at the churning of the milky ocean, so he raised up the earth from the nether world by taking the form of a boar.

CHAPTER FORTYTWO

Narasiṁhadvādaśīvrata

Durvāsas said:

1. Similarly one may worship Viṣṇu in the prescribed manner on Dvādaśī on the bright half of the month of Phālguna.

2-3. He should worship the feet as Narasiṁha, thighs as Govinda, waist as Viśvabhuk, chest as Aniruddha, neck as Śitikaṇṭha, head as Piṅgakeśa, disc (Sudarśana) as Asuradhvaṁsin (destroyer of Asuras) and conch as Toyātmā, with sandal, flowers and fruits.

4-5. A pot together with two white clothes and a gem inside should then be placed in front and over that in a vessel made of copper or wood or reed a golden image of Narasiṁha with the usual materials.

6. After performing worship on it, on Dvādaśī day it should be given to a Vaidik Brahmin.

7. I shall now tell you the result gained through this Vrata by the king named Vatsa.

8. In the land of Kimpuruṣas there was a righteous king named Bhārata and he had a son named Vatsa.

9. Vatsa was conquered by his enemies and was completely robbed of his treasury, and he went with his wife to the hermitage of sage Vasiṣṭha.

10. Vasiṣṭha then asked him the purpose of his visit.

The king said:

11-12. O sage, I have been deprived of my kingdom and robbed of my treasury by the enemies, and without any one to help me, I have now come to you. Be pleased to advise me.

Durvāsas said:

13. Thus said, Vasiṣṭha told him about this (Narasiṁha) dvādaśīvrata, and he observed it accordingly.

14. At the end of the vrata, lord Narasiṁha was pleased, and he gave him a cakra (disc) to smash his enemies in battle.

15. With that weapon, the king won back his kingdom, and after performing numerous Aśvamedha sacrifices, attained Viṣṇuloka.

16. This holy Dvādaśīvrata is thus narrated to you. Now you may do whatever you desire to do so.

CHAPTER FORTYTHREE

Vāmanadvādaśīvrata

Durvāsas said:

1. In the same manner, in the month of Caitra (Meṣa),

Viṣṇu should be worshipped on the Dvādaśī day after due fasting.

2-3. The feet should be worshipped as Vāmana, the waist as Viṣṇu, belly as Vāsudeva, chest as Saṅkarṣaṇa, neck as Viśvabhṛt, head as Vyomarūpin, the arms as Viśvajit and the conch and disc by their own names (Pāñcajanya and Sudarśana).

4. After worship to the great lord in this manner, place in front, as before, the pot of water with gem within duly purified.

5. As before, place on it in a vessel (of the material mentioned earlier) a golden image of Vāmana with a white yajñopavīta.

6. Near it should be placed the Kamaṇḍalu (spouted vessel), a small umbrella, wooden sandals, rosary and seat of kuśa grass.

7. All these together should be given to a Brahmin in the morning uttering "May Viṣṇu in the form of the dwarf be pleased".

8. The story of the appearance of Vāmana in this month (Caitra) should then be recited. This is the rule. (Here is a story in this connection).

9. There was once a king named Haryaśva. He was childless and so he performed penance for an issue.

10. When he was performing a sacrifice for the purpose, Viṣṇu came to him in the form of a Brahmin.

11. He asked the king the aim of his deed. The king replied that it was for getting a son. The Brahmin asked him to continue what he was doing.

12. Saying thus to the king, he suddenly disappeared.

13-14. The king completed the rites and then gave (the image with all the associated things) to a poor Vaidik Brahmin saying "O Lord, just as to the issueless Aditi you were born as son, by the same truth may I also get a child".

15. By this vrata a son was born to him by name Ugrāśva and he became an emperor.

16-17. One without a son gets a son, one who wants wealth gets it, one who is deprived of his kingdom regains it. And after death he goes to Viṣṇu's abode and after remaining there for long, takes birth as a man and becomes an emperor like Yayāti, son of Nahuṣa.

CHAPTER FORTYFOUR

Jāmadagnyadvādaśīvrata

Durvāsas said:

1. In the same manner in the month of Vaiśākha (Vṛṣabha), one should perform saṅkalpa (on Dvādaśī day) and after bathing using mud, go to the place of worship.

2-3. There he should worship Viṣṇu in the following manner. The feet should be worshipped as Jāmadagnya, belly as Sarvadhārin (bearing everything), waist as Madhusūdana, thighs as Śrīvatsadhārin, hands as Kṣarāntaka, the beard as Śitikaṇṭha, the conch and disc by their own names (Pāñcajanya and Sudarśana) and head as Brahmāṇḍadhārin.

4. After worshipping thus, he should place a pot in front as before and put on it a pair of clothes.

5. A golden image of Jāmadagnya (Paraśurāma) having an axe in the right hand, should be put in a rotten vessel and then placed on it.

6. Worship should then be made with sandal and flowers of various kinds.

7. Keeping awake the whole night with devotion, it should be given to a Brahmin early in the morning the next day.

8. I shall now illustrate the result accruing from this vrata.

9. There was a mighty king by name Vīrasena. He had no sons and so he began to perform intensive penance.

10. When he was thus doing severe penance, the great sage Yājñavalkya came to him.

11. Seeing the effulgent sage thus come to him, the king rose up with folded hands.

12. The sage who was honoured thus, asked the king about the aim of his penance.

The king said:

13. O sage, I am now without a son, and so I perform these austerities so that this body of mine may steadily decline (leading to death).

Yājñavalkya said:

14. O king, enough of this severe penance. Surely you will

get a son without difficulty.

The king said:

15. O sage, be pleased to tell me how I will beget a son without difficulty.

Durvāsas said:

16. Asked by the king thus, the sage told him about this (Jāmadagnya)dvādaśīvrata to be performed in the bright fortnight in Vaiśākha.

17. By observing it with due fasting, the king got a son, the well known Nala, who even now is remembered in the world as one to be considered as with a sacred name.

18. Such is the result of this Dvādaśīvrata.

19. One who observes it will get good sons, learning, prosperity and resplendence in this life.

20. In the world beyond, he remains in the world of Brahmā for one kalpa attended by numerous Apsarases.

21. Then he will be reborn as an emperor and live for thirty thousand kalpas.

CHAPTER FORTYFIVE

Rāmadvādaśīvrata

Durvāsas said:

1. In the month of Jyeṣṭha (Mithuna) similarly, after saṅkalpa in the prescribed manner, one should worship the lord with flowers of different kinds.

2-4. He should worship the feet as Rāma, waist as Trivikrama, belly as Dhṛtaviśva (the holder of the universe), chest as Saṁvatsara, neck as Saṁvartaka, hands as Sarvāstradhārin (the bearer of all weapons), the conch and disc by their names (Pāñcajanya and Sudarśana) and head as Sahasraśiras (thousand-headed). After this, as before, the pot should be placed in front.

5. As before, the golden images of Rāma and Lakṣmaṇa

covered in clothes, should be worshipped in the prescribed manner, and should be gifted to a Brahmin the next morning by him who desires to accomplish his wishes.

6-7. When the advice of Vasiṣṭha was sought by Daśaratha when he was without a son, it was this that was suggested to him by the sage.

8. Grasping the secret, the king observed this and the result was Viṣṇu in a fourfold form became his sons, being pleased with him.

9. Such is the result in this world. I shall tell you the effect in the world beyond.

10. The performer enjoys the pleasures of heaven as long as Indra remains its lord. Then he takes birth as a king who would perform a hundred sacrifices (and thus becomes one like Indra himself).

11. One who performs this vrata without any desire gets all his sins removed and in the end attains eternal bliss.

CHAPTER FORTYSIX

Kṛṣṇadvādaśivrata

Durvāsas said:

1-2. In the month of Āṣāḍha (Karkaṭaka) also, one may take due saṅkalpa, and after worshipping Viṣṇu in the hands as Cakrapāṇi, neck as Bhūpati, conch and disc as Pāñcajanya and Sudarśana and head as Puruṣa, and place the pot in front as before.

3. Then on a cloth over it should be placed the golden image of Viṣṇu as Vāsudeva and the other vyūhas (Saṅkarṣaṇa, Pradyumna and Aniruddha).

4. After worship with sandal, flowers etc., it should be gifted to a Vaidik Brahmin, as before.

5. Now listen to the benefits arising from this vrata performed in the prescribed manner.

6. In the Yadu clan there was a great man named Vasudeva

He had a highly devoted wife named Devakī, but she was without a child.

7. Once Nārada came to their house, and being received with due respect, he said:

8. "O Vasudeva, please listen to this matter relating to the worship of god, after knowing which I have rushed here to tell you.

9. Earth went to the assembly of gods and said that she was unable to bear the weight (of the demons) straining her and requested them to kill (these evil-doers).

10. Thus requested, Devas thought of going to lord Nārāyaṇa, but the moment they thought of him, he appeared before them.

11-12. The great lord himself then told Devas that he would accomplish their desire by taking birth as a human being, but he would be born only to her who, with her husband, observes the fast (on Dvādaśī) in the bright half of the month of Āṣāḍha.

13. Assured thus, Devas went away, and I came here to tell you about this so that you can get a worthy son.

14. By performing this Dvādaśī vrata, Vasudeva got the son named Kṛṣṇa and gained great prosperity.

15. After enjoying great affluence, he attained in the end final beatitude. Thus I have told you about the observance of Dvādaśī vrata in Āṣāḍha.

CHAPTER FORTYSEVEN

Buddhadvādaśīvrata[1]

Durvāsas said:

1. In the month of Śrāvaṇa (Siṁha) on the Ekādaśī day of the bright half, observe the vrata as before, and worship Viṣṇu with sandal and flowers.

2-3. Worship the feet as Dāmodara, waist as Hṛṣīkeśa, belly

1. The colophon at the end of the chapter gives this name but its significance is not clear.

as Sanātana, chest as Śrīvatsadhārin, hands as Cakrapāṇi, neck as Hari, head as Muñjakeśa and tuft as Bhadra.

4. After worship in this manner, place the pot in front as before, and place over it covered in a pair of clothes, the golden image of the lord as Dāmodara.

5. After worship with sandal and flowers in proper form, give it to a Vaidik Brahmin as before.

6-7. Now listen to the account of the power of this vrata which is capable of removing all sins.

8. In the Kṛtayuga there was a mighty king by name Nṛga. He was wandering in the forest for hunting.

9. Riding on his horse, he happened to enter into the interior of the dense forest full of tigers, lions, elephants, snakes and aborigines.

10. Being alone in a lonely place, he was sad and dismounting the horse, spread Kuśa grass and slept on it.

11. In the night there came near him a multitude of fourteen thousand hunters for hunting.

12. They saw there the king adorned with golden jewels and full of high effulgence.

13. They quickly ran to their master and reported to him, and he immediately started to kill the king and take away the gold and gems he was adorning on his body.

14. The other hunters also rushed there to snatch away the horse from the sleeping king.

15. At that time there arose from the king's person a divine lady decked with sandal and garlands and ornaments white in colour.

16. With a Cakra held in her hand, she killed all the hunters, and then entered his body.

17. As she was entering into the body, the king rose up.

18. Seeing her disappear in his own body and seeing all those base men killed there, the king mounted the horse and went to the hermitage of sage Vāmadeva.

19. Bowing to the sage with reverence, he asked him to be pleased to tell him as to who that lady was and who the killed hunters were.

Vāmadeva said:

20. O king, in the previous life you were a Śūdra, but you performed this Dvādaśī vrata on hearing about it from Brahmins.

21. You observed the vrata on Dvādaśī in the bright half of Śrāvaṇa month.

22. By this vrata you became a king and the goddess (of this vrata) protects you always from all dangers.

23. She who killed all these base and cruel men and protected you is this goddess.

24. Even this one goddess is capable of protecting from all dangers and bestowing (on the devotee) a kingdom. Twelve of them[1] will well bring about the position of Indra.

CHAPTER FORTYEIGHT

Kalkidvādaśīvrata

Durvāsas said:

1. In the same manner, on the Ekādaśī of the bright half of the month of Bhādrapada (Kanyā), one may worship the lord of lords in the prescribed manner.

2-3. He should worship the feet as Kalkin, the waist as Hṛṣīkeśa, the belly as Mlecchavidhvaṁsaka, neck as Śitikaṇṭha, arms as Khaḍgapāṇi, hands as Caturbhuja and head as Viśvamūrti.

4-5. After worship in this manner, he should place, as before, a pot in front and over it a golden image of Kalkin in a white cloth and with sandal and flowers, and in the morning it should be gifted to a Vaidik Brahmin.

6-7. O sage, now listen to the result accruing from this vrata:

Once there was a powerful king named Viśāla in Kāśī. Deprived of his kingdom by his kinsmen, he went to Gandhamādana and from there reached Badarī in a canoe, bereft of all his royalty.

8. There came the great and ancient sages Nara and Nārā-

1. The goddesses of the Dvādaśīs of all the twelve months.

yaṇa, who are worshipped by all gods.

9. Seeing the king there immersed in contemplation of the Supreme Being Viṣṇu, they were very much pleased and asked him to seek a boon from them who had gone there pleased by his meditation.

The king said :

10. "I do not know who you are and from whom I should seek the boon. I wish to get boon from him whom I am worshipping".

11. Said thus, they asked : "O king, whom are you worshipping and what boon do you wish to get ? We wish to know this. So please tell us".

12. The king replied that he was worshipping Viṣṇu and then remained silent. They then said :

13-14. "It is by the grace of that same god (Viṣṇu) that we are offering you a boon now. So tell us what you desire".

The king said:

15. Grant me the boon by which I will be able to propitiate the lord of sacrifices (Viṣṇu) by various sacrifices.

Nara said:

16. Lord Nārāyaṇa who looks after the entire world, is performing penance with me at Badari.

17. He formerly took the form of a fish (Matsya), then that of a tortoise (Kūrma), afterwards that of a pig (Varāha) and then assumed the form of man-lion (Narasiṁha).

18-19. Then he was born as a dwarf (Vāmana), and later on as the mighty son of Jamadagni (Paraśurāma). Then he took birth as the son of Daśaratha (Rāma) and killing all the base and vile people, established order in the world.[1]

20-22. One may worship Narasiṁha for ridding oneself of sins, Vāmana for removing all stupefaction, Paraśurāma for wealth, Rāma for annihilation of enemies, Balarāma and Kṛṣṇa for begetting sons, Buddha for physical charm and Kalki for victory.

1. One verse relating to Kṛṣṇa and Kalkin seems to be missing here.

23. He then told him about this Dvādaśī. And observing this, the king became an emperor, and by his name Badari came to be known as Viśālā.

24. After ruling the country for long, the king retired to the forest. By performing several sacrifices he attained final beatitude.

CHAPTER FORTYNINE

Padmanābhadvādaśi

Durvāsas said:

1. In the same manner, on the Dvādaśī day in the bright half of the month of Āśvayuja (Tulā) lord Padmanābha should be worshipped.

2-3. The feet should be worshipped as Padmanābha, the waist as Padmayoni, the belly as Sarvadeva, the chest as Puṣkarākṣa, the hands as Avyaya, the weapons as before, and head as Prabhava, and then, as already described earlier, the pot should be placed and over it the golden image of Padmanābha.

4. After performing worship with sandal, flowers etc., early in the morning the next day it should be gifted to a Brahmin.

5. Listen to the result accruing from the observance of this.

6. In the Kṛtayuga there was a valiant king named Bhadrāśva. His kingdom also came to be known by his name Bhadrāśva.

7. Once sage Agastya came to him and said that he would stay with him for a week. The king, with bowing head, agreed with pleasure.

8. The king's wife by name Kāntimatī was so beautiful that she had the splendour of a dozen suns.

9. She had five hundred co-wives but they were all devoted to her and they attended on her like servants.

10-11. Agastya saw her in her radiant beauty, the co-wives earnestly serving her and the king being delighted at her happiness.

12. He was very glad to see all this and exclaimed, "O Lord of the worlds, how good in this !"

13. On the second day seeing the beaming queen, Agastya exclaimed, "The whole world has been acquired".

14-15. On the third day, seeing her he said, "Fools do not know lord Viṣṇu, who by a single day's propitiation has given this king this gift".

16-18. On the fourth day, he threw up his arms and exclaimed, "well done, lord of the world !, well done, women and Śūdras !, well done, Brahmins !, well done Kṣatriyas !, well done Vaiśyas !, well done Bhadrāśva ! , well done Agastya !, well done Prahlāda !, well done Dhruva !" Saying thus Agastya danced in joy before the king.

19. The king with his queen, seeing him thus immersed in joy, asked him the cause of his delight.

Agastya said:

20-21. "You are a foolish king, all your followers are fools, your priests are also so, since they do not understand me".

22. Told thus, the king with folded hands, requested him to be sympathetic and tell him clearly so that he could understand.

Agastya said:

23. "In the former life, this queen was a servant in the house of the Vaiśya Haridatta, and you were her husband, a Śūdra serving in the same household.

24-25. The Vaiśya, observing Dvādaśī in the month of Āśvayuja, went to the temple of Viṣṇu and after worshipping there with flowers, incense etc., left you both there to keep guard and to keep the lamps burning.

26. When the Vaiśya was gone, you were both engaging yourselves in keeping the lamps burning throughout night.

27-28. In course of time both of you died, and due to the merit you had acquired (by attending to the duty assigned to you by the Vaiśya in the temple), you were born in the family of Priyavrata and this queen, who was originally servant of the Vaiśya, became your wife.

29-30. If this is the result of simply keeping the lamp burning in the temple for another's sake, it is beyond words to state the effect of doing such a thing for one's own sake. Hence, I said 'O lord of the worlds, how good is this !".

31-32. The merit acquired by the worship for one year in Kṛtayuga, is acquired by the same for half a year in Tretāyuga, by quarter of a year in Dvāparayuga and by the mere utterance of the name 'Nārāyaṇa' in Kaliyuga.

33. Hence, I exclaimed 'the whole world has been acquired'.

34. The result of burning the lamp before Viṣṇu for author's sake is what has been gained by you. Hence, I exclaimed 'Fools do not know the effect of serving Hari'.

35. Since the Brahmins and Kṣatriyas perform with devotion sacrifices of various kinds they were hailed by me.

36. I do not find in this world anything more worthy than the worship of Viṣṇu. Hence, I congratulated myself saying 'O Agastya, well done'.

37. That woman is blessed who attends on her husband, because that kind of service is an indirect service of god. A Śūdra who does so, is even more blessed.

38. That woman and that Śūdra are blessed, if they attend on the twice-born. Hence, I said "Well done, women and Śūdras"

39. Although born in the Asura clan, Prahlāda proclaimed that he knew none other than Puruṣottama (Viṣṇu). Hence I said "Well done Prahlāda."

40-41. Dhruva who belonged to the line of Brahmā, went to the forest when he was but a boy, and there worshipping Viṣṇu attained an extremely glorious position. Hence I said 'Well done Dhruva !".

42. Hearing these words of the great Agastya, the king sought his advice, but the sage was leaving for the tīrtha Puṣkara.

43. Bhadrāśva followed him to get his advice, and he was then told about this Dvādaśīvrata by the sage.

Durvāsas said:

44. "O sage, I have told you this much". Agastya then told the king:

45. "I am leaving for Puṣkara, but you will be blessed with good sons". So saying, the sage suddenly disappeared.

46. By observing this Padmanābhadvādaśī as prescribed and with fasting, the king attained the height of glory in this world.

47. Enjoying all pleasures surrounded by children and grandchildren, he finally reached the world of Viṣṇu with the blessings of Padmanābha.

CHAPTER FIFTY

Dharaṇīvrata

Durvāsas said:

1. After going to Puṣkaratīrtha, sage Agastya returned to the palace of Bhadrāśva in the month of Kārttika.

2. The righteous king duly received him with *arghya*, *pādya* etc., and offered a seat. He then asked him with curiosity.

The king said:

3-4. O sage, formerly you told me about the observance of Dvādaśī in the month of Āśvina. Now be pleased to tell me what is sacred in the month of Kārttika.

Agastya said:

5. O king, Dvādaśī in the month of Kārttika is spoken of as most sacred. I shall tell you about its observance and results. Listen to me with rapt attention.

6. In the manner detailed earlier, take the saṅkalpa and perform bath.

7-10. Then perform worship to Lord Nārāyaṇa. The head should be worshipped as Sahasraśiras (thousand-headed), the hands as Puruṣa (Supreme Man), neck as Viśvarūpin (universal form), weapons as jñānāstra (weapon of knowledge), chest as Śrīvatsa, belly as Jagadvasiṣṇu (the abode of all the worlds), waist as Divyamūrti (divine-bodied), feet as Sahasrapāda (thousand-footed), and the whole body together as Dāmodara. Thus perform worship in the reverse order (from head to foot).

11-12. After worship in this manner, place in front four pots smeared with white sandal and with gems within, decorated in the neck with flower garlands and placed in copper receptacles filled with sesamum and (a little) gold.

13. Consider these four pots (of water) as representing the four oceans. In their midst, as before, place the golden image of Viṣṇu wearing yellow cloth and in the form of a yogin.

14. After worship in the prescribed manner, keep awake (the whole night).

15. Then perform Vaiṣṇava sacrifice for the lord as Yogīśvara (the great yogin)in the sixteen-petalled cakra[1] devised by yogins.

16. In the morning give four pots to Brahmins, and the fifth containing Yogīśvara with particular devotion (to an exalted person like the preceptor).

17-18. Giving (to an ordinary Brahmin) is equivalent to the acquisition of Vedas, giving it to one steeped in Vedic knowledge brings double the result, giving it to an Ācārya of the Pāñcarātras[2] brings about the result a thousand-fold, and giving it to one who is learned in the secrets of all this makes the result a crore time more.

19. When the guru is available, if ignoring him the gift is given to another, it becomes useless and leads to the donor's downfall.

20-21. Persuade the guru to accept it, and then think of others, because, learned or otherwise, the guru is lord Janārdana. Whether he follows the proper path or not he is highly important.

22. If any one, after resorting to the guru, falls out with him, he is put to torment in the hell for numerous yugas.

23. After worshipping Viṣṇu and giving gifts thus, Brahmins should be fed according to one's means and given dakṣiṇā.

24. The Creator formerly performed this Dharaṇīvrata and attained his position and the eternal Brahman.

25. Similarly, the Haihaya king named Kṛtavīrya got the son named Kārtavīrya and attained the eternal Brahman.

26. Performing this vrata, Śakuntalā got through Duṣyanta the son Bharata who became an emperor.

1. Specified mystic figure with sixteen points engraved on a metal plate.

2. The Vaiṣṇavas who follow the Pañcarātrāgama.

27. The emperors referred to in the Vedas, all got their positions by performing this vrata.

28. When Dharaṇī (Earth) sank into Pātāla, she performed this vrata and hence it is known as Dharaṇīvrata.

29. When the vrata was completed, the earth was raised by Viṣṇu in his form as Varāha and placed over the water like a canoe.

30-31. O sage, I have thus told you about this Dharaṇīvrata. He who listens to this and he who performs this, becomes freed from all sins and gets merged in Viṣṇu.

CHAPTER FIFTYONE

Agastyagītā I

Varāha said:

1-2. After hearing the account of Dharaṇīvrata from sage Durvāsas, Satyatapas went to a slope of Himālaya mountain where the river there was Puṣpabhadrā (beautiful with flowers) the stone Citraśilā (beautifully shaped) and the banyan tree Bhadravaṭa (particularly attractive), and building a hermitage there, spent the rest of his life in contemplation.

Earth said:

3. Thousands of aeons have elapsed since I performed this Vrata, and now I have forgotten all about it.

4-5. By your blessing I now begin to get a recollection of all that. I am, therefore, anxious to know more.

6. Therefore, kindly tell me what Agastya did after returning to the residence of Bhadrāśva.

Varāha said:

7. When the sage returned, Bhadrāśva asked him about Mokṣadharma.

Bhadrāśva said:

8. O sage, by what means is the bondage of worldly exis-

tence snapped, and by what means the sorrows in life can be got over ?

Agastya said:

9. O king, listen well to this story relating to what is distant and what is near and based on the division into the seen and the unseen.

10. At the time when there was no day, no night, no direction, no heaven, no gods and no sun, a king named Paśupāla was looking after numerous beasts.

11. He once went to see the eastern ocean, and there, on the shore of that limitless expanse of water, saw a forest full of snakes.

12. There were eight trees and a freely flowing river. Five important persons were there moving horizontally and upwards. One of them was holding an effulgent woman.

13. The woman was holding on her chest a person having the splendour of a thousand suns and with three colours and three divisons.

14. Seeing the king, all of them became silent and still, and as soon as the king entered the forest, became combined into a single being.

15. The king was then encircled by the serpents, and he began to think about how he could kill them and effect his escape.

16. When he was thus thinking, another person having the three colours, white, red and yellow, came out of his body.

17. He asked by gesticulation where he should go. Just then there arose Mahat.

18. The king was covered by that and asked to be alert in mind. He was then confronted by the woman (who was really Māyā).

19. He was thus engulfed by Māyā. Then the lord of all beings caught him in his possession.

20. Then five other persons came there and surrounded him.

21. All these hid themselves within the king's person when the serpents came united to attack.

22. The king then appeared highly resplendent and his all sins disappeared.

23. In him were unified earth, water, fire, air and ether and all their qualities.

24. Thus Paśupāla unified all these that stood around him.

25. Seeing the king then, the tri-coloured person said to him:

26-27. "O king, I am your son, please command me to do what you wish. We decided to bind you, but we were defeated and bound by you, and we now remain hidden in your body. When I have become your son, everything else will arise of its own".

28. Told thus, the king spoke to the man.

29. "You (say you) are my son, and as a result other things arise. But I don't desire to have attachment to any of the pleasures men may have".

30. So saying he released the son, and with him others also. And freed from them, he stood alone.

CHAPTER FIFTYTWO

Agastyagītā II

Agastya said:

1. The king made himself into a tri-coloured being and produced a tri-coloured son named Aham (Ego).

2. The son got a daughter Avabodha (consciousness) and she got a son Vijñāna (knowledge).

3. He got five sons comprehending all comprehensible objects and named Akṣa and the rest (Eye etc).

4. These (sense-organs) were the Dasyus (hostile aborigines) who were subjugated by the king.

5. In their abstract form they made an abode for themselves (in the king's person), a city consisting of nine outlets, a single pillar, four pathways, and numerous rivulets and ponds.

6. All the nine entered the city together and soon Paśupāla became the concrete Puruṣa.

7. Established in that city, the king brought the Vedas there by contemplating on them.

8. The king also arranged there for all the Vratas, rules and sacrifices laid down in them.

9. The king once felt distressed and evoked the karmakāṇḍa (the scripture of ritualistic action), and then the Supreme lord remaining in yogic slumber, got forth a son with four faces, four hands and four feet and embodying the four Vedas.

10. From then onwards every object of sense came to be under the king's perfect control.

11. He found alike the sea and the forest, the grass and the elephant as a result of his invocation of the Karmakāṇḍa.[1]

CHAPTER FIFTYTHREE

The Story of Paśupāla[2]

Bhadrāśva said:

1. O sage, you have narrated this story in reply to my question. But how did it arise and by whom was it made ?

Agastya said:

2. This curious story is there and it relates to every object in the world. Its implication is the same in your body, my body, and every other being's.

3-4. Desiring to originate it and thinking of the means for it, he who arose from Paśupāla with four feet and four faces is its originator as well as propagator.

5. His son named Svara is considered as an embodiment of truth. He expounded the significance of the four Vedas to four persons and thus became venerable.

6. The first of these four was Catuḥśṛṅga (four-horned) and the second Vṛṣa (bull), the third followed their path and the fourth followed them with devotion.

7. They all heard the story of Satyamūrti (Svara). The second (Vṛṣa) then resorted to Brahmacarya.

8. As a result of Vṛṣa's dominance there arose in men the

1. The whole of this Agastyagitā is an allegory based on the principles of Sāṅkhya philosophy.

2. Many verses in this chapter are obscure.

capacity to govern servants, riding on bulls and living in the forest.

9. When he was speaking, there arose his sons suddenly fourfold, singlefold and twofold.

10. The fourfaced seeing the permanent and transient objects, thought of the means of seeing his father.

11. "The great virtues which were there in my father, I am not able to see in any of the sons of Svara.

12. The Veda proclaims that the grandson with the grandfather's name (will be like him), and this cannot be different in the case of Svara's sons.

13. I should see those virtues in some one here. But what shall I do ?" He was thinking in this way.

14. While he was thinking thus, a weapon from his father appeared there and with that Svara was churned.

15. When the churning was in progress, the fourfaced saw the head appearing like a cocoanut fruit covered in a tenfold way.

16. The four-footed then cut it off like a sesamum plant.

17. Then he cut off what had become rootless.

18. At that part arose ten[1] and afterwards the five.[2]

19. He cut them again and they were all flaming.

20. When that was cut off, a small object, onetenth of the original size, appeared.

21. That too was cut off, but then arose another small like that and white and calm.

22-23. And he saw in that his own father small like a molecule and indistinct. He then became happy and so too the father Svara.

24. Such was the man Svara, his trunk was Pravṛtti (action) and head Vivṛtti (inaction).

25. Thus arose the story and it has been narrated to you.

26. This is the earliest of all stories. He who understands its significance, performs true action.

---

1. The ten indicates the indriyas, five jñānendriyas for perception and five karmendriyas for action.

2. The five represents the five elements, Earth, Water, Fire, Air and Ether.

CHAPTER FIFTYFOUR

Vrata for attaining the best husband

Bhadrāśva said:

1. O sage, be pleased to tell me who should be worshipped by a person desirous of getting knowledge and how he should be worshipped.

Agastya said:

2. Lord Viṣṇu alone is to be worshipped by all always, even by Devas. I shall tell you the means by which one can get boons from him.

3. He is the ultimate truth conveyed by the Vedas and sought by sages and the common people, and He is the Supreme God. Worshipping him will never be in vain.

4. The vrata to propitiate Viṣṇu told by the great Nārada to the Apsarases is well known.

Apsarases said:

5. O divine sage, son of Brahmā, we wish to have husbands. Please tell us how we can get Lord Nārāyaṇa as our husband.

Nārada said:

6. It is the rule that a question like this should be asked after respectful prostration, but you did not observe it because of your pride of youth.

7. Still, since you have uttered the name of the great Viṣṇu and what you seek is to attain him as husband, I feel you have made some amends for your fault.

8. I shall now tell you about the vrata by which Viṣṇu will give boons on his own and become the husband of the seekers.

Nārada said:

9. On the auspicious Dvādaśī day in the śuklapakṣa in Vasanta (spring season), one should fast and worship Viṣṇu at night in the prescribed manner.

10. A circle of red flowers should be made (round the idol) and the whole night should be spent without sleep and with dance

and song, vocal and instrumental.

11. The (lord's) head should be worshipped as Bhava, the waist as Anaṅga, the hands as Kāma, the belly as Suśāstra, the feet as Manmatha, and the whole body as Hari.

12. The devotee should then bow in all directions.

13. In the morning gifts should be given to a Vaidik Brahmin who is free from bodily defect.

14. After propitiating the Brahmins, the vrata should be concluded. If you observe all this, Viṣṇu will certainly become your husband.

15. The lord should also be worshipped with fine sugarcane juice and flowers like jasmine.

16. Since in your pride you did not bow to me before asking me about this, you have shown me an insult and you cannot escape (fully) from its effect.

17. Therefore in this very lake here you stand now, you will happen to laugh at sage Aṣṭāvakra and incur his curse.

18-19. You will get the great Hari as your husband, but you will face the insult of being carried away by the cowherds. But the lord will still be your husband.

Agastya said:

20. After saying this, the divine sage Nārada disappeared. They performed all that they were told to do, and Viṣṇu became pleased with them.

CHAPTER FIFTYFIVE

Śubhavrata

Agastya said:

1. O great king, listen to the best of vratas namely Śubha, by which Lord Viṣṇu may be attained.

2. This should be started on the first day in the bright fortnight of the month of Mārgaśīrṣa and on Daśamī take food only once.

3. Then at noon on that Daśamī day worship Viṣṇu. And on the Dvādaśī day, perform Saṅkalpa as before.

4. Fasting on that day, give away yava grain to Brahmins and utter the name of Hari while performing Dāna, Homa and Arcana.

5. Spend four months like this, and in the next four from Caitra month observe similarly but give barley meal as gifts to Brahmins.

6. In the next three months from Śrāvaṇa give paddy grain as gift.

7. In the month of Kārttika also observe in the same manner and on Dvādaśī worship Viṣṇu with great purity and devotion in the name of the month.

8. With full control of the senses and with saṅkalpa as before, perform rituals on Dvādaśī.

9-10. (For this) on Ekādaśī day instal a golden image of Earth, with the great mountains in front of Viṣṇu, on a pair of white clothes over layers of different grains.

11. Offer to the deity five gems (gold, silver, ruby, emerald and pearl) and keep awake the whole night.

12. In the morning invite twentyfour Brahmins and give each a cow with dakṣiṇā.

13. Also a pair of clothes, a ring (for the finger), bangles and earrings in gold.

14. The king may give a village each to the poor (Brahmins).

15. Along with the land gift, a pair of golden cows as well as a pair of clothes also may be given, according to capacity.

16. A cow decorated with all ornaments may also be specially given. In this way the Lord becomes pleased.

17. The image of Earth may also be made of silver and this may be given to the Brahmin along with the other associate materials thinking of Viṣṇu.

18-19. He should also be fed and given slippers and umbrella uttering 'May lord Viṣṇu of universal form be always pleased with me'.

20-21. The merit acquired by such feeding and gifts cannot be described even in the course of many years. Still, I shall tell you a little of it. Listen to my account of what was achieved by this vrata.

22. In the Kṛtayuga there was a saintly king named Dṛḍhavrata. He asked Lord Brahmā as to what he might do to get a son. Brahmā told him about this vrata and he performed it.

23. At the close of the vrata, the universal god (Viṣṇu) appeared before him and asked him to seek a boon.

The king said:

24. "Bless me with a son, O Lord, who will be longlived, very famous, highly virtuous, proficient in the Vedas and inclined to perform sacrifices".

25-26. The king continued: "Grant me also, O great god, the position of a sage by attaining which one will have no cause to regret".

27. Lord Viṣṇu granted the boons sought and disappeared. And a son by name Vatsaśrī was born to him.

28. He became very learned, well versed in Vedas and Vedāṅgas and performed many sacrifices, and his fame spread over the whole world.

29. The king, having attained this son by the blessing of Viṣṇu, retired to perform intensive penance.

30. With full control of the senses and absolute fasting, he began to meditate on Viṣṇu in the Himālayas and always utter the praise of Viṣṇu.

Bhadrāśva said:

31. O sage, what was the praise uttered by him and what happened to him who was praising the lord in that manner?

Durvāsas said:

32. Resorting to the Himālayas and with mind fully immersed in Viṣṇu, the king praised him.

The king said:

33. "I bow to Janārdana of the form of water, the permanent as well as the transient, reposing in the milky ocean, the holder of the earth, the final resort of all beings, beyond all senses and the foremost among the enjoyers of the whole universe.

34. O lord, you are the first principle, the ultimate truth, all-pervading, most ancient, the best among men, beyond senses,

the foremost among those who have mastered the Vedas. Save me, O holder of the conch, mace and weapons.

35. "O Viṣṇu, the Eternal, all that you have done at the entreaties of Devas and Asuras is for the sake of bringing about creation, though you are the ultimate.

36. Still, you assumed the form of the tortoise and other animals and you are spoken of as having taken birth several times, though actually all this is not there.

37. I bow to you, O Narasiṁha, Vāmana, Paraśurāma, Rāma, Vāsudeva, Buddha, Kalkin, Śambhu, the destroyer of the enemies of the gods.

38. I bow to you, O Nārāyaṇa, Padmanābha, Puruṣottama, worshipped by all gods and the foremost of all-knowing.

39. O eternal god, I bow to you who assumed the fierce man-lion form, the tortoise-form expansive like the mountain, the fish-form extensive like the ocean and the boar form.

40. All this (assumption of different forms) is for the sake of creation (of the world). Really you have no form whatsoever. To facilitate meditation, a form is conceived for you, the ancient Man.

41. You are the first sacrifice by yourself. You are the accessories of the sacrifice. You are the offering in the sacrifice. You are the sacrificial animal. You are the priest and the clarified butter. Groups of gods and sages sacrifice for you.

42. The entire world, animate and inanimate, is in you. In you are the gods, time and fire. O Janārdana, you are undivided. Please grant me my desire.

43. I bow to you Hari, lotus-eyed. I bow to you the finite and infinite. I seek refuge in you. Lift me up from the worries of the world".

44. Thus praised by the great king standing under a big mango tree, the lord became very much pleased.

45. And he came there in the form of a dwarfish Brahmin. As soon as he came, the big mango tree also became a small one.

46. Seeing that great wonder, the saintly king began to think about how the big tree became small.

47. Then he was able to understand that the arrival of the Brahmin was the cause and that this very fact showed, that the visitor was the lord himself.

48. He prostrated before that Brahmin and prayed.

49. "O Lord, you are certainly the great Viṣṇu come here to bless me. Be pleased to show me your genuine form".

50. Thus requested the lord appeared before him in his original form bearing the conch, disc and mace, and told him:

51. "O great king, ask me the boon you wish to get. When I am pleased, the whole world to me is but a sesamum seed".

52. Told thus, the king became extremely delighted and asked for mokṣa and nothing else.

53. Thus requested, the lord said again:

54. "Since at my arrival this expansive mango tree (*āmra*) became small (*kubja*), this tīrtha will hereafter be known as *Kubjakāmra*.

55. Not only Brahmins, but even the animals, when they give up the body here, will get salvation that is the yogin's."

56. After saying thus, the lord touched the king with the tip of his conch and immediately he attained salvation.

57. Therefore, O king, you too resort to this lord so that you may not revert to worldly existence.

58. He who listens to this story and he who recites it daily in the morning, attains liberation.

59. And, O king, he who performs this holy Śubhavrata, will get great prosperity and, in the end, will be merged in Him.

CHAPTER FIFTYSIX

Dhanyavrata

Agastya said:

1. I shall now tell you about the Dhanyavrata by performing which even a poor man becomes quickly rich.

2. In the tithi Prathamā in the bright half of the month of Mārgaśirṣa, worship in the night Viṣṇu in the form of fire.

3. Worship the feet as Vaiśvānara, the belly as Agni, chest as Havirbhuja, hands as Draviṇoda, head as Saṁvarta and the entire body as Jvalana.

4-5. After duly worshipping Janārdana in this manner, prepare an altar of fire in front and perform homa in it with the above mantras. Then eat cooked barley with ghee.

6. In the dark half of the month also the worship should be done in the same manner. This may be continued for four months.

7. During the next four months from Caitra eat milky food with ghee and during the four months from Śrāvaṇa eat barley meal. The vrata is thus brought to a close.

8. At the end of the vrata make a golden image of fire, cover it with a pair of red clothes, decorate it with red flowers and anoint it with saffron.

9-10. Then give the image to a Brahmin of faultless body along with the pair of red clothes uttering the following mantra.

11. "I am gratified (*dhanya*), I perform righteous deeds (*dhanyakarmā*), all my actions are for good (*dhanyaceṣṭa*), I am blessed (*dhanyavān*). Let me be happy by this *Dhanyavrata*".

12. Thus saying make the gift of the image with money to the Brahmin. The result is that one becomes highly satisfied without actual enjoyment or suffering in the world.

13. It is quite certain that by this vrata alone, one attains in this life abundant happiness, wealth and grain (food).

14. The fire (in the vrata) burns away all sins in the former lives and, as a result, brings about liberation.

15. He who listens to this and he who recites it with devotion, both become highly blessed.

16. It is said that long long ago, this was performed by Dhanada who was born to a Śūdra woman.

CHAPTER FIFTYSEVEN

Kāntivrata

Agastya said:

1. I shall now tell you about the important Kāntivrata by performing which the Moon regained his lost resplendence.

2. It is well known that the Moon was attacked by consump-

tion due to the curse of Dakṣa and that he regained his lustre by performing this vrata.

3. O king, on the Dvitīyā tithi in the bright half of the month of Kārttika, spend the whole night by worshipping Viṣṇu as Bala-Keśava.

4. The feet should be worshipped as Baladeva and the head as Keśava.

5. After worshipping Viṣṇu in this form, an image of the moon of two digits (in gold) should be worshipped with *arghya* etc., and with the (prescribed) mantras.

6. "I bow to the great soul Soma, the overlord of the world of sacrifice, the holder of amṛta and the great ordainer". (This should be uttered).

7. In the night should be eaten cooked barley with ghee.

8. For the four months from Phālguna milky food should be taken and in Kārttika homa with barley should be conducted.

9. During the four months from Āṣāḍha homa with sesamum should be performed, and only sesamum food should be taken.

10. At the end of one year, the golden image of the moon covered in a pair of white clothes and decorated with white flowers should be gifted to a Brahmin.

11-12. At the end of the year, a silver image[1] of the moon covered in a pair of white clothes and decorated with white flowers may also he given to a Brahmin after similarly honouring him.

13. "O Nārāyaṇa in the form of Soma, by your grace, one becomes lustrous, learned and lovely; I bow to you". (This should then be uttered).

14. By making the gift to the Brahmin with this mantra, a man becomes resplendent.

15. In days of yore, this vrata was performed by Soma himself and Viṣṇu was very much pleased by it.

16. And he rid him of his consumption and gave him the digit called 'Amṛta'. This digit was acquired by Soma at night.

17. He regained his full form and became the king of the stars. On the Dvitīyā day the Aśvinīdevas should be acclaimed as Soma-eaters. They are known as Śeṣa and Viṣṇu.

1. The silver image seems to be an alternative for the golden image for those who cannot afford to give it.

18. O king, there is no god other than Viṣṇu. All the other gods are himself in different names.

CHAPTER FIFTYEIGHT

Saubhāgyavrata

Agastya said:

1. I shall now tell you about Saubhāgyavrata by performing which prosperity accrues to man and woman alike.

2. On Tṛtīyā tithi in the bright half of the month of phālguna one should perform this vrata with purity of body and mind in the night.

3-4. He should worship Hari with Lakṣmī or Rudra with Umā. Lakṣmī is identical with Umā and Hari is identical with Rudra. It is so declared in all Śāstras and Purāṇas.

Any Śāstra or Kāvya which states otherwise is not worthy of its name.

5-6. Viṣṇu should be considered as Rudra and Lakṣmī as Gaurī. He who speaks of difference between them is lowly (Adhama) and should be considered an atheist outside the field of dharma.

7. Knowing this well, Hari together with his consort should be duly worshipped with the prescribed mantras.

8. The feet should be worshipped as Gambhīra, the waist as Subhaga, the belly as Devadeva, and face as Trinetra (three-eyed), the head as Vācaspati and the entire body as Rudra.

9-10. Worshipping thus with sandal, flowers etc., either Viṣṇu with Lakṣmī or Śiva with Gaurī, homa should be performed in front with honey, ghee and sesamum in the name of Saubhāgyapati (lord of prosperity).

11. Cooked wheat should be taken on the floor and without oil and caustic elements.

In the dark half of the month also, the observance is the same.

12. In the months of Āṣāḍha etc., the fast should be broken with barley food, and in Kārttika etc., with food made by Śyāmāka grain.

13-14. Then on Tṛtīyā tithi in the bright half of the month of Māgha a golden image of Rudra and Gaurī or of Viṣṇu and Lakṣmī should be made according to means.

15-16. The image should be given to a deserving Brahmin who is a good Vedic scholar but without means for food or one who closely observes the precepts. It will be better if the recipient is a devotee of Viṣṇu.

17-18. It will be particularly meritorious if six vessels are given to the Brahmin containing honey, ghee, sesamum oil, molasses, salt and cow's milk one in each.

19. By observing this, prosperity and beauty in seven lives are gained, be the performer man or woman.

CHAPTER FIFTYNINE

Avighnavrata

Agastya said:

1. I shall now tell you about the Vighnahara (Avighna) Vrata by which, O king, obstacles are warded off.

2. This vrata should be performed on Caturthī tithi in the month of Phālguna. Food should be taken only at night and it should be of rice mixed with sesamum.

3. The homa also should be of the same material (sesamum), so too the gift to the Brahmin.

4. This should be done for four months and in the fifth a golden image of Gaṇeśa should be worshipped and gifted to a Brahmin together with milky food in five vessels and sesamum.

5. All obstacles can be got over by performing this vrata.

6. When Sagara faced impediments while performing Aśvamedha sacrifice, he got them removed by this vrata.

7. When Rudra was destroying Tripura, he did the same to accomplish his aim. And I too did the same while drinking the ocean.

8. This was done by many kings and by those that seek penance or knowledge, to remove obstructions.

9. Pūjā (worship) should be performed to Gaṇeśa (invoking him as) Śūra, Dhīra, Gajānana, Lambodara and Ekadaṁṣṭra, and homa also should be done to keep off obstacles.

10. By doing this all obstacles vanish, and by gifting the image of Vināyaka, one attains great gratification.

CHAPTER SIXTY

Śāntivrata

Agastya said:

1. O king, I shall now tell you about Śāntivrata by performing which all householders get peace of mind—Bliss. Listen.

2. It should be performed on Pañcamī tithi of the bright half (starting from) the month of Kārttika. During the year hot things should be avoided in food.

3-4. In the night Viṣṇu should be worshipped in his form reposing Śeṣa. The feet should be worshipped as Ananta, the waist as Vāsuki, the belly as Takṣaka, the chest as Kārkoṭaka, the neck as Padma, the hands as Mahāpadma, the face as Śaṅkhapāla and the head as Kuṭila.

5. Worshipping (the great serpents) as contained in Viṣṇu, pūjā may be offered to them separately also.

6. With them in mind, Viṣṇu should be bathed with milk, and then homa should be performed with milk and sesamum.

7. At the end of the year, Brahmins should be fed and a golden image of a serpent should be gifted to one of them.

8. O king, he who observes this vrata with a devoted mind, will certainly get full peace of mind and freedom from the fear of snakes.

CHAPTER SIXTYONE

Kāmavrata

Agastya said:

1-2. O king, listen to me. I shall tell you now about Kāmavrata by which whatever pleasure is desired is obtained by anyone who performs it on the Ṣaṣṭhī day eating only fruit.

3-4. On Pañcamī day in the bright half of the month of Pauṣa one should take meal, but on Ṣaṣṭhī only fruit and afterwards silently pure rice in the company of other Brahmins. Or (even on that day) he may take fruit alone and on the Saptamī day have (the usual) meal.

5. Homa also should be performed after worshipping Viṣṇu as Guha (Skanda) in the prescribed manner. This should be done for one year.

6. The worship of Viṣṇu should be in his names as Ṣaḍvaktra (six-faced), Kārttikeya (son of Kṛttikā), Senānī (commander), Kumāra and Skanda.

7. At the close of the vrata, Brahmins should be fed and a golden image of Skanda should be gifted to one of them, saying.

8. "O lord Kumāra, may all my wishes be accomplished by your mercy due to my devotion. O Brahmin, receive it soon".

9. When this (image) is given to the Brahmin along with the clothes the desires of the worshipper begin to get fulfilled in this life itself.

10. A sonless man gets a son, a needy man gets money, the deposed king regains kingdom. There need be no doubt in this matter.

11. In days of yore, this vrata was performed by Nala when he was living (in servitude) in Ṛtuparṇa's capital.

12. Similarly by several other deposed kings was this vrata observed to succeed (in regaining kingdom).

CHAPTER SIXTYTWO

Ārogyavrata

Agastya said:

1. Now I shall tell you about another vrata called 'Ārogyavrata which removes sins of every kind.

2. This vrata is to be observed by performing worship (to the Sun-god) in the names of Āditya, Bhāskara, Ravi, Bhānu, Sūrya, Divākara and Prabhākara.

3. The rule is that on the Ṣaṣṭhī day food may be taken; on Saptamī day the sun should be worshipped (without food) and on the Aṣṭamī day food may again be taken.

4. One who performs this worship of the Sun duly for one full year, gets health, wealth and grain in this life, and gets in the other world a place from where he need not return.

5-6. In days of yore, the glorious and valiant king by name Anaraṇya propitiated the god by this Vrata, as a result of which the god was pleased and he bestowed upon him sound health.

Bhadrāśva said:

7. Was that king sickly that he is spoken of as getting healthy ? O sage, how did he happen to get the disease ?

Agastya said:

8. The king was, no doubt, glorious, famous, handsome, mighty and healthy.

9. But once he happened to go to the Mānasa lake frequented by hosts of gods. He saw there in the middle of the lake a big white lotus.

10. And within that an effulgent man of the size of the thumb, two-armed and clad in red silk.

11-12. Seeing him, he called his charioteer and spoke to him: "Bring that lotus to me. Wearing this on my head before the whole world, I shall become highly praiseworthy. So bring it quickly". Told thus, the charioteer entered the lake.

13. He went near it in order to catch it. But the moment he touched the lotus, a boom emanated from it and, terrified by that sound, he fell down dead.

14. By the impact of that sound, the king lost his complexion, might and prowess and became a leper.

15. Seeing the transformation of that kind, the king was grief-stricken and began to think about how it happened.

16-17. When he was pondering thus, sage Vasiṣṭha, the son of Brahmā, came there and asked him: "O king, how has your body become afflicted in this way? Tell me what I may do for you".

18. Asked thus by Vasiṣṭha, the king told him about the lotus and all that happened.

19. After hearing that, the sage said: "O king, you are lucky. But you are also unlucky and hence you have become a leper".

20-21. Told thus, the king shivering with fear and with folded hands, asked him: "O sage, I am righteous, how could I be otherwise"? Be pleased to tell me the cause of my leprosy."

Vasiṣṭha said:

22. "This lotus is called 'Brahmapadma' and it is well known over the three worlds. Its very sight is equivalent to the sight of all gods.

23. Somewhere in this lake, it will be seen for six months. On seeing it, he who enters water gets cleansed of all sins and attains supreme beatitude.

24. This is the form of Brahman in the originating stage. Seeing this and then plunging in water, brings about liberation.

25. O king, your charioteer saw this and was immersed in water. But you came here to catch hold of it and so you have committed a sin and, as a result, become a leper.

26-27. Since you were able to see this (lotus) I said you are lucky. But since you became stupefied (so as to attempt at plucking it) I said you are unlucky".

28. Saying thus to the king, Vasiṣṭha disappeared.

29. The king, grasping what Vasiṣṭha had said, came there every day and saw the lord (in the lotus) (and got cured of the disease).

30. The gods too call it the golden lotus. Seeing the Brahmapadma with Hari within it in the Mānasa lake, one attains the supreme Brahman from where he does not return.

31. O king, there is another reason also for your becoming leprous. The sun remains within this lotus.

32-33. He is really the eternal Supreme self. You thought of wearing that on the head thinking you would become famous thereby and so sent the charioteer to fetch it. That very moment you became afflicted by leprosy.

34. Therefore, O king, you also perform this vrata and by its power you will be cured of leprosy.

CHAPTER SIXTYTHREE

Putraprāptivrata

Agastya said:

1. O king, now listen to the brief account of the Putraprāptivrata. I am going to give you.

2. This Putraprāptivrata (the vow for getting a son) is to be performed fasting on the Aṣṭamī tithi in the dark half of the month of Bhādrapada.

3. The *Saṅkalpa* should be made on the Saptamī day and the worship to Viṣṇu as Kṛṣṇa lying in Devakī's lap surrounded by the mothers, should be conducted on Aṣṭamī.

4. On the Aṣṭamī day, early in the morning, Viṣṇu should be worshipped with full concentration of mind.

5. Then homa should be performed with barley, black sesamum, ghee and curd. Brahmans should be fed and given dakṣiṇā.

6. Then the performer of vrata may take food, first Bilva leaves, and then with oils and other items.

7. Doing in this way on the Kṛṣṇapakṣa Aṣṭamī every month, an issueless person begets children.

8-10. It is known that in ancient times the valiant king Śūrasena who was issueless, performed penance in the Himālayas, and the Lord himself told him about this vrata, and accordingly he performed it and got a son Vasudeva by name who later on performed many sacrifices. And the saintly king (Śūrasena) gained salvation.

11. Thus, O king, I have told you about Kṛṣṇāṣṭamī. (In this Vrata), at the end of the year, a pair of cows should be gifted to a Brahmin.

12. Such is the Putravrata narrated to you. By performing it one gets freed from all sins.

CHAPTER SIXTYFOUR

Śauryavrata

Agastya said:

1. I shall now tell you about another vrata called Śauryavrata (the vow for valour) by which even a timid man becomes valiant all of a sudden.

2. On the Navamī day in the month of Āśvayuja one should undertake absolute fasting. Taking the *saṅkalpa* on the Saptamī day and remaining without food on Aṣṭamī, on the Navamī day flour should be taken first in all reverence.

3. Feeding the Brahmins, goddess Durgā who is Mahāmāyā, Mahābhāgā and Mahāprabhā should be worshipped.

4-5. Observing in this way for one whole year, at the end of the vrata, young girls should be fed, and, according to means, given golden garments. The goddess should then be implored saying, "May the goddess be pleased with me".

6. By performing thus, a deposed king gets back his kingdom, the ignorant man gets knowledge and the fear-stricken man gets valour.

CHAPTER SIXTYFIVE

Sārvabhaumavrata

Agastya said:

1. I shall now tell you briefly about the Sārvabhaumavrata (vow for emperorship) by performing which properly, a king can become an emperor.

2-4. On the Daśamī tithī in the bright half of the month of Kārttika, one should take food only in the night and offer pure *bali* to the different quarters with flowers of various kinds, after offering worship to Brahmins, and pray with devotion to the quarters saying, "May you all be favourable to me in life after life". So saying *bali* should be offered to them with pure mind.

5. Food should not be taken in the night, but well-cooked food with curd may be taken before and after.

6. He who performs so, for one year, gains victory in different quarters.

7. If he performs this in the prescribed manner without food starting from Ekādaśī in the bright half of the month of Mārgaśīrṣa and continues for one year, Kubera gets pleased and grants abundant wealth.

8. It is a great vrata relating to Viṣṇu if on Ekādaśī, whether in the bright half or dark half of the month, one fasts and takes food on Dvādaśī day.

9. Such observance destroys even great sins.

10. Then there is Dharmavrata, which should be started in the night of Trayodaśī in the bright half of the month Phālguna. It is Raudravrata starting in Caturdaśī in the dark half, from the month of Māgha and continuing for one year.

11. It is Pitṛvrata when it is performed on the Amāvāsyā day. All these have been now told to you.

12. If one continues these vratas for fifteen years, one gets reward according to their intensity.

13. O king, performing them according to the prescribed rules, is equivalent to performing thousands of Aśvamedha and hundreds of Rājasūya sacrifices.

14-15. Even a single vrata is capable of destroying all sins. A king who performs all of them gets the whole universe under his control and finally attains the celestial region called Virāja.

CHAPTER SIXTYSIX

Nāradīya Pañcarātra

Bhadrāśva said:

1. I am eager to know whatever wonder you have seen or heard. Please tell me.

Agastya said:

2. Lord Janārdana is himself of the nature of wonder. The wonders I have seen about him are many and varied.

3. O king, when sage Nārada once went to Śvetadvīpa he saw there many effulgent men bearing the conch, disc and lotus.

4. Seeing them he began to ponder over as to who was Lord Viṣṇu among them.

5. He was unable to know who was the Lord Kṛṣṇa (Viṣṇu) with conch, disc and mace, to whom he could offer worship.

6. Baffled thus, he began to meditate on lord Kṛṣṇa, the great Nārāyaṇa.

7. By this meditation for a thousand divine years, the lord became pleased with him.

8. He appeared before him and asked him what boon He could give him.

Nārada said:

9. I have meditated on you for a thousand years. If you are pleased with me, tell me how I may attain you.

The great lord said:

10. O sage, those who perform sacrifice with Puruṣasūkta and those who learn the Vedic Texts attain me.

11. In the absence of Vedas and Śāstras, those who do sacrifice in the manner ordained in the Pāñcarātra attain me.

12. The Pāñcarātra is for Brahmins, Kṣatriyas and Vaiśyas For Śūdras and others what is laid down is going to the temple and utterance of my names but not my worship.

13-14. O sage, I declared this in the most ancient times for the multitude. Any one who follows it and becomes my devotee, will retain this in his mind when the fruits of his actions disappear.

15. Others who are engulfed by the feelings caused by Rajas and Tamas, become indifferent towards me.

16. In Kṛta, Tretā and Dvāpara yugas, those with the *sattva* element (predominating) reach me, but in Kali people have a preponderance of Rajas and Tamas.

17-18. Listen to me Nārada, now, I give you another boon. This rare Pañcarātra doctrine of mine will fully dawn upon you by my blessing. You need have no doubt in this matter.

19. I can be attained through the Vedas, Pāñcarātra, Bhakti and Yajña, but not by anything else even if resorted to for crores of years.

20. Telling this to Nārada, the great lord disappeared, and Nārada too went to heaven.

CHAPTER SIXTYSEVEN

The Wonder of Viṣṇu

Bhadrāśva said:

1. Who are the two women in this world, one black and the other white, and who is both black and white ?

2. Who is this pure person, who became sevenfold ? Who is the lord who is twelve-fold and who has two bodies and six heads?

3. How was conjugal unity brought about through the rising sun? How was this world expanded?

Agastya said:

4. The white woman and the black woman are sisters. The woman who is of the dual colour, black and white, is the night.

5. The person who being one became sevenfold, is the ocean which is seven in number.

6. He who is twelve-fold and has two bodies and six heads is the year and the two bodies are the two movements (northward and southward), the six faces are the six seasons and thus the person is verily the year.

7. The conjugal unity is the day and night brought about by the sun and the moon, and from this dual god arose the propagation of the world.

8-9. O king, Viṣṇu should be considered the Supreme God. One who does not do the rites ordained by the Vedas, can never see him.

CHAPTER SIXTYEIGHT

Yugadharma

Bhadrāśva said:

1. How should this great lord, the omnipresent Supreme Soul, be known in four yugas?

2. What are the practices to be observed in each yuga by the castes? How can a Brahmin who contacts a woman not his own, can get himself purified?

Agastya said:

3. In the Kṛtayuga the earth becomes connected with Devas by Vedic rituals. In the Tretāyuga the same is accomplished through sacrifices.

4. In the Dvāparayuga by the mingling of Sattva and Rajas, the king reigns according to the extent of his righteousness. In Kaliyuga Tamas predominates.

5-6. In the Kali age Brahmins stray from the path of righteousness and the Kṣatriyas, Vaiśyas and Śūdras become mostly lowcastes without truth and purity. Then the world gets spoiled and the dharma of the castes begins to disappear.

Bhadrāśva said:

7. How can a Brahmin, Kṣatriya, (Vaiśya) and Śūdra purify himself if he happened to have sexual connection with a prohibited women. Is such a connection tolerated at all?

Agastya said:

8. A Brahmin can cohabit with (women of all) the four

(castes), a Kṣatriya with three (avoiding Brahmin), a Vaiśya with two (avoiding Brahmin and Kṣatriya) and Śūdra with his own (only).

9. To the Kṣatriya the Brahmin woman is prohibited, to the Vaiśya the Brahmin and Kṣatriya women are prohibited and to the Śūdra all these three.

10. Manu has declared that to a man in the lower caste a woman of the higher caste is prohibited; so too the mother, mother's sister, mother-in-law and brother's wife.

11. To one in the lower caste, a woman in the higher caste is fully excluded; so too the daughter-in-law, daughter, the frend's wife and grand-daughters.

12-13. The women of the washerman class and similar others are also of the prohibited category. Cohabiting with a woman of the prohibited category produces great sin.

14. The atonement for a Brahmin for such prohibited cohabitation is *prāṇāyāma* (control of breath in the prescribed form) for a hundred times.

15-16. The sin acquired by a Brahmin by prohibited association with the woman of a different caste, even during a long time, disappears by reciting the *Gāyatrī mantra* with *praṇava* ten times and by *prāṇāyāma* three hundred times. Even the sin of killing a Brahmin (disappears by such a practice), then should we say about the other (less grave) sins?

17. It may also be noted that the Brahmin who is able to realise the Supreme god by meditation and worship is no touched by sin.

18. The learner of the Vedas is not affected even if he happens to commit numerous sins.

19. By meditating on Viṣṇu, learning the Vedas, giving gifts and performing sacrifices for Hari, a Brahmin always remains pure and gets over all obstacles.

20. I have thus told you all that you asked me about. I have briefly stated what has been said by Manu and others in detail.

CHAPTER SIXTYNINE

The Wonder of Nārāyaṇa

Bhadrāśva said:

1. O Sage, be pleased to tell me what happened to you in your body that you are long-lived.

Agastya said:

2. O king, this body of mine is associated with many interesting things. It is purified by Vedic knowledge and it wil remain for numerous kalpas.

3. Wandering over the whole world, O king, I once went to the great land Ilāvṛta near mount Meru.

4. There I saw a beautiful lake, near it a great hermitage and within it a frail sage performing penance.

5. Seeing him who was reduced to a skeleton and was wearing torn bark garment, I was wondering who he was.

6. In order to gain his confidence, I exclaimed: "O sage, I have come to you, please give me something".

7. The sage said: "Welcome to you, O great Brahmin, please remain here. I shall show hospitality to you".

8. At these words of his, I entered the hermitage and saw the sage glowing with lustre.

9. Seeing me standing on the floor, the sage hummed and immediately there arose splitting the earth five virgins.

10. One of them took a golden seat and offered it to me. Another held water in her hand and a third began to wash my feet with it.

11. Two others holding fans stood on my sides. The sage again hummed.

12. As a result, a large golden canoe appeared in that lake beautifully floating.

13. In that canoe were hundreds of virgins holding golden pots. Seeing them the sage told me:

14. "O Brahmin, all this is for your bath. Please enter the canoe and have your bath".

15. Then I entered that canoe, but soon the canoe sank into the lake.

16. When I was thus immersed in water, I saw that place, that sage and myself at the top of mount Meru.

17. O king, I then saw the seven oceans, the seven principal mountains, and the seven islands constituting the earth.

18. Even now I remain thinking of that glorious world and how and when I could get there (again).

19. I have now satisfied your curiosity regarding the great lord and what happened to my person. What else do you wish to ask?

CHAPTER SEVENTY

Rudragītā I

Bhadrāśva said:

1. O sage, what Vrata, Tapas or Dharma was done by you to get at that world again?

Agastya said:

2. No one can think of getting at those worlds without worshipping Viṣṇu with devotion. When once he is worshipped, all of them are easily attainable.

3. Thinking, thus, O king, the eternal Viṣṇu was worshipped by me with sacrifices in which dakṣiṇā was liberally given.

4. As I was worshipping him in his form as sacrifice for a long time, Devas who were invoked in the sacrifice came there together with Indra.

5-6. When Indra and the other gods were remaining in their positions in the sky, the great god Rudra arrived there. He too stood in his position.

7-9. Seeing all the gods, sages and great serpents arrive there, the sage Sanatkumāra, son of Brahmā, came there in a very minute aerial car resembling the sun and he, a great yogi who could know the past, present and future, prostrated before Rudra.

10-11. At the sight of these Devas, sages like Nārada, and Sanatkumāra and Rudra, I asked who among them was the greatest to whom sacrifices could be offered. Then in the presence of gods, Rudra told me:

Rudra said:

12. Listen to me all of you Devas, Devarṣis, Brahmarṣis, and you intelligent Agastya in particular.

13-14. He for whom sacrifices are to be performed is the great and omnipresent lord Nārāyaṇa from whom the entire universe has arisen and in whom it is dissolved along with Devas.

15-16. That great lord put himself to a three-fold transformation. With Sattva predominating in him, he associated himself with Rajas and Tamas, and created out of his navel Brahmā seated in the lotus. Brahmā associated himself with Rajas and Tamas and created me.

17-18. Lord Hari is Sattva and he is the ultimate. Brahmā, the four-faced god, who arose from the lotus is Sattva and Rajas. That which is with Rajas and Tamas is no doubt, myself.

19. There is the trio constituted of Sattva, Rajas and Tamas. Sattva is of the nature of Nārāyaṇa and all living beings are liberated by it.

20. By Rajas associated with Sattva arises this creation which has got Rajas predominating. This is well known as the creation of Brahmā.

21. The actions not laid down in the Vedas but are, however, based on Śāstras, are called Raudra (pertaining to Rudra) and that is not commended for people.

22. Actions not out of Rajas, but purely out of Tamas, lead people to ruin both in the present world and in the world beyond.

23. Sattva pertains to Nārāyaṇa and living beings have Sattva as the means of liberation, and Nārāyaṇa is considered as of the nature of sacrifice.

24. In the Kṛtayuga, Nārāyaṇa is worshipped in his pure and minute form. In the Tretāyuga he is worshipped in the form of sacrifice and in the Dvāpara yuga according to Pāñcarātra.

25. In the Kaliyuga he is worshipped in the manner laid down by me in various Tāmasic forms and with the motive of animosity.

26. There is no god above him in the past, present or future.

He who is Viṣṇu is Brahmā and he who is Brahmā is Maheśvara too.

27. Men who are learned in the three Vedas and adepts in sacrifices have declared that he who draws a distinction among us three, is sinful and wicked and faces downfall.

28. O Agastya, listen. I shall tell you about the early times when people were not having devotion to Hari.

29-30. In olden times, the people of the Bhūloka (Earth) performed sacrifice to Janārdana, and went to the Bhuvarloka, and from there worshipped Him and attained heaven being liberated in the gradual manner.

31. (Even) after being thus liberated, everyone began to meditate on Hari, and He being present everywhere, appeared before them.

32. He asked them all as to what he might do for them. They then bowed to him and said:

33. "O great god, all people have been now liberated. How then will creation proceed and who will go to hell?"

34. Thus asked by Devas, lord Janārdana told them: "During the (first) three yugas, most people reach me.

35. But in the last yuga (Kali) those who attain me will be few. I then create the force of stupefaction which deludes people.

36. O you Rudra, you produce the Mohaśāstra (the science of stupefaction). With a little effort you produce delusion".

37. So saying, the great lord concealed himself and I was made very manifest.

38. From then onwards people became more interested in the śāstras which I promulgated.

39. Following the Vedic path, (worshipping) lord Nārāyaṇa and finding unity (in all the three gods), people get liberation.

40. Those who consider me as different from Viṣṇu or Brahmā, are driven to do sinful deeds and reach hell.

41. It is for the delusion of those who are outside the Vedic fold that I introduced the śāstra called Naya, Siddhānta etc.

42. This is the rope (Pāśa) that binds men (Paśu) and that should be snapped. Therefore, it is the Pāśupata śāstra which is Vaidik.

43. O sage, my body is of the Vedas. This truth is not known by those who propound other śāstras.

44. I am to be known through the Vedas and particularly by the Brahmins. I am the three yugas and also Brahmā and Viṣṇu.

45. I am the three guṇas Sattva, (Rajas and Tamas), the three Vedas and the three fires, and three worlds, the three Sandhyās[1] and the three Varṇas.[2]

46. I am the three *savanas*[3], the three bonds in the world.

47. He who knows this and also knows me as Nārāyaṇa, the lotus-born Brahmā and myself as one made different by the qualities (has right knowledge). I am essentially one, it is ignorance that produces the sense of difference.

CHAPTER SEVENTYONE

Rudragītā II

Agastya said:

1. Said thus by Rudra, all the gods and sages bowed to him; I too did the same.

2. After bowing thus, when I looked at him, I saw in his body Brahmā.

3. I also saw in his heart lord Nārāyaṇa in an extremely minute form glowing like the Sun.

4. Seeing this all the sacrificing sages were wonder-struck and hailed him uttering the Sāma, Ṛk and Yajurvedas.

5. Then they asked Parameśvara (Rudra) how in one and the same god all the three gods are seen.

Rudra said:

6. O learned men, whatever is offered in the sacrifice for me, is shared by all the three of us.

1. Morn, noon and evening.
2. Brāhmaṇa, Kṣatriya, and Vaiśya
3. Vedic rites to be performed in the morning, noon and evening.

7. O great sages, there is no diversity among us, and discerning people do not find any such thing".

8. Thus said by Rudra, O king, all the sages asked him about the purpose of Mohaśāstra (which deludes people).

The sages said:

9. You have produced a separate śāstra to stupefy the world. Be pleased to tell us why you have done this.

Rudra said:

10. There is in Bhāratavarṣa a forest called Daṇḍaka. There a Brahmin named Gautama was performing severe penance.

11. Brahmā was very much pleased at this, and he asked the ascetic to seek a boon from him.

12. Thus asked by Brahmā, the creator of the worlds, he requested, "Give me abundance of crops and grain". And Brahmā granted it.

13-14. Getting this boon, the ascetic built a large hermitage at Śataśṛṅga and there he used to reap every morning the ripe grain and cook it at noon and offer sumptuous food to Brahmins.

15. He was doing this for a long time, but once a severe drought occurred which lasted for twelve years.

16. Distressed at this drought and very much famished, all the sages in the forest went to Gautama.

17. Seeing them all in his hermitage, Gautama bowed to them and asked them to stay there.

18. They remained there eating a variety of food till the drought was over.

10. Then those sages felt a desire to undertake a pilgrimage.

20. Knowing this the great sage Mārīca spoke to the sage Śāṇḍilya.

Mārīca said:

21. "O Śāṇḍilya, I say for your good that sage Gautama is like your father. Without telling him we should not leave here for penance".

22. When told thus, the sages laughed and said, "Have we sold ourselves to him by taking his food"?

23. Again they spoke of leaving the place. They also created a magical cow and left it at the hermitage.

24. Seeing that cow wandering in the hermitage, Gautama took some water in his hand and splashed it on its body (to drive it out).

25. Then that magical cow fell down like a drop of water.

26. Seeing it thus hurt, he turned to the sages starting to leave and asked them with reverence:

27. "O Brahmins, please tell me why you are going leaving me, your devotee".

The sages said:

28. "O sage, so long as the sin of killing the cow remains in you, we shall not eat your food".

29. Told thus, Gautama who knew what was righteous, asked them to tell him what was the atonement for the sin of having killed the cow.

The sages said:

30. "This cow is not dead but has only become unconscious. Bathed in the water of Gaṅgā, it will doubtless rise up.

31. The atonement is only with regard to one that is killed. So penance may be performed. Please don't be angry". So saying they all left.

32. When they were gone, Gautama went to the great mount Himālaya to perform severe penance.

33. For one hundred and one years I was worshipped, and, being pleased by that, I asked him to seek a boon.

34. He sought me the river Gaṅgā in my matted hair to be made to follow him.

35. I then let off the river from one part of my head and Gautama led it to the place where the cow was lying.

36. Washed by that water the cow rose up, and the river became great with holy water and sacred spots.

37. Seeing that great wonder, the seven sages came there in aerial cars saying "Well done, well done.

38. Blessed you are O Gautama, who is there equal to you in that you have brought this Gaṅgā to this Daṇḍaka (forest)".

39. Then Gautama was wondering as to how he became the cause for hurting the animal.

40. He realised then that it was all the result of the magic adopted by the sages (who were living in his hermitage) and cursed them who were sages only in appearance.

41. "You will all be outside the three Vedas and ineligible to perform Vedic acts".

42. Hearing the curse of Gautama thus pronounced on those sages, the Seven Sages told him: "Although your words will have due effect, you should not mean it for all time.

43. In the Kali age let these Brahmins become such as to be ungrateful to those who do them good.

44. But, burnt by the fire of the woods of your curse, let them in the Kali age become devotees.

45. But let them he outside the fold of Vedic rites. Let this river also have the secondary name Godāvarī.

46. In Kaliyuga those who come to this river and give gifts of cows and other materials according to their capacity, will delight themselves with the gods.

47-48. If at the time when Jupiter is in Leo one takes bath there and propitiates the manes according to the rules, they will go to heaven even if they have fallen in hell, and those who are already in heaven will get final release.

49. You will attain great fame and gain eternal liberation".

50. Then the seven sages went to Kailāśa where I was with Pārvatī and told me:

51. "In the Kali age many will have your form with crown of matted hair assuming by themselves ghostly forms and wearing liṅgas.

52. For their sake, give a śāstra to all these people under the influence of Kali".

53. Requested by them thus, I produced a Saṁhitā which contained rules for Vedic rites as well.

54. This Saṁhitā was named Niśśvāsa, and Bābhravya and Śaṇḍila were absorbed in it.

55. Deluded by me, people out of selfish motives, will promulgate their own śāstras in Kaliyuga.

56. The *Niśśvāsasaṁhitā* with a lakh of verses alone is authoritative and that gives the discipline regarding Pāśupata.

57. This follows the path of the Vedas, and whatever is outside its scope should be considered as impure.

58. The Vedāntins in Kaliyuga resort to Rudra. Fickle-minded people frame their own śāstras, but I don't remain with them.

59-60. In yore, I assumed the fierce Bhairava form for the sake of the gods and for the annihilation of the wicked demons and laughted terribly.

61. Out of my tears which fell then on the earth, arose innumerable terrific beings.

62. They were fond of flesh and wine and women and were out to create terror in the world.

63. The Brahmins cursed by Gautama will be born in their clan. Among them those who follow the rules I have laid down and are of good conduct, will attain heaven and get liberation.

64. Those who doubt the doctrine I have laid down, ridicule my followers and go to hell.

65. Formerly burnt by the fire of Gautama and now by my words they go to hell and we need not doubt this.

***Rudra continued*:**

66. Told thus by me, the sons of Brahmā (the seven sages) went away. Gautama too returned to his abode.

67. I have thus told you what Dharma is. He who is averse to this naturally is prone to do only wicked things.

CHAPTER SEVENTYTWO

Determination of Prakṛti and Puruṣa[1]

Varāha said:

1. Agastya asked the omniscient Rudra; "Who is the most ancient one and the creator of everything?"

Agastya said:

2. Yourself, Brahmā and Viṣṇu constitute a trio and the three Vedas. Like the flame of the lamp (you illumine everything) and permeate all śāstras.

1. Actually the chapter deals with the identity of Brahmā, Viṣṇu and Śiva.

3. O god, tell me at which time are you Rudra, at which time Brahmā and at which time Viṣṇu.

Rudra said:

4. Viṣṇu is the Supreme Brahman and in Vedas and śāstras he is spoken of as having three forms. But this is not known to the ignorant.

5. From the root *viś* meaning 'to enter' with the Nominative singular suffix we get the word 'Viṣṇu'. He is the eternal and the supreme among all gods.

6. This Viṣṇu who is spoken of as having a tenfold form as well as of a single form is the Āditya with all yogic powers.

7. The great god for the sake of Devas assumes human form in every yuga and praises me.

8. For the sake of the world as well as gods, I worship these two forms of the lord (divine as well as human) in the Śvetadvīpa (white island) in Kṛtayuga.

9. At the time of creation, I extol the fourfaced (Brahmā) and become time. And in that Kṛtayuga, Brahmā, Devas and Asuras extol me always.

10. People who seek pleasures sacrifice to me in my form as liṅga (phallus), and those who seek liberation sacrifice to me mentally in my form as the thousand-headed. It is to this form that the universal god Nārāyaṇa himself offers sacrifice.

11. Those who perform Brahmayajña daily propitiate Brahmā, because the Veda is Brahmā.

12. The Supreme Brahman is enshrined in the names Nārāyaṇa, Śiva, Viṣṇu, Śaṅkara and Puruṣottama.

13. For those who perform Vedic rituals, we Brahmā, Viṣṇu and Maheśvara are the spirits of the mantras. There need be no doubt in this matter.

14. I am Viṣṇu as well Brahmā with the eternal Vedas. The three (gods) are really one and the wise men should not consider them as different.

15. He who considers otherwise is a sinner and he goes to the terrible hell.

16. I am Brahmā and Viṣṇu and the Vedas Ṛk, Yajus and Sāman. The difference is only in this manner.

CHAPTER SEVENTYTHREE

Vairājavṛtta

Rudra said:

1. O great Brahmin, listen to another interesting wonder.

2. I was created by Brahmā and ordered to create beings, but being unable to do it, I immersed myself in water.

3-4. There, while for a moment I was fully absorbed in contemplating on the great lord in the size of the thumb, there arose from the water eleven persons blazing like fire at the time of deluge and heating the water with their radiance.

5. I asked them who they were thus come out of the water and imparting to it much heat and where they were going.

6. Though asked thus, those great beings did not speak anything, but simply went away.

7. Then came an effulgent person cloud-like in complexion and with eyes like the lotus.

8. I asked him who he was and who the other persons were and also the purpose with which they came.

The man said:

9. The effulgent persons who came out here and went away are Ādityas who appeared at the meditation of Brahmā.

10. Brahmā performs creation and they are for the protection of the created.

Śambhu (Rudra) said:

11. "Please tell me, O lord, how I can know this great Person".

12-13. Asked thus by Rudra, the Man replied: "I am the eternal lord Nārāyaṇa reposing in water. You are given a divine eye, and see me with that carefully".

14. Told thus, when I looked at him, I found him to be the same as the lord of the size of the thumb (whom) I was meditating on) with a lotus in his navel.

15. I saw Brahmā (in that lotus) and myself near him. Seeing that great Being I was full of pleasure.

16-17. O great Brahmin, I had then an urge to extol him, and I accordingly praised that Universal Soul with the following hymn.

Rudra said:

18. I bow to that eternal being, the pure soul, with numerous forms and thousand hands, the foremost among the effulgent, extensive in body and pure in action.

19. I bow to that great Śambhu, resplendent like a thousand suns and blazing like the fire, the remover of all ills of the world, the holder of all knowledge, the bearer of the disc, and praised by all Devas.

20. I bow to you always, the originless and eternal, reposing on the serpent Śeṣa, great lord, lord of all beings, the chief of Maruts, the master of all, the lord of the world, the master of the entire universe.

21-22. O Nārāyaṇa, lord of water, the bestower of good to the whole world, lord of the universe, the universal eye, the moon, the sun, the eternal, with form to be inferred, the embodiment of ambrosia, the eternal, with effulgence excelling fire, the omnipresent, protect me always who have sought refuge in you, O remover of the perils of Devas.

23. I see your innumerable faces and in their midst Brahmā, the creator of the worlds. I bow to you, O my grandfather.

24. O the first and great god, you are resorted to by those with mind purified by following the path of knowledge after numerous births in the cycle of saṁsāra. I bow to you.

25. He who understands you to be the one beyond Prakṛti (Matter), is not subject to the activity of the Guṇas (the three qualities Sattva, Rajas and Tamas) and realises you in the extensive as well as the minute aspects.

26. You are the root of speech, but you are without organs. You are without action, but you have not given up action. You are not one in Saṁsāra, but you have a body of pure abstracts.

27. You in your four-armed form are known by those who perform sacrifices, but it is a matter for wonder that your supreme form is not known even by Devas.

28. Therefore, gods like Brahmā contemplate on your avatāras. Even Brahmā does not know your ultimate form.

29. But I, having been purified by penance, am able to know you, the most ancient. And my father Brahmā has become known to many Purāṇas.

30. Even those like me cannot know you except through

penance. But you, who cannot be known even by those like Brahmā, can be known by continuous meditation on you.

31. Those who know the Vedas gain superior mental power through your grace and they alone know you.

32. To him who has realised you, manhood or godhood is not delectable. You are of universal form. You are minute as well as big.

33. You are expensive as well as minute. O God, still you are quite attainable. Those who keep out from you fall in hell. When you, the lord, are there, why speak of Vasus, Ādityas, Maruts and Bhūmi ?

34. My praises are all for you who are extensive and supreme soul, and so, O eternal one, be pleased to accept them from me, a staunch devotee.

35. O Viṣṇu, give me omniscience when you command me to perform creation.

36. Four-faced (Brahmā) or crore-faced, only he who is pure of mind will be able to narrate your countless qualities.

37. He who with pure mind contemplates on you unswervingly, in his mind you remain. I bow to you.

38. O lord, this hymn thus came out of my mind. Be pleased to purify me, fear-stricken by the course of saṁsāra.

Varāha said:

39. Thus praised by the great Rudra, Lord Viṣṇu was pleased and spoke in a voice majestic like thunder.

Viṣṇu said:

40. O God, husband of Umā, everything is well for you. Please seek a boon. There is no difference between us. We are one and the same.

Rudra said:

41. I am engaged by Brahmā, O lord, to perform creation. Give me for that the threefold knowledge required.

Viṣṇu said:

42. "You are the abode of all knowledge. You are doubtless omniscient and worshipped by Devas always".

43-44. Told thus, Rudra said again, "O lord, give me another boon by which you will take a form with which you will worship me and bear me and get a boon from me, and as a result of that you will become the most worshipful among gods.

Viṣṇu said:

45. "For the sake of gods, I will take incarnations and then I will worship you and you will give me boons.

46. As for bearing you, O lord of Umā, I shall bear you for a hundred years assuming the form of a cloud".

47. So saying, Viṣṇu became a cloud, drew up Rudra from the water, and said:

48. "The eleven persons who came out earlier, are Vairājas and they have gone to the earth with the name 'Ādityas'.

49. The twelfth part of mine has descended on earth with the name 'Viṣṇu' and will worship you".

50. So saying, Nārāyaṇa, out of his own part produced a divine cloud full of sound, and it is not known where he disappeared.

Rudra said:

51. Thus this great Hari who is omnipresent and omnipotent, became a giver of boon to me in yore, as a result of which I am supreme among gods.

52. There is no god above Nārāyaṇa in the past or future. This is the secret propounded by the Vedas and Purāṇas.

53. I have thus told you how Viṣṇu is to be propitiated.

CHAPTER SEVENTYFOUR

Cosmology

Varāha said:

1. The sages then asked the ancient, eternal and omnipresent Rudra, three-eyed and holder of the trident.

The sages said:

2-3. You are beyond us and the Devas. So we ask you a

question. O lord of Umā, be pleased to tell us about the magnitude of the earth and the position of mountains in detail.

Rudra said:

4-5. In the Purāṇas this earth is considered to be the world. So I shall briefly describe this earth. Please listen.

6. The great Nārāyaṇa who pervades all over the worlds, who is atomic, unknowable, pure and whose ultimate form can be known by Supreme knowledge alone, who is indicated as broadchested, wearing yellow garment and holding the earth, and who is spoken of as beyond the three qualities Sattva, Rajas and Tamas, and as neither long nor short, neither big nor small etc., and who is of the nature of pure knowledge, created water. Having created that, the primordial man Nārāyaṇa, who pervades the entire world, and is of the nature of all gods, sacrifices and water, produced from his navel a lotus during his yogic slumber. In it arose the creator Brahmā, the great god, the repository of the Vedas. He produced the repositories of knowledge like Sanaka, Sananda, Sanātana and Sanatkumāra, and then Svāyambhuva Manu and those from Marīci to Dakṣa. From Svāyambhuva Manu created by the lord, further creation began to proceed. He had two sons, Priyavrata and Uttānapāda.

7. Priyavrata had ten sons, Āgnīdhra, Agnibāhu, Medhas, Medhātithi, Dhruva, Jyotiṣmān, Dyutimān, Havya, Vapuṣmān and Savana. Priyavrata established seven of his sons in seven islands. Āgnīdhra was made the lord of Jambūdvīpa, Medhātithi the lord of Śākadvīpa, Jyotiṣmān the lord of Krauñca, Dyutimān the lord of Śālmalī, Havya the lord of Gomeda, Vapuṣmān the lord of Plakṣa and Savana the lord of Puṣkara. Savana, the lord of Puṣkara had two sons Mahāvīti and Dhātaka. Their regions were known after their names. Thus Dhātaka had Dhātakikhaṇḍa and Kumuda had Kaumuda.[1] Jyotiṣmān, the lord of Śālmalī[2], had three sons, Kuśa, Vaidyuta and Jīmūtavāhana. Their regions came to be known after them. Dyutimān had seven sons, Kuśala, Manugavya, Pīvara, Andhra, Andhakāraka, Muni and Dundubhi and seven regions in Krauñca came to be known after them.

1. Kumuda seems to be another name for Mahāvīti.
2. This contradicts with the earlier statement that Dyutimān is the lord of Sālmali.

8. Jyotiṣmān, the lord of Kuśadvīpa,[1] had seven sons, Udbhida, Veṇumān, Rathapāla, Manas, Dhṛti, Prabhākara and Kapila and they had regions with their names. Medhātithi, the lord of Śaka, had seven sons, Nābhi, Śāntabhaya, Śiśiramukha, Udama, Nanda, Śivakṣemaka and Dhruva. They had regions with their names. Nābhi had Hemakūṭa, Kimpuruṣa, Naiṣadha, Harivarṣa, Merumadhya, Ilāvṛta, Nīla, Ramyaka, Śveta, Uttarakuru, Mālyavān, Bhadrāśva, Gandhamādana and Ketumāla. This is the division of the earth in Svāyambhuva Manvantara. In every aeon seven kings each thus rule the earth. This happens in every aeon.

9. I shall now narrate the creation by Nābhi. Nābhi begot in Merudevī the son named Ṛṣabha, his son was Bharata. To Bharata his father gave the region to the South of Hemādri called the great Bhārata. Bharata's son was Sumati. Bharata gave his kingdom to Sumati and retired to the forest. Sumati's son was Tejas, his son Indradyumna, his son Parameṣṭhī, his son Pratihartā, his son Nikhāta, his son Unnetā, his son Abhāva, his son Udgātā, his son Prastotā, his son Vibhu, his son Pṛthu, his son Ananta, his son Gaya, his son Naya, his son Virāṭa, his son Sudhīmān.

10. Sudhīmān had hundred sons and by them was the population increased. The Bhāratavarṣa with its seven islands is occupied by them.

11. This earth is enjoyed by their descendants. There are seventyone aeons like Kṛta, Tretā etc.[2]

12. Incidentally I have given an account of Svāyambhuva Manvantara. Know this well.

CHAPTER SEVENTYFIVE

Jambūdvīpa and Meru

Rudra said:

1. I shall now tell you in detail about the Jambūdvīpa and the number of oceans and islands in it.

---

1. Earlier Jyotiṣmān is spoken of as lord of Krauñca.

2. The Yugas are generally given as only four, Kṛta, Tretā, Dvāpara and Kali.

2. Also the number of regions in it, the different rivers etc, and again their extent and the movements of the sun and the moon.

3. It is not easy to describe thousands of islands within the seven major ones by which the whole universe is filled.

4. I shall say about the seven islands and also about the sun and moon, about which people propound logical authority.

5. But it is not possible for logic to accomplish what is unthinkable. And what is beyond nature is really unthinkable.

6. I shall, therefore, describe Jambūdvīpa as it is and the dimensions of its different regions.

7. It is one hundred and one thousand yojanas[1] in extent and is strewn all over with human settlements.

8. It is full of Siddhas and Cāraṇas[2] and is beautiful with mountains full of rocks and minerals.

9. It has numerous rivers arising from the mountains and is globular.

10. In this remains the great lord surrounded by nine (creators?). It is encircled by the saline ocean.

11. In the expansive Jambūdvīpa there are six broad and long mountains.

12. There are oceans on the east and west. There is Himavān full of snow and Hemakūṭa full of gold.

13. There is the big mountain Niṣadha which gives pleasure in all its parts and the mount Meru which is of four (main) colours and contains gold.

14. It (Meru) is round and uniform in shape and has variegated colours. It has in it groups of Prajāpatis.

15. It arose from the navel of the great Brahmā. It is white in colour on the eastern side and this represents the Brahmin.

16. On the southern side it is yellow and this represents the Vaiśya.

17. On the western side it is black like the bee and this represents the Śūdra symbolising service.

18. On the northern side it is red in colour and this represents the Kṣatriya. This is the division according to colour.

---

1. One Yojana is equal to eight miles.
2. Siddhas and Cāraṇas are semi-divine beings.

19. The blue parts contain Vaiḍūrya stones, the pale white parts contain gold. The parts with the colour of peacock feathers contain highly pure gold.

20. These mountains have Siddhas and Cāraṇas in them. Their internal extent is nine thousand (yojanas).

21. In the middle is the region Ilāvṛta on which stands Meru. It spreads thousands of yojanas on all sides.

22. Mahāmeru stands in the middle like smokeless fire. It is half a Vedi in extent on the northern and southern sides.

23. There are six regions there each with a mountain. The periphery of each region is one yojana.

24. Two each of these are for the thousands of Kṣatriyas. Their extent is that of Jambūdvīpa.

25. Occupying one hundred thousand yojanas are two mountains, Nīla and Niṣadha.

26. Smaller than these are the white Hemakūṭa and the peaky Himavān, Niṣadha has the same dimension as Jambūdvīpa.

27. A twelfth part of it is the dimension of Hemakūṭa and Himavān has the dimension of a twentieth part of Hemakūṭa.

28. An eighth part of Himavān lies between the east and west. Because of the expansive nature of the island, there appears increase and decrease.

29. In the regions, just as there are mountains, there are settlements of people.

30. It is not easy to go from one settlement to another since each is surrounded by steep mountains and rivers.

31. Different kinds of beings live there. In the region of Himavān, the people are the Bhāratas.

32. In Hemakūṭa the people are Kimpuruṣas. After Hemakūṭa is Niṣadha. The settlement there is Harivarṣa.

33. After Harivarṣa is Ilāvṛta. After Ilāvṛta is the well known Ramyaka which is blue.

34. After Ramyaka is the well known Hiraṇmaya which is white. After Hiraṇmaya is Śṛṅgavān where we get Kuru.

35. Like a bow are two regions in the south and north. Of the four islands, Ilāvṛta is square-shaped.

36. Half a Vedi of Niṣadha on the southern side is low and half a Vedi on the northern side is peaky.

37. On this southern side are three regions and there are three on the northern side too. Between these, where the Meru stands, is Ilāvṛta.

38. Its extent is thirtyfour thousand yojanas. On its eastern side is the mountain Gandhamādana.

39. In its length, breadth and height it is similar to mount Mālyavān. In the middle is the golden mount Meru.

40. It is full of gold and has four colours. All the vital elements and living beings arose from it.

41. Taking the original indefinite form of earth as a lotus, Meru may be considered as its pericarp, and from it to have evolved the four major (outer) petals and the definite form with five qualities.

42. Then arose all activities and men of virtue living for several kalpas.

43. The best of Men (the Lord), who is the great yogin, the great God to be contemplated upon by the whole world, is attained by the great men who have realised the self.

44. His form is imperishable, endless and pervades the whole universe and he does not possess body constituted of bones, flesh and marrow.

45. He is all-pervading and bears all forms because of his being a yogi and the great Master. Because of him there arose in the world the great lotus.

46. In that great lotus arose the great lord, the four-faced (Brahmā).

47. He is the chief of the creators and the overlord of the whole world. The seeds of creation have arisen from him.

48. The creation is now explained in detail. That water full of gems is the body of Viṣṇu.

49. The earth arose in the form of the lotus with forests and lakes. It is this world lotus that expanded itself.

50. I shall recount this expansion in its order, please listen O Brahmins.

There are four regions in it.

51. There is the mighty mountain Meru. It has different colours. On the eastern side it is white.

52. It is yellow on the south, black on the west and red on the north.

53. The white part of Meru is for the clan of kings. It shines like the rising sun and like fire without smoke.

54. It is eightyfour thousand yojanas in height, sixteen thousand yojanas deep and sixteen thousand yojanas in length.

55. It has a table-land thirtytwo thousand yojanas in extent. The area of its expanse is thrice this.

56. One division of it has ninety thousand yojanas.

57. Beyond that is one of six thousand yojanas more.

58. This mountain is divine and is full of celestial herbs. The houses (built) in it are all of gold.

59. In this big mountain, groups of Devas, Gandharvas, Nāgas, Rākṣasas and Apsarases delight themselves.

60. All round the Meru are auspicious abodes. There are four regions on its four sides.

61. They are Bhadrāśva on the east, Bhārata on the south, Ketumāla on the west and Kuru on the north.

62. The pericarp of this lotus covers several thousand yojanas.

63. It has fifteen stamens each a yojana long and their interspaces (at the bottom) occupy eightyfour yojanas each.

64. The stamens pervade a space of thirty thousand yojanas.

65. The length is one hundred thousand and the breadth eighty thousand (yojanas). There are four parts of fourteen thousand yojanas.

66. Listen now to the account about what I told you as the pericarp.

67. It is attractive with hundreds of jewelled petals of various colours, golden and shining like the rising sun.

68. It has a thousand protrusions and thousand depressions and is fully circular.

69. In it there is the assembly of Brahmā with splendidly jewelled arches and full of Brahmarṣis.

70. It is known by the name Manovatī in all the worlds. The glory of the great lord, resplendent like a thousand suns, is well marked there.

71. The groups of Devas propitiate the four-faced Brahmā with sacrifices and prayers.

72-74. Also by those great men who have given up all desires by those who are of good mind and taken to righteous living, devoted to please the manes and gods, and by those householders who are full of humility, inclined to honour guests and of detached mind.

75. Those who with a resolve get their sins removed by their yogic practices like yama, niyama etc, attain the commendable white Brahmaloka.

76. The final position is beyond a height of fourteen thousand yojanas.

77. Above that is the beautiful black place luminous like the rising sun in the mountain full of gems and minerals.

78-80. The mountain with the circular base is thirty thousand yojanas and from a place in it which is ten yojanas long starts the river which begins flowing upwards and then falls on the earth. This flows through Amarāvatī, the city of gods.

81. Thrown out by this river, the sun, the moon and the stars rise and set and render service.

82. The Brahmins propitiate all the eight great mountains.

CHAPTER SEVENTYSIX

The cities of the eight Dikpālas

Rudra said:

1-2. On the resplendent eastern part of Meru full of different minerals and in the form of a circular extension, there is the city of the immortals full of mighty gods and demons, full of gold and with well-devised pathways and arches.

3- To its north-east with hundreds of spires and extensive lakes, decerated with flowers and flags, is the prosperous city of Indra named Amarāvatī abounding in Devas, Yakṣas, Apsarases and sages.

6. In the interior of Amarāvatī there is a hall full of diamonds and other gems, which is well known as the assembly Sudharmā.

7. In it remains the thousand-eyed Indra, husband of Śacī, surrounded by Siddhas and other divine beings.

8. Indra, revered by all other gods, is the president of this assembly. The great sun is there.

9. On its side, as broad and splendid like it, is the city of Agni, called Tejovatī.

10. Next is the beautiful city of Vaivasvata (Yama), well known as Saṁyaminī.

11. On the fourth direction is the city of Nirṛti, called Kṛṣṇavatī.

12. The fifth, on the northern side, is the city of the lord of waters (Varuṇa), called Śuddhavatī.

13. Beyond that in the north is the city of Vāyu, called Gandhavatī.

14. On its right is the beautiful city of Kubera, called Mahodaya with a hall of Vaiḍūrya gems.

15. On the eighth quarter is the city of Īśāna, called Manoharā.

16. This world of gods, prayed for by people in their different āśramas (stages of life) is svarga (heaven).

CHAPTER SEVENTYSEVEN

The Meru Mountain

Rudra said:

1. The middle of Meru, which is considered as the pericarp of the world-lotus, has (a circumference) of one thousand yojanas.

2. Its bottom is (in circumference) fortyeight thousand (yojanas).

3. In it there are thousands of mounts and those at the extremity of the eight quarters are the mounts that indicate the limit.

4. Among these, two named Jaṭhara and Devakūṭa are on the eastern side.

5. O great Brahmins, listen to my account of this Meru, the golden mountain, in respect of its parts in different directions

6. There are four prominent parts in the four directions and fourteen parts at the top, because of which the earth, with its seven islands, moves.

7. Its extent is ten thousand yojanas and its vertical and horizontal parts are covered with yellow orpiment.

8. It has caves full of red arsenic and is strewn with golden gems. It has numerous fine mansions and playgrounds.

9. On its eastern part is the mountain Mandara, on its south Gandhamādana, on the west Vipula and on the north Supārśva.

10. On their peaks are four great trees which are resorted to by gods, demons and Apsarases.

11. At the peak of the Mandara mountain is the big tree called Kadamba with hanging branches.

12. Its flowers have the size of big pots and they blossom throughout the year and have high fragrance.

13. The entire area where its smell spreads is very sacred.

14. This is the tree of trees and is famous, beautiful and auspicious.

15. Lord Viṣṇu, meditated upon through efficacious mantras, remains in it.

16. This is also called 'Bhadrāśva', because this great god remains in it surveying the whole world.

17. On the peak of the southern mountain is the Jambū tree in a cluster with big branches full of flowers and fruits.

18. From that fall down at the top of the mountain fruits by name Atisa, sweet and fragrant and like ambrosia.

19. From this great mountain arise many rivers which make the places fertile.

20. There we get gold named Jāmbūnada glowing like fire and used by the gods for their decoration.

21-22. Devas, Gandharvas, Yakṣas and Rākṣasas drink the juice of the jambu fruit which is like ambrosia and delight themselves in the southern region which is known as Jambūloka. People call it Jambūdvīpa.

23. In the mountain Vipula on the south, there is the very big tree called Aśvattha with a big trunk spreading all around. It is the abode of all noble qualities.

24. It bears beautiful fruits big like pots throughout the year.

25. Because of the flags fluttering in this region, resorted to by Devas and Gandharvas, it is known as Ketumāla (literally one having a row of flags). O Brahmins, listen to this name.

26. At the time of churning the milky ocean, a garland and a banner appeared here and hence it is known as Ketumāla.

27. At the top of the peak of Supārśva we get the big tree Vaṭa.

28. It has got a big trunk; it spreads over three yojanas, grows also downwards and is highly clustered by hanging branches.

29. It bears golden fruits big like pots.

30. Adding lustre to the tree are the mind-born sons of Brahmā, the younger brothers of Sanatkumāra.

31. They are seven in number and are known as Kurus. They are calm in mind and free from passion.

32-33. They are eternal and they remain in this region which goes by their name. These Kurus are the lords of the region.

CHAPTER SEVENTYEIGHT

Mandara and other mountains

Rudra said:

1-8. I shall now tell you about the four great mountains and about the lakes in them, which are beautiful, from which blow the gentle and sweet-smelling breeze, which have rivers flowing out of them, each of which have nine regions frequented by the celestial couples, which are full of gems and sacred spots, which always sound with waterfalls, which are full of lotuses, lilies, and other beautiful plants.

9. The lake in the eastern mountain is Aruṇoda, the one in the southern is Mānasa, the one in the western is Asitoda and the one in the northern is Mahābhadra. All these are full of lilies of various colours.

10. I shall tell you now about the mounts around Aruṇoda, listen to me.

11-12. They are Vikaṅka, Maṇiśṛṅga, Supātra, Upala,

Mahānīla, Kumbha, Suvindu, Madana, Veṇunaddha, Sumedas and Niṣadha, all of them holy.

13. The mounts around Mānasa, I shall now enumerate.

14-16. They are Triśikhara, Śiśira, Kapi, Śatamakṣa, Turaga, Tāmrābha, Viṣa, Śvetodana, Samūla, Sarala, Ratnaketu, Ekamūla, Mahāśṛṅga, Gajamūla, Śāvaka Pañcaśaila, Kailāsa and Himavān.

17. The mounts on the next, namely on the west (around Asitod a) I shall now give you.

18-20. They are Kapila, Piṅgala, Bhadra, Sarasa, Kumuda, Madhumān, Garjana, Markaṭa, Kṛṣṇa, Pāṇḍava, Sahasraśiras, Pāriyātra and Śṛṅgavān. I shall tell you now about the mounts around Mahābhadra in the north.

21-23. They are Haṁsakūṭa, Vṛṣahaṁsa, Kapiñjala, Indraśaila, Nīla, Kanakaśṛṅga, Śataśṛṅga, Puṣkara, Meghaśaila, Virāja and Jāruji.

24. In this manner know the places, towns and lakes in order from the north.

CHAPTER SEVENTYNINE

The Valleys of Meru I

Rudra said:

1-2. Between the mountains Asita (Kṛṣṇa) and Kumuda is the valley which is three hundred yojanas long and hundred yojanas broad and full of all kinds of birds and beasts.

3. In it there is a beautiful big lake with sweet water and huge lotuses, white and red, in which are seated gods, demons, Gandharvas and the great snakes.

4. Its placid water is resorted to by all. It is called Śrīsaras and it always sparkles.

5-7. Amidst that array of lotuses there is a particularly big lotus shining like the sun, astounding in its size, spreading with a crore of petals and attractive filaments, and with the bees humming all around. In it is seated the great goddess Lakṣmī, the embodiment of prosperity.

8-9. On the bank of that lake is the forest of Bilva trees always full of flowers and fruits wherein live Siddhas. It is two hundred yojanas in length and hundred yojanas in breadth.

10. It has numerous big trees as high as half a krośa with thousands of branches.

11. They bear thousands of fruits green and grey, smelling sweet and tasty like nectar.

12. The place is filled with the fruits falling from these trees and it is known all over the world as Śrīvana.

13. It has eight peaks. Many Devas and bilva-eating sages, live in it. Lakṣmī, adored by groups of siddhas, ever remains there.

14-15. Between the mountains Ekācala and Maṇiśṛṅga there is a lotus-grove, two hundred yojanas long and a hundred yojanas broad, resorted to by Siddhas and Cāraṇas.

16. The flower there appears as if held by Lakṣmī. There are big peaks as high as half a krośa.

17. With branches full of flowers, the whole place is made reddish yellow.

18-19. In this the flowers are each three cubits long and two cubits broad and with filaments of the colour of red arsenic and sweet-smelling. It always hums with inebriate bees and there are in it gods, Gandharvas, Rākṣasas and Yakṣas, and also Kinnaras, Apsarases and Nāgas.

20. There is the hermitage of the divine Kaśyapa in it and also other hermitages.

21. Between Mahānīla and Kakubha (Kumbha?) there is the river Sukhā, and on its bank is a big forest fifty yojanas long and thirty yojanas broad.

22. This forest is Tālavana (forest of Palmyras) with the trees rising to a height of half a krośa.

23. These trees are full of big, strong and juicy fruits of the colour of collyrium.

24. The whole place smells sweet and it is resorted to by Siddhas. This bears close resemblance to Airāvata, the great elephant.

25-26. Between Airāvata, Rudra (Kailāsa)? and Devaśīla (Pañcaśaila?) there is a tableland formed of a single rock, thousand yojanas long and hundred yojanas broad, without any kind of trees or plants, and with but a small stream of water.

27-28. Thus has been narrated, O Brahmins, the valleys in order around Meru.

CHAPTER EIGHTY

Valleys of Meru II

Rudra said:

1. Let us now see the valleys on the southern side occupied by Siddhas. Between Śiśira and Pataṅga is the white land which is without women and trees. But its sugar-cane-like peak has trees, and around it there is the grove of Udumbara trees full of birds.

2. In this grove, the trees bear fruits as big as large tortoises. It is resorted to by all the eight kinds of demigods.[1]

3. In this region flow many rivers which are full of clear and sweet water. In it there is the hermitage of Kardama Prajāpati frequented by many sages and men. Around it there is a forest extending to a hundred yojanas.

Between the mountains Tāmrābha and Pataṅga there is a big lake hundred yojanas broad and twice as long, full of different kinds of lotuses glowing like the rising sun and resorted to by Siddhas and Gandharvas.

4. In the middle is a tall peak, hundred yojanas long and thirty yojanas broad, full of a variety of minerals. At its top is a broad pathway leading to a vast enclosure with a jewelled porch. Within it is the city of Vidyādharas. Therein lives the Vidyādhara king by name Puloma with numerous attendants.

5. Between the mountains Sumūla and Vasudhāra, there is the place called Bilvasthalī, fifty yojanas long and thirty yojanas broad.

6. The Bilva trees there bear fruits big like pitchers, the ground there is strewn with these fruits, and it is resorted to by Guhyakas and the like who eat these fruits.

Between Vasudhāra and Ratnadhāra there is the Kiṁśuka

1. The demigods are Vidyādharas, Apsarases, Yakṣas, Rākṣasas, Gandharvas, Kinnaras, Piśācas and Guhyakas.

forest, a hundred yojanas long and thirty yojanas broad, spreading smell of the blossoms over a hundred yojanas. It has abundant water and is used by the Siddhas.

7. In it is the abode of Āditya. This god, the sun, appears month after month. Devas and others bow to Prajāpati, the creator of the world.

Between Pañcakūṭa and Kailāsa, there is the expansive land which is one thousand yojanas long and hundred yojanas broad, white like the swan, unapproached by trivial beings, and which is like the ladder to heaven.

8. Let us see now the valleys on the western side. Between Supārśva and Śikhiśaila there is a stony plateau which is untouchably hot for ever. In its middle is a part, a hundred yojanas in extent, which is the place of fire. Here fire which is the destroyer of the world, blazes for ever without fuel.

Between the mountainas Kumuda and Añjana is the Mātuluṅgakasthala (the place of Pomegranate), inaccessible to beasts and covered by yellow fruits.

In it is the holy pond used by Siddhas. This grove is Bṛhaspati's.

Then between the mountains Piñjara and Gaura there are lakes extending to hundreds of yojanas. They are full of big lilies.

9. In it is the abode of the great lord Viṣṇu.

Between the mountains Śukla and Pāṇḍura there is a single rock ninety yojanas long and thirty yojanas broad without trees. In it there is a pond of still water with different kinds of lotuses. In its middle is a big banyan tree spreading over five yojanas. Beneath it sits lord Śiva wearing blue cloth, praised by Yakṣas and others.

Between the mountains Sahasraśikhara and Kumuda is a sugar-cane-like peak, fifty yojanas long and twenty yojanas broad, full of birds and numerous trees bearing tasty fruits. In it is the divine hermitage of Indra.

Between Śaṅkhakūṭa and Ṛṣabha there is the beautiful grove of Punnāga trees extending over several yojanas and bearing sweet-smelling fruits as big as bilvas. In it live the Nāgas and others inebriated with the juice of the Punnāga fruits.

10. Between the mountains Kapiñjala and Nāga, there is the place, two hundred yojanas long and one hundred yojanas

broad, occupied by various kinds of people and with grapes and dates in abundance.

Between Puṣkara and Mahāmegha is the place, one hundred yojanas long and sixty yojanas broad, called Pāṇitala, without trees and plants. On its sides are four big forests and lakes extending over several yojanas. In it there are fierce valleys, ten, five, seven, eighty, thirty and twenty yojanas long.

CHAPTER EIGHTYONE

The domains of Devas in the Mountains

Rudra said:

1. I shall now state about the domains of Devas in these mountains At the top of the mountain called Sītā is the pleasure spot of Indra. Therein is the big grove of Pārijāta trees. On its eastern side is the Kuñjara hill. At its top there are eight cities of Dānavas.

2. In the mountain Vajraka there are many cities of Rākṣasas. They are called Nīlakas and they are capable of changing their shapes. In the mountain Mahānīla, there are fifteen thousand cities of Kinnaras. They are the regions of fifteen Kinnara kings like Deva datta, Candra and others. In the mountain Candrodaya we get golden underground cities wherein live Nāgas. The Dānavas are established there under an arrangement with Garuḍa. In (the mountain) Veṇumān there are three cities of Vidyādharas, each thousand yojanas in length and hundred yojanas in breadth. These are the regions of Vidyādhara Kings like Ulūka, Romaśa and Mahāvetra.

3. In each of these Garuḍa is established. In the mountain Kuñjara Paśupati (Śiva) is permanently established. In Vasudhāra the great god Śaṅkara (Śiva) on the bull remains with his retinue of crores of Gaṇas. In this live Vasus.

4. At the tops of Vasudhāra and Ratnadhāra there are eight and seven cities (respectively) for Vasus and seven sages. In the great mountain Ekaśṛṅga is the seat of four-faced Brahmā.

In the mountain Gaja the goddess herself takes abode with her retinue.

5. In the mountain Vasudhāra is the city, the abode of sages, Siddhas and Vidyādharas with forts and gateways. In it live the militant Gandharvas called Anekaparvatas with their chief Rājarāja. In Pañcakūṭa there are Devas and Rākṣasas, in Śataśṛṅga Dānavas, and there are hundred cities of Dānavas and Yakṣas.

6. On the western portion of Prabhedaka there are the cities of Devas, Dānavas, Siddhas and others. At the top of this mountain there is a big slab. The moon descends on it every new moon day. On its northern portion is Trikūṭa. Brahmā remains in it sometimes. There we get the abode of Fire. Fire in concrete form is worshipped by gods.

7. On the north, in the mountain Śṛṅga, we get the abodes of gods. On its eastern part is the abode of Nārāyaṇa, in the middle that of Brahmā and in the west that of Śiva. There we see a few cities of Yakṣas. On the north, in the mountain Jātuccha, there is a lake covering an area of thirty yojanas. In it lives the hundred-headed serpent-king Nanda.

8. Thus are the eight Devaparvatas (mountains of gods). They have the colours of gold, silver, ruby, cat's eye, vermillion etc., in order. This part of Earth is full of millions of houses of Siddhas and Vidyādharas. On the side of Meru is the world of Siddhas full of Kesara trees. The earth is in the form of a lotus. This is the general description given in the Purāṇas.

CHAPTER EIGHTYTWO

The descent of the rivers

Rudra said:

1. Now listen to the descent of the rivers. From what is known as the ocean of the sky, starts the river of the sky. This river is always agitated by the elephant of Indra. (As a result) it falls at the top of Meru in eightyfour thousand streams. And flowing upto the foot of the Meru, it forms into four and follows

a clockwise direction for six thousand yojanas with the names Sītā, Alakanandā, Cakṣus and Bhadrā. Among them the one that reaches earth slashing eightyone thousand mountains is known as Gaṅgā.

2. Now we describe Amaragaṇḍika on the side of Gandhamādana. It is thirtyone thousand yojanas long and four hundred yojanas broad. This region is Ketumāla with mighty men black in complexion and beautiful women lotus-like in complexion. There we get big jack trees. The son of Brahmā is the lord there. The people here drink water, are free from decay and disease and live for ten thousand years. On the eastern side of Mālyavān is the Pūrvagaṇḍikā and from Ekaśṛṅga extends Mānasa for one thousand yojanas. This region is known as Bhadrāśva.

3. There we get the forest of wholesome Rasāla trees. The mangoes are black, men white, women lotus-coloured and their life is one thousand years. There are five great mountains, Śailavarṇa, Mālākhya, Korajaska, Triparṇa and Nīla. The regions watered (by the streams from these mountains) have the same names.

4. Those regions consume the water from the rivers Sītā, Suvāhinī, Haṁsavatī, Kāsā, Mahāvaktra, Candravatī, Kāverī, Surasā, Ākhyāvatī, Indravatī, Aṅgāravāhinī, Harittoyā, Somāvartā, Śatahradā, Vanamālā, Vasumatī, Haṁsā, Suparṇā, Pañcagaṅgā, Dhanuṣmatī, Maṇivaprā, Subrahmabhāgā, Vilāsinī, Kṛṣṇatoyā, Puṇyodā, Nāgavatī, Śivā, Śaivālinī, Maṇitaṭā, Kṣīroda, Varuṇatālī and Viṣṇupadī. Those who drink the waters of these rivers live for ten thousand years and become devotees of Rudra and Umā.

CHAPTER EIGHTYTHREE

The regions and rivers in the mountain Naiṣadha

Rudra said:

1. Bhadrāśva and Ketumāla have been described in detail. Now are described the major mountains, regions and rivers on

the western side of the great mountain Naiṣadha. The seven major mountains, Viśākha, Kambala, Jayanta, Kṛṣṇa, Harita, Aśoka and Vardhamāna, have given rise to crores of others. The regions occupied by people there are also known by the same name (as of the mountains).

2. The settlements upto Sauragrāma like Sātapa, Kṛtasurā, Śravaṇakambala, Māheyācala, Kūṭavāsa, Mūlatapa, Krauñca, Kṛṣṇāṅga, Maṇipaṅkaja, Cūḍamala and Somīya and those upto the end of the sea, like Kurakuñja, Suvarṇataṭa, Kuha, Śvetāṅga, Kṛṣṇapāda, Vida, Kapila, Karṇika, Mahiṣa, Kubja, Karanāṭa, Mahotkaṭa, Śuka, Nāka, Sagaja, Bhūma, Kakurañjana, Mahānāha, Kiki, Saparṇa, Bhaumaka, Coraka, Dhūmajanma, Aṅgāraja, Madhureya, Śukeya, Cakeya, Śravaṇa, Mattakāśika, Godāvāma, Kulapañjāba, Varjaha and Modaśālaka consume the water flowing from these mountains.

3. Among these rivers, Plākṣā, Mahākadambā, Mānasī, Śyāmā, Sumedhā, Bahulā, Vivarṇā, Puṅkhā, Mālā, Darbhavatī, Bhadranadī, Śukanadī, Pallavā, Bhīmā, Prabhañjanā, Kāmbā, Kuśāvatī, Dakṣā, Kāsavatī, Tuṅgā, Puṇyodā, Candrāvatī, Sumūlāvatī, Kakupadminī, Viśālā, Karaṇṭakā, Pīvarī, Mahāmāyā, Mahiṣī, Mānuṣī, Caṇḍā are the more important. The others are small rivers and they are in thousands.

CHAPTER EIGHTYFOUR

The regions on the South and North of Meru

Rudra said:

1. Now are duly described the people who live on the northern regions as well as those who live on the southern side.

2. O Brahmins, listen to what I say. In the region to the south of Meru and north of Śveta, there is Ramyaka belonging to Vāyu.

3. The people there are born pure, highly intelligent and free from old age and disaster.

4. The extremely big banyan tree grows there. Drinking the juice of its fruits, all the people there attain divine form and live for ten thousand years.

5. To the north of Śveta and south of Triśṛṅga, we get the region named Hiraṇmaya where flows the river Hairaṇvatī.

6. The mighty Yakṣas, who can assume any form at will, live there. The duration of their life is eleven thousand years.

7. Many live there for fifteen thousand years.

8. The breadfruit and jack trees flourish there. By the juice of their fruits alone, one can live for many days.

9. In Triśṛṅga with its peaks of gems and gold, from its northern peak, upto the southern ocean[1], is the northern Kuru. There we get sappy trees and many juice. In those trees are clothes and ornaments. The land is full of gems and the sands are golden. People dropped from heaven live there, with duration of life of thirteen thousand years.

10. On the western side of this island, after four thousand yojanas, we get the celestial region Candradvīpa covering an area of one thousand yojanas. In its middle are two waterfalls called Candrakānta and Sūryakānta. Between them is the great river Candrāvartā with numerous tributaries and many trees (on the banks).

11. On the northern side of Kuru is the celestial region Sūryadvīpa covering an area of one thousand yojanas washed by the waves of the ocean. In its middle is a great mountain, a hundred yojanas in extent. From it arises the river called Sūryāvartā. The abode of the Sun is there. Therein live the people with the Sun as their god and having the same complexion as his, with duration of life of ten thousand years.

12. On the western side of this island, after four thousand yojanas, we find in the ocean the island called Bhadrākara covering an area of one thousand yojanas. Therein is the abode of Vāyu adorned by numerous gems. There Vāyu remains in corporal form. There the people are golden in colour and live for five thousand years.

---

1. Perhaps the northern ocean is meant.

CHAPTER EIGHTYFIVE

The nine divisions of Bhārata

Rudra said:

1. Thus has been described the arrangement in the world-lotus. Now listen to the ninefold division of Bhārata. These (divisions) are Indra, Kaseru, Tāmravarṇa, Gabhasti, Nāgadvīpa, Saumya, Gandharva, Vāruṇa and Bhārata (proper). Each is surrounded by an ocean and is one thousand yojanas in extent. There are seven major mountains.

2. These major mountains are Mahendra, Malaya, Sahya, Śuktimān, Ṛkṣa, Vindhya and Pāriyātra.

3. There are minor mountains like Mandara, Śāra, Dardura, Kailāsa, Maināka, Vaidyuta, Vārandhama, Pāṇḍura, Tuṅgaprastha, Kṛṣṇagiri, Jayanta, Airāvata, Ṛṣyamūka, Gomanta, Citrakūṭa, Śrīparvata, Cakorakuṭa, Śrīśaila and Kṛtasthala. There are smaller mountains also. In the settlements in these dwell Āryas and Mlecchas. They drink water in the rivers flowing there.

4. The rivers are Gaṅgā, Sindhu, Sarasvatī, Śatadru, Vitastā, Vipāśā, Candrabhāgā, Sarayū, Yamunā, Irāvatī, Devikā, Kuhū, Gomatī, Dhūtapāpā, Bāhudā, Dṛṣadvatī, Kauśikī, Nisvīrā, Gaṇḍakī, Cakṣuṣmatī and Lohitā, all rising from the foot of the Himālayas. Vedasmṛti, Vedavatī, Sindhuparṇā, Candanābhā, Nāśadācārā, Rohīpārā, Carmaṇvatī, Vidiśā, Vedatrayī and Vapantī arise from Pāriyātra.

5. Śoṇa, Jyotirathā, Narmadā, Surasā, Mandākinī, Daśārṇā, Citrakūṭā, Tamasā, Pippalā, Karatoyā, Piśācikā, Citrotpalā, Viśālā, Vañjukā, Bāhuvāhinī, Śuktimatī, Virajā, Paṅkinī and Rātrī arise from Ṛkṣa. Maṇijālā, Śubhā, Tāpī, Payoṣṇī, Śīghrodā, Veṣṇā, Pāśā, Vaitaraṇī, Vaidipālā, Kumudvatī, Toyā, Durgā, Antyā and Girā arise from the base of the Vindhya. Godāvarī, Bhīmarathī, Kṛṣṇā, Veṇī, Vañjulā, Tuṅgabhadrā, Suprayogā and Bāhyakāverī arise from the foot of Sahya.

6. Śatamālā, Tāmraparṇī, Puṣpāvatī and Utpalāvatī arise from Malaya. Triyāmā, Ṛṣikulyā, Ikṣulā, Trivindālā, Mūlinī and Vaṁśavarā have their origin in Mahendra. Ṛṣikā, Lūsatī, Mandagāminī and Palāśinī have their source in Śuktimān. These are the main rivers arising from the major mountains.

The others are minor rivers. This Jambūdvīpa is one lakh yojanas in extent.

CHAPTER EIGHTYSIX

Śākadvīpa

Rudra said:

1. Now know about Śākadvīpa. It is double the extent of Jambūdvīpa and the saline ocean surrounding it also is double the size. There live in it blessed people, long-lived and free from famine, decay and disease. There are seven major mountains here which have the saline ocean on one side and milky ocean on the other.

2. On the east is the extensive mountain called Udaya. To the west of it is the mountain named Jaladhāra, also called Candra. Indra drinks its water and then pours it down (as rain). In it there is another mountain called Śvetaka. It has six parts. Here the people play a good deal. There is another mountain called Rajata. It is also known as Śāka. Beyond it is Āmbikeya. It is also called Vibhrājasa.

3. The same is called Kesarī. The wind arises from there. The regions are also known after the mountains, as Udaya, Sukumāra, Jaladhāra, Kṣemaka and Mahādruma as principal names. The other names of the mountains are also applied. In the middle is the Śāka tree. There are seven main rivers with two names each. These are Sukumārī, Kumārī, Nandā, Veṇikā, Dhenuḥ, Ikṣumatī and Gabhasti.

CHAPTER EIGHTYSEVEN

Kuśadvīpa

Rudra said:

1. Now listen to Kuśadvīpa, the third. Kuśadvīpa is surrounded by the milky ocean, and is double in extent of the Śāka-

dvīpa. There are seven major mountains here also, each with two names such as Kumuda, also called Vidruma. The high Hemaparvata is also Droṇa, Puṣpavān is also Kaṅka, Kuśeśaya is also Agnimān, and the sixth Mahiṣa is also Hari. Agni remains there.

2. The seventh is Kakudhra; it is the same as Mandara. These are the mountains in Kuśadvīpa. The divisions in it have also two names each. Kumuda is Śveta, it is named first. The high Lolita is also Veṇumaṇḍala. Valāhaka is Jīmuta and is the same as Rathākāra. Droṇa is Hari and is the same as Balādhana.

3. The rivers there have also two names. Pratoyā is also called Praveśā. The second is Śivā, also called Yaśodā. The third is Citrā, also known as Kṛṣṇā. The fourth is Hrādinī, also called Candrā. The fifth is Vidyullatā, also called Śuklā. The sixth is Varṇā, it is the same as Vibhāvarī. The seventh is Mahatī, the same as Dhṛti. These are the main rivers. The others are minor ones. This is the arrangement in Kuśadvīpa.

4. Śākadvīpa and its position have already been narrated. In its middle is a big mass of Kuśa grass. The Kuśadvīpa is surrounded by an ocean of curd, equal to amṛta, and double the size of the milky ocean.

CHAPTER EIGHTYEIGHT

Krauñcadvīpā

Rudra said:

1. The fourth is Krauñca, double the dimensions of Kuśadvīpa, surrounded by an ocean also double in size. In it also there are seven mountains. The first in Krauñca is Vidyullatā or Raivata, then is Mānasa or Pāvaka. Then is Andhakāra or Acchodaka. Then is Devāvṛta which is called also Surāpa. After this is Deviṣṭha, also called Kāñcanaśṛṅga.

2. After Devananda we get Govinda or Dvivinda. Then is Puṇḍarīka, which is the same as Toyāsaha. These seven mountains in Krauñcadvīpa are all high and full of gems.

3. The regions in Krauñca are: Kuśala or Mādhava, Vāmaka or Saṁvartaka, Uṣṇavān or Saprakāśa, Pāvaka or

Sudarśana, Andhakāra or Sammoha, Munideśa or Prakāśa and Dundubhi or Anartha.

4. There are seven rivers: Gaurī, Kumudvatī, Sandhyā, Rātrī, Manojavā, Khyāti and Puṇḍarīka.

5. Gauri is Puṣpavahā, Kumudvatī is Ārdravatī, Sandhyā is Raudrā, (Rātrī) is Sukhāvahā, (Manojavā) is Bhogajavā, Khyāti is Kṣiprodā, Puṇḍarīka is Bahulā. The minor rivers have different colours and flow in different regions. Krauñcadvīpa is surrounded by (an ocean of) ghee and beyond it is Śālmali.

CHAPTER EIGHTYNINE

Śālmalidvīpa and others

Rudra said:

1. I shall now speak about the people in the remaining three islands. Listen to the account of the fifth, Śālmali.

2. Śālmali is double the size of Krauñca island.

3. This is surrounded by the sea of ghee. It is also double in size. There also we get seven principal mountains, and the same number of rivers. The mountains are big, yellow and full of gold and have the names Sarvaguṇa, Sauvarṇa, Rohita, Sumanasa, Kuśala, Jāmbūnada and Vaidyuta. The regions are also of the same names.

4. Then is the sixth, Gomeda. This is twice the size of Śālmali. There are only two mountains in it, Avasara and Kumuda. The ocean is of Sugarcane juice.

Puṣkara is double its size. In it there is the mountain called Mānasa. This is divided into two and is surrounded by sweet water spreading to the same area as itself.

5. Then is this broad earth forming part of the expansive universe.

These are the regions enumerated. In every aeon Lord Nārāyaṇa assumes the form of a boar and raises it up by a tusk and restores it to its original position.

6. I have thus told you about the dimensions of the earth. May good befall you, O Brahmins. I shall now retire to my abode in Kailāsa.

Varāha said:

7. Saying thus, Rudra immediately left for Kailāsa. All the gods and sages also departed.

CHAPTER NINETY

The Goddess of Creation

Earth said:

1. Some consider the holy Śiva, some Viṣṇu and others Brahmā as the supreme being.

2. I have great curiosity to know who among these is superior and who inferior. Please enlighten me.

Varāha said:

3. O goddess, Nārāyaṇa is the supreme god. Then is Brahmā who arose from him. From Brahmā arose Rudra the omniscient.

4. The wonders Rudra accomplished are numerous. I shall tell you all of them.

5. In the beautiful peak Kailāsa, full of many kinds of minerals, resides the three-eyed lord Śiva.

6. Once this god, who is bowed to by all beings, was in the company of Pārvatī, surrounded by his Gaṇas.

7. Some among the Gaṇas were lion-faced and were roaring like lions. Some were elephant-faced and others horse-faced.

8. Some were crocodile-faced, others boar-faced, yet others mule-faced and donkey-faced.

9. A few were goat-faced and a few others fish-faced. In all, they were all innumerable and holding weapons. Some were singing, some dancing, some running and some jumping.

10. The mighty ones were laughing, clapping and roaring. Some of the leaders were fighting throwing stones at one another.

11. Many were engaged in single combat. Thus were the Gaṇas surrounding Maheśvara.

12. While the Gaṇas were thus mirthful and the lord was playing with his spouse, there came Brahmā in great hurry together with Devas.

13. The great god Rudra, seeing Brahmā arrive there, honoured him and said:

14. "O Brahmā, tell me quickly the object of your hurried visit to me".

Brahmā said:

15. "There is a great Rākṣasa named Andhaka. Being much harassed by him, Devas came to me for help.

16. I then told them that they may go to Śiva and that is why they are here now".

17. Saying this, Brahmā looked at Śiva and at the same time called to his mind the great god Nārāyaṇa.

18. Lord Nārāyaṇa thus came to be between the other two. And Brahmā, Viṣṇu and Maheśvara came to be unified.

19. They looked at each other minutely, and as a result of the unified looks of the three, a goddess arose.

20. This deity was young and resplendent, had the complexion of the blue lotus and had dark and curly hair.

21. She had shapely nose and forehead and wellformed mouth. All that the god Tvaṣṭā (the celestial architect) had described as five-tongue was well descernible in her.

22. Seeing her, Brahmā, Viṣṇu and Maheśvara asked her who she was and what she wanted to do.

23. That goddess who had the three colours black, white and yellow said:

24. "O great gods, I was born out of the combination of the looks of all the three of you. How do you fail to know me to be the goddess representing your energies ?".

25. Then Brahmā and others were pleased and gave her a boon saying: "O goddess, we name you Trikalā, protect this universe always.

26. You will have other names also based on your attributes, and all these will produce different achievements.

27. There is another thing also. You have three colours. Assume three different forms one with each colour".

28. Thus told by the gods, she became triplicated, one white, another red and the third black.

29. The white body is Brahmā (because of Brahmā element) and creation proceeds from it calmly as ordained by Brahmā.

30. The beautiful body red in colour, is Vaiṣṇavī (because of Viṣṇu's element) and bears conch and disc.

31. She protects the whole universe and is known as Viṣṇu-māyā.

32. The body black in colour bears the trident and holds a fierce face. She destroys the universe.

33. The broad-eyed white goddess with the aspect of Brahmā, took leave of him and disappeared.

34. She hid herself in the Śveta mountain and began to perform severe penance desirous of attaining omniscience.

35. The red goddess with the aspect of Viṣṇu took leave of him and went to the Mandara mountain for performing severe penance.

36. The fierce-looking black goddess with the aspect of Rudra, similarly went to perform penance at the Nīla mountain.

37. Then for a long time Brahmā started to create beings, but he could not progress.

38. When the creations made out of the mind of Brahmā thus failed to multiply he began to seriously think about the cause of it.

39. When Brahmā, thus, meditated with his yogic powers, he knew about the goddess performing severe penance at the Śveta mountain.

40. Then he went to the place of her penance and told her who was absorbed in contemplation.

Brahmā said:

41. O beautiful goddess, why do you do this penance? I am pleased with you. You may seek of me a boon.

Sṛṣṭi said:

42. "O god, I don't wish to remain confined to a single place. I seek of you the boon to make me present everywhere".

43. God Brahmā, being thus requested by Sṛṣṭi (the goddess of creation), told her that she would be present everywhere.

44. Told thus, the beautiful Sṛṣṭi dissolved herself in Brahmā.

45. From then onwards, the creation by Brahmā began to grow.

46. Seven arose from Brahma's mind, from them other sages, from them yet others, and from them still others. Thus there are four series of beings.

47. Thus was established beings moving and stationary and all that is expressible by words.

48. Thus was established all that is past and future.

CHAPTER NINETYONE

Sarasvatī and others

Varāha said:

1. O fair lady, hear what that goddess did who was made triple by the great god Śiva.

2. The form of the goddess of creation which is beautiful and white, is known as Ekākṣarā (of one syllable) and also Sarvākṣarā (of all syllables).

3. She is also known as Vāgīśā (highest speech) and sometimes as Sarasvatī. She is Vidyeśvarī and Amitākṣarā.

4. She is Jñānanidhi (the abode of all knowledge) and also Vibhāvarī. All the names that are soft and all the names related to knowledge pertain to her.

5. The broad-eyed, beautiful and red-coloured Vaiṣṇavī is another. Raudrī is the third.

6. All the three arose really out of Rudra. It is really a single goddess who is in three froms.

7. Thus have I told you about ancient creation. The entire world of movable and immovable objects is pervaded by her.

8. Brahmā praised the goddess by whom his creation was made to grow.

Brahmā said:

9. Hail O goddess, that arose from truth, firm and eternal, the mother of all, all-pervading.

10. You bestow all achievements, all intelligence and good progeny.

11. You are Svāhā, you are Svadhā, you are the origin of everything, you are Praṇava and the source of all Vedas.

12. You are the source of all gods and demons, all Yakṣas, Gandharvas and Rākṣasas, all animals and all plants.

13. You are Vidyā, Vidyeśvarī, Siddhā, Prasiddhā and Sureśvarī.

14. You know everything, you give all success, you are present everywhere, you are free from all doubts, and you destroy all enemies.

15. You hold all knowledge and bestow all good. I bow to you.

16. He who unites with his wife after her menstrual bath, gets good progeny by your blessing. You destroy all enemies and always remain victorious.

CHAPTER NINETYTWO

The greatness of Vaiṣṇavī

Varāha said:

1. The goddess Vaiṣṇavī who went to Mandara for performing penance, was the great power representing Rajas.

2. She was doing penance all by herself (at the place) Viśālā. After a long time, her mind became agitated.

3-4. As a result of this agitation there arose hundreds of beautiful damsels with black curly hair and red lips, wearing bracelets and anklets.

5-7. Seeing them all, the goddess created a city with numerous mansions with golden balconies, crystal stairs and water fountains, with jewelled windows and gardens, all on broad roads.

8. The ladies thus created were innumerable, but I shall tell you the names of the more important among them.

9-12. Vidyutprabhā, Candrakāntī, Sūryakāntī, Gambhīrā, Cārukeśī, Sujātā, Mañjukeśinī, Ghṛtācī, Urvaśī, Śaśinī, Śīlamaṇḍitā, Cārukanyā, Viśālākṣī, Dhanyā, Candraprabhā, Girisutā, Sūryaprabhā, Amṛtā, Svayamprabhā, Cārumukhī, Śivadūtī, Vibhāvarī, Jayā, Vijayā, Jayantī, Aparājitā and several others in hundreds occupied that fine city.

13. All these in the retinue of the goddess were bearing the rope and the noose, and she herself was seated on the throne.

14. Attended on by these, she began to perform the vrata called Kaumāra.

15. While she was thus engaged in penance, duly attended on by them, there appeared before her Nārada, the son of Brahmā.

16-17. Seeing that great sage, she directed Vidyutprabhā to give him a seat and water for washing the feet.

18. Thereupon Vidyutprabhā offered to Nārada *āsana* (seat), *pādya* (water for feet) and *arghya* (holy water).

19. When Nārada bowed to her and took his seat, she asked him in great joy.

20. "O great sage, welcome to you. From which world are you coming now ? Be pleased to say with what purpose you have come ?".

21-22. Asked by the goddess thus, Nārada who knew all the worlds, said: "From Brahmaloka I went to Indraloka and from there to Rudra's mountain (Kailāsa). From there I have come here to see you". Saying so, he looked intently at the goddess.

23. Seeing her for a while, Nārada became wonder-struck.

24. "How wonderful is her form, how wonderful is her lustre, how wonderful her courage, how wonderful her selflessness in that she is undergoing all this strain.

25. In no other woman can this beauty be seen, be she belong to Devas, Gandharvas, Siddhas, Yakṣas, Kinnaras or Rākṣasas". Thinking thus, his wonder was redoubled.

26. He bowed to her and then jumped into the sky and quickly went to the city of the Rākṣasa chief.

27. That city was known as Mahiṣa and was within the ocean. He went there to the Asura whose form was like a buffalo.

28. When he saw the sage, he duly honoured him with devotion.

29. Thus pleased, Nārada told him about the matchless beauty of the goddess doing penance.

Nārada said:

30. "O lord of Asuras, by means of a boon, the entire universe has become yours. Now hear about a jewel among damsels,

31. From Brahmaloka I happened to go to the Mandara mountain. There I saw a city, Devīpura, full of hundreds of young women.

32. The chief among them is performing penance. Like her we cannot find one among gods, demons or Yakṣas.

33. I have not seen one like her in all my wanderings all over the world.

34. She is honoured by Devas, Gandharvas, Ṛṣis, Siddhas, Cāraṇas and Daityas.

35. Seeing that benevolent goddess, I rushed here to you. She cannot be won without winning Devas and Gandharvas".

36. Thus informing him, Nārada immediately disappeared.

CHAPTER NINETYTHREE

The discussion of Mahiṣāsura with his ministers

Varāha said:

1. When Nārada was gone, Mahiṣāsura began to think of the beautiful damsel spoken about by him.

2. Thinking of her, he never got peace of mind. He summoned his chief minister by name Alaṁśarman.

3-4. He had eight ministers who were learned, valiant and just. They were Praghasa, Vighasa, Śaṅkukarṇa, Vibhāvasu, Vidyunmālī, Sumati, Parjanya and Krūra. These were the principal ones. They asked their king to tell them what they should do.

5. Determined to get the damsel mentioned by Nārada, the king told them:

Mahiṣa said:

6. Sage Nārada spoke to me about a young woman. She cannot be obtained without defeating the king of gods.

7-8. You, therefore, consider the matter well and tell me how gods can be defeated and how this woman can be obtained. Please tell me quickly.

9. Thus asked, they began to say. First Praghasa said to him:

10. "O lord, she who was spoken of by Nārada to you, is the supreme power that has assumed the form of the goddess Vaiṣṇavī.

11. A king who desires the wife of his preceptor, the wife of another king or the women in attendance on him, or cohabits with a woman prohibited for him, brings about his own doom.

12. After Praghasa, Vighasa said, "O king, what Praghasa said about that goddess is true.

13. If we all agree, then what should be done by one desirous of success, is to get that virgin goddess in marriage.

14-15. In a matter relating to a virgin, one should not act by oneself. If you all agree to what I say, then let the ministers go to her nearest relative and seek her hand for you.

16. We will first try negotiation failing which we will try to get the approval by gifts. If we still fail we try the method of threat, and finally, if necessary, we will fight.

17. If by all these processes, we fail to achieve our aims, we will march forward and carry her away by force".

18. Vighasa's proposal was gladly approved by all the other ministers. They said:

19. "Vighasa has said now what best we can do in this matter. Let that be done and let us send a messenger now.

20. The messenger should be pure in mind, valiant and learned in polity.

21. We should know from him about her appearance, complexion, valour, might, relations and residence.

22. After knowing all this, we may think of the further action to be taken".

23. The king accepted the suggestion and applauded the minister Vighasa.

24. All of them then considered as to who should be sent as messenger and finally chose Vidyutprabha, who had magical powers, for the purpose.

25. Vighasa then told him: "Be victorious over the army of gods. Mobilise the Rākṣasa army with all its four constituents.

26. O lord of Asuras, when the gods are defeated by you, that damsel will naturally come to you.

27-28. When the guardians of the quarters, Maruts, Nāgas, Vidyādharas, Siddhas, Gandharvas, Rudras, Vasus, Ādityas, are all overcome, you will become Indra.

29. When Indra's harem with numerous women, and the women among Devas and Gandharvas fall to you, she too will certainly do so".

30-31. Thus said, the king ordered the commander-in-chief Virūpākṣa, black like the cloud and collyrium, to get ready the army with the elephants, horses, chariots, and soldiers, in order to defeat gods and Gandharvas.

32. Commanded thus, Virūpākṣa immediately got ready the invincible army.

33. Each Rākṣasa in the army was adequate to defeat one god in battle.

34. Even the chieftains were nine crores in number. Thousands of Rākṣasas constituted the infantry.

35. The entire force was assembled and made to march with a view to defeating the force of gods.

36. With a variety of weapons in hands and with ferocious looks, the soldiers in the army danced in delight and uttered loud cries at the prospect of victory over the gods.

CHAPTER NINETYFOUR

The fight between gods and demons

Varāha said:

1. Then the mighty demon Mahiṣa, who could assume any form at will, started for mountain Meru on an elephant.

2. Reaching Indra's city, he challenged Indra and gods for battle.

3. Taking their weapons and riding on their battle vehicles, the gods accepted the challenge.

4. Then started the exciting battle between great warriors full of war cries from both sides.

5. The (eight) Vasus were attacked by eight Rākṣasas, namely Añjana, Nīlakukṣi, Meghavarṇa, Valāhaka, Udarākṣa, Lalāṭākṣa, Subhīma and Svarbhānu.

6-9. The twelve Ādityas were engaged by twelve Rākṣasas, namely, Bhīma, Dhvāṅkṣa, Dhvastakṣṛṇa, Śaṅkukarṇa, Vajraka, Jyotivīrya, Vidyunmālī, Raktākṣa, Vidyujjihva, Atikāya, Mahākāya and Dīrghabāhū.

10-12. Similarly, the eleven Rudras were to face eleven Rākṣasas by name Kāla, Kṛtānta, Raktākṣa, Haraṇa, Mitrahā, Nala, Yajñahā, Brahmahā, Goghna, Strīghna and Saṁvartaka.

13. The other Rākṣasas engaged the other devas and Mahiṣa himself engaged Indra.

14. Mahiṣa was very valiant and was highly haughty that he could not be killed by any male, because of a boon from Brahmā, be he Śiva himself.

15. Numerous Asuras were killed by Ādityas, Vasus and Rudras. Many in the army of Devas were also killed by the Rākṣasas.

16. In the end Indra was defeated, and the gods, unable to face the piercing weapons, took to their heels.

17. The Asuras reached Brahmaloka and began to harass Devas further.

CHAPTER NINETYFIVE

Death of Mahiṣāsura

Varāha said:

1. Then Vidyutprabha, who was sent as the messenger, reached the place of the goddess where there were hundreds of young women, and said:

Vidyutprabha said:

2. "O goddess, there was a sage named Supārśva who was one among the first of creations.

3. To him was born the valiant and resplendent Sindhudvīpa.

4. He was performing severe penance without food in the city Māhiṣmatī.

5. One day princess Māhiṣmatī of incomparable beauty was moving about playing with her friends.

6. She chanced to reach the valley of the Mandara mountain.

7-8. There she saw the penance-grove of sage Asvara which was full of bowers and trees like Bakula, Lakuca, Candana, Spandana, Sāla and Sarala.

9. Seeing this beautiful hermitage, princess Māhiṣmatī thought.

10. "I shall frighten out this sage from this penance grove and shall myself enjoy here with my friends".

11. Thinking thus, she transformed herself into a buffalo with sharp horns, along with her friends.

12. She then went to the sage to frighten him.

13. When frightened by them, the sage was able to see by his internal eye that she was the Asura princess, and in anger he cursed her.

14. "Since you are frightening me by assuming the form of a buffalo, you be a buffalo itself for a hundred years for your misconduct".

15. Cursed thus, she was shivering with fear, and she fell at his feet with her friends and sought his pardon.

16. He was very much moved and said in mitigation of the curse: "When once you give birth to a son with this form, there will be the end of the curse. My words will never be in vain".

17. Told thus, she went to the bank of river Narmadā where Sindhudvīpa was performing penance.

18. There a young and beautiful Rākṣasa girl by name Indumatī, bathing naked, was seen by this sage.

19. Then he had an emission which he dropped in a stony crevice at the river (and it got mixed with the water).

20. Finding the water fragrant (with it), Māhiṣmatī told her friends that she would drink it. She then drank the water containing the emission of the sage.

21. As a result she conceived and in due time brought forth, a son named Mahiṣa, intelligent and valiant.

22. O goddess, this Mahiṣa who has vanquished the army of gods, now desires to marry you.

23. This great Asura, having subjugated all the three worlds, will give you everything you desire.

24. O goddess, you will be doing a great thing if you offer yourself to him".

25. Told thus by the messenger, the goddess simply laughed and did not utter a word.

26. When she was laughing, he saw in her belly all the three worlds and he became stupefied.

27. Then the doorkeeper of the goddess, by name Jayā, spoke what was in the mind of her mistress.

Jayā said:

28. "You have now spoken seeking the hand of this goddess (for your master). But the vrata she has undertaken is a ceaseless one.

29. There are so many damsels here attending on her. Even one among them is not available to you. Then why speak of the goddess. Therefore, O messenger, please go before something untoward befalls you".

30. The messenger departed. Immediately there appeared sage Nārada from the sky.

31. He quickly prostrated before the virgin goddess, took the seat offered to him and said after bowing to all the others there.

32. "O goddess, I am sent to you by the gods.

33. The gods have been defeated in battle by the asura Mahiṣa, and now he is attempting to capture you.

34. And I have been asked by the gods to tell you that you should be firm in killing him".

35. Soon Nārada disappeared and the goddess ordered her retinue to get ready for battle.

36. Thus ordered, they all took ferocious forms holding sword, shield and arrows, and stood ready for battle to destroy Asuras.

37. Then the entire army of Asuras quickly came away from the army of gods to the place where this army of women was ranged.

38. The women fought with them and soon destroyed their force with all its four divisions.

39. The heads of many were smashed or cut down. The chests of many were broken and goblins were drinking the blood therein.

40. The trunkless heads of many of the Asuras were rolling on the ground.

41. Thus very soon the Asura army was vanquished and the attack now turned towards Mahiṣāsura.

42. Then the whole army raised a cry of fear, and Mahiṣa asked the commander why it was so.

43. The Asura named Yajñahanus, who had assumed the form of an elephant, told him that this was because of the army of women striking ferociously at the Asura force.

44. Mahiṣa then darted forth towards these women to strike them with his mace.

45. He straightaway went to the spot where the goddess worshipped by Devas and Gandharvas was standing.

46-47. Seeing him advance towards her, she assumed a form with twenty hands, holding bow, sword, spear, arrows, trident, club, mace, disc, sling, rod, rope, flag and lotus.[1]

48. The twenty-armed goddess appeared riding on a lion. She then meditated on the fierce Rudra who is the cause of destruction.

49-50. Rudra immediately arrived there. She bowed to him and said that she would gain victory over the Asuras by his mere presence there.

51. Then she defeated all the Asuras except Mahiṣa. Afterwards she darted towards him.

52. When he saw her, Mahiṣa rushed towards her. He alternately fought and fled.

53. He sometimes fought and sometimes withdrew. The fight went on in this manner for ten thousand divine years.

54. The entire universe was realing with fear in the tumult of the battle.

55. Finally in the mountain Śataśṛṅga, he was trodden upon and killed with the trident.

56. His head was cut off with the sword, As he was killed by the goddess, his soul went to heaven.

57. Then Devas led by Brahmā, delighted at the annihilation of Mahiṣa, praised the goddess.

Devas said:

58. Bow to you, O goddess, the great, majestic and fierce,

---

1. Only thirteen items are mentioned here and not twenty.

victorious, the cause of the existence of the world, three-eyed and omnipresent.

59. Knowledge and nescience, meditation, the object of meditation, the slayer of Mahiṣāsura, present in everything, the lord of all, of universal form, Vaiṣṇavī.

60. Free from fear, permanent, with eyes like the lotus petal, engaged in holy vows, of frightening form.

61. The bestower of prosperity and success, learning and ignorance, immortal, auspicious, the energy of Śiva, Viṣṇu and Brahmā, prostrated by all gods.

62. Holding the bell in hand, bearing the weapon trident, the destroyer of terrible Mahiṣa, fierce in form, uneven-eyed the great illusion, the exuder of ambrosia.

63. Well disposed towards all beings, the very essence of all beings, the supporter of all beings, the source of all Vidyās, Purāṇas and Śilpas.

64. Bow to you, O mother, you are the repository of all powers and all the secrets of the Vedas.

65. Bow to you, O great goddess, pure, the embodiment of forbearance.

66. We all seek refuge in you, O supreme goddess, as a result of which we never meet with any reverse in battle.

67-68. He who recites this Stotra with devotion escapes from ferocious animals like the tiger, from robbers and from the displeasure of kings, gets release from fetters and lives happily.

Varāha said:

69. Thus extolled by gods, she asked them to seek of her a boon.

The gods said:

70. "The boon we seek is that you may be pleased to fulfil all the desires of those who recite this stotra of yours".

71. Saying 'Let it be so', the goddess sent the gods off and herself remained there.

72. O Earth, he who knows this the second birth of the goddess, becomes free from grief and attains the eternal abode free from all misery.

CHAPTER NINETYSIX

The exploits of Raudri

Varāha said:

1. O Earth, listen to the Vrata of Raudrī, representing the power of Tamas, who went to the Nīla mountain for performing penance.

2. With the aim of protecting the world by means of penance for a long time, she resorted to five fires.[1]

3-4. While she was thus performing great penance, there lived in a city rich with gems and full of forests in the midst of the sea, a powerful Asura king named Ruru who had got a boon from Brahmā. He was a source of terror to gods.

5. He was like a second Namuci,[2] and had as his followers crores of Asuras.

6. For a long time he fought against gods with a view to capturing the cities of the deities guarding different quarters.

7. As the great Asura was rising with his army, the water in the sea began to swell and enter the valleys of mountains filling them with crocodiles and big fish.

8. From within that water issued forth the Asura army with variegated weapons and armour.

9. Came out from it big elephants with Asuras seated on them and loudly tinkling with bells tied on them.

10. Crores of horses having white streamers came out with riders seated on golden pedestals.

11. Similarly, came out a ceaseless stream of chariots with good wheels, shaft and poles, fitted with mechanical contrivances, and equalling in speed the chariot of the sun.

12. In the same manner rushed forth the infantry with quivers, bows and arrows, quickly striking at all those that came in the way.

13. After coming out of the waters, they vanquished the gods and darted towards the city of Indra with all the four divisions of the army.

14. The Asura king Ruru fought Devas with fierce club, hammer, rod and arrows.

---

1. The five fires are those on the four sides, the fifth being the sun.
2. Namuci was a demon killed by Indra.

15. In the battle,the Asuras inflicted serious injury on Devas and so too Devas on the Asuras. In the end, Devas with their leader Indra were defeated and they ran away.

16. When Devas were thus taking to their heels, Asuras chased them.

17-18. Running in great fear, gods came to Nīla mountain where the goddess Raudrī was doing penance. They understood her to be Kālarātri, the cause of all destruction.

19. Seeing Devas thus fear-stricken, she told them aloud not to be afraid.

The goddess said:

20. O gods, why are you so worried. Tell me the cause of your fear.

The gods said:

21. "O great goddess, protect us from the powerful Ruru, the king of Asuras, who is pursuing us".

22. Told thus by the gods, she of matchless valour, simply laughed a while.

23. As she was laughing, from her mouth arose numerous goddesses of strange forms, and the whole world became covered by them.

24. They were ferocious, with expansive breasts, holding noose, goad, trident, bow and arrows.

25. They remained around the goddess in crores.

26. They soon fought against Asuras and annihilated their entire force.

27. The army of Devas together with the army of Kālarātri fought Asuras and sent them all to Yama's abode.

28. The great demon Ruru alone was left there.

29. He then discharged towards the gods a magical power which made them all fall into a swoon.

30. When Devas were thus in a state of forced sleep, the goddess struck at Ruru with her trident.

31. When he was struck, his trunk (*carma*) and head (*muṇḍa*) got separated from each other.

32. Since the *carma* and *muṇḍa* of the demon Ruru were separated thus, she came to be known as *Cāmuṇḍā*.[1]

33. Because of her terrific form engaged in destruction, she was known as *Kālarātri* (the night of time).

34. Her attendant goddesses are legion and they always stand around her.

35. They all felt extemely hungry and so requested the goddess to give them food.

36. Thus requested, she began to think about food for them, but could not find an immediate solution.

37. She then meditated on Lord Rudra, and as a result the three-eyed god appeared before her.

38. He then asked her to tell him what her desire was.

The goddess said:

39. These mighty attendants of mine are in need of food. Please give them something suitable to eat. Otherwise, O lord, they may be eating me.

Rudra said:

40. "O resplendent Kālarātri, I shall tell you about the food for them. Please listen.

41-42. She who, while in pregnancy, wears the cloth of another woman, or touches a man (other than her husband), let her be (the food) for some of them on earth.

43. Where there are foibles among the ignorant, the occasion may be taken advantage of as an offering for some of them.

44. Others may take advantage of crevices in rooms for child-birth and snatch away the newborn ones.

45. Still others may satisfy their hunger by possessing the bodies of women standing with tears in houses, fields, lakes, tanks and gardens thinking of men (other than their own husbands)".

46-47. Telling the goddess thus and seeing Ruru and his army lying dead, the three-eyed god began to praise her.

Rudra said:

48. "Hail goddess Cāmuṇḍā, hail the snatcher of all beings, hail omniscient Kālarātri, bow to you.

1. Usually the name is taken as due to her killing the two demons, Caṇḍa and Muṇḍa.

49. O you of universal form, the auspicious, pure, three-eyed, fierce, benevolent, the great illusion, the great beginning.

50. Speedy like the mind, victory, the cause of growth, fierce-eyed, settler of all agitation, the great devastation, attractive in body, the lover of dance.

51. Fierce, black-coloured, remover of sins, with noose and and rod in hand, of frightening appearance.

52. Cāmuṇḍā, with flaming mouth, sharp teeth, mighty, sitting in a hundred vehicles, sitting on the dead.

53. Possessed of threatening big eyes, striking terror in all beings, furious.

54. Kāli, Karāli, Kālarātri, bow to you".

55. Thus praised by god Rudra, the great goddess became very much pleased and asked him to seek any boon he wished.

Rudra said:

56. "May you be pleased to grant desires of those who recite this stotra of yours.

57. He who recites this with devotion thrice a day, may attain sons, grandsons, cattle and affluence.

58. He who listens to this account of the Triple power, may he be freed of all sins and made to attain beatitude".

59. Having praised the goddess Cāmuṇḍā thus, lord Rudra disappeared and the gods retired to their abodes.

60. He who knows about the origin of the goddess in this three-fold form, becomes freed from all bondages and attains supreme bliss.

61. A king who has lost his kingdom, regains it free from all troubles, if for one year he worships her fasting on Aṣṭamī, Navamī and Caturdaśī.

62. This Triple power brings success in diplomacy.

63. This great goddess of creation, when white, is of Sāttvic nature and pertains to Brahmā. The same, when red, is of Rājasic nature and is called Vaiṣṇavī (pertaining to Viṣṇu).

64. The same, when black, is of Tāmasic nature and is known as Raudrī (pertaining to Rudra).

65. Just as the same supreme soul manifests itself in three forms (Brahmā, Viṣṇu and Rudra), so the same power manifests itself in three different forms based on function.

66. He who listens to the origin of this Triple power, becomes free from all sins and attains the highest bliss.

67. He who listens to the same on the Navamī tithi with great attention, becomes free from fears and attains a kingdom.

68. He who keeps it written in his house, gets it immune from fire, thiefs and snakes.

69. He who worships the book in which it is written, gets the whole world in his favour. He gets children, money, grain, kine and noble women.

70. He who has it in his house, gets jewels, horses, cows, servants, servant maids and all other kinds of wealth.

Varāha said:

71. O Earth, I have now told you about the secret and the greatness of Rudra.

72. Cāmuṇḍā has different forms numbering nine crores. Cāmuṇḍā is the Tamasic power which pertains to Rudra.

73. Vaiṣṇavī has different forms numbering eighteen crores. Vaiṣṇavī is the Rājasic Power of protection which pertains to Viṣṇu.

74. Brāhmī has different forms countless in number.

75. O Earth, to each one of these Śiva creates a form of himself to be their husbands.

76. So Rudra becomes pleased with those who worship them and grants all that they desire.

CHAPTER NINETYSEVEN

The greatness of Rudra

Varāha said:

1. O Earth, now listen to the origin of Rudra Vrata, by knowing which one gets freed from all sins.

2. The red-eyed and tawny-coloured Rudra who was created by Brahmā in his third birth, was borne by him in pleasure on his shoulder.

3-4. When he was thus on the shoulder, the fifth head of Brahmā told Rudra the Ātharvaṇa mantra by which release is obtained.

5. "O Kapālin, Rudra, Babhru, Bhava, Kairāta, Suvrata, my valiant and broad-eyed son, do protect this world".

6. When Rudra was thus addressed by the names which he would be getting in future he was angry at the word 'Kapāla' used and clipped off that (fifth) head.

7. The head was clipped off by the nail in the left thumb, but it got attached to the hand.

8. Having plucked out the head, Rudra, however, spoke to Brahmā in humility.

Rudra said:

9. O lord, please tell me how this cut-off head can be made to fall from my hand and how I can make atonement for this sin.

Brahmā said:

10. "O Rudra, perform the vrata called Kāpālika by your own prowess and following the right Samayācāra."

11. Thus said by Brahmā, Rudra went to the holy mountain Mahendra to make atonement for his sin.

12. Remaining there, Rudra broke that head into three. He separated the hair on the head and with it made his yajñopavīta.

13. He made a bead of the bones. One part of the skull, full of blood, remained in his hand.

14-15. Another he made into smaller parts and placed them on his matted hair. Then the great god wandered over the whole earth with its seven islands, bathing in the holy Tīrthas every day; first he bathed in the sea and then in the Ganges.

16. He went to river Sarasvatī and then the confluence of the Ganges and Yamunā. He then went to river Śatadru and from there to the great river Devikā.

17. He then bathed in Vitastā, Candrabhāgā, Gomatī, Sindhu, Tuṅgabhadrā, Godāvarī and Gaṇḍakī.

18. He went to the great Śiva temple in Nepal and then to Dāruvana in Kedāra.

19. He visited Bhadreśvara and then the very holy Gayā and there propitiated the Pitṛs.

20. Thus, O Earth, he quickly traversed the whole earth.

21-22. In the sixth year of his wandering, his only dress,

a lion cloth tied to the waist-string, fell down and he became the naked Kāpālika.

23. Wandering again for the next two years from one holy place to another, he attempted to cast off the piece of skull in his hand but could not.

24. For another two years he continued the same but in vain.

25. He then spent one year in the holy Himālaya mountain.

26. For another year also he did the same in great excitement.

27. The next two years Rudra wandered about visiting very ancient holy places.

28. O Earth, in the twelfth year, he went to Vārāṇasī and had his bath there.

29. When he was dipping himself in river Gaṅgā there, Brahmā's skull in his hand released itself.

30. This tīrtha in Gaṅgā, thereafter came to be known as 'Kapālamocana'.

31. Going to the place Harihara and bathing in Devāṅgada and worshipping Someśvara, he went to Cakratīrtha.

32. Bathing there and worshipping the deity Trijaleśvara, he went to Ayodhyā and from there to Vārāṇasī.

33. At the end of twelve years, the skull in his hand was made to fall by the force of the Gaṇas moving in the borders.

34. This place became the holy tīrtha named Kapālamocana.

35. He bathed in the Gaṅgā there, worshipped Viśveśvara and became free from the sin of Brahmahatyā.

36. The tīrtha Kapālamocana is well known in the world, by bathing in which one gets absolved of the sin of killing a Brahmin.[1]

37. Seeing the skull fall, Brahmā arrived there together with Devas, and said:

Brahmā said:

38. "O Rudra, be you the propounder of the righteous path in the world. Since you wandered in the world with *Kapāla*

1. Verses 31 to 36 seem to be an interpolation stating the same matter as in the verses before with the change that the skull was made to fall by the Gaṇas instead of its dropping on its own accord.

(skull) in hand, the Vrata relating to you will be known as *Nagnakāpāla*.

39. Since you attained reddish-brown colour while wandering in the Himālaya, the Vrata will be known as *Bābhravya*.

40. Since you became *Śuddha* (purified) in this place, the Vrata will be *Śuddhaśaiva*, highly purificatory.

41. I will impart the śāstras only to those who duly worship you at first.

42. He who performs these Vratas which you did first, will be absolved of even the sin of killing a Brahmin.

43. The Vratas performed by you as a Nagnakāpāla (naked holding the skull), Bābhravya (as pure Śiva), will be known by the respective names.

44. Following this, those who duly worship you, to them you may impart briefly with the rituals all śāstras, the Pāśupata Śāstra in particular".

45. Told thus by Brahmā, Rudra became extremely pleased, and hailed by Devas, he went to Kailāsa.

46. Brahmā departed with Devas to the celestial world, and then Devas went to their abodes.

Varāha said:

47. I have thus told you about the greatness of Rudra and what he did in this world.

CHAPTER NINETYEIGHT

Mokṣa of Satyatapas[1]

Earth said:

1-2. O lord, you said formerly that there is much that is interesting to be said about Satyatapas, the Brahmin who became a hunter and who saved Āruṇi from a tiger and propitiated Durvāsas and then went to Himālayas.

1. In the text the chapter is named *Parvādhyāya*.

3. I am now very much eager to know this. Be pleased to tell me.

Varāha said:

4. Satyatapas was a Brahmin in the line of Bhṛgu, but because of his association with Dasyus (a cruel uncivilised tribe), himself became one like them.

5. After a long time, by the contact with sages, he became a Brahmin again and got instruction from Durvāsas in particular.

6. On the northern side of mount Himavān there is a holy river called Puṣyabhadrā, on its bank a beautiful slab called Citraśilā and a big banyan tree called Bhadra.

7. There Satyatapas was performing severe penance.

8. Once when he was cutting with his axe sticks (for homa), he happened to cut his left fore finger.

9. At the broken part there were only ashes, neither blood nor flesh nor marrow. He put the broken finger in its place and it got united as before.

10. This wonder was seen by a Kinnara couple that had resorted to the banyan tree Bhadra the previous night.

11. When the couple returned to Indraloka in the morning, they were asked by Indra and Yakṣas, Gandharvas and Kinnaras there to tell them if there was anything wonderful to be narrated.

12-15. The Kinnara couple then narrated about their being near Rudrasaras, the wonder relating to Satyatapas they saw on the bank of river Puṣyabhadrā, the exudation of ashes from his broken finger and all that.

16-17. Surprised at this, Indra suggested to Viṣṇu that they may go to the place of wonder mentioned by the Kinnara pair on the slopes of the Himālayas.

18. Viṣṇu then transformed himself into a boar and Indra into a hunter, and both went near the sage (Satyatapas).

19. Viṣṇu in the form of the boar appeared within the sight of the sage, alternately revealing and hiding himself.

20. Soon appeared there Indra also (in the guise of the hunter) with bow and arrow in hand and asked sage Satyatapas:

21. "O sage, did you see here a big boar? I want to kill it for the food of my family".

22. Asked thus, the sage began to think: "If I show him the boar now, it will surely be killed by him.

23. If I don't, his family will famish. This hunter with his wife and children, is in great hunger.

24. The boar hit by the arrow has sought refuge in my hermitage. What shall I do?".

25. When thus in a dilemma, a thought occurred to him, and he exclaimed:

26. "The eye is directed to see the moving objects and the tongue is directed to speak to the hunter. There is no eye now to see or the tongue to speak. Does the tongue really have the eye?".

27. Hearing this, both Indra and Viṣṇu were pleased, and showing their genuine forms, offered to grant him a boon.

Hearing this Satyatapas said:

28. "Really there is nothing to be asked, after seeing you both before me here in this earth. I am fully gratified.

29. Still I shall ask: One, when Brahmins honour other Brahmins at the sight of the new moon and full moon with devotion, let their acquired sin disappear in the course of a month.

30. Another, let me attain full liberation".

31. They granted him both the boons asked for and disappeared. Satyatapas too felt in his heart to have become one with Brahman.

32. While the sage was thus remaining there fully gratified, his guru Āruṇi came there after going round the world visiting the holy spots.

33. In great devotion he honoured the Guru with a seat, Pādya, Ācamana and Godāna.

34. Āruṇi then spoke to him, seeing him full of humility and freed from all sins.

Āruṇi said:

35. "You have achieved in full the aim of penance and you have now become Brahman. Now it is the time for your liberation along with me,

36. Arise, my son, we shall go to the supreme Abode, after reaching which there will be no rebirth".

37. Then both of them, Satyatapas and Āruni, meditated on Lord Nārāyaṇa and became merged in him.

38. He who listens to this Parvādhyāya in full or reads it to others, attains all that he desires.

CHAPTER NINETYNINE

Greatness of Tiladhenu[1]

Earth said:

1. She who is Māyā and arose out of the body of Brahmā who was born of Avyakta, became the eight-armed Gāyatrī and fought Caitrāsura.

2. The same goddess became Nandā to achieve the purpose of Devas. Then she became Vaiṣṇavī at the instance of Brahmā for killing Mahiṣāsura. Be pleased to tell me how all this was done.

Varāha said:

3. She is the goddess Gaṅgā very much loved by Lord Śiva. Being given his own abode, she is omniscient.

4. In Svāyambhuva (time), she killed as Vaiṣṇavī in the Mandara mountain the demon Mahiṣa.

5. Then in the Vindhya as Nandā, the demon Caitra was killed.

6. Or (it may also be understood) she is the power of knowledge and Mahiṣa the embodiment of ignorance. Doubtless, ignorance is to be overcome by knowledge.

7. For the embodied form we get the story. For the abstract form the place is the heart itself. This is proclaimed by Vedic statements and established by the exponents of the Vedas.

8. Now listen, O Earth, to the propitiation of Viṣṇu, the greatest of gods, as a result of which the five great sins are destroyed and sons and wealth are acquired.

1. Hollow metal cow filled with sesamum.

9. And he who is oppressed by poverty and diseases like leprosy and is issueless, attains quickly prosperity, long and healthy life and children.

10. He who sees Lord Nārāyaṇa with goddess Lakṣmī in the maṇḍala with due rites.

11. The lord who is self-born and is the embodiment of mantra, as directed by the priest.

12. During all Dvādaśī days, particularly on the Dvādaśī day in the bright half of the month Kārttika.

13. Or during the change of month or solar and lunar eclipses.

14. To him occurs great happiness, dissolution of all sins, and other deities also get propitiated.

15. The priest should test for one year whoever approaches him, be he Brahmin, Kṣatriya or Vaiśya, as to his conduct and eligibility as true devotee.

16. The devotee should also treat the priest with the same constant devotion as for Viṣṇu.

17. At the end of the year he should propitiate the priest saying.

18. "O worthy lord, I desire by your grace all prosperity in this world and then to cross this ocean of worldly existence".

19. Thus should he worship the Guru taking him to be Lord Viṣṇu before him.

20. Thus worshipped, the Guru should on the Daśamī day in the month of Kārttika, get him clean the teeth with mantras using the twig of a sappy tree and sleep near the deity.

21. He will see dreams and he should tell them to the Guru, who will then know whether it augurs well or ill.

22. On the Ekādaśī day the devotee should fast and go to the temple after bath.

23. Then Guru should prepare the maṇḍala on the floor according to prescription and draw there the cakra Ṣoḍaśāra, Sarvatobhadra or Aṣṭapatra[1] and ask the devotee to see it.

24. Then he should cover the eyes of the devotees with white cloth and ask them to enter the place of worship in the order of their Varṇa (Brāhmaṇa, Kṣatriya and Vaiśya).

---

1. These are diagrams of different kinds to be drawn on the floor according to specifications.

25. The maṇḍala Navanābha should then be arranged with different colours.

26. Then worship should be done for the Dikpālas in their respective positions in the maṇḍala, Indra in the east, Agni in the south-east.

27. Yama in the south, Nirṛti in the south-west, Varuṇa in the west, Vāyu in the south-west.

28. Kubera in the north and Īśāna in the north-east.

29. At the centre of the *Padma* (lotus in the middle of the diagram), worship should be done to the great lord Viṣṇu.

30. In the petal on the east of the Padma, worship should be offered to Balabhadra, in the one on the south to Pradyumna, in the one on the west to Aniruddha and in the one on the north to Vāsudeva, the destroyer of all sins.

31. (Of the four objects in the hands of Viṣṇu) the conch should be placed on the north-east, the disc on the south-east, the club on the north-west and the lotus on the south-west.

32. In the north-east, again, may be placed the mace (*musala*). Garuḍa should be on the right and Lakṣmī on the left of the lord.

33. The bow and the sword are to be placed in front, special position is to be given for Śrīvatsa (the mark on Viṣṇu's body) and Kaustubha (the jewel he wears).

34. After performing worship to lord Janārdana in this way, in the petals in the diagram on the eight directions, a pot each filled with water should be placed. A ninth pot pertaining to Viṣṇu also should be placed (in the middle).

35. The water in the pot pertaining to Viṣṇu should be poured on the devotee desirous of mokṣa.

36. The water in the pot pertaining to Indra (the one placed on the east) should be poured on him who is desirous of prosperity and the same in the one pertaining to Agni (the one placed on north-east) on him who is desirous of great fame.

37. The water in the pot pertaining to Yama (the one placed on the South) should be poured on the devotee desirous of long life, and the same on the one relating to Nirṛti (placed on the south-west) on him who desires the annihilation of the wicked.

38. The water in the pot pertaining to Varuṇa (the one placed on the west) should be poured on him who is desirous of tranquility and the same on the one relating to Vāyu (the one

placed on the north-west) on him who desires the destruction of his sins. The water in the pot pertaining to Kubera (the one placed on the north)should be poured on him who desires wealth.

39. The water in the pot pertaining to Īśāna (the one placed on the north-west) should be poured on him who desires knowledge or kingship.

40. Even when bathed in the water of one of these, one becomes free from sins, acquires profound knowledge and attains great skill. What then, when he is bathed in all the nine? All his sins disappear, he becomes equal to Viṣṇu and becomes a king.

41. The Guru may also perform worship to the guardian deities of different directions (Indra and others) one after another in the respective spots.

42. And then lead there the blind-folded devotees and make them circumambulate the maṇḍala.

43. The rituals relating to Varuṇa, Vāyu and Soma should then be performed and the order of propitiation should be told.

44. Namely, high Brahmins, Vedas, Viṣṇu, Brahmā, Rudra, Āditya, Agni, the lokapālas (deities guarding the eight directions), the planets, preceptor, Vaiṣṇavas and the devotee who has taken the vow.

45. Then the homa should be performed with the mantra *Om namo Bhagavate sarvarūpiṇe huṁ phaṭ svāhā.*

46. Homa should be made in the blazing fire with the (above) Ṣodaśākṣara mantra, and rituals like Garbhādhāna should be done.

47. The offering should be made thrice in fire in front of the deity. At the end of the homa, the devotee who has undertaken the vow should give dakṣiṇā to the Guru.

48. A king may give as dakṣiṇā elephants, horses, jewels, gold and land; others according to capacity.

49. O Earth, the merit attained by this cannot be described even for a hundred years.

50. If the person with the vow listens to Varāha, it is equivalent to reciting the Vedas, Purāṇas and mantras.

51-52. He gets double the merit of reciting them at Puṣkara tīrtha, Prayāga, Kurukṣetra or Vārāṇasī or during eclipses or Viṣu.

53. Even Devas perform penance and meditation, and wonder when they will be born in Bhāratavarṣa.

54. Become devotees with vow, listen to Varāha, and leaving the body with its sixteen elements.

55. Reach the position from which there is no return. They think so and say the same.

56. An old story is illustrated in this connection in the form of conversation between Vasiṣṭha and Śveta.

57. In the region Ilāvṛta there lived a highly saintly king named Śveta.

58. He wished to gift away all his verduous land and consulted sage Vasiṣṭha on the matter.

59. "O great sage, I wish to give away the entire continent of mine to Brahmins. Please permit me". Vasiṣṭha told the king.

60. "O king, give them food conducive to all times. If food is given, what does become not given?

61. The gift of food is superior to all other gifts. All beings arise from food, and they all grow by food.

62. Therefore, O king, resort to giving food". The king, however, did not follow the advice of Vasiṣṭha.

63. He called Brahmins and gave them gems, cloth, ornaments and fine urban land with money.

64. He even gave them majestic elephants. After this, once having conquered the whole earth, he called his family priest Vasiṣṭha again and told him:

65. "O great sage, I wish to perform a hundred Aśvamedha sacrifices".

66. He then performed the sacrifice and gave the Brahmins gold, silver and copper but not food or drink thinking it to be an insignificant thing.

67. O Earth, this affluent king, in due course, became dead.

68. In the world beyond, he became oppressed by hunger, and thirst in particular.

69-70. He went to the mountain Śveta and from there collected from the place where his mortal body was cremated, all the bones and began to lick them.

71. He then got into his aerial car and returned to heaven. (He used to do this quite often).

72. After a long time, the king was seen thus licking the bones by sage Vasiṣṭha. The sage asked him why he was feeding on his own bones.

73. Thus asked by Vasiṣṭha, king Śveta replied.

74. "O sage, I am hungry and as I have not gifted food or drink, so hunger and thirst overpower me".

75. Told thus by the king, Vasiṣṭha addressed him again.

76. "What can I do for you, particularly now that you are hungry. What is not given never serves any one at any time.

77. By giving gold and gems, one enjoys pleasures. But by giving food and drink, one attains everything.

78. That was not given by you, being under the impression that it was a trifle.

Śveta said:

79. Please tell me how I can attain its fruit, although I have not given food. I request you most earnestly.

Vasiṣṭha said:

80. There is one way to attain it. I shall tell you that. Please listen.

81. In days of yore, there was a famous king named Vinītāśva. He began a great sacrifice called Sarvamedha.

82. During the sacrifice, he gave to the Brahmins cows, elephants and money, but not food, just as you did.

83. After a long time he died in river Gaṅgā and because of the great merit he had acquired, he went to heaven as you too did.

84-85. He too became very much hungry in the same manner and went to the Nīla mountain on the bank of the river Gaṅgā, in a resplendant aerial car and saw there his own body.

86. He also saw there on the bank of Gaṅgā his priest and asked him the cause of his hunger (and the means to overcome it).

87-88. The priest asked him to quickly make gifts of Tiladhenu, Jaladhenu, Ghṛtadhenu and Rasadhenu so that he may be rid of his extreme hunger.[1]

---

1. These are models of cows with sesamum, water, clarified butter and sugarcane juice inside.

89. The effect will last as long as the sun and moon are in the sky".

The king then asked him again:

Vinītāśva said:

90. O Brahmin, tell me how Tiladhenu (cow of sesamum) is to be given so that I may peacefully enjoy heaven.

The priest said:

91. Listen to me. I shall tell you how Tiladhenu is to be given.

92. Four Kuḍavas make one Prastha. The cow should be of sixteen prasthas and the calf of four prasthas. The nose should be of sandal and the tongue of gur.

93. The tail should be adorned with bells and the horns should be made of gold.

94. The body should be of bronze and hoofs of silver. As is the cow (so should be the calf). This should be then given to the Brahmin.

95. On its back should be placed antelope's skin and the rope should be adorned with gems.

96. The gift should be made with mantra and with herbs uttering.

97. "May I get food, may I get water good, O cow of sesamum given to the Brahmin, I hold you with devotion for the sake of my family. I bow to you, may you be pleased to grant my desire".

98. Give away Tiladhenu in this way. I fulfil all your desires.

99. He who listens to this intently or makes the gift or makes one give such a gift, gets freed of all sins and reaches the abode of Viṣṇu.

CHAPTER ONE HUNDRED

Greatness of Jaladhenu

The priest said:

1. I shall now tell you about Jaladhenu. On a holy day clean the floor of the size of a cow's skin with cowdung.

2. In its middle, place a pot full of water with perfumes, camphor and sandal paste.

3. Consider that as the cow and another full of water as the calf.

4. Place on all sides the tender sprouts of Dūrvā grass and duly decorate with garlands.

5. Put on the pot fine gems and different kinds of fine fragrance.

6. Place also different kinds of grain on all sides.

7. Place four vessels on the four sides respectively filled with ghee, curd, honey and gur.

8. The face should be of gold, horns of lead and eyes of pearl.

9. The back should be of copper and (the rest of) the body of bronze and hairs to be of darbha. The tail should be of strings with black bells.

10. There should be garlands on the neck, gur on the face and teeth should be of seashells. The tongue should be of strings with black bells.

11. The feet should be of Sugarcane with sandalpaste and flower. Cover it then with cloth and place it on an antelope's skin. Then give it to a Brahmin after giving him sandalpaste and flowers.

12-13. The person to whom it is given should be good, learned in Veda, one with a family and devoted to duty.

14. He who gives the gift, sees it or hears about it and he who receives it, all get freed of their sins.

15. Even those who have the sin of killing a Brahmin, father or cow, or of drinking liquor or of adultery with his teacher's wife, get absolved of it and go to Viṣṇu's abode.

16. The performer of an Aśvamedha with all gifts and dakṣiṇas and the giver of a Jaladhenu are equals.

17. The giver of Jaladhenu may live on water alone for a day and the receiver in the same manner for three days.

18. The giver of Jaladhenu goes to the place where rivers are full of milk and ponds are full of honey and where always swells the music of the Apsarases.

19. He who gives Jaladhenu, he who causes it to be given and he who receives it, all get merged in Viṣṇu.

20. He who speaks about the greatness of the gift of Jaladhenu and he who listens to it go to heaven, getting rid of all sins.

CHAPTER ONE HUNDRED AND ONE

Greatness of Rasadhenu

The priest said:

1. I shall now tell you about the rules of the gift of Rasa dhenu in brief.

2. On the floor smeared (with cowdung) place an antelope's skin covered with kuśa grass and over it a pot filled with sugarcane juice (and also the metal cow) and a calf of one-fourth its size on its side.

3. Its feet should be of sugarcane sticks and hoofs should be of silver.

4-5. The horns should be of gold, the tail of cloth, the udder of butter, the face and tongue of gur.

6. The teeth should be of fruits and back made of copper, the hairs of flower and eyes of pearl. It should be well decorated and scented with sandal paste.

7. Seven (different kinds of) cereals should be placed near it and lamps lit on the four sides.

8. Four vessels filled with sesamum should be placed one on each side.

9. The person desirous of heaven should make the gift of Rasadhenu.

10. The giver and the recipient attain the result of drinking the sacrificial soma juice if they fast for a day before the gift.

11. Those who see the gift being made also attain salvation.

12. With the mantras stated before, the donor should pray and then give it to the recipient.

13. Besides himself he leads to a permanent position in heaven ten generations of his ancestors and ten generations of his successors.

14. Thus I have told you, O king, about Rasadhenu. Follow it and attain supreme bliss.

15. He who reads this account every day or listens to it in reverence, goes to the world of Viṣṇu, being freed of all sins.

CHAPTER ONE HUNDRED AND TWO

The greatness of Guḍadhenu

The priest said:

1. I shall now tell you about Guḍadhenu, the gift of which accomplishes all desires and endows wealth.

2. On the floor smeared (with cowdung) place an antelope's skin covered with kuśa grass. Spread a cloth on it and place in it the cow made of gur along with the calf and a bronze milking vessel.

3. The face should be of gold and teeth of pearls. The neck should be full of gems and nose of sandal paste.

4. The horns are to be of Agaru sticks and the back of copper. The tail is to be of silk and well decorated.

5. The feet are to be of sugarcane and hoofs of silver. A velvet cloth is to be put on it and fitted with bells.

6. The ears are to be of brass and the udder to be of butter. Different kinds of fruits are to be placed all around.

7. The best Guḍadhenu is one which is four ādhāras (in weight), its calf may be half or one-fourth its weight.

8. The medium is the one with half its weight and the inferior is the one with a quarter of the weight. The poor may have it of the size according to capacity.

9. Then according to means, worship should be performed to this, as also for the Brahmin to whom it is to be given.

10. This is to be done with sandal paste, flowers, ghee and other offerings and lamp.

11. It should be given to a Vedic Brahmin, preferably one who has performed sacrifices, with a hundred pieces of gold, or half or even a quarter of it.

12. And in the absence of capacity even for that, with a hundred or fifty, together with ear-rings, umbrella and footwear.

13. And then should be uttered the mantra: "O virile Guḍadhenu, the bestower of all prosperity, be pleased to provide me with food and drink as a result of this dāna".

14. The mantras cited before may also be recited.

15. The giver should face east while giving it to the Brahmin.

16. The gift of such a cow is proclaimed to be efficacious in removing the sins committed through thought, word or deed and of all that is false.

17. Those who witness the gift of such a cow attain salvation. The rivers in that place flow with milk and marshes produce ghee. The sages and Siddhas flock there.

18. The giver takes himself and those in the past ten and future ten generations in his family to the world of Viṣṇu.

19. For this dāna the equinoxes, solstices and the new moon and full moon days are particularly meritorious.

20. The gift should be made only to a deserving person and with full sincerity.

21. It then fulfils all wishes, removes all sins, provides enjoyment and finally liberation.

22. By the blessing of Guḍadhenu one enjoys all prosperity, good health and long life.

23. All adversity is overcome and the abode of Viṣṇu is attained.

24. Never does he, at any time, meet with any distress or discomfort.

25. He who recites this or listens to this or advises others on its basis, lives in this world with all happiness and in the world beyond for long honoured by the gods.

CHAPTER ONE HUNDRED AND THREE

Greatness of Śarkarādhenu

The priest said:

1. Listen, O king, similarly to the account about Śarkarādhenu (cow of sugarcandy).

2. On the floor smeared (with cowdung) place antelope's skin and over it kuśa grass and then cow made of sugarcandy.

3. The best is one made of four weights of sugarcandy and its calf of one-fourth the quantity; the medium is one of half this quantity and the inferior one of a single unit of weight. In all cases the calf is to be of one-fourth the weight of the cow.

4. (The money to go with it) may be above one hundred and eight, but it may also be according to one's capacity and without straining oneself.

5. Cereals of different kinds should be placed on all the four sides.

6. The face and horns should be of gold, eyes of pearls and tongue of flour. The face should be smeared with sugar.

7. Round the neck should be a silken band. The feet should be of sugarcane, the hoofs of silver and udder of butter.

8. The ears should be of grass. The cow should be adorned with five gems and white chowries and cloth should be thrown over it.

9. It should then be decorated with sandalpaste and flowers and given to a poor, good and intelligent Brahmin with a family.

10. It should not be given to one who is bad or jealous.

11. Solstices, equinoxes and other holy days are particularly good for this dāna.

12. It is particularly good if it is given to a deserving Vedic Brahmin who happens to come to the house.

13. The gift should be made facing east or north and keeping the cow faced east and holding its tail, and the calf on its northern side.

14. The mantras prescribed for the gift should be recited and the Brahmin to whom it is to be given should be honoured with ear-rings.

15. In his hand should be placed sandalpaste and flowers and dakṣiṇā according to one's means.

16. Without looking at his face, the gift of the cow should be made. The giver may live on sugarcandy for one day and the recipient for three days.

17. The cow is the remover of all sins and bestower of all that is wished for. So one who gifts it attains all desires.

18. Those who see the gift being made, also attain salvation.

19. He who listens to this or reads this becomes purified of all sins and attains the abode of Viṣṇu.

CHAPTER ONE HUNDRED AND FOUR

The greatness of Madhudhenu

The priest said:

1. I shall now tell you about Madhudhenu (cow of honey) which removes all sins.

2. On the floor smeared (with cowdung) and on which is placed antelope's skin with kuśa grass spread over it, the cow of honey made with sixteen pots of it and the calf of a fourth of its size should be placed.

3. The face should be of gold and the horns of Agaru. The back should be of copper and dewlap of bands of silk.

4. The feet should be of sugarcane covered with white velvet. Gur should be smeared on the face and sugar on the tongue.

5. The hips should be of flowers and the teeth of fruits. The hairs should be of darbha grass and the hoofs of silver.

6. The ears should be of brass. Seven cereals should be spread all round in the prescribed manner and measure.

7. Four vessels of sesamum should be placed, one on each side. The cow should then be adorned with a pair of cloths and jewels on the neck.

8. A bronze milking vessel is also to be placed. Worship should then be done with sandalpaste and flowers.

9. It may be gifted to a deserving Brahmin at any time, but the solstices, equinoxes, change of month and eclipses are particularly sacred.

10. The Madhudhenu is to be given to a poor Vedic Brahmin who has performed sacrifices and is born in the region Āryāvarta.

11. The gift is to be made with water and dakṣiṇā, uttering the mantras and holding the cow by its tail.

12. This cow pleases all gods and is for the well-being of all.

13. It is to be given to the Brahmin saying, "O Madhudhenu, I bow to you; may all my ancestors be pleased.

14. I bow to you again; I hold you, O yielder of wishes, for the sake of my family."

15. After the cow, umbrella and footwear also should be given.

16. After giving the cow, the giver may live on milk and honey for a day and the recipient similarly for three days.

17. Now listen to the good that arises out of it.

18. In the place where this gift is made, rivers flow with honey and marshes turn into pāyasa. Sages and Siddhas flock there.

19. The giver enjoys all pleasures in this world and goes to the world of Brahmā. After living there long, he returns to the earth.

20. Then he enjoys pleasures in abundance and goes to the world of Viṣṇu.

21. In addition for himself, he acquires union with Viṣṇu for ten past generations and ten future generations in his family.

22. He who listens to this or recites to others gets free from all sins and goes to the world of Viṣṇu.

CHAPTER ONE HUNDRED AND FIVE

The greatness of Kṣīradhenu

The priest said:

1. Listen, O king, I shall tell you about Kṣīradhenu (cow of milk) now.

2. On the floor smeared with cowdung over an area of a cow's hide, spread Kuśa grass over a black antelope's skin.

3. Place on it a small heap of cowdung and over it a pot full of milk, and another, a fourth of its size, to represent the calf.

4. The face is to be of gold, the horns of sandalwood or Agaru, ears to be of brass.

5. The mouth is to be of gur, tongue of sugar, teeth of white seeds and eyes of pearl.

6. The feet are to be of sugarcane, the hairs to be of darbha grass. A white velvet is to be thrown over it. The back is to be of copper and the rest of the body of bronze and tail of silken threads.

7. The udder is to be of butter, the hoofs to be of silver and the five gems.

8. Vessels of sesamum are to be placed on the four sides and those containing seven grains all around.

9. The Kṣīradhenu is to be arranged like this, and it should be covered with a pair of cloths and worshipped with sandal-paste, flower, dhūpa, dīpa etc.

10. Then it should be given away to a Brahmin together with clothes, ear-rings, footwear and Umbrella.

11. Reciting the mantras *āpyāyasva* etc. and *āśrayaḥ sarva-bhūtānām* etc.

12. The mantra *āpyāyasva* etc., is also for propitiating the Kṣīradhenu. The other mantra is to be recited by the recipient also.

13. This is the rule about this gift. Those who see the gift being made also reach heaven.

14. O king, listen to the benefit of making the gift with a thousand gold coins or a hundred ones or even according to capacity.

15. He who does this remains in the world of Indra for sixty thousand years.

16. He then goes to the world of Brahmā with his departed ancestors and enjoys there for a long time.

17. Anointed with fine perfume and wearing divine garlands, he ascends an aerial car and goes to the world of Viṣṇu.

18. Which is resplendent like the twelve suns and where swells the vocal and instrumental music and where dance the Apsarases. Living there long he finally becomes one with Viṣṇu.

19. O king, he who listens to this or recites this with devotion, gets rid of all sins and goes to the world of Viṣṇu.

CHAPTER ONE HUNDRED AND SIX

The greatness of Dadhidhenu

The priest said:

1. O king, now listen to the rules of gifts of Dadhidhenu (cow of curd).

2. On the floor smeared with cowdung over the area of a cow's hide and strewn with flowers, spread kuśa grass over an antelope's skin.

3. Then spread the seven cereals and install a pot of curd, and another, a fourth of its size, to represent the calf.

4. Place on it a pair of clothes and then perform worship with flowers and sandal paste.

5. Give it away to a good-natured Brahmin from a good family and endowed with qualities like patience and the like, holding it by the tail.

6. And giving along with it coins, ear-rings, footwear and umbrella and uttering the mantra *dadhikrāvṇo* etc.

7. The giver of Dadhidhenu may live on curd alone for a day and the recipient in the same manner for three days.

8. Those who see the giving away of Dadhidhenu also attain salvation.

9. He who listens to this or recites it for others, gets the result equivalent to Aśvamedha sacrifice and goes to the world of Viṣṇu.

CHAPTER ONE HUNDRED AND SEVEN

The greatness of Navanītadhenu

The priest said:

1. O king, now listen to the rules relating to Navanītadhenu (cow of butter) by which one gets freed from all sins.

2. On the floor smeared with cowdung for an area of a cow's hide, spread a black antelope's skin.

3. Place on it a pot containing butter of the measure of one prastha, and another, a fourth of its size, to represent the calf on its northern side.

4. The cow should have horns of gold, eyes of pearl, tongue of gur.

5. Lips of flower, teeth of seeds, dewlap of white threads.

6. Udder of butter, feet of sugarcane, back of copper, hoofs of silver and hair of darbha grass.

7. Four pots of sesamum are to be placed, one on each side.

8. Place a pair of clothes on it, decorate it with sandalpaste and flowers, kindle lamps on all sides and then give it away to a Brahmin.

9. The mantras stated for the other Dhenus, should be recited here also, (and in addition).

10. "When the ocean was churned by devas and asuras, the divine ambrosia that arose is this butter. I bow to you, O butter, the elixir of all beings."

11. Uttering this, the cow should be given to a Brahmin with a family to support, and he should take it to his house.

12. The giver may live on butter for one day and the recipient similarly for three days.

13. He who witnesses the gift of Dadhidhenu gets free from all sins and becomes merged in Śiva.

14. He remains in the world of Viṣṇu with his ancestors as well as descendants till the end of the world.

15. He who intently listens to this or recites it to others, becomes purified and remains in the world of Viṣṇu.

CHAPTER ONE HUNDRED AND EIGHT

The greatness of Lavaṇadhenu

The priest said:

1. O king, now listen to the rules relating to Lavaṇadhenu (cow of salt).

2. On the floor smeared (with cowdung), spread kuśa grass over an antelope's skin and place on it a cow made of salt of the measure of sixteen prasthas, and a calf a fourth of its size.

3. The feet are to be of sugarcane, face and horns of gold, hoofs of silver.

4. The mouth to be of gur, teeth of fruits, tongue of sugar, nose of sandalpaste, eyes of jewels and ears of leaves, abdomen of sugarcandy and udder of butter.

5. The tail of silken threads, back of copper, hair of darbha and the milking vessel of bronze. It should be decorated with bells and jewels.

6. Worship should be performed with sandalpaste, flowers and incense. A pair of cloths should be placed on it and the whole thing gifted to a Brahmin.

7. This gift may be made at any time if it is to ward off evil effects of planets or stars. But eclipses, change of month and solstices are special occasions for it.

8-9. The recipient should be a Brahmin who is well-versed in Vedas, is of good conduct and of a good family.

10-11. This should be done along with a pair of cloths, gift and a woolen shawl and gold according to one's ability.

12. Holding the tail and according to the prescription laid down before.

13-15. The (special) mantra should be uttered "O Brahmin, I bow to you; receive this cow adored by all gods, who knows the tastes of all beings and who is veritably Rudra. O goddess, I bow to you; fulfil all my desires".

16. Such a gift with a thousand or hundred gold pieces, leads one to the heaven of Śiva.

17. He who listens to this intently or recites for others, is removed from all sins and goes to the world of Rudra.

CHAPTER ONE HUNDRED AND NINE

The greatness of Kārpāsadhenu

The priest said:

1. O king, I shall now tell you about the Kārpāsadhenu (cow of cotton) the giving of which leads one to the world of Indra.

2. (This is particularly effective when performed, during equinoxes and solstices and the beginning of the year, and also when the planets are unfavourable or when calamity is foreboden by dreams.

3. Its proper place, O king, is a temple, other sacred spots or where there is a herd of cows.

4. On the floor smeared with cowdung, spread darbha grass and sesamum and place on it the cow (made of cotton) adorned with cloths and sandalpaste and perform worship with incense, lamp and sweets.

5. The best (cow) is the one weighing four bhāras, the medium is the one weighing just half of it and the inferior the one weighing a quarter, but the weight need not be insisted on.

6. The calf should be of one-fourth the weight of the cow.

7. The horns should be of gold, the hoofs of silver, the teeth of different fruits and gems.

8. Then the cow should be invoked with full concentration of mind and gifted to a brahmin with full sincerity.

9. This should be done according to the prescriptions formerly given and with the mantra:

10. "The multitude of Devas will not be there without you. O goddess, raise me up out of this ocean of saṁsāra and protect me."

---

1. One *bhāra* is equivalent to 2000 *palas*.

CHAPTER ONE HUNDRED AND TEN

The greatness of Dhānyadhenu

The priest said:

1. O king, listen. I shall tell you about Dhānyadhenu (cow of grain) by the very mention of which goddess Pārvatī gets pleased.

2. One gets absolved of all sins, like the moon becoming free from the clutches of Rāhu, by performing it during equinoxes, solstices and in the month of Kārttika.

3. The gift of Dhānyadhenu brings about the merit equal to that of ten cows.

4. As in the earlier cases, worship is to be done on the floor smeared with cowdung and covered with antelope's skin.

5. The best (Dhānyadhenu) is the one made of four droṇas of grain, the medium the one made of just half of it. But the quantity need not be insisted upon.

6. The calf should be one-fourth of the cow.

7. The horns should be of gold and the hoofs of silver. The nose should be of 'gomeda' gem or of Agaru or sandalwood.

8. The teeth should be of pearl and mouth of curd and honey. The ears are to be of leaves and the milking vessel of bronze.

9. The feet are to be of sugarcane and tail of silk. There should also be a variety of fruits and gems.

10. The rules are as before, and after performing worship it should be given to a Brahmin together with footwear and umbrella.

11. At the auspicious time, the giver should bathe, dress himself in white cloth, circumambulate the Brahmin thrice and prostrate before him.

12. He should then utter: "O brahmin learned in the Vedas, be pleased to receive this gift so that the great lord Viṣṇu may be pleased.

13-15. Lakṣmī is associated with Viṣṇu, Svāhā with Agni, Śacī with Indra, Gaurī with Śiva, Gāyatrī with Brahmā, Jyotsnā (moonlight) with Candra, Prabhā (lustre) with Sūrya, Buddhi (intellect) with Bṛhaspati and Medhā (intelligence) with Munis (sages). But O goddess (cow), all these remain in you".

16. Saying this, the offering should be made to the Brahmin. He should then be circumabulated and his pardon sought for any lapses unknowingly made.

17. The benefit acquired by the gift of Dhānyadhenu is equivalent to the acquisition of the entire earth with all its gems.

18. Therefore, O king, the gift of Dhānyadhenu should be made as it gives enjoyment and release.

19. It gives prosperity, longevity and health in this life, and a place in the world of Śiva, taken there in a brilliant aerial car attended on by Apsarases.

20. He stays there till he thinks of birth when he comes to earth as the lord of Jambūdvīpa.

21. O king, he who listens to this, becomes freed from all sins, goes to the world of Rudra and is honoured there.

CHAPTER ONE HUNDRED AND ELEVEN

The greatness of Kapilādhenu

The priest said:

1. I shall now tell you about the most important Kapilā dhenu (the brown cow), the giver of which attains the world of Viṣṇu.

2. Following the prescriptions given before, give the (brown coloured) cow along with the calf, well decorated and provided with gems.

3. All the holy places in the world are contained in the head and neck of the brown cow, as ordained by Brahmā.

4-5. He who sprinkles on his head early morning the water poured on the head and neck of the brown cow, burns away all his sins accrued during thirty years, like fire burning away faggots.

6. Circumambulating such a cow is equivalent to circumambulating the whole earth.

7. He who circumambulates it even once, burns away sins acquired in ten births.

8. He who bathes in the urine of the brown cow gets merit equal to that of bathing in Ganges.

9. Bathing in it once, removes sins acquired during the whole life.

10. Lord Brahmā has declared that giving away one brown cow is equivalent to giving away hundred other cows.

11. Even the smell of burning bones of a dead cow is a purifier.

12. Caressing the cow and actually rearing it give the benefit of making the gift of a hundred cows for the cure of ailments.

13. He who gives to a hungry cow grass and water every day gets the merit of performing a Gomedha sacrifice.

14. He gets many aerial cars and is attended on by celestial damsels like so many brilliantly glowing lamps.

15. The different colours of the 'brown cow' species are, first golden brown, second yellowish brown, third rosy red, fourth gurlike brown.

16. Fifth variegated colour, sixth whitish yellow, seventh whitish brown, eighth blackish brown.

17. Ninth reddish brown, tenth tawny in tail, eleventh white in hoof.

18. Such cows with good features and well decorated should be given to a Brahmin. That brings about enjoyment here and liberation hereafter.

19. Giving enjoyment and liberation, it leads one to the path of Viṣṇu.

CHAPTER ONE HUNDRED AND TWELVE

The greatness of cow at childbirth, list of Purāṇas

The priest said:

1. O king, listen to the account of the double-faced cow (the cow just giving birth to the young one) narrated to the Earth in days of yore. This produces great merit.

Earth said:

2. What are the characteristics of the sacred cow referred to as Kapilā created by you in connection with sacrifice?

3. How many varieties of it are distinguished by Brahmā ?

4. O Mādhava, what merit accrues by the gift of a cow in the process of childbirth? I wish to know all this in detail.

Varāha said:

5. O goddess, know the truth about it, sacred and removing all sins, by hearing which one certainly becomes free from all acquired sins.

6. The Kapilā (brown cow) is for Agnihotra and other sacrifices. It was made by Brahmā out of all effulgence.

7. The Kapilā is the holiest of the holy and the most auspicious. It gives important merit.

8. It is the best of all penances, the foremost of all vows, the most important among gifts and the most imperishable of all wealth.

9. It is equivalent to all holy spots in the world and all temples accessible as well as inaccessible.

10. The Brahmins should perform Agnihotra morning and evening with the ghee, curd and milk of Kapilā.

11. They are used with great devotion in Agnihotra, in the offerings with mantras and in hospitality for guests.

12. Those who do so move in aerial cars dazzling like the sun.

13. The Kapilā with its several varieties was made by Brahmā from out of the middle part of the solar globe. Its eyes are brownish yellow. It provides happiness, success and intelligence.

14. All the varieties of Kapilā mentioned before, if they have the right characteristics, are great indeed, and they lead to liberation.

15. In confluences they are particularly efficacious. They have Agni in their tail and face and have complexion like the fire and hence called Āgnāyī.

16. One who receives Kapilā as a gift from a Śūdra should be considered as most lowly like a Caṇḍāla.

17. Therefore let not a Brahmin receive the offering from Śūdras. They are to be kept far away like dogs during sacrifices.

18. They are discarded by the manes during new moon and full moon. They should not be spoken to and nothing should be received from them because they do only sinful deeds.

19. Those (Śūdras) who drink (the milk of) Kapilā make their forefathers eat the filth in the earth for long.

20. Note what happens to the Śūdras who feed on the milk, ghee and butter of the Kapilā cows.

21. They go to the terrible hell called Raurava.

22. After living there for a hundred crores of years, they are born as dogs.

23. After the life as dogs, they become faecus-eating worms stinking deep. They are born again and again there and never get release.

24. Once a Brahmin receives a gift from a Śūdra, his ancestral manes fall into filth.

25. No other Brahmin shall speak with him or share a seat with him. He is to be kept afar.

26. The Brahmin who, however, chances to speak with him or share a seat, shall perform Prājāpatyakṛcchra ceremony for purification.

27-28. The aim is achieved by the thousandth part (of the merit) of the dāna of a single cow. Why then speak of the numerous other gifts?

29. The parturient cow should be gifted to a poor, good-natured Vedic Brahmin.

30. The cow in the condition of the young one just coming out of its womb is to be considered as earth itself.

31. Those who make the gift of Kapilā remain in the Brahmaloka honoured there for as many crores of years as there are hairs in the cow and its calf.

32. Make horns of gold and hoofs of silver, or place gold and silver in the hand of the Brahmin.

33. And place the tail of the Kapilā on his hand pouring water and uttering clearly (the mantras).

34. This gift becomes certainly equivalent to the gift of the whole earth full of gems and mountains and forests and oceans.

35. By this gift, which is thus equal to the gift of the earth,

one becomes honoured and goes with his ancestral manes to the supreme abode of Viṣṇu.

36-37. By the gift of the cow, one gets fully purified even if he has incurred the sins of stealing the property of the Brahmin, killing a cow, destroying the foetus, deceit, defiling the Brahmin, ridiculing prescribed rites and similar others.

38. On the day of the gift of the double-faced cow, the giver may feed on milk or milky preparations.

39-40. (The gift should be accompanied by) a thousand gold pieces, half of it or a quarter of it, or a hundred or even fifty or according to means. There need not be any stipulation in this respect.

41. (The giver should utter): "Receive this double-faced cow. I give this to you so that I may have good progeny and peace of mind. Let this bring about prosperity".

42. (The recipient should utter): "O cow, I receive you particularly for my family. O mother of gods, I bow to you. Let good befall me".

43. (The giver should then say): "I bow to you again and again. May good befall me always". (He should utter the mantra)." May the heaven give you and the earth receive you. Who gave this to whom?"

44. The Brahmin should then be allowed to go and the cow should be taken to his house.

45. O Earth, he who also gives this gift of the parturient cow gets the merit of the gift of the whole of the earth with its seven islands.

46. The congregation of Devas always worship (the Kapilā) who is beautiful like the moon and golden in complexion.

47-48. He who reads these rules (about Kapilā) early morning, pure of mind and with full control of the senses, gets rid of sins acquired during one whole year. The sins are blown away like dust by the wind.

49. If this is read at the time of Śrāddha, the food becomes particularly purified and the manes eat it with pleasure.

50. If this is read before Brahmins on Amāvāsyā day, the manes become pleased for a hundred years.

51. He who listens to his gets purified of all sins accumulated during the year.

The priest said:

52. I have thus told you this secret, the greatness of the cow, formerly narrated to Earth by Varāha.

53. He who gifts Tiladhenu on the dvādaśī day of the bright half of the month of Māgha, gets all wishes fulfilled and goes to the abode of Viṣṇu.

54. On the dvādaśī day of the bright half of the month of Śrāvaṇa, the gift of the real cow should be made along with gold.

55. O king, the gift of any kind of cow at any time is capable of removing all sins.

56. I have thus briefly told you this extensive matter relating to the gift of cows which fulfils all desires of men.

57. (You may do this). Otherwise you will continue to be tormented much by hunger (and thirst).

58. O king, now is the month of Kārttika when the whole earth is full of fresh plants.

59. Devas, Rākṣasas and Yakṣas all mingle in this.

60. A golden cow with fruits and gems may be given to the priest particularly on the dvādaśī day or pañcadaśī day (new moon or full moon) in the month of Kārttika.

61. This will be equivalent to the gift of the whole world.

62. He who performs a yajña with dakṣiṇā of ten thousand (gold pieces), really covers only a part of the universe.

63. But he who performs this (gift of the cow) covers the whole universe, whatever is offered in fire, gifted, read or recited.

64. Hearing this, the king gave the sage a golden pot representing the universe.

65. He then got his desires fulfilled and went to heaven.

66. Therefore, O king, you too do the same.

Told thus by Vasiṣṭha, the king too did the same and attained supreme abode by reaching which one becomes free from all sorrow.

Varāha said:

67. O Earth, I have thus told you about this great and sanctifying treatise Varāha Purāṇa.

68. This arose from the omniscient (Viṣṇu), and from him Brahmā learnt it.

69. Brahmā imparted it to his son Pulastya and the latter to Paraśurāma.

70. Paraśurāma imparted it to his disciple Ugra, who, in turn, gave it to Manu. In that line I have told you now.

71. Another dissemination of the same also you may know. I learnt it from the omniscient (Viṣṇu) and you have now got it from me.

72. From you, sages like Kapila will know by the power of their penance. In due course this will be learnt by Vyāsa.

73. He will have a disciple by name Romaharṣaṇi. He will impart it to Śaunaka and none else.

74. The teacher Dvaipāyana (Vyāsa) knows eighteen Purāṇas namely, Brāhma, Pādma, Vaiṣṇava, Śaiva, Bhāgavata.

75. Nāradīya, Mārkaṇḍeya, Āgneya, Bhaviṣya.

76. Brahmavaivarta, Laiṅga, Vārāha, Skānda.

77. Vāmana, Kaurma, Mātsya, Gāruḍa and Brahmāṇḍa.

78. O Earth, he who gets them or reads with reverence on the dvādaśī day in the month of Kārttika, begets children.

79. Lord Nārāyaṇa is always present in the house in which these are kept written.

80. He who listens to this continuously, and after listening worships (this Purāṇa) Varāha.

81. And performs worship of Viṣṇu with sandalpaste, flowers and clothes, and propitiates Brahmins.

82. And the king who worships along with his subjects and according to his ability, gets freed from sins and attains merger in lord Viṣṇu.

CHAPTER ONE HUNDRED AND THIRTEEN

The hymn on the Lord

Om, bow to Varāha, bow to the son of Brahmā, bow to Sanatkumāra.

1. Bow to that Varāha who raises up the earth with ease, and within whose hoofs mountain Meru tinkles.

2. May this Viṣṇu, the lord of all, the destroyer of demons

Mura, Naraka and Rāvaṇa, who, in the form of the boar, raised by the tip of the tusks the earth full of mountains and rivers and encircled by the ocean, for removing the fear of his devotees, whom the sinless saints easily attain, remove all adversities.

3-4. Earth who was thus raised up in the former kalpa asked the great lord in all reverence.

Earth said:

5. O lord, in every aeon you and you alone raise me up. Otherwise, O Keśava, my body cannot move, not even my hands.

6. When the lord was consoling her, came there Sanatkumāra and, blessing her, he said.

Sanatkumāra said:

7. O Earth, you who are Viṣṇu's and prosper by him, tell me what wonder you have seen when you were held by him.

8. Please tell me also what you have heard from him.

9. Hearing these words of the son of Brahmā (Sanatkumāra), Earth said:

Earth said:

10. "O great Brahmin, listen to the essence of the great secret he told me in response to my request.

11. He told me about what should be done by a devotee of Viṣṇu in order to release himself from the miseries of worldly existence.

12. He told me the great secret of the eternal and ever valid dharma".

13. Hearing these words of Earth, the great sage Sanatkumāra brought there the ascetics from his place Kokāmukha.

14. He then spoke to Earth.

Sanatkumāra said:

15. "O lovely goddess, tell me now what I sought of you, namely the essence of dharma and the path to salvation".

16. Earth then bowed to that great sage and spoke to him in sweet words.

Earth said:

17. "O sages, may you all be ready to hear what I have learnt from Viṣṇu." They said, "yes, O goddess, tell us".

(She then said praising Viṣṇu):

18. "When the world was without sun, moon, stars and fire, when the quarters were all still and nothing was known.

19. When the wind did not blow, the fire did not blaze and the lightning did not flash, when the star did not shine and the zodiac did not appear, and nothing was there.

20. And when the Vedas were lost, you assumed the form of a fish, entered the underworld, recovered the Vedas and restored them to Brahmā.

21. O lord, during the churning of the ocean, you became a tortoise and held the Mandara mountain.

22. Then, when I was sinking into the nether world, you took the form of the boar and lifted me up from the ocean with a single tusk.

23. When hiraṇyakaśipu became haughty because of a boon, he was destroyed by you in the form of man-lion.

24. O lord, once I was seen by you exhilirated by the extermination of the Kṣatriyas, in your form as Paraśurāma.

25. Then by your prowess the demon Rāvaṇa was vanquished, and in the form of the dwarf, O lord, Bali was bound.

26. I am not in the least able to know your actions. How do you raise me up and why do you create beings in me ?

27. And even after creation, nothing could be known. The wind does not blow, fire does not blaze.

28. The sun and moon are not there, no stars, no planets; no Mars, no Venus, no Jupiter.

29. No Saturn, no Mercury, no Indra, Kubera, Yama or Varuṇa or Devas.

30. No trinity, Brahmā, Viṣṇu and Śiva.

Being distressed,[1] Earth sought resort in Brahmā.

31. Having gone there, she said in a plaintive tone: "O grand-father, I am sinking with the mountains and forests in me, because of my unbearable burden. Be pleased to save me".

---

1. The portion from here upto the end of verse 40 is out of place here and seems to be an interpolation.

32. Hearing the words of Earth, the grandfather of the world, meditated for a while and told her.

33. "O earth, I am helpless to save you in this sad predicament of yours.

34. Rush to Viṣṇu, the originator of all, who stands with bow and arrow and who has magical powers.

35. All activity is due to him alone. He is capable of saving all, then why say about you".

36. Earth with folded hands approached him, who was lying in yogic repose on the serpent Ananta.

Earth said:

37. On account of my burden, I sought the help of Brahmā, but he sent me away saying:

38. 'O fair goddess, I am unable to save you, please go to Viṣṇu.

39. He will hold you if you happen to sink in the ocean'.

40. O lord of the worlds, I have now come to you with supplication. Be pleased to protect me.

41. You are Āditya, Candra, Yama, Kubera, Indra, Varuṇa Agni and Vāyu. You are the quarters main and subsidiary, and all that is permanent and transient.

42. You are (the avatāras) Matsya, Kūrma, Varāha, Narasiṁha, Vāmana, (Paraśu)rāma, Kṛṣṇa, Buddha and Kalki.

43. Your greatness in this manner is known by yogic powers, and you remain the same aeon after aeon.

44. The earth, air, ether, water and light, and sound, touch, colour, taste and smell, are all yourself.

45-46. The planets and stars, (units of time like) kalā, kāṣṭhā and muhūrta, the entire milky way and the pole stars are all your effulgence.

47. The month, fortnight and day, the seasons, the half-year and the year are all yours.

48. The rivers, oceans, mountains and snakes are all yourself.

49. You are (the mountains) Meru, Mandara Vindhya, Malaya, Dardura, Himavān and Niṣadha.

50. You bear the disc and the bow. You are Sāṅkhya-yoga.

You are the tradition of the world, you are the adorable Nārāyaṇa.

51. You are diminutive as well as extensive, you are the sacrifice permanent. You are the greatest of all yajñas and of the sacrificial pillars.

52. You are Sāma among the Vedas, and Mahāvrata in all its detail. You are thunder as well as rain and you are truth as well as untruth.

53. You generate ambrosia and sustain with it the whole world. You are satisfaction, supreme satisfaction and the most ancient Man.

54. You are all that is movable and stationary in the world and all action. You are the lord of all the seven worlds.

55. You are time, you are death. You are the origin and cause of all beings. You are the beginning, middle and end. You are intelligence, intellect and memory.

56. You are the sun, aeon, ascetic penance. You are measureless, you are all that is to be known and the greatest of all sages.

57. You are Ananta among the snakes and Takṣaka among serpents. You are the (winds) Udvaha and Pravaha, and Varuṇa and the sea.

58. You project the world in sport, you are the gods in the homes. You pervade everything, nourish everything. You are the mind.

59. You are energy of every kind and the brightest of all flashes. At all times you are the biggest of all trees.

60. O lord, you are attention, you are the dispeller of all evils. You are the source of all the four types of beings, egg-born, earth-born, sweat-born and womb-born.

61. You are the great Garuḍa and you bear everything. You are the sounds of all drums, and the pure sky.

62. You are Jaya and Vijaya[1]; all the domestic deities are your manifestations. You are all-pervasive.

63. You are Bhaga, Liṅga, and the supreme soul. You are to be worshipped by all. I bow to you, O lord, again and again.

64. O lord Kṛṣṇa, it behoves you who have in you all the

1. These two are the doorkeepers of Viṣṇu.

worlds and the entire time, to protect me when I am sinking down."

65. He who recites this hymn of Viṣṇu is cured of all diseases and freed from all bondages.

66. The issueless man gets issue, the poor man gets wealth, the man without a life gets one and the girl without a husband gets one.

67. He who recites this in the morning and evening goes to the world of Viṣṇu. There need be no doubt in this matter.

68. Even if this is mechanically recited (without knowing the meaning), one gets a place in heaven for a thousand years.

CHAPTER ONE HUNDRED AND FOURTEEN

The Varāha incarnation—Questions of Earth

Varāha said:

1. Lord Nārāyaṇa was extremely pleased when he was extolled.

2. He then meditated for a while and spoke to Earth in a sweet voice.

3. "With great reverence have you told me what you badly need. I shall do what you wish.

4. I shall hold you along with your mountains, forests, rivers and oceans and the seven islands".

5. Comforting Earth thus, the lord assumed the form of a big boar full of effulgence.

6. It was six thousand yojanas long and three thousand yojanas broad, and thus covered nine thousand yojanas.

7. The whole earth with its mountains, forests, islands and cities was raised up by the left tusk.

8. Some mountains were clinging, some falling. It all looked like clouds of various farmations and colours at evening time.

9. The earth clinging to the white tusk of the boar looked like the clod of clay with a lotus stalk.

10. It was thus held in the tusk for a thousand years.

11. Time then passed and then set in the seventyfirst Kalpa, the lord of which was Kardama Prajāpati.

12. That was the Varāha kalpa wherein the mutual regard for Viṣṇu and Earth was the highest.

13. Earth extolled that eternal Person and sought complete resort in him.

Earth asked:

14. O lord, what is the foundation and what is the practice of different actions (for man) to be done from time to time ?

15. What is the nature of evening sandhyā ? Do all those who perform rites get the same result?

16. How do we know the measure regarding the consecration invocation and release (of deities for worship and of agaru, candana, dhūpa etc.?

17. How is pādya (water for washing feet) to be offered, how is unguent to be applied, how is the lamp to be waved and how are the roots and fruits to be offered ?

18. What are the rules for the seat and the bed for the deity, how is worship to be performed and how many are the vital airs to be instilled ?

19. What is the merit to be acquired in the morning and evening sandhyās. What are the rituals in the śarat (autumn) season, what are they in śiśira (winter) ?

20. What are the rituals to be performed in vasanta (spring) and what are they in grīṣma (summer) ? What are they in prāvṛṭ (rainy season) ? What is laid down for the end of the year ?

21. What are the flowers and the fruits that can be used ? Who are entitled to offer worship and who are prohibited ?

22. By what actions does one attain Viṣṇu ? How do these actions take one to the level beyond that of food ?

23. What is the size of the idol to be used and how is it to be installed ? what is the nature of fasting and what is its duration ?

24. What are the rules regarding cloths (to be used in worship), yellow, white and red ?

25. What are the constituents of Madhuparka ? What are the benefits that accrue from it ?

26. To what worlds do we go by taking in Madhuparka ?

27. What is the measure of Madhuparka to be offered? What kinds of flesh, fruit and leaves are to be mixed with it?

28. What are the rites of invocation to be observed?

29. What are the mantras to be used in offering food after due invocation?

30. After food, what are the things to be done by the devotee so that there may not be any fault?

31. What is the food for those who pray to you eating only once a day?

32. What is the place of those in the life beyond, who worship you following the rules?

33. What position do those get who worship you with the rituals Kṛcchra and Sāntapana?

34. What position do those get who worship Kṛṣṇa, living on air alone?

35. What position do those get, O Kṛṣṇa, who worship you living on food without salt and chillies?

36. What position do those get who worship you living on milk alone?

37. What position do those get who worship Viṣṇu with vows and tending cows?

38. What position do those get who worship with great devotion and live on begging alms?

39. What position do those get who worship living as householders but feeding on what is offered to them?

40. What position do those get who always serve you in your temples and die there?

41. To what worlds do those go who end their lives in your temples performing penance with the five fires?

42. What position do those get who end their lives by performing penance with the five fires but lying on a bed of thorns?

43. What position do those devotees get who do the same in bed of thorns but lying without touching the earth?

44. What position do those get who worship you lying in the cowshed?

45. What position do those devotees get who worship you living on vegetables alone?

46. What position do those get who worship you living on grains and Pañcagavya ?[1]

47. What position do those get who worship you living on gruel and cowdung ?

48. What is the position, O Nārāyaṇa, for those who worship you feeding on flour ?

49. What is the position for those who serve you lighting a lamp on their heads ?

50. What is the position for those who carry lamps on their heads and worship you always thinking of you and drinking milk alone ?

51. What is the position for those devotees of yours who eat stones alone ?

52. What is the position for those devotees who feed on the dūrvā grass ?

53. What is the position for those who follow their own traditional avocations and pray to you kneeling ?

54. What is the position for those who worship you lying flat and holding a lamp ?

55. What position do they get who worship you holding a lamp between their legs ?

56. What position do they get who worship you turning their faces away ?

57. What position do they get lying with face downwards, giving up their family and possessions ?

58. Be pleased to give me answers for all these that I have asked you in the interest of the world.

59. O Mādhava, every movement depends on you. You are knower, you are the father; in you is the decision regarding all dharma.

60. Therefore, you alone can answer all these which have a bearing on Sāṅkhya-yoga.

61. How should your devotee who has offered you Madhuparka, be consigned to fire when he is dead ?

62. What place do your devotees attain who remain in water or in your temples ?

---

1. Pañcagavya is a preparation consisting of cow's milk, curd and ghee from it and its urine and cowdung.

63. What place do they attain who utter your name Nārāyaṇa, though calling one's own son ?

64. What place do those warriors attain who die in battle uttering your name ?

65. O lord, I am your disciple and servant. So be pleased to tell me this secret dharma.

66. For my sake please impart me this secret.

CHAPTER ONE HUNDRED AND FIFTEEN

Origin of different dharmas (*Karmas of different castes*)

1. Hearing these words of Earth, lord Nārāyaṇa said: "O goddess, I shall tell you about the actions that lead to the pleasures of heaven.

2. O Earth, I shall answer your questions relating to the existence and attitude of devotees that are laid down.

3. I am never pleased with petty-minded people even if they make a thousand dānas, perform hundreds of sacrifices and offer a lot of money.

4. I am pleased with him who (tried to) know me with steadfast mind even though he may have many faults.

5. Now that you ask me about the actions that lead to the pleasures of heaven, I shall tell you. Please listen.

6. Those people who bow to me always, at midnight, in darkness, at noon or afternoon, although of diverse minds.

7. Who with unfailing devotion to me observe fast on Dvādaśī day.

8. Realise me in the fruition of their devotion.

9. The good man with clean mind devoted to me gets a place in heaven by the very desire.

10. I shall tell you about those actions in the path of devotion that lead to my realisation.

11. Those devotees who fast on Dvādaśī day certainly attain me.

12. He who after fasting, offers me libations of water saying 'Bow to Nārāyaṇa' and looks at the sun.

13. Remains honoured in heaven for as many thousands of years as there are drops in the water of libation.

14-15. Now listen to what happens to those pious people who worship me on dvādaśī day with due rites and with white flowers and incense.

16. Putting flowers on the head and dressing in white cloth he may utter the mantra: "May the worshipful lord Hari be pleased to accept these flowers."

17. Sandal paste is to be offered with the mantra: "Bow to lord Viṣṇu, be pleased to accept the sandalpaste which gives out its scent fully and slightly alternately or fragrant sandalpaste".

18. The incense is to be offered with the manta: "May lord Acyuta receive the incense at the main ritual".

19. He who makes my image according to Śāstras reaches my abode and becomes four-armed.

20. Thus have I told you, O goddess, this mantrapūjā which brings about happiness and which is dear to me.

21. He, who being devoted to my service, eats (only) the grains śyāmāka,svastika, godhūma, mudgaka, śāli, yava, nīvāra and kāṅguka, attains (the divine) conch, disc, plough and club.

22. O Earth, I shall now tell you what actions the Brahmins devoted to me should do.

23. Free from ego and attending seriously to the six duties ordained,[1] with full control of senses, living on alms and unconcerned about loss or gain.

24. Engaged in my service, free from malignity, following the prescribed rules, fully unbiased, and neither senile nor childish.

25. Performing deeds beneficial to the people at large, and full of concentration of mind, such a Brahmin attains me.

26. I shall now tell you about what the Kṣatriyas devoted to me should do.

27. Free from bias, munificent in gifts, pure, keen on sacrifices, devoted to my service, free from ego.

28. Reserved in speech, capable of knowing merit, always considerate towards other devotees, free from malice, avoiding all prohibited deeds, learning from the master.

---

1. The six duties of the Brahmin are *adhyāpana* (teaching) *adhyayana* (learning), *yajana* (performing sacrifice), *yājana* (making others perform sacrifice), *dāna* (giving gifts) and *pratigraha* (receiving gifts).

29. Eager to show respect to others, without a trace of avarice, such a Kṣatriya attains me.

30. I shall now tell you about what the Vaiśya devoted to me should do.

31. Doing the duties ordained to him, without the motive of gain or loss, doing the duties by his wife at the proper time, free from greed, calm in mind.

32. Remaining pure, skilful, fasting when worshipping me.

33. Always honouring his guru, considerate towards other devotees, such a Vaiśya always remains mine and I always remain his.

34. I shall now tell you about what the Śūdra should do in order that he may be mine.

35. Husband and wife always pious, devoted to me and ever engaged in doing service to me.

36. Knowing the appropriate place and time for their actions, unstained by Rajas and Tamas.

37. Free from ego, pure in mind, humble, hospitable, free from greed and malice, and full of sincerity.

38. Fond of prostrating (before me), ever thinking of me, such be the actions of the Śūdras.

39. Leaving thousands of sages, I always look after Śūdras. Such are the duties of devotees in the four castes which you wished to know.

40. So much about the four castes. Now listen to another matter relating to yoga (of attaining me).

41. Giving up (thoughts of) gain and loss, delusion and desire.

42. Without thinking of heat and cold, what is obtained and what is not, without preference among what is hot, bitter, sweet, sour and saline.

43. Giving up attachment towards wife, children, father and mother and concentrating on service to me.

44. Steadfast, proficient, serious and determined.

45. Always earnest, averse to all other actions, doing things appropriate to his age, eating the minimum, maintaining family prestige.

46. Full of compassion, honouring all, highly patient, keeping silence when necessary, particularly when observing vows.

47. Performing rites prescribed for morning, noon and evening, not taking food without giving it to others.

48. Doing all actions with me in the mind, answering calls of nature and bathing at the right time.

49. Always eager to offer me sandalpaste, flowers and incense.

50. Eating sometimes roots, sometimes fruits, sometimes milk, sometimes what is got by begging, and sometimes living simply on air.

51. Sometimes eating once in four days, at other times once in six days, often once in ten days or once in a fortnight or once in a month.

52. Those that do all this in seven lives, become yogins and attain me.

CHAPTER ONE HUNDRED AND SIXTEEN

Happiness and unhappiness

Varāha said:

1. O blessed one, now listen to the benefits that accrue to those that perform actions in the manner stated above.

2. With full concentration of mind, free from ego, always devoted to me, full of forbearance, tranquil and with senses controlled.

3. Taking in roots and fruits and leaves at times on the Dvādaśī day, feeding mainly on milk and abstaining from meat.

4. Observing continence on Ṣaṣṭhī, Aṣṭamī, Amāvāsyā and Caturdaśī, particularly on dvādaśī.

5. He who performs rites according to the rules of yoga, gets purified, acquires merit and goes to the world of Viṣṇu.

6. For him there is no fatigue, no decay, no stupor, no illness. He gets eighteen hands endowed with bow, arrow, sword, mace and the like.

7. The benefit that accrues as a result of actions in this manner and worship of mine, is the residence in my world for sixty thousand and sixty hundred years.

8. O Earth, I shall now tell you what is unhappiness. Please listen.

9. Is there anything more unhappy than a man being unable to attain me because of his ego and delusion enveloping him?

10. Is there anything more unhappy than a man being unable to attain me because of his eating anything and trading on anything and not prostrating before me?

11. Is there anything more sorrowful than being the man who at the time of Vaiśvadeva sees a guest coming but, without giving him food, himself eats.

12. Is there anything more unhappy than the man whose food Devas do not partake of because of differentiation in preparation?

13. Is there anything more despicable than a person who is unhappy in adversity, establishes illicit contact with another's wife, torments others and is slow-witted?

14. Is there anything more pitiable than a person who spends all his life till death grasps him, in his house without doing righteous deeds in profusion?

15. Is there anything more contemptible than the person who runs after elephants, horses, chariots and other vehicles?

16. Is there anything more sorrowful than this that some eat meat, some eat it with grain and others eat dry food?

17. Is there anything more disquieting than the fact that some sleep in ornamental beds of costly cloth and others sleep on the grass in the floor?

18. Is there anything more disturbing than the fact that some people are handsome and some ugly although this may be the result of their own deeds?

19. Is there anything more distressing than the fact that some are virtuous and learned in all śāstras while others are seen dumb?

20. Is there anything more annoying than the fact that wealthy personal are niggardly while poor people are generous?

21. Is there anything more condemnable than the man who, having married two wives, favours one and discards the other?

22. If the three castes, Brāhmaṇa, Kṣatriya and Vaiśya, are engaged in sinful actions, can there be anything more detestable?

23. Having got human birth, if one does not strive to attain me, can there be anything more deplorable?

24. I have thus told you about the actions leading to unhappiness which you asked me.

25. Now I shall tell you about the actions leading to happiness which you asked me.

26. Let all actions be dedicated to me. Those that are otherwise lead to unhappiness.

27. Is there anything more happy than eating the food remaining after offering it to me?

28. Is there anything more happy than observing rites in the morning, noon and evening, particularly the last?

29. Is there anything more happy than offering food to the gods, guests and men in general and then oneself taking it?

30. Is there anything more happy than giving a supplicant something instead of sending him away disappointed?

31. Is there anything more happy than propitiating the manes on Amāvāsyā day every month?

32. Is there anything more happy than giving food of barley to those that have come seeking food, without a trace of unwillingness on the face?

33. If a person with two wives looks upon both alike, is there anything more happy for him?

34. He, who with pure mind, always observes non-violence, attains happiness.

35. If, on seeing the beautiful wife of another, the mind does not flutter, can there be greater happiness?

36. Can there be greater happiness for a person if he is able to see as mere stones gold and gems like pearl?

37. Can there be anything more happy than giving up life in the midst of the battle which delights the horses and elephants?

38. He who lives contented condemning wrong actions for attaining the ends, is prone to be happy.

39. Can there be greater happiness for a woman who pleases her husband considering him to be everything for her in life?

40. Can there be anything more gratifying if a man, in spite of his being rich, is learned and has full control of the senses?

41. If one is forbearing of an offence, is not dispirited in adversity, and knows everything well, can there be a greater cause for pleasure?

42. He who leaves off his mortal coil in my temples, be that

with any desire or without any desire, can there be anything more happy for him ?

43. Is there anything more happy than honouring the parents like gods ?

44. Can there be anything more happy than cohabiting with the wife with full attention every month after the course ?

45. He who worships me like this, never ceases to be mine and I never cease to be his.

46. Thus have I told you the directions for the good for the sake of the world in reply to your question.

CHAPTER ONE HUNDRED AND SEVENTEEN

The thirtytwo offences

Varāha said:

1. O blessed goddess, now listen to the rules of food, about eating food as well as avoiding it.

2. The food has a bearing on attaining me, because the man who follows dharma reaches me even if he chances to do an inauspicious act.

3. Let the prescribed food be taken always. Vrīhi and Śāli grains (cereals) are to be used

4. I shall tell you about the grains (food) prohibited, because to use them is an offence.

5. The first offence, which I always dislike is to worship me after taking another's food.

6. The second offence, which obstructs dharma, is to touch me after a sexual contact.

7. The third offence, O earth, is to attend to me after seeing a woman in her courses.

8. The fourth offence, one which I never tolerate, is to serve me after touching a dead body and without undergoing the necessary purification.

9. The fifth offence, which I do not brook, is to touch me after seeing a dead body and without taking ācamana.

10. The sixth offence, which I do not forgive, is to go for answering calls of nature in the midst of my worship.

11. The seventh offence, O Earth, is to serve me wearing blue cloth.

12. The eighth offence, O Earth, is to talk much while engaged in my service.

13. The ninth offence, O Earth, is to worship me without purifying oneself according to the rules.

14. The tenth offence which displeases me, is to do me service with an angry mind.

15. The eleventh offence is to consider in my worship prohibited objects as conducive to merit.

16. The twelfth offence is to worship me wearing cloth made red with saffron.

17. The thirteenth offence is to touch me in darkness.

18. The fourteenth offence is to serve me wearing black cloth.

19. The fifteenth offence is to serve me wearing unwashed cloth.

20. The sixteenth offence is to eat food even unknowingly (while engaged in my worship).

21. The seventeenth offence is to approach me after eating fish and meat.

22. The eighteenth offence is to approach me after eating goose (and other waterbirds).

23. The nineteenth offence, O Earth, is to come to me after touching my lamp-bearer.[1]

24. The twentieth offence, O fair goddess, is to approach me after going to the cremation ground.

25. The twentyfirst offence, O Earth, is to approach me after eating oil-cake.

26. The twentysecond offence is to take pork as food conducive to attaining me.

27. The twentythird offence, O Earth, is to approach me after drinking liquor.

1. The word is *dīpaka*. What it means here is not quite clear.

28. The twentyfourth offence, O Earth, is to approach me after eating vegetables with saffron.

29. The twentyfifth offence, O Earth, is to approach me putting on the garment of another.

30. The twentysixth offence, O Earth, is to eat fresh food without offering it first to the gods or manes.

31. The twentyseventh offence, is to go to the tank (for bathing) with footwear on.

32. The twentyeighth offence, O virtuous one, is to come to me after tormenting the body.

33. The twentyninth offence, which never takes one to heaven, is to approach me with undigested food (in the abdomen).

34. The thirtieth offence is to offer me incense without offering sandalpaste and flowers.

35. The thirtyfirst offence, O noble one, is to open the door (of my temple) without sounding the drums.

36. The thirtysecond offence should be taken as the most serious.[1]

37. I shall now tell you about Dṛḍhavrata (strong vow) by observing which one attains me.

38. Learning the Śāstras, always remaining devoted to me and rendering service to me, following non-violence, being compassionate to all beings, affable to all, pure, clever.

39. Controlling senses completely, without committing any offence, being generous, righteous, well attached to the wife.

40. Observing the rules prescribed for the four castes, (he who worships me attains me).

41. She who is devoted to the preceptor, devoted to the husband and looks after the family (also attains me by worshipping me).

42. The man who is my devotee reaches me even if he gives up his wife, but awaits here the devoted wife.

43. I shall now tell you about the best of all actions.

44. Even sages who follow the path of devotion are not able to easily realise me, what then about ordinary men ?

45. Those sinful people who are attached to other gods, are deluded by my magical power and do not attain me.

1. It is simply stated as mahāparādha. What it is, is not given.

46. O Earth, those who resort to me desirous of liberation, get purified and get places allotted (in my world).

47. I told you all this because of the fact that I hold you with great energy.

48. This should not be instructed to a slanderer, a fool, an uninitiated or the cunning.

49. Nor to the vowless, base or the impious.

50. To none other than the devotees of mine.

51. I have thus told you all this about dharma for the sake of the world. What else have you to ask me now?

CHAPTER ONE HUNDRED AND EIGHTEEN

Rituals in Idol worship

Varāha said:

1. O blessed one, listen to the expiation that my devotee is to offer.

2. Take the tooth stick. Do not light the lamp till the ground is touched.

3. As soon as the lamp is lighted, wash the hands and then approach the idol.

4. Bow to the feet and offer the toothstick with the mantra.

5. "O the abode of the worlds, excelling the sun in lustre, endless, middle, receive this universal toothstick".

6. In accordance with the rules explained to you, O Earth, the teeth should be cleaned.

7. The flower placed on the head of the idol the previous day should be taken and placed on one's own.

8. The hand should then be washed with water and the face of the idol should be sprinkled with a little water.

9. The mantra for it is this and by reciting it one gets release from the world:

10. "O lord, receive these waters by their quality and soul." The faces of all deities should be washed in this way. By the same mantra should be offered sandal paste, incense, lamp and food.

11. Then handfuls of flowers should be offered saying "O

lord Nārāyaṇa, who look after the devotees, I bow to you," and then utter the mantra.

12. "I bow to the sacrificer of those who know the mantras, and the creator of all beings". Further flowers should be offered.

13. The devotee, with due knowledge and purity of mind, should worship the lord in this manner and then throw himself down with all his actions.

14. Making the body fall in this way, he should seek the grace of the lord and with hands folded over the head, utter this mantra:

15. "Getting clear consciousness by the mantras I pray O lord, when you are pleased and by your wish only even the yogins attain liberation.

16. Since I am your servant as you have stated, be pleased with me".

17. After doing all this seriously he should quickly go behind.

18. The idol should then be bathed in oil first and then in ghee.

19. Then with full concentration of mind, the devotee should offer oil with the mantra:

20. "O lord of the worlds, I am offering this oil with affection and with my hand to you who pervade the whole world. I have said 'Pardon me.' I bow to you again and again."

21. With this mantra it should be first applied to the head.

22. Then the right hand, then the left and afterwards the back and then the waist.

23. Then cowdung should be smeared on the floor.

24. I shall tell you what benefits accrue by this anointing.

25. The man who bathes the idol in ghee or oil remains in heaven for as many thousands of years as there are drops in them.

26. He who does this is honoured in my world.

27. Now I shall tell you about the application of unguents by which the body is purified and I am pleased.

28. The unguent should be made of lodhra, the juice of fig and the leaves at Madhūka, Aśvaparṇa, Rohiṇa and Karkaṭa.

29-30. The ingredients may be either crushed by the hand or otherwise made into powder and then applied. It makes my body pleasant.

31. For complete fulfilment, after the application of the unguent, the bathing (proper) should be done.

32. Then the whole body of the idol should he rubbed with (the fruits of) Āmalaka and Vasugandha.

33. Taking then the pot of water this mantra should be uttered:

34. "O sinless lord, you are the god of gods, you have no beginning, you are supreme, be pleased to accept this bath for your visible form". Thus should the bath be conducted by those who follow my path.

35. The water for bath may be taken in golden or silver pot, and if they are not available, in copper pot.

36. After this ritual of bath, sandalpaste should be applied with the mantra.

37-38. "O Mādhava, all scents from flowers and all colours are liked by you. These which arise in different worlds are combined by you in Satyaloka. I am now applying the same on your body in pure form. Being pleased by my devotion, do me the favour of accepting it".

39. After applying sandal (with the perfumes) perform other edifying actions.

40. Adorn me with garlands of the prescribed kind and continue the ritual.

41. Then offer handfuls of flowers and utter the mantra:

42. "O Acyuta, accept these clean flowers, waterborn as well as land-born in this season, for my release from this worldly existence".

43. After this may be offered incense from fragrant substances with the mantra.

44-46. "Be pleased to receive this incense the essence of the great trees mixed with many ingredients, for the sake of deliverance from worldly existence. This for peace for all Devas, peace for me and peace for all devotees. I bow to you. O lord of the worlds, there is no saviour for me other than you".

47. After this, adorn the idol with sandalpaste, unguents and garlands. Then decorate with white and yellow silk garments.

48. Then with hands folded over the head and remaining in meditation, he should utter.

49. "May this please lord Puruṣottama, of the nature of bliss, the abode of Lakṣmī, the creator, protector, overlord, lord of all beings, the primordial being. I dress you in beautiful yellow silk".

50. After this, I should be provided seat in a pedestal of flowers.

51. Then naivedya should be offered uttering 'Om'.

52. "O lord, receive this (naivedya) which is the giver of life and mutually pleasing."

53. After this he should quickly give water for washing the mouth.

54. The naivedya given should be pure and the water for washing is essential for making it acceptable.

55. After thus offering food and water, betel leaf and arecanut should be given with the mantra.

56. "O lord of the worlds, receiving this tāmbūla which is an ornament to all gods and which is mixed with all fragrant substances, be pleased to remain in this idol of yours in this house.

57. Please receive this fine decoration for your mouth reverentially given by me".

58. The devotee who worships me in this way gets liberated and remains in my great world for ever.

CHAPTER ONE HUNDRED AND NINETEEN

Food forbidden in worship

1. Hearing the rules of rituals in worship which lead to liberation, Earth asked again the pleasant lord.

Earth said:

2. "I have heard from you now about the efficacious actions that lead to attaining you. Be pleased to tell me what are the materials to be used for it".

3. Hearing the words of Earth, Varāha was much pleased and spoke these words of virtue.

Varāha said:

4. The mantras to be utilised (have been said. Now I shall tell you about the materials).

5. The seven kinds of grain together with milk and vegetables and the (fruits of) Madhūka and Udumbara (are commendable).

6. There are others in hundreds and thousands which I may tell you.

7. I shall say about the grains that can be used. Listen to me with attention.

8-9. The vegetable Cillika, the fragrant raktaśāli, the long śāli, the big śāli, good saffron, fine honey, the sweet-smelling śivasundarī, śīrika and kulaśālika and different kinds of cooked barley are commended in worship.

10-11. Green gram, black gram, horse gram, sesamum,panicseed, gavedhu, makuṣṭa, vāhija, and śyāmāka are all permitted.

12. All this I accept if devoutly offered; also the flesh of deer, goat and hare.

13. All these are dear to me in the worship meant to attain me.

14. When the goat is offered in sacrifice by the Vaidic Brahmin, a part of it comes to me as my share.

15. The milk, curd and ghee of the buffalo should be avoided. The devotee of Viṣṇu should avoid its meat, even the food cooked in its milk.

16. The birds that are to be used also in my worship, I shall tell you now.

17-18. The flesh of the birds lāvaka, vārtika and kapiñjala are used in my temples.

19. He who does the worship following these instructions (and restrictions) does not commit any fault and good befalls him.

20. Those who worship me in this manner with all the rituals attain their goal.

CHAPTER ONE HUNDRED AND TWENTY

The worship of Sandhyā

Varāha said:

1. O Earth, I shall tell you the great secret of crossing the worldly existence which you asked me about.

2. My devotees, duly taking bath, approach me with full control of mind and eating but a trifle of food.

3. O blessed one, my form is eternal. I am the one that permeates all beings.

4. It is I that is above, below and the sides, as also at the quarters and subquarters.

5. Obeisance should, therefore, be made to all these by the devotees desirous of salvation.

6. I shall also tell you this secret that by worshipping these my followers acquire great fame.

7. With concentration of mind, the devotee should turn to east and take water in both hands held together.

8. He should then say *Om namo nārāyaṇāya* (Bow to Nārāyaṇa) and then utter:

9. "I bow to that great and merciful primordial man, the most important in all the worlds, Nārāyaṇa the origin of dharma. I offer sacrifice to him".

10. Then turning to west and similarly holding water he should utter Dvādaśākṣara (*Om namo bhagavate vāsudevāya*) and then the mantra:

11. "I extol that eternal being, the most ancient, whose desire is never in vain, the first creator who manifests himself in all objects".

12. Then holding water in the same manner he should turn to the north and uttering *Om namo nārāyaṇāya* recite the mantra:

13. "I offer sacrifice to that most divine being, the most ancient without beginning or end, of eternal form, the originator of life and the world, the most tranquil, unique, the liberator from the woes of worldly life".

14. Then inmediately turning to the south (similarly holding water in the hands) he should utter *Om namaḥ puruṣottamāya* and recite the mantra:

15. "I offer sacrifice to the great being of endless forms, the

first, the truth, the righteous, of the form of time, for liberation from worldly life".

16. Then remaining steady like wood and fully controlling the senses and concentrating the mind on Viṣṇu, he should utter the mantra.

17. "I offer sacrifice to the lord of the worlds, with the sun and moon as his eyes, the foremost of all in the worlds, the drinker of soma juice, the liberator from death and worldly existence".

18. The devotee of mine who desires beatitude may do this wisely and sincerely during morning, moon and evening.

19. This is the secret of all secrets, the highest of yoga and the best of Sāṅkhya.

20. This should not be inparted to the dunce, the cheat or the crooked; it can be imparted only to the good, initiated disciple.

21. These secret instructions given by Viṣṇu should be well borne in mind and never be forgotten even at the time of death.

22. He who learns this well and follows the instructions, always finds a place in my mind.

23. He who worships the sandhyā in this manner, whatever be his form here, reaches my abode.

CHAPTER ONE HUNDRED AND TWENTYONE

The absence of birth

Varāha said:

1. O Earth, listen to me. I shall tell you the essence of all *dharma* by which one can remain without entering into birth.

2. One is not able to realise the self even after performing the prescribed rites with purity of mind.

3. But he who performs the duties by me, becomes blessed and able to distinguish between right and wrong.

4. He who bears heat and cold alike, overcomes thirst and hunger, speaks the truth, is not jealous, persevering even if poor.

5. Is devoted to his own wife and discards the women of others, is honest and dedicated to the Lord.

6. Sets on the good from the bad, is well disposed towards Brahmins, speaks endearingly to them, and is attached to my service.

7. Such a person never goes to a cursed womb, but reaches my abode.

8. O Earth, I shall tell you another thing regarding my devotee's never going to a bad womb.

9. He who refrains from all sorts of injury, is kindly disposed towards all beings, is pure-hearted, considers alike a stone and gold.

10. Never keeps in mind any insult received, is always aware of his duties and speaks only the truth.

11. Turns away from all falsehood, is firm in truth, never speaks ill of any one even privately,

12. Cohabits with his wife for the sake of progeny soon after her period, and is steadfast in my devotion.

13. Never goes to a bad womb, but reaches me.

O Earth, I shall tell you another thing. Please listen.

14. The eternal dharma of man is seen in one way by Manu, in another way by Āṅgirasa.

15. In yet another way by Śukra and still another way by Gautama, in a different way by Soma, still differently by Rudra.

16. Yet differently by Śaṅkha and more differently by Likhita, similarly by Kāśyapa and so too by Dharma.

17. Agni and Vāyu found *dharma* differently; so also Yama, Indra and Varuṇa.

18. Kubera found it in one way and Śāṇḍilya in another; Pulastya and Āditya still differently.

19. Pitṛs found it yet differently and Svayambhū too. Each propounder found it according to himself.

20. Each man should follow *dharma* according to his faith and should not dispute about it with others.

21. He should stand in the path of righteousness and should not despise virtuous deeds.

22. Such a person never falls into a heinous womb, but reaches my world.

Listen, O Earth, I shall now tell you about another thing.

23. By which people are able to cross this ocean of births.

24. He who has control of his senses, has overcome anger and is free from desire and delusion, helps himself by always

worshipping god, guests and preceptors, abstains from injury and does not partake of meat or liquor.

25. Who never even thinks of cohabiting with a Brahmin woman, makes gift of Kapilā cow to the Brahmin and attends on old men.

26. Does not discriminate among his own sons, consoles a Brahmin when he is angry.

27. Who touches the Kapilā cow in devotion, never outrages the modesty of a virgin, does not cross fire, and does not dispute with the son.

28. Does not pass urine in water, is respectful towards the teacher, is not talkative.

29. And endowed with such qualities (like these) resorts to me; he never goes to a womb, but reaches my world.

CHAPTER ONE HUNDRED AND TWENTYTWO

The greatness of Kokāmukha—the story of the fish and cricket

Varāha said:

1. "O Earth, listen to the secret of secrets by which even those that have become animals are cleared of all their sins.

2. He who maintains continence on the eighth and fourteenth days of each lunar fortnight, he who, having taken the food offered by another, does not speak ill of it.

3. Who even from childhood is devoted to me, who is happy with whatever he gets, who honours his parents.

4. He who does not live in strain, who is virtuous and discreet, liberal in gifts, enjoys life, restrained but independent in all actions.

5. Who, even in his youth, does not do anything prohibited, who is kind towards all beings, and is full of energy.

6. Who is of desireless mind and never covets another's wealth, such a person reaches my world.

7. O lovely damsel, this is a secret which is not easily comprehended even by gods. Listen to what I say further.

8. He who is sympathetic and does not harm any being and he who gives up life at Kokāmukha, becomes dear to me and he does not swerve even in mind".

9. Hearing these words of Viṣṇu, the saintly Earth asked the Lord who was in the form of a boar.

Earth said:

10. "O Mādhava, I am your disciple, servant and devotee. I deserve to be told the great secret.

11-12. Leaving out Cakra, Vārāṇasi, Aṭṭahāsa, Naimiṣa and Bhadrakarṇa, why do you praise Kokā.

13. Again, leaving out Dviraṇḍa, Maṇḍaleśvara and Kedāra, why do you praise Kokā ?

14. So too while there are Devadāruvana, Jāleśvara and Durga, why do you praise Kokā ?

15. Similarly, when there are Gokarṇa, Jālmeśvara and Ekaliṅga, why do you praise Kokā ?"

16. Thus asked in great reverence, the Lord in the form of the boar replied:

Varāha said:

17. What you say is true. I shall, therefore, tell you about the special nature of Kokāmukha.

18. All the places mentioned by you pertain to Rudra and they are resorted to by the Pāśupatas. But Kokā pertains to the Bhāgavatas.

19. I shall tell you what happened in this Kokāmukha of mine.

20. A hungry hunter was once wandering about in this Kokā country.

21. He saw in a shallow pond a fish and caught it in his net. But the mighty fish escaped from his hand.

22. Immediately a vulture saw it. It swooped down, caught it and swiftly flew away.

23. But the vulture was unable to carry it far, and the fish fell down at Kokāmukha. By the special power of that place, it became a handsome prince (in Śaka kingdom).

24. After a long time, the wife of this hunter happened to pass by there with meat in her hand.

25. A female cricket, desirous of the meat, hopped on it again and again and annoyed her.

26. She struck it with an arrow and hurled it down on the ground.

27. The cricket fell before me in Kokā, and she was born as a beautiful princess in Candrapura.

28. She duly grew up and mastered all the sixtyfour arts, but developed an aversion for men.

29-30. She disliked even a man who was highly virtuous, quite handsome and brave in war.

31. After a long time, however, she married a young Śaka.

32. Having thus got each other in wedlock, they lived a happy and virtuous life.

33. He never parted company with her and she never parted company with him. They never wasted even a minute.

34. A long time they spent in mutual love. She served him with humility and regard.

35. He too (enjoyed himself) in the same way.

36. Once, in the afternoon, the Śaka prince became afflicted by severe headache.

37. All the expert physicians tried their best with all their recipes, but the headache did not subside.

38. For a long time he was unable to know himself being deluded by the *māyā* of Viṣṇu.

39. The period (of their transformation into human form) was drawing to a close.

40. Still they were strongly attached to each other, and neither left the other even for a moment.

41. Then the beautiful princess asked her husband: "Are you doing well ? How is it that you are having this headache ?

42. Please tell me the truth, if you have any consideration for me.

43. Numerous expert physicians are treating you, but the headache still remains".

Thus asked by his wife, he said:

44. "Have you forgotten that the human life we are having now is a mixture of pleasure and pain.

45. You should not ask this question now that we are in the ocean of *saṁsāra*". So was that young lady spoken to by her husband.

46. After a long time, when both were sleeping, she again asked him:

47. "O my lord, please give me an answer to what I asked you long ago.

48. Is there anything to be hidden (from me)? Otherwise why do you hide facts. You should certainly tell me if I am your beloved".

49. Pressed thus, the Śaka prince told her out of love and regard:

50. "Give up this human form and remember what you were formerly. If you are interested in knowing about your previous life.

51. Please go to my parents and propitiate them. They are honourable and my mother kept me in her womb.

52. After honouring them and getting their consent, we will go to Kokāmukha and there I shall tell you the whole thing.

53. Although it is difficult even for gods to know about the previous life, I shall tell you about it there".

54. Then that beautiful damsel went to her parents-in-law and prostrated at their feet. She then told them:

55. "Please listen, I have a submission to make before you. With your permission, both of us wish to go to the holy Kokāmukha.

56. Since the purpose is serious, you should not object to this.

57. So far we have not asked of you anything. Therefore, it behoves you to grant the present request.

58. Your son is suffering from an incurable headache and at noon he becomes practically lifeless.

59. Because of this he has to forego all pleasures. There is no remedy for this other than going to Kokāmukha.

60. This secret has never been told to you. I wish to go quickly to that supreme abode of Viṣṇu. Contemplation by the husband and wife is always efficacious".

61. Then the great king of the Śakas, held his daughter-in-law by the hand and told his son:

62. "Why do you think of going to Kokāmukha?

63. You have got here elephants, horses, chariots and other

vehicles and women beautiful like Apsarases. This country with all its seven constituents like treasury and fort is all for you.

64. So too our friends and this throne. O son, take all this. My life rests in you, so too progeny".

65. Hearing these words of the father, the prince held his feet and spoke in humility.

66. "Enough of the kingdom, treasury, vehicles and army. I wish to go to Kokāmukha quickly.

67. Only if I survive after this terrible headache that has caught hold of me, can this kingdom, army and treasury be of any avail to me.

68. By going there my headache will surely disappear".

69. At these words of the son, the king of Śakas gave permission for him to go to Kokāmukha and blessed him.

70. The citizens, traders, beautiful ladies and courtesans followed him to Kokāmukha.

71. When they reached Kokāmukha, the princess asked her husband:

72. "Be pleased to tell me now what you promised to tell me at Kokāmukha, now that we have reached that place".

73. O Earth, when asked thus by the beloved, the prince laughed and embracing her said:

74. "Now night has fallen and let us sleep well. I shall tell you tomorrow all that is in my mind".

75. At daybreak both of them had their bath. They put on silk garments and bowed to Lord Viṣṇu. He then held her by the hand.

76. And pointed out at the north-east part the remains of some bones and said:

77. "These are the bones of my former body. I was then a fish moving about in the pond in this Kokā country.

78. I was caught in a net by a hunter, but I slipped out of his hand and fell down on the ground.

79. I was then caught by a vulture and torn by its nails. But when I was being carried away by it, I slipped again and fell down here.

1. The seven constituents (*saptāṅga*) are the king, minister, kingdom, forts, treasury, army and friends.

80. My head hit the ground and thus developed this headache of mine. I alone know this and none else.

81. I have now told you what you asked. You may now go wherever you please".

82. Then that lady of faultless limbs and of a hue like the red lotus spoke to the husband again in a piteous tone:

83. "In order to know this, I did not disclose what I was in my former birth. Now I shall tell you that, please listen.

84. I was a cricket flying in the sky. Once overcome with hunger and thirst I was sitting on the branch of a tree thinking of my food.

85. Just then there came a hunter with a big mass of flesh of the many animals he had killed that day.

86. Placing the mass of flesh near his wife, he went to fetch firewood for cooking the flesh, as he was hungry.

87. When he kindled fire (and began cooking a part of the flesh), I swiftly flew there and began to cut the flesh (left with his wife).

88. But it was too heavy for me to carry away and so I remained there itself.

89. After eating the (cooked) flesh, the hunter was much pleased, but, not seeing the mass of flesh, looked for it everywhere.

90. Then he saw me eating the mass of flesh. At once he took his bow and discharged an arrow towards me.

91. The arrow hit me and hurled me down from the mass of flesh I was eating.

92. Then I moved about here and there practically dead.

93. But by the power of this holy place, I was born a princess and became your beloved with the memory of my former life.

94. See here the remains of the bones of my former body".

She told her husband again:

95. "O blessed soul, you have been brought to this Kokāmukha.

96. By the power of this place even animals get birth as human beings and in high families.

97. O famous prince, whatever *dharma* is there spoken by Viṣṇu, I follow, because that gives us supreme joy in the world of Viṣṇu".

98. At this narration, the prince was wonderstruck remembering the previous birth.

99. The princess, fully knowing what was to be done in that place, herself did certain rites fully devoted to her husband.

100. Hearing this, others also performed whatever prescribed rite that was to their liking.

101. Then the couple gave gifts of food and gems in great delight to deserving Brahmins.

102. Others who were given presents, also gave them to Brahmins because of their devotion to Viṣṇu.

103. Remaining there steadfast in devotion they went to Śvetadvīpa (the white island).

104. The prince also, following the tenets of my worship, cast off his human form and reached Śvetadvīpa. All the people there realise their own selves.

105. They are all clad in white, adorned with divine jewels, effulgent, tall and fine-looking.

106. The women also have divine jewels, are resplendent and pure, and absorbed in contemplating on me.

107. Thus have I told you about the matchless Kokāmukha where the fish and the cricket attained each other.

108. Some may perform the Cāndrāyaṇa ceremony, some may live on water alone. But every Brahmin shall follow the *dharma* laid down by Viṣṇu.

109. Even those couples who have a lot of grain and gems, perform the rites laid down by me for my devotees.

110-111. All those who move about serving me, go to the Śvetadvīpa after death by the power of the place, the power of their deeds and my own power.

112. So it was that the prince also went there after giving up his human form.

113. Even his servants who were devoted to me cast off their mortal frame and reached my world.

114. There all are resplendent and every one realises the self.

115. All the women there have the smell of the lotus, are free from *māyā* and in the company of their beloved persons. They reach Śvetadvīpa due to my blessing.

116. This is virtue, this is fame, this is power, this is renown.

117. This is the greatest of actions, the highest of penances, the best of narratives and the worthiest of deeds.

118. I have now told you about the highest of *dharmas*. This should not be told to a choleric, a fool or a jealous person.

119. Nor should it be told to a non-devotee, the unlistening or the arrogant. It should be imparted only to the calm and the initiated.

120. It should not be imparted to the disputing man even if he is learned.

121. He who remembers this at the time of death, gets removed of all sins and never takes birth again.

122. I have thus told you, O Earth, this great and inv gorating story. Those who go to Kokāmukha attain supreme bliss as did the fish and the cricket.

CHAPTER ONE HUNDRED AND TWENTYTHREE

The greatness of flowers, sandalpaste etc.

Sūta said:

1. On hearing about the greatness of Kokā with its emphasis on *dharma*, the Earth became wonderstruck.

Earth said:

2. "How wonderful the greatness of Kokā narrated by lord Varāha, that even animals attain supreme bliss.

3-4. Now, O lord, by your grace I wish to know what I have already asked you, namely, by what *dharma*, penance or action can people see your benign face ?"

5. Requested thus by the goddess Earth, the lord laughed and began to tell her:

Varāha said:

6. "What you ask is quite proper. I shall tell you that secret which leads to release from *saṁsāra*.

7. When the rainy season is over and the autumn sets in with the sky clear and the moon fully bright.

8. With the weather neither hot nor cold, when the swans sing in delight and the smell of the lotus, lily and kalhāra spreads.

9. There on the Dvādaśī day in the month of Kumuda, (Kārttikà) if one worships me, what merit he attains I shall tell you.

10. O Earth, such a person becomes my devotee and not of any other so long as these worlds last.

11. Performing actions relating to me on Dvādaśī day he shall utter the following mantra for my worship:

12. "You are praised by Brahmā and Rudra. You are adorable and adored by the sages. Dvādaśī has come. Awake, arise. The clouds are gone. The moon is full. O lord of the worlds, I offer you the flowers of autumn for the sake of *dharma*. For worshipping you who have arisen, sacrifices are performed, the Vedas are recited by the awakened, O lord of the worlds".

13. Doing in this way on Dvādaśī day, my devotees attain supreme bliss.

14. Thus have I told you about the autumnal action aimed at getting release from *saṁsāra* for my devotees.

Thus is the action of awakening.

15. I shall now tell you about the actions to be performed in winter by doing which the devotees attain supreme bliss.

16. Although tormented by cold winds, remaining firm in devotion and with unchanging mind.

17-18. Worshipping me with the flowers available in winter, kneeling down on the floor and with folded hands, the following mantra is to be uttered:

19. "O lord of the worlds, you are winter, the snow is impenetrable and uncrossable. Lead me out of this *saṁsāra*, O lord of the three worlds".

20. He who performs worship with this mantra in full devotion, attains supreme bliss.

21. O Earth, I shall tell you another thing, please listen.

22. The month Mārgaśiras is very dear to me; so too the month Vaiśākha. I shall tell you the result of offering flowers to me then.

23. He who makes offerings to me then with a steady mind, goes to Viṣṇuloka and remains there for nine thousand nine hundred years.

24. The offering of even a single turmeric produces great effect. So one should wisely offer turmeric and flowers.

I shall tell you more about the efficacy of turmeric.

25-26. During the three months Kaumuda, Mārgaśīrṣa and Vaiśākha, he who offers me with constant mind the *vanamālā* of beautiful flowers and sweet sandal on the Dvādaśī days.

27. Attains the merit of worshipping me for twelve years.

28. In Kaumuda the flower of Śāla with sandal, in Mārgaśiras the flower of lotus with sandal (are important in my worship). Thus have I told you about the result of worship with turmeric".

29. After hearing all this, Earth laughed and then spoke to him in all humility.

30. "O lord, there are twelve months (consisting of) three hundred and sixty days. Of these why two (months) alone are particularly praised by you, and even there why Dvādaśī alone?"

31. Asked thus by the Earth, he laughed and told her words of *dharma*.

32. "O goddess, I shall tell you why these two are particularly dear to me.

33. (Worship of Dvādaśī day) is more important than all sacrifices. By this one attains the same result as by giving gifts of land to a thousand Brahmins.

34. I wake up in the month of Kaumuda and remain alert in Vaiśākha.

35. O Earth, these remove all ailments and, therefore, with steady mind in Kaumuda and Vaiśākha, one should take turmeric in the hand and utter the mantra:

36-37. "O lord, command me. Vaiśākha and Kārttika are eternally great. Accept this turmeric and increase all *dharma*. Bow to Nārāyaṇa", and then make the offering.

38. I shall now tell you about the qualities and results of offering flowers. After turmeric, one should take flowers in the hand and say 'Om, bow to Vāsudeva' and then utter the following mantra:

39. "O lord, command me. Make my mind favourable to worship you with these flowers. Accept them with sandalpaste. I bow to you".

40. He who worships me offering me these, never again takes birth, is never fatigued and never feels hungry.

41. He remains in my world for a thousand divine years.

42. Such is the effect of each flower offered. Such is the greatness that arises from flowers and sandal about which you asked.

CHAPTER ONE HUNDRED AND TWENTYFOUR

Worship in the Seasons

Varāha said:

1. On the Dvādaśī day in the bright half of the month of Phālguna, the devotee should collect the fragrant flowers blooming in spring.

2. Flowers that are white or pale yellow and auspicious and offer them in the prescribed manner with a pleasant mind.

3. This ritual relating to the great God is to be done by one who knows the rules and rituals and is clean.

4. This is to be done according to rules and uttering the prescribed mantra and with pure mind.

5. First should be uttered 'Om, I bow to Nārāyaṇa' and then the mantra: "I bow to you, the lord of Devas, holding the conch, disc and mace; I bow to you, the lord of the worlds; I bow to you, the great hero.

6. Splendid is the spring season with the trees full of fragrant and honeyed flowers".

7. He, who worships in this manner in the month of Phālguna, goes to my world and is never born again.

8. I shall now tell you the result of worship on the Dvādaśī day of the bright half of the month of Vaiśākha which you asked about.

9. When the Śālas and other trees are in full bloom, the devotee should collect the flowers of the Śāla for my worship.

10. Performing the rituals and honouring other devotees, he should lay them before me.

11. O Earth, the sages praise with Vedic mantras. Gandharvas and Apsarases sing and play instruments and dance.

12. The entire celestial world praises this most ancient and best Man. The Siddhas, Vidyādharas, Yakṣas, Piśācas, Uragas (snakes) and Rākṣasas praise the god of all beings and the lord of all worlds.

13. The Ādityas, Vasus, Rudras, Aśvins and Maruts praise the god of gods who alone remains when everything else disappears.

14. Then Vāyu, Viśvedevas and Aśvins praise lord Keśava who remains from the most early times.

15. Then Brahmā, Soma, Indra and Agni come together and praise the lord of all worlds.

16-17. Nārada, Parvata, Asita, Devala, Pulastya, Pulaha, Bhṛgu, Aṅgiras and many other sages like Mitrāvasu and Parāvasu, praise the lord of all beings and the greatest of yogins.

18. Hearing the reverberating sound of the praise by Devas, lord Nārāyaṇa told Earth:

19. "Do you hear this sound mixed with the recitation of the Vedas? Do you hear the sound of Devas?"

20. The lotus-eyed Earth endowed with all forms and qualities replied to the lord in the form of the boar:

21. "O lord, Devas desire that this boar form of yours be there for ever and they are all engaged towards that end".

22. Then lord Nārāyaṇa told Earth: "I know that they have come here seeking this.

23. I have held you, with ease at the tip of one of my tusks, O Earth, for a thousand divine years.

24. And you are quite safe. To see this have come here the celestials, Ādityas, Vasus, Rudras, Skanda, Indra and Brahmā".

25. Hearing these words of Viṣṇu, Earth fell down at his feet with hands folded over the head.

26. She then requested the great lord in the form of the boar: "I who sank deep in the netherworld was raised by you.

27. I seek refuge in you as your devotee. You are my lord and saviour. What is *Karma*? By what *karma* can life's aim be achieved?

28. How can you be propitiated? By what action can you be worshipped? I wish to do that which will be conducive to my happiness.

29. Being engaged in your service, I never feel fatigue or strain, nor do old age and birth and death affect me.

30. Where do the gods, demons and people, as also Rudra, Indra and Brahmā remain in pleasure ?

31. What actions do those perform that realise you, O Mādhava ? What food do they take and what practices do they follow ?

32. What should be the actions of the Brahmins, what should be the actions of the Kṣatriyas ? What actions should the Vaiśyas do and what the Śūdras ?

33. By whom is yoga attained, by whom penance ? What result does he attain who is devoted to you ?

34. What should be the nature of living of your devotees ? What food shall they take and what drink ? What is the nature of their actions ?

35. Which directions do they take ? How can they attain cessation from birth, particularly in a despicable family ?

36. By what action can they avoid being born as animals ? Tell me all this by which they attain happiness ?

37. By what action can they avoid old age and rebirth, O Acyuta ? By the power of which action can they get relief from *saṁsāra* ?"

38. Thus requested by Earth, the lord replied.

39. "Know how my devotees are led to the path of liberation and what mantras please me.

40. The mantra: "O Mādhava, you are indeed the month Mādhava which is the chief of all months. May you be seen in the spring season when approached with sandal-paste. Lord Nārāyaṇa who is the greatest hero in all the seven worlds and ever present in sacrifices is invoked".

41. In summer also worship should be done as I have directed, and the following mantra, which is for the good of all devotees, should be uttered:

42. "In summer occurs the most important of months. May you be seen, O lord, in summer so that all my sufferings may cease".

43. O lovely damsel, my worship is to be performed in this way in summer so that there may not be any more births or deaths (for the devotee).

44. As long as there are flowering trees and sweet smelling objects like sandal, so long I may be worshipped in this manner.

45. In the rainy season also my worship may be performed. By this the intellect becomes pure and the soul never becomes subject to *saṁsāra*.

46. I shall tell you another thing conducive to release from *saṁsāra*.

47. After consecrating me, I should be ritualistically worshipped using the buds of Kadamba tree and the flowers of Sarala and Arjuna. The mantra *Namo Nārāyaṇāya* (Bow to Nārāyaṇa) should be uttered and then:

48. "The blessed people who contemplate on you and worship you find you of the hue of the cloud. May you enter into sleep, O lord of the worlds, during this rainy season seeing the colour of the cloud".

49. He who performed my worship on Dvādaśī day in the month of Āṣāḍha, never falls into *saṁsāra* at any time.

50. I have thus told you about the worship in the different seasons, by which the devotees cross *saṁsāra*.

51. This secret is not known even to the gods, other than lord Nārāyaṇa in this form of the boar.

52. This should not be communicated to the uninitiated, the uneducated or the envious, nor to an undeserving disciple or one who finds fault with scripture.

53. This should not be read to those who slaughter cows or those who are wicked, as it will result in rapid loss of wealth and virtue.

54. It should be read only to devotees and those who are wedded to *dharma*.

55. I have thus told you what you desired to know in full, what else do you ask me?

CHAPTER ONE HUNDRED AND TWENTYFIVE

Māyācakra

Sūta said:

1. After listening to the actions to be performed in the six seasons, Earth again asked Lord Nārāyaṇa.

2. "You have explained the auspicious and sacred actions to be performed, that indeed gladden your mind.

3. Knowing these from you, O Mādhava, I have become free from stain like the moon in autumn.

4. I am now eager to know another secret which you may be pleased to enlighten me about, namely.

5. What is it that you speak of as my *māyā* (illusory power); what is its nature, O Viṣṇu.

6. I wish to know this great secret, namely the meaning of *Māyā*."

7. Viṣṇu, who is the very repository of *māyā*, laughed a little at this, and then told Earth:

8. "You ask this quite earnestly, but why do you ask this since you see it yourself?

9. But know this that even Rudra, Indra and Brahmā have not known me fully even now; then how can you, O Earth, know my *Māyā*?

10. Where the clouds shower rain, there water accumulates, but there are also places without any water. This is due to my *māyā*.

11. The moon wanes in one fortnight and waxes in the next, and does not appear at all on new moon day. This is really due to my *māyā*.

12. In winter, the water in the well is warm, but in summer it is cool. This really is due to my *māyā*.

13. The sun sets in the west and rises in the east the next morning. This is due to my *māyā*.

14. The generative fluid is in the female and the semen is in the male. In the womb they combine to form a being. This is due to my *māyā*.

15. The soul entering the embryo knows pleasure and pain, but when once born, it forgets the whole thing. This is due to my *māyā*.

16. The soul depends upon its own actions, but is quite unaware of it and is free from desire. But by its actions it is led elsewhere. This is due to my *māyā*.

17. Living beings are born (in the human and animal world) by the combination of semen of the male and the generative fluid of the female.

18. The fingers, feet, hands, head, waist, hip, belly, teeth, lips, nose, ears, eyes, cheeks, forehead and tongue, all these are produced in association with my *māyā*.

19. By the same *māyā* do they deteriorate like fire transforming the food eaten and the liquids drunk.

20. Sound, touch, colour, taste and smell all act in a living being due to food. All this is by my *māyā*.

21. The cause of the effects on stationary and mobile objects in each season is not known because of my *māyā*, O fair damsel.

22. The celestial waters as well as terrestrial waters by which the rivers are flooded are all due to my *māyā*.

23. During the rainy season, all ponds and lakes are full of water, but in summer season, they all dry up. This is due to the power of my *māyā*.

24. The river arising from the peak of Himavān with the name Mandākinī and flowing in earth with the name Gaṅgā is because of my *māyā*.

25. The clouds drawing water from the saline ocean and showering it on the land as sweet water is due to my *māyā*.

26. Beings afflicted by disease take in medicine. The efficacy of such medicines is due to my *māyā*.

27. That in spite of medicine, a being sometimes dies is because of the fact I take it away making the medicine ineffective.

28. First the embryo is formed, then the child is born, afterwards he becomes a youth and finally becomes old. In due course the senses are lost. All this is due to my *māyā*.

29. The seed sown in the field sprouts and then gets foliage. by my *māyā*.

30. From a single (aggregate) seed grow numerous plants and they all become perennial because of my *māyā*.

31. People say that Garuḍa is the vehicle of Lord Viṣṇu. Really I become Garuḍa and bear myself.

32. Different gods are made to be pleased by the offerings in sacrifices. Really it is I that please them by my *māyā*.

33. All people believe that the gods always eat the sacrificial offerings. Really the sacrifices propitiating the gods are due to my *māyā*.

34. All people consider Bṛhaspati as the sacrificer. Actually it is I that do the sacrifice by my *māyā Āṅgirasī*.

35. All people believe that Varuṇa protects the sea. It is I that protect the sea by my *māyā Vāruṇi*.

36. All people take it that Kubera is the lord of wealth. It is I that protect that wealth by my *Kuberamāyā*.

37. All people think that Vṛtra was killed by Indra. Vṛtra was really killed by me by *Aindrī māyā*.

38. All people believe that the sun remains constant by itself. But the fact is that by producing Meru by my *māyā*, I hold the sun.

39-40. All people take it that water (in the ocean) is consumed (by the submarine fire). Really it is I that sit at the mouth of Baḍavā (the submarine fire) and consume the water. And by producing wind by my *māyā*, the water is lodged in the clouds.

41. All people ask "Where is water deposited ?" Even the gods do not know where *amṛta* remains. By my *māyā* the medicine remains (in the herbs) in the forest.

42. All people think that it is the king who protects his subjects. It is I that really rule the earth by producing *Rājamāyā*.

43. Twelve suns appear at the time of deluge. I enter them, O Earth, and create *māyā* in the world.

44. O Earth, it is by (the heat of) rays of the sun that all cooking is made possible. But it is really my Aṁśumayī *māyā* in the form of these rays.

45. The Saṁvarta clouds (at the time of deluge) pour down water in torrents. It is really I that fill the world with water by my *māyā sāṁvartikī*.

46. O Earth, that I repose over the serpent Śeṣa is because of my Anantamāyā.

47. What I do by *Varāhamāyā* you already know.

48. Do you not know that the Devas are all enveloped by my *Vaiṣṇavī māyā* ?

49. O beautiful damsel, I have raised you up from the big ocean and held you (in my tusk) seventeen times by my *māyā*.

50. That I remain in this water is also due to my *māyā*.

51. I create Brahmā and Rudra and hold them. But due to the power of my *māyā* they do not know it.

52. The group of Pitṛs resplendent like the sun, I hold by my *Pitṛmayī māyā* ultimately, but apparently by you.

53. I shall now tell you how by the power of *māyā* a sage was made to enter the womb of a woman".

54. Extremely eager to hear this, Earth said with folded hands.

55. "What was the difficult task done by that sage that gave him womanhood and was made to enter a woman's womb ?

56. I am very much curious to know this. What was the sinful action of the great Brahmin that brought him womanhood ?"

57. Hearing the words of Earth, Lord Viṣṇu was very much pleased and spoke to her in sweet words.

58. "O lovely goddess, listen to this. By my exciting *māyā Rohiṇī*, Somaśarmā was tormented.

59. He had numerous lives exalted, ordinary and despicable, but became a Brāhmaṇa again because of my *māyā*.

60. That he was led to the womb of a woman was not because of any prohibited action or offending deed of his.

61. He was always worshipping me and performing deeds that would please me. He was always meditating on my attractive form.

62. After a long time, I was very much pleased with his penance, devotion and unchanging mind.

63. I then appeared before him and asked him to seek a boon.

64. I said: "O Brahmin, ask of me anything you have in mind, gems, gold, cows or even a kingdom free from trouble.

65. If you desire heaven where you get all pleasures, beautiful women and gems and gold in abundance,

66. And where there are celestial Apsarases, I shall give you".

67. Hearing my words, the Brahmin prostrated before me and said:

68. "If you will not feel angry, I shall tell you what boon I desire now that you have offered me many things to choose from.

69. I don't desire gold, cows, women or kingdom; nor do I desire Apsarases or abundant wealth.

70. I do not wish even one among the thousand heavens. I wish to know only about your *Māyā* by which you play".

71. Hearing his words, I spoke to him: 'O virtuous Brahmin, what have you to do with *Māyā*? Why do you ask about this irrelevant thing?

72. Deluded by *Viṣṇumāyā*, even the gods do not know about it".

73. Hearing my words, the great Brahmin spoke being induced by *māyā*:

74. "If you are pleased with me, O great god, by my actions or penance, give me the boon I have asked".

75. Then I asked that ascetic Brahmin to go to the place called Kubjāmraka on the bank of the river Gaṅgā and take bath there in order to know *Māyā*. He then circumambulated me and went there.

76. O goddess, at Kubjāmraka he carefully placed on the bank his staff, vessel and bundle of cloth.

77. Then performing the prescribed rites for the bath, he got down on the river.

78. As soon as his whole body was immersed in water, he found himself in the womb of a woman in a hunter's hut.

79. Troubled by being deposited there, he thought: "what a pity ! what bad deed did I do that I am now in the hell of the womb of the wife of a hunter?

80. Fie on my penance, fie on my righteous deeds, fie on the effects of these, fie on my life, that now I am placed in the womb of this wife of the hunter full of filth.

81. With three hundred bones, nine openings, full of urine and faecal matter and flesh and blood.

82. Foul smelling, unbearable, full of air, phlegm and bile, with numerous diseases.

83. Or why say all this? I am undergoing a lot of suffering.

84. Where is Viṣṇu? Where am I? Where is Gaṅgā? Having been placed in this womb, I have to face all the consequences".

85. While he was thinking like this, he was cast out of the womb, and falling on the earth, he lost all his reminiscence.

86. The Brahmin was born as a girl in the hunter's house which, however, was affluent.

87. Being deluded by the *māyā* of Viṣṇu, the girl did not remember anything (about her previous life).

88. In due time she was well married and she begot sons and daughters.

89. She ate permitted as well as prohibited food and drank permitted as well as prohibited drink. She also killed several creatures.

90. Deluded by *māyā* she could not discriminate between good and bad actions or good and bad utterances; so too between permitted and forbidden contacts.

91. After fifty years, I decided to call back that Brahmin (now living as the hunter's wife).

92. In order to wash dirty cloth, she went to the Ganges with a pot and, placing the cloth and the pot on the bank, plunged into the water.

93. When she dipped herself into the river being oppressed by heat and sweat, she was retransformed into the ascetic Brahmin holding the staff and vessel.

94. He found himself holding the staff and the vessel. He could see the bundle of cloth he had placed formerly on the bank.

95. When knowledge dawned upon him as before, he was able to know the power of the *māyā* of Viṣṇu.

96. He took his original clothes from there and began, as before, his yogic practice sitting on the sands of Ganges.

97. Then he understood himself and also what happened. He cursed himself for having done heinous things.

98. He felt sorry for the loss of his *ācāra* in the despicable life he was subjected to.

99. (He repented:) "I was born in the family of a hunter. I ate forbidden food. I killed many creatures, terrestrial, celestial and aquatic.

100. I drank forbidden drinks and traded on prohibited things. The prohibitions relating to contacts and utterances were not observed by me.

101. Doubtless I ate in the home discarded food. I gave birth to sons and daughters begot in me by the hunter.

102. What a crime have I done? But who thinks of this

that I have been brought to this state of being the wife of a hunter ?"

103. In the meantime the hunter became angry and came to that Māyātīrtha in the Ganges together with his children.

104. He searched there for his devoted and beautiful wife and asked every ascetic he saw there about her.

105. (He wailed:) "O my dear, where have you gone leaving me and the children at home ? The little girl cries for breast-milk".

106. (He asked the sages:) "Did you find my wife who came to the bank of the Ganges with a pot in hand to fetch water" ?

107. People flocked there and they saw the ascetic with the pot near him.

108. Seeing the cloth and the pot and not the wife, the hunter was grief-stricken and he lamented a lot.

109. "The cloth and pot are left on the bank of the river, but my wife who took them here is not to be seen.

110. Can it be that some crocodile snatched her away for delicious food.

111. I never spoke to her anything harsh even in dream.

112. Perhaps she is devoured by some spirit, goblin or demon. Or some (sudden) disease caught hold of her when she entered the river (and she became senseless and was carried away by the stream).

113. What bad thing did I do in my former life that my wife met with her end this way ?

114. O my dear wife who used to follow my mind always, look at these pitiable children moving about in fear here and there.

115. Look at me, my dear, and the three little sons and the four daughters.

116. The boys cry to see you. The daughters seek your help. How cursed am I !

117. You certainly know that I am hungry and thirsty. Please be kind to assuage my grief".

118. To the hunter who was wailing like this and was restlessly moving about, the Brahmin said without going near him.

119. "After being with you and giving you pleasure, she has departed never to return.

120. Go away without uselessly lamenting any more. Bring up these children with the necessary food. They should never be given up".

121. Hearing these words of the ascetic, the grief-stricken hunter said in soft tone :

122. "O great sage, the upholder of *dharma*, I am really consoled by your sweet words".

123-124. When the hunter spoke thus, the ascetic spoke again feeling great pity for him.

125. "Please don't cry. I shall tell you the truth. It was I that was your wife. When I came to the bank of this Ganges, I was transformed like this."

126. Hearing the words of the ascetic, the hunter felt much consoled and spoke to him again.

127. "O Brahmin, what do you say? This is mystifying. How can a woman be transformed into a man?"

128. The Brahmin felt very sad at this and told that fish-hunter softly.

129. "Go to your house with these children and give them the attention they deserve".

130. In spite of the persuation of the Brahmin, the hunter was at a loss to know, and so asked him again.

131. "What wrong had you done in the past that you became a woman, as you say, and how did it happen?

132. And having become a woman, by whatever fault, how did you become a man again? Please tell me".

133. At this the ascetic replied to that fish-hunter in the Māyātīrtha in Ganges.

134. "O hunter, hear my story. Really I did not do anywhere anything which I should not have done.

135. I was taking food only once a day and that too was never of any prohibited article. Janārdana (Viṣṇu) the lord of the worlds, was worshipped by me by various rites with a view to seeing Him.

136. After a long time, Janārdana appeared before me and asked me to seek a boon.

137. I did not, however, desire any boon and requested that I may be shown his *Māyā*.

138. The lord told me: "Enough of *māyā*, O Brahmin (Ask

something else)". But I insisted on the *māyā* being shown to me.

139. Then he said that I will know what *māyā* is and asked me to take bath in the Ganges at the place called Kubjāmraka.

140. Anxious to know about *māyā*, I immediately went there, and placing my staff, vessel and cloth on the bank, dipped myself in the river after performing the due rites.

141. I am unable to know what happened then. But I was born as a hunter's daughter and became your wife.

142. For some reason I entered the Ganges again and I become the old ascetic again.

143. See here my old vessel, staff and cloth. Though this is after fifty years, the river Ganges has kept them all intact".

144. As he said this, the hunter disappeared and none of his children could be seen there.

145. O Earth, the Brahmin then performed penance with upward breath and arms held upwards and living on air alone.

146. In the afternoon he offered water ritualistically.

147. Sitting in the Vīrāsana pose, he worshipped me with the prescribed flowers.

148. The Brahmins going for bath in the Ganges asked him.

149. "In the forenoon you placed your bundle, cloth and vessel here, and went to the fishermen (hunters). Did you forget this that you did not return soon ?"

150. Hearing these words of the Brahmins, the ascetic simply remained quiet, contemplating on the self.

151. Then, O goddess, the Brahmin thought: "Now fifty years are over and it is Amāvāsyā today.

152. Then why do these Brahmins say that I left these things here just this forenoon ?"

153. Just then I appeared before him and asked him.

154. "Why are you stupefied ? What have you seen ? Finding you perplexed, I came here".

155. Asked thus by me, he prostrated before me and told me with great distress, frequently heaving.

156. "O preceptor of the whole world, these Brahmins tell me that I left this staff, this vessel and this cloth here in the forenoon and I returned in the afternoon and whether I forgot them.

156 (a) Actually I was born as daughter to a hunter, was married to another hunter and remained in that state for fifty years.

157. I bore three sons and three daughters by him probably as a result of my misdeed in earlier lives.

158-59. Once I happened to go to the Ganges for bath and when I dipped myself in it, leaving my cloth bundle on the bank, I became converted into the Brahmin again.

160. What fault d d I commit when I was worshipping you or performing penance ?

161. Did I eat any prohibited food or commit any error in worship to you ?

162. Please tell me the truth as to why I had this hell ? Please know that I am extremely tormented by these thoughts.

163. I was eager to know about *māyā* and so I asked you about it. I do not remember to have committed any sin to be put to hell like this".

164. Noting his pitiable lament, I told the distressed Brahmin:

165. "O Brahmin, don't be sorry. There is no fault in you nor have you committed any error in worship by which you were afflicted and made to have a hinferior birth.

166. I asked you formerly to seek a boon, but you chose to have knowledge of *māyā*.

167. I offered you heavenly pleasures or worldly pleasures if such was your desire. But you wanted to get the knowledge of *māyā*.

168. You have, therefore, seen *Vaiṣṇavī māyā* according to your desire. There is no day, no afternoon nor the life of yours in the hunter's house for fifty years.

169. I shall tell you another thing about the *Vaiṣṇavī māyā* which you desired to know.

170. You did neither good nor bad. Everything is due to *māyā* which stupefies all.

171. You have not done any bad action or swerved from the proper path. Nor have you committed anything wrong in worship or in penance.

172. The suffering you were subjected to was the result of your actions in previous birth. I shall tell you about it.

173. This predicament of yours was the result of the sin incurred by your failing to revere the Brahmins who were devoted to me.

174. My devotees are really my own manifestations. Those who honour such Brahmins really honour me. I am known by them.

175. People should know that my devotees deserve to be worshipped by those desiring to attain me.

176. Particularly in Kali age, I am manifest in Brahmins. Therefore, those who honour Brahmins do really honour me.

177. He who is irreproachable and desires to attain me, let him turn his attention towards my devotees.

178. O Brahmin, you have now accomplished your desire. When you die, you will surely reach my place, Śvetadvīpa".

179. So saying, the lord disappeared. The Brahmin too cast off his mortal coil at Māyātīrtha and reached Śvetadvīpa.

180. By the power of *māyā* he attained bow, arrow, quiver and sword and supreme valour and remains always seeing me.

181. O Earth, why do you ask about *māyā*? You cannot know *māyā*. My *māyā* is incomprehensible even to gods and Rākṣasas.

182. I have now told you about this mighty *māyā*. This is called 'Māyācakra' and it brings about good.

183. This is the greatest of all narratives, the highest of penance, the best of merits and the most important of all paths.

184. This should be narrated to devotees and not to non-devotees. This should not be recited in the midst of the bad or those who find fault with scripture.

185. The Brahmin should recite it before devotees, and not before those who dishonour scripture.

186. O Earth, he who recites it with due adoration, attains result equivalent to reciting it a dozen times in my presence.

187. And at the end of his full life, becomes my perpetual devotee and never takes birth in any inferior family.

188. He, who listens to this great story also, is never born dull and never takes birth in any inferior family.

189. I have thus told you what you desired to know. What else do you wish to ask?

CHAPTER ONE HUNDRED AND TWENTYSIX

The greatness of Kubjāmraka—the story of the serpent and ichneumon

1. Hearing about the power of Māyā from the lord, Earth asked Varāha again:

Earth said:

2. What you have to say about Kubjāmraka is endless, I know. But I am not able to grasp well even what you have said.

3. You may, therefore, tell me about the sacredness and glory of Kubjāmraka.

Varāha said:

4. I shall tell you all this which is conducive to the welfare of the world at large, the glory of Kubjāmraka and holy spots there.

5. Hear this in full, O goddess, how this Kubjāmraka came into being and about the holy places there, and also what accrues to a person who bathes or dies there.

6. O Earth, in the seventeenth aeon when the whole earth was one mass.

7. And after killing the demons Madhu and Kaiṭabha according to the desire of Brahmā and collecting all the waters together for my repose.

8. I was not able to see sage Raibhya who was deep in my devotion, scrupulously performing all the prescribed actions.

9. Very intelligent, virtuous, pure, clever, who had controlled all his senses, who performed penance with upraised hands for one thousand years.

10. Another thousand years by living on water alone and then for five hundred years on moss.

11. I was very much pleased by the supreme devotion of Raibhya and I was well worshipped by him.

12. Then I saw that great sage performing penance at the foot of a mango tree on the bank of the Ganges.

13. This was pointed out to me by some one, but when I came near that mango tree, he became a dwarf.

14. This place thus came to be called 'Kubjāmraka' (the place of the mango with the dwarf). People who die there go to my world.

15. I shall tell you another thing, O Earth, namely what that sage said.

16. When I saw him as a dwarf, he crawled towards me with his knees and began to speak.

17. Seeing him bow to me, I was much pleased and I offered him a boon.

18. Hearing my words, that virtuous sage spoke sweet words.

19. "If you, O lord Janārdaṇa, are so pleased, may you remain in this place for ever.

20. I pray you to be here as long as the world lasts.

21. This is the one boon which I have in mind. May you grant this if you are pleased.

22. May I have devotion for you always. I do not wish to have devotion for any one else".

23. Hearing these words of sage Raibhya, I said "Let it be as you desire".

24. Then, O Earth, the Brahmin said after contemplating for a while:

25. "O protector of the worlds, I wish to know from you about the greatness of this great *tirtha*.

26. As well as of the other tīrthas in this place."

27. (I said then:) "O Brahmin, I shall tell you what you wish to know.

28. In this holy and pleasant Kubjāmraka there is a *tirtha* with the shape of a lily, by the mere bath in which people attain heaven.

29. In the months Kaumuda, Mārgaśīrṣa and Vaiśākha, after austerities.

30. One who ends one's life here attains heaven, be the person a man, woman or eunuch.

31. I shall tell you about another, O Earth. Please listen. That is the *tīrtha* known as Mānasa.

32. By bathing in this, one goes to the divine garden Nandana and enjoys there with Apsarases for a thousand divine years.

33. At the end of this period of thousand years, he is born in a big family with abundant wealth and virtues.

34. If he dies there on the Dvādaśī day in Kaumuda, he attains great merit and reaches my world.

35. I shall tell you about another. Please listen, O Earth. It is known as Māyātīrtha by which people understand *māyā*.

36. By bathing there, one attains great fame and remains my devotee for ten thousand years.

37. Gets abundant wealth and reaches the abode of Kubera. He gets the capacity to go wherever he likes for a thousand years.

38. If one dies in the Māyātīrtha, he becomes a *māyāyogin* and reaches my world.

39. I shall now tell you, O Earth, about Sarvatīrtha which has the efficacy of all *tīrthas*.

40. By bathing there on the Dvādaśī day of Vaiśākha month, one enjoys heaven for fifteen thousand years.

41. If one gives up life there giving up all attachment, one attains my world.

42. O fair goddess, I shall tell you now about the little known *tīrtha* called Pūrṇasukha.

43. While the whole of the river Ganges is cool, in Pūrṇamukha it is warm.

44. By bathing in this, one goes to the world of Soma and remains there for fifteen thousand years.

45. Then he is dropped from heaven and takes birth as a Brahmin, pure, clever and a devotee of mine endowed with all good qualities.

46. If he dies there on Dvādaśī day in the bright half of the month Mārgaśīrṣa, he goes to my world.

47. And finds me there in my effulgent form with four hands. He will have no more births or deaths.

48. O Earth, listen to my account of another *tīrtha* with full concentration.[1]

49. If a person with unflinching devotion for me bathes in this tīrtha at any time, he goes to heaven and remains there for ten thousand years.

50. At the termination of his period in heaven, he is born again as a virtuous and wealthy devotee.

51. After severe austerities, if one gives up life here on Dvādaśī day in the bright half of the month Vaiśākha.

52. One will have no more birth or death, nor langour or fear, and becoming free from all attachments, goes to my world.

53. I shall now tell you, O Earth, about the *tīrtha* called Karavīra which brings about happiness to all.

---

1. The name of the tirtha is not given. Presumably it is Amaratirtha.

54. I shall tell you about its characteristics by which it may be known.

55. If the man with knowledge and devoted to me, on the Dvādaśī day in the month of Māgha, when the Karavīra plant (oleander) is full of flowers.

56. Takes bath in it in midday after the prescribed rituals, gets the power to move and live anywhere travelling in a divine car with a thousand women dancing in attendance.

57. If one dies there on the Dvādaśī day in the month of Māgha, he sees me, Brahmā and Śiva.

58. O Earth, I shall tell you about another *tīrtha* which I formerly told to that Brahmin.

59. That is called Puṇḍarīka, and this is particularly dear to me in Kubjāmraka.

60. I shall tell you about its characteristics by which it may be identified.

61. At noon on Dvādaśī day there moves in it a tortoise as big as a chariot's wheel. Listen to what I have to say about it.

62. Bathing there confers the same merit as performing the Puṇḍarīka sacrifice. There need be no doubt in this.

63. If one happens to die there, he regains consciousness, becomes famous.

64. And after enjoying the merit of performing ten Puṇḍarīka sacrifices, becomes highly purified and ascetic.

65. Gains great attainments and gets a permanent place in my world.

66. I shall tell you about another. Please listen. That is the Agnitīrtha in Kubjāmraka, proclaimed as efficacious for the sinless on Dvādaśī day.

67-68. The Dvādaśī in the bright half of the months of Kaumuda, Mārgaśīrṣa, Āṣāḍha and Mādhava are particularly important for this.

69. I shall tell you the characteristics by which this *tīrtha* of mine can be identified.

70. So you listen with attention. None other than the pure Bhāgavatas who master my *Saṁhitās* know the *Śāstra* relating to me.

71. I ask you again to listen, for I am going to tell you about the result accruing by bathing or dying there.

72. The man who bathes in Agnitīrtha in Kubjāmrka which is a Vaiṣṇava tīrtha of great efficacy.

73. Attains the merit equivalent to that of seven Agnimedha sacrifices.

74-75. If one dies there on Dvādaśī day after remaining there for twenty days, he reaches my world.

76. I shall tell you about the characteristics of this tīrtha which it can be known (as I already promised).

77. During the hot season it is cool, and during the cold season it is warm. Such is this Āgneyatīrtha, O Earth, and through this people are able to cross the ocean of the woes of worldly life.

78. I shall now tell you about another *tīrtha* in Kubjāmraka, called Vāyavyatīrtha which arose from *dharma*.

79. He who bathes there after performing the daily ablutions, attains the merit of Vājapeya sacrifice.

80. If anyone dies in this Vāyutīrtha after performing worship for fifteen days, he will not have birth or death again in this world.

81. He becomes four-armed and remains in my world.

82. I shall tell you about its further characteristics to facilitate its identification.

83. The leaves of the Aśvattha (Pipal) tree always flutter there during all the twentyfour Dvādaśī days in the year.

84. I shall now tell you about another *tīrtha* in Kubjāmraka, known as Śakratīrtha which helps us to cross the ocean of *saṁsāra*.

85. In that Śakratīrtha, O Earth, Śakra (i.e., Indra) always resides with Vajrāyudha in his hand.

86. He who dies in this highly holy Śakratīrtha after fasting for ten days, reaches my world.

87. I shall tell you its characteristics for the sake of identification. Please listen attentively.

88. Five trees stand on its southern side and that is its identification mark.

89. I shall now tell you about another *tīrtha* in Kubjāmraka where Varuṇa performed penance for twelve thousand years.[1]

90. What merit accrues to a person bathing there, I shall tell you.

---

1. This tīrtha was probably named Varuṇatīrtha.

91. Also for the person who dies there. The former goes to the world of Varuṇa and remaining there for eight thousand years acquires the power to go anywhere he likes.

92. He who dies there after giving up all attachment and fasting for twenty years, reaches my world.

93. Listen to what I say about its characteristics.

94. There is a uniform waterfall in it which neither increases in the rainy season nor decreases in the summer season.

95. (I shall now tell you about) the *tīrtha* called Saptasamudraka in Kubjāmra. He who offers ablutions there gains the merit of three Aśvamedha sacrifices.

96. He soon reaches heaven and after living there for fifteen years, is born again as a noble Brahmin.

97. He becomes an expert in Vedas and Vedāṅgas and performs Soma sacrifice.

98. He who gives up life there, after acquiring full detachment and control of senses and fasting for seven days, reaches my world.

99. O fair damsel, listen to my account of its characteristics namely what strange thing occurs in it on the Dvādaśī day in the month of Vaiśākha.

100. Mixed with the placid water of Ganges, in this tīrtha the water turns milky in colour.

101. Soon the colour changes into yellow and then red. Then it becomes emerald-coloured and finally gets the colour of pearl. This *tīrtha* is to be identified by this.

102. Now I shall tell you about another tīrtha in Kubjāmraka named Mānasaras which is dear to all devotees.

103. He who bathes there goes to Mānasasaras and sees there Devas and Rudra, Indra and Maruts.

104. If one dies there after fasting for thirty days and with full detachment, he reaches my world.

105. I shall tell you about its identification mark.

106. It extends over fifty krośas and can be known only by those Bhāgavatas who do their duties scrupulously and not by ordinary people.

107. I told about this to Raibhya particularly because he was an aspirant of mokṣa.

108. I shall tell you another thing, O Earth, about a wonder that once occurred in Kubjāmraka.

Please listen.

109. Near the place where the offerings made to me (in my temple there) were thrown out, a female serpent was moving about without any fear.

110. She was eating the sandalpaste, garlands and the cakes and fruits offered.

111. After some time an ichneumon came there and he chanced to see this serpent. Then occurred a furious battle between the two.

112. At noon on the Dvādaśī day in the month of Māgha, the ichneumon was fatally bitten by the serpent in my temple.

113. The ichneumon too bit the serpent injecting his venom and thus both died.

114. The serpent was born as a noble princess in Prāgjyotiṣa (Assam) and the ichneumon was born as a prince in Kosala (Bihar), handsome, virtuous and learned.

115. They grew up in all happiness and steadily like the moon in the bright half of the month.

116. But whenever the princess saw an ichneumon, she wished to kill it and whenever the prince saw a serpent he too wished to kill it.

117. When they came of age, due to my blessing, the king of Kosala celebrated the marriage of his son with the daughter of the Prāgjyotiṣa king.

118. This alliance gave great jubilation to the kings of Kosala and Prāgjyotiṣa.

119. They were attached to each other firmly like the lac and the stick or smoke and fire.

120. Like Śacī and Indra playing in the Nandana garden, they were deep in love.

121. But although they were so deep in love, they never transgressed limits, like the ocean not transgressing the shore.

122. Seventyseven years they spent like this, without, however, knowing that fact, as they were under my *māyā*.

123. One day, while they were sporting in the garden, the prince saw a female serpent and he wanted to kill it immediately.

124. Although he was prevented from doing so by his beloved, he did not desist from it. Indeed Garuḍa kills a snake at its very sight !

125. So he too, although prevented, did kill that serpent mercilessly.

126. The princess was very much offended by this and became very cross with him and did not speak a word.

127. Just then the princess saw an ichneumon coming out of a burrow before her in search of food.

128. Seeing the ichneumon who came out to eat the snake (which was killed), the princess became angry and started to kill it.

129. Although prevented from doing so by the prince, she killed it.

130. Seeing the beautiful ichneumon killed, the prince was very sorry and he asked her.

131. "The husband is always to be respected by a woman. Then why did you kill this ichneumon which is auspicious and liked by kings, in spite of my warding you off from that action ?"

132. Hearing these words of her husband, the daughter of the king of Kosala replied to him angrily:

133. "Although I repeatedly prevented you from killing that serpent, you killed it. Therefore, although you attempted to prevent me from killing this ichneumon, I killed it".

134. The prince then told her in hard and threatening words.

135. "The serpent has fierce fangs and dreadful poison. It bites men who die as a consequence. So I killed this venomous creature.

136. We are kings who protect the people. It is our duty to suitably punish whoever swerves from the right path.

137-38. Those who harass innocent people and those who molest women out of lust are to be punished even with death according to the rules of kingship.

139-40. I only discharged my duty as a king. But what crime has the ichneumon committed ? It is an innocent creature considered as beautiful, auspicious and sacred for royalty.

141. Since you killed the ichneumon in spite of my attempt to ward you off, you are no more my wife and I am no more your husband.

142. I do not kill you because the royal rules do not permit the killing of a woman". So saying he returned to his city.

143. Thus anger took away their mutual love.

144. In course of time, the king of Kosala came to know of the incident of killing the snake and the ichneumon and the consequent unpleasantness between the couple.

145. He ordered his chamberlains and ministers to bring there his son and daughter-in-law.

146. In accordance with the king's command they duly brought there the prince and his wife before the king.

147. Seeing the son and daughter-in-law, the king said:

148. "O my son, where has gone that intense love between you ? How have you become cross to each other ?

149. The love between you was fast like the lac on the stick. You used to consider each as the image of the other.

150. You were always closely united. It is not proper on your part to reject this good-natured and dutiful wife.

151. She never said anything unpleasant even to the servants. On the contrary, she was always eager to feed them sumptuously. It is not proper for you to discard such a person.

152. *Dharma* is our asset. That indeed is caused by women. It is true that *dharma* rests on women, the son and the family".

153. Hearing these words of the father, the prince fell at his feet and said:

154. "O father, your daughter-in-law has no blemish in her. But she killed an ichneumon even when I prohibited her.

155. Then I got angry seeing that creature killed before me and in that anger I told her.

156. 'Hereafter you are not my wife and I am not your husband'. This is the reason and nothing else".

157. Hearing this, the princess of Prāgjyotiṣa bowed her head and said:

158. "An innocent and frightened serpent was quickly killed by him in spite of my repeated attempts to ward him off from that action.

159. Seeing the serpent killed, I got angry and did not speak any more. Please know this".

160. Hearing his son as well as daughter-in-law, the king of Kosala said to them before the people assembled there.

161. "The serpent was killed by him and the ichneumon was killed by you. What was the cause of anger at this, I wish to know.

162. "O son, when the ichneumon was killed, why did you

get angry ? O princess, when the serpent was killed why did you get angry ?"

163. At this the Kosala prince softly spoke to his father.

164. "Why should this question be put to me ? Ask her, O king. Then you will know".

165. Hearing the words of the son, the king of Kosala uttered words in order to maintain *dharma*.

166. "Tell me, son, what is in your mind that brought about the break in your mutual love.

167. Sons are the closest relations (of the father) in everything. Those who hide the truth when asked by the father, are the lowest and despicable.

168. Right or wrong, the sons who do not answer the father when questioned fall into the hell called Raurava full of hot sands.

169. Pleasing or displeasing, those who answer the father when questioned, go to the world that is for the speakers of truth.

170. You should certainly tell me here the reason for the loss of love between you".

171. Thus said by the king, the Kosala prince said before that assembly of men:

172. "Let all these people go to their homes. Tomorrow morning I shall tell you what is most essentially to be told".

173. When the day dawned, the Kosala king was woken up by the sound of drums and the music of the minstrels.

174. The prince then had his auspicious bath and came to the doorway of the royal chamber.

175. The chamberlain announced the arrival of the prince to the king and conveyed his desire to meet him.

176. The king asked the chamberlain to usher in the prince immediately.

177. Thus ordered by the king, the prince was led into the chamber.

178. The prince prostrated before his father. The king asked him to sit down and expressed his blessings.

179. The people saw the king and the prince seated together and looking auspicious both within and without.

180. The king then asked the son to give him reply to what he had formerly asked namely the cause of estrangement between him and his beloved wife.

181. Then the prince told his father.

182. "I should certainly tell you what you asked me about, although it is not going to be of any help in this.

183. It is really a secret and if you wish to know it, come along with me to the place called Kubjāmra.

184. There I shall tell you, O Kosala king, this secret which you have asked one about".

185. Hearing these words of his son, the king agreed out of his affection for him.

186. When the prince was gone, the king said to his ministers who had assembled there.

187. "O ministers, listen to what I say now after due deliberation. We are now to proceed to Kubjāmra.

188. Make the necessary arrangements. Get ready the elephants and horses". They replied, "We shall do so at once".

189. In the course of a week they made everything ready, elephants, horses, bulls, vehicles, money and cows.

190. Also gold, gems, cloths, food and everything else that was necessary. Then they informed the king that everything was ready.

191. Then, O Earth, the great king called his son and asked him: "How can we start, O son, leaving the country void".

192. Hearing the words of the father, the prince bowed to him, and told him softly.

193. "My younger brother, who is born of the same mother, may be endowed with the kingdom".

194. The Kosala king then observed: "When the elder son is there, how can the younger son be considered for this ?".

195. At these words of the father, the prince of Kosala spoke to him impelled by *dharma*.

196. "I give my full consent for you to give the kingdom (to my younger brother). The acceptance of this will not involve him in any transgression of *dharma*.

197. Having gone to Kubjāmra, I will not return from there. O father, I swear this in the name of truth and *dharma*".

198. Consented thus by the elder son, the younger son was duly installed on the throne.

199. After a long time, the king reached the place called Kubjāmraka with his family and attendants and with all the necessary equipment.

200. Then he performed the prescribed rites in that *tīrtha* and gave there abundant gifts of food, cloth, gold, cows, elephants, horses and land.

201. After many days, the king once asked his son who came near him, about the secret of estrangement between him and his wife.

202. "O son, this is the holy spot sanctified by the feet of Viṣṇu.

203-4. We have given as gifts here a lot of money and gems according to rules. Now tell me the truth why this beautiful daughter-in-law, who is noble and virtuous and who never commits any wrong, has been given up by you without any real cause".

205. The prince then told the father: "Let this night pass. May you sleep. Tomorrow morning I shall tell you everything".

206. Then, when the night was gone and the sun was rising, he took his bath in the Ganges and put on silken dress.

207. He then worshipped me and circumambulated his father and said as follows:

208. "Come, father; let us go. You ask me the secret. Please know it from me".

209. Then the prince, the princess and the king went to the place where the remains of the offerings made to me were heaped.

210. Going close there, the prince held his father's feet in respect and said:

211. 'O king, I was an ichneumon living at the foot of the plantain. Once I chanced to go to this place where the remnants of offerings to the Lord are thrown.

212. I saw there then a female serpent crawling about eating the sandalpaste, flowers and other things there.

213. Seeing that fierce serpent, my eyes turned red with anger and soon I jumped upon her.

214. A terrible fight ensued but none noticed it. It was on the Dvādaśī day of the month of Māgha.

215. In the course of the fight, when I was guarding myself, the serpent bit me on my nose.

216. The poison from me got into the serpent too. Thus both of us were dead.

217. After a lapse of time, when our anger and stupor were gone, I was born as the son of the Kosala king.

218. The serpent was killed in these circumstances, mainly because of my anger. This is the secret I have to communicate to you."

219. After this narration by the prince, the daughter-in-law said: "I was that serpent moving about in the remanants thrown out from the lord's offerings.

220. During the fight I was crushed down by the ichneumon. I was then born as the daughter of the king of prāgjyotiṣa, and then I became your daughter-in-law.

221. Because of that anger inherent in me, I killed that ichneumon. This is the secret I have to tell you".

222. After listening to what his son and daughter-in-law had to say, the king went to Māyātīrtha and died there.

223-24. O lovely Earth, the prince and the princess then went to Puṇḍarīkatīrtha and died there and went to the supreme heaven lorded over by Janārdana.

225-26. The king, the prince and the princess then reached the Śvetadvīpa due to my blessings.

227. All their attendants became highly meritorious and they also got entry into the Śvetadvīpa.

228. Thus have I told you about the splendour of Kubjāmraka, as I narrated to the great Brahmin Raibhya.

229. This is a sacred narrative which deserves to be recited by people of all the four castes and in all ceremonies.

230. This is the best of all lustre and the highest of all penance. This should not be recited in the midst of fools.

231. Nor should it be recited amidst cow-slaughterers or those who condemn the Vedas and Vedāṅgas; so too before those who harbour ill-will to their teachers or speak ill of śāstras.

232. This should be recited in the assembly of Bhāgavatas or of those who are initiated.

233. He who recites it at dawn liberates ten generations of his ancestors and ten generations of his successors. He who dies reciting this, attains a four-armed form and resides in my world.

234. Thus, O Earth, have I told you about the place Kubjāmraka. What else do you propose to ask for the good of my devotees?

CHAPTER ONE HUNDRED AND TWENTYSEVEN

The initiation of the Brahmin

Sūta said:

1. After listening to the account of the many acts of *dharma* meant to bring about liberation, Earth told Janārdana the lord of the worlds.

2. "O the power of this place, by hearing the prowess of which I, who was feeling great weight, now feel much lighter and also much purified and free from stupor, O great lord !

3. I am known in the world as having come out of your mouth (and that is quite proper).

4. I now ask you again, O lord, a doubt regarding *dharma*, namely by what dharmic rites initiation is effected.

5. I am very eager to know this great secret in order to know *dharma* in full. So be pleased to tell me".

6. Hearing these words of Earth, the lord in the form of the boar replied in a dense tone resembling thunder.

Varāha said:

7. "O goddess, listen to the truth of my eternal *dharma*, which even the gods concentrating on yoga are unable to know.

8. This auspicious *dharma* which is now being spoken by me, I alone know and in this world my devotees.

9. O auspicious one, listen to the details of initiation (*dīkṣā*) leading to release from *saṁsāra* which you ask me about.

10. Listen to the process of this *dīkṣā* which brings about all good and which is different for the different castes.

11. By this the people are able to escape from further births if they repose their minds in me.

12. Let the person (who wishes to be initiated) go to the preceptor and tell him "O preceptor, I am your disciple. Please instruct me". And after getting his consent collect the materials for *dīkṣā*, like,

13. Honey, ghee, Kuśa grass, sandal paste, flowers, incense, lamp,

14. Antelope's skin, Palāśa stick, spouted vessel, pot, clothes, footwear, white *yajñopavīta*.

15. Support poles, vessel for *arghya*, cooking vessel with ladle, sesamum, paddy and barley, different kinds of fruits, water.

16. Other kinds of food and drink that are acceptable and agreeable to him.

17. He shall also collect the necessary grains, gems and crystals.

18. All these should be then presented to the preceptor at his feet.

19. The Brahmin who wishes for prosperity and desires to be initiated should hold the feet of the preceptor and ask him what he might do for him.

20. Then with the approval of the preceptor, he shall prepare a spacious altar, a square in shape and sixteen cubits in dimension, and place pot in it.

21. Over a mass of grain according to rules. The pot should then he filled with water with mantras and tender sprouts and flowers should be placed in it.

22-23. The rituals, as directed by the preceptor, should be performed there and the materials formerly enumerated should be brought to the centre of the altar.

24. Four pots filled with water and decorated with mango twigs should be placed, one on each side.

25. They should be wound all round with white threads. Vessels containing presents like cloth and the like should be placed near each pot.

26. They should then be gifted away uttering the mantra according to the direction of the preceptor.

27. The person desirous of initiation should then follow the preceptor to a temple of Viṣṇu.

28. After washing the hands and feet, the preceptor shall then sit facing the east and tell the disciples the following:

29. "If a Bhāgavata (devotee of the Lord) does not stand up (in respect) on seeing other Bhāgavatas, it is equivalent to harassing me.

30. After performing *kanyādāna* (giving a daughter in marriage), if one does not observe the subsequent rites, he harasses eight generations of his manes.

31. He who mercilessly torments a dutiful wife, goes to the company of the lowborn oppressers.

32. Disciples who have committed the sin of killing a Brahmin or similar other sins, or kill cows or remain ungrateful, should be avoided.

33. Trees like Bilva, Udumbara and other sacred trees (which are of use in ceremonies) should not be cut down.

34. If the disciple desires ultimate mokṣa, he should be told about what is good to eat and what is bad.

35. Karīra is good. The fruit of Udumbara can be used before it gets petrid.

36. Pork and fish should not be eaten by Brahmins, particularly by those who are to be initiated.

37. Let him not be fault-finding and let him not harm any. Let him not be a tale-bearer or a thief.

38. Seeing a guest coming, he should go out to receive him and converse with him.

39. Lord Viṣṇu has ordained that one should not even think of having illicit contact with the wife of the preceptor, the wife of the king and any Brahmin woman.

40. Lord Viṣṇu has ordained again that one should not set one's mind on gold, jewels or a young girl.

41. Seeing another's affluence and one's own penury, one should not be angry or jealous. This should be an all-time maxim".

42. Thus should the disciple be told. He should then symbolically offer an umbrella and footwear in the form of two pairs of Udumbara leaves in the middle of the altar.

43. So too a razor and a cup full of water. Then I should be invoked with the following mantra:

44. "Om, bow to seven oceans, seven islands, seven mountains and to the thousands of creations and to all. All these live in my heart. What showers down goes up again.

45. Om, lord Vāsudeva, make your presence here as you deem fit. I utter your mantra. Considering your commands to us, kindly come here in this spot of the earth upraised by you. This aspirant of initiation prays for your favour".

46. After uttering this mantra, he should prostrate on the ground by his knees and head.

47. "Om, welcome, I am the welcomer".

48. By the above mantra, O Earth, having invoked the lord, *arghya* and *pādya* should be offered according to direction.

49. The mantra is: "O lord of the worlds, all that is given by the grateful Rudra to the grateful Devas and Asuras and the Brāhmaṇas, may that all be given to you, accept it all, O lord".

50. After offering the *arghya* and *pādya* in this manner, he should take the razor and utter this mantra:

51. "O disciple, may Varuṇa protect you whose head I shave. By this water of Viṣṇu this *dīkṣā* serves to terminate *saṁsāra* '.

52. One pot of water should be given to the workman (barber), who should shave the head without any bleeding (due to scratching or cutting by negligence).

53. The disciple should then take his bath quickly (and then perform other rites) conducive to *mokṣa*.

54. He should then kneel down on the floor and utter the following mantra:

55. "Om, I know all Bhāgavatas, all Dīkṣitas and Gurus (preceptors). Let all of them who have become Dīkṣitas by the favour of Viṣṇu be pleased with me".

56-57. Then saluting all the devotees there and kindling the fire, he should offer in the fire seven times the mixture of ghee, honey, fried paddy and black sesamum, and then rice mixed with sesamum twenty times. Then sitting on the knees, he should utter the following mantra:

58. "The Aśvins, the quarters, sun, moon, and my own self, may they all please listen to my declaration of truth.

59. The earth is held by truth, the earth remains by truth, the sun moves by truth and the wind blows by truth".

60. After declaring this truth, the Brahmin should propitiate the preceptor in due form.

61. Circumambulating the lord preceptor thrice, he should hold his feet in respect and utter the following mantra:

62. "I accidentally got initiation by the blessing of my preceptor. May he forgive me for whatever lapse there may be on my part.

63. After this supplication, he should be seated at the middle of the altar facing east.

64. The spouted vessel should then be held as also the white *yajñopavita* and then he should utter the following mantra:

65. "By the blessing of Viṣṇu I attained my aim, and got

initiation together with the spouted vessel (kamaṇḍalu). By taking it in my hand, I am initiated into duty and action".

66. Then the preceptor and the disciple together shall circumambulate uttering this mantra:

67. "By moving about placing myself lower and lower, I secured the preceptor and attained initiation, by your blessing O preceptor".

68. By this mantra, the head shall be touched by the feet. Then he can wash (if necessary) and put on the prescribed clothes (given by the preceptor saying).

69. "Wear these clothes, O disciple, and then take the spouted vessel for purification in all rituals".

70. The mantra is: "Receive these vessels containing pleasant sandal paste, pure and favourite to Viṣṇu, and helping to obtain mokṣa".

71. After *madhuparka*, the following mantra is to be recited: "Be pleased to accept this *madhuparka* which cleanses the devotees".

72. Then propitiate the preceptor by holding his feet in respect and by bowing to him with hands folded over the head. Then bearing in mind the instruction of the preceptor, this mantra is to be uttered, namely.

73. "May all Bhāgavatas listen. This great preceptor dissolved all worldly desires in me. I am his disciple and servant. I got a Guru, who is like a God".

74. O Earth, I have thus told you about the initiatory rites of the Brahmin. Know about the same relating to the other three castes.

75. The same rites are applicable to them also (with the necessary modifications) The preceptor and the disciple both attain their aim.

CHAPTER ONE HUNDRED AND TWENTYEIGHT

Initiation of other castes. Gaṇāntika, Comb, Collyrium and Mirror

Varāha said:

1. I shall now tell you about (the initiation of) the Kṣatriya.

2. Giving up all weapons which he has practised to wield, let him attain initiation with the mantra mentioned before.

3. He should gather all materials which I had mentioned earlier except one, namely the skin of the black antelope. The staff of Palāśa also is not to be used.

4. Instead, the skin of the black goat is to be given, and the staff of the Aśvattha is to be used.

5. An altar of twelve cubits is to be made and all that I have said earlier should be done.

6-7. Thus arranging all the materials for the initiation of the Kṣatriya, he should touch my feet and utter the following mantra:

8. "Giving up all weapons, giving up all deeds of the Kṣatriya and giving up, in fact, everything, I have resorted to Lord Viṣṇu for crossing the stream of successive lives".

9. Then standing on my side and holding my feet, he should utter the following mantra:

10. "O lord of lords, I shall not touch any weapon, I shall not speak ill of others. I shall follow only such things as are laid down for liberation proclaimed by you in your boar form".

11. Then he should do all those things as directed, with sandal, leaves, incense etc.

12. Then food should be given to the pious devotees according to practice.

13. O goddess, I have thus told you about the initiation of the Kṣatriya who desires to attain my grace.

14. I shall now tell you about (the initiation of) the Vaiśya.

15. Giving up all actions of the Vaiśya and turning everything towards me, the third caste attains the aim.

16. Collecting all the materials I have enumerated before, an altar of ten cubits should be prepared.

17. As before it should be smeared with cowdung. He should then cover himself with goat skin.

18-19. Then holding a staff of Udumbara in the hand, he should circumambulate the pure devotees thrice, and kneeling down utter the mantra:

20. "I, this Vaiśya, have come to you, giving up all my actions as a Vaiśya. By your blessing, I got initiation. May you be pleased to give me liberation".

21. After saying this and doing things to gain my favour, he may hold the feet of his preceptor and utter the mantra:

22. "Giving up my cultivation, cattle rearing, business and trade, I have been able to get initiation into your worship by your grace.

23. After bowing to the Lord, the devotees should be fed without fault.

24. Such is the initiation of the Vaiśya to worship following my path for release from *saṁsāra.*

25. I shall also tell you about the initiation of the Śūdra by which he gets freed from all sins.

26. All the materials which I had formerly detailed for initiation should be procured.

27. The altar should be of eight cubits and the skin should be that of the blue goat for the Śūdra.

28. The staff should be of bamboo and the cloth should be blue. Then prostrating before me, he should utter the mantra:

29. "I, this Śūdra, have given up all actions of Śūdra and all forbidden food".

30. The Śūdra desirous of initiation should say like this, giving up all desires, free from all sins and with pure consciousness.

31-32. Then he should hold the feet of the preceptor in his hand and utter the following mantra for propitiating him.

33. "For the sake of relief from Saṁsāra I am doing such actions as are ordained for getting the grace of Viṣṇu.

34. After uttering the mantra he should perform circumambulation and prostrate before him again.

35. He should then perform worship with sandal and flowers and, without fail, feed (devotees).

36. Such is the initiation of Śūdra. I have thus told you about this pertaining to all the four castes.

37. I shall also tell you about the colour of umbrellas for different castes.

38. The white umbrella is for the Brahmin, red for Kṣatriya, yellow for Vaiśya and blue for Śūdra.

Sūta said:

39. After hearing about (the initiation regarding) the four castes, Earth bowed to Varāha and asked again.

Earth said:

40. "I have now heard about initiation for different castes. (I wish to know) what should be done by the initiated".

41. Hearing these words of Earth, the resplendent Lord in the form of boar answered.

Varāha said:

42. "Listen to what I tell you in reply to your question. The observance is called Gaṇāntika and it should be always considered as secret".

43. Hearing these words of Lord Nārāyaṇa, Earth was pleased and satisfied.

44-45. Then the lotus-eyed goddess who was a devotee herself and was attached to other devotees, spoke to lord Nārāyaṇa with folded hands.

Earth said:

46. "O Mādhava, what are the rules to be observed by those that are fully devoted to you and are initiated?

47. How should you, who are unknowable, be contemplated upon by these people according to their capacity?"

48. Hearing these words of Earth, the Primordial Being replied in sweet words:

Varāha said:

49. I shall tell you in truth what you ask, namely, how I am to be contemplated upon by one dedicated to me.

50. The (use of) Gaṇāntika (rosary) is an ancient practice pertaining to my contemplation and it is of a secret nature.

51. This should be received by those who are pure and initiated and with the prescribed mantras.

52. He who is a Bhāgavata and receives this Gaṇāntika with sight and touch, for him the initiation is successful and he has no duty left.

53. He who receives Gaṇāntika sanctified by mantra, the initiation is called Āsurī.

54. He who receives the Gaṇāntika should meditate on me with pure heart.

55. He who meditates by the Gaṇāntika performs the equivalent of contemplation for a thousand lives.

56. I shall tell you how the mantra is to be imparted to the disciple for the good of the world.

57. The day suitable is Dvādaśī in the months of Kaumuda, Mārgaśīrṣa and Vaiśākha.

58. The follower of my path may receive Gaṇāntika on that day after avoiding non-vegetarian food for three days.

59-60. Kindling fire before me and installing the Gaṇāntika on a bed of Kuśa grass, the preceptor as well as the initiated disciple shall utter *Namo Nārāyaṇāya* and recite this mantra:

61. "O disciple, receive her who was born out of the right side of Lord Nārāyaṇa, and who was held by the first grandfather Brahmā".

62. Then taking the Gaṇāntika with this mantra, the preceptor shall give it to his dear disciple with the following mantra:

63. "O my disciple, receive this goddess who was born out of the right side of the lord Nārāyaṇa, and on contemplating on whom you will get liberated and never take birth again".

Earth said:

64-65. After conducting the bath what should be done? By what mantra should decoration be done so that the action may lead to the state of non-action?"

66. Hearing these words of Earth, the lord of the worlds, Janārdana, replied in words of *dharma*:

Varāha said:

67. "O goddess, I shall tell you in truth what you seek to know, namely the bathing and decoration (of the rosary) which the worshippers perform.

68. In these relating to water (for conducting the bath) and the offerings, the comb, collyrium and mirror are important. Now know what the mantras for this are.

69. After bathing me (as represented in the Gaṇāntika) white silk should be offered as garment. Then collyrium and comb should be offered.

70-71. Then kneeling down with a sense of dedication to me, he should hold the comb (and the collyrium) in his hand and utter the following mantra:

72. "O great lord, be pleased to accept this comb in my hand and arrange your hair with it.

73. O the most supreme being, this collyrium is for your eyes by which you are able to see all the three worlds".

74. Then bathing should be done for the deity with the following mantra:

75. "O lord of lords, with folded hands I pray that you may be pleased to accept for your bath the water contained in this golden pitcher".

76. Then *Namo Nārāyaṇāya* should be uttered and the following mantra should be recited:

77. "This worship by mantra I have attained by your grace O Mādhava. I have been given the Gaṇāntika too. May there not be anything unrighteous for me any more".

78. He who follows this after getting it from the preceptor, goes to my world.

79. This Gaṇāntika should not be given to a bad disciple or to an envious or wicked person. It can be entrusted only in the hands of the good disciple.

80. The best should have one hundred and eight (beads), the medium fiftyfour and the inferior half of that (twentyseven).

81. The best should be of *rudrākṣa*, the medium of *putrajīvaka* and the inferior of *padmākṣa* (seeds).

82. The truth and efficacy of this rosary is not easy to know even by hundreds of lives.

83. It should not be touched by an impure person and it should not be in hands of women.

84. It should be hung up high and should not be touched by the left hand. It should not be shown to others, but worshipped with contemplation.

85. I have, thus, told you this secret leading to liberation. This should be scrupulously guarded. Being purified, my devotee reaches my world".

86. Hearing these words of Viṣṇu, the ascetic Earth, again asked the great lord:

87. "How should the mirror be offered to you by which you could see your own form in it?".

88. Hearing these words of Earth, Varāha said, "O goddess, listen to the rule relating to the offering of the mirror.

89. After saying *Namo Nārāyaṇāya*, the following mantra should be recited.

90. "Your ears are the Vedas and Agni, mouth the Brahmin,

nostrils Aśvins, eyes the Sun and the Moon, the face is like the moon, body the entire universe. See this form in this mirror".

91. He who performs my worship in this manner, liberates seven generations in his family.

92. These are the mantras, these are the modes of service. All this should be done with pleasure and satisfaction by those desirous of beatitude.

CHAPTER ONE HUNDRED AND TWENTYNINE

Further Rituals in Worship[1]

1. After bowing to the lord, Earth said again.

Earth said:

2. "I wish to know this, namely the mode of worship of the *sandhyā* in your system".

3. Hearing these words of Earth, the great lord in the form of boar said:

Varāha said:

4-5. O Earth, I shall tell you this secret which you have asked, by which all devotees are able to get liberation from *saṁsāra*.

6. The worship of *sandhyā* is laid down in this way.

7. Holding water in the joined palms with great reverence, and meditating for a while, the following mantra is to be uttered:

8. "The source of the worlds, the primordial indistinct form, all the gods, Brahmā, Rudra, all in *dhyānayoga* bow to Vāsudeva in Sandhyā; we too every day in the sevenday week for release from *Saṁsāra*; O Vāsudeva, I bow to you".

9. He who recites this mantra of mantras and penance of penances, reaches my world.

10. He who recites this secret of secrets, never gets stained by sins.

---

1. In the text the title is given as *Caturvarṇadikṣā*.

11. This should not be imparted to any one other than an initiated person.

12. O goddess, I shall tell you another matter, namely the offering of lamp by devotees.

13. After performing the due rites, the lighted lamp should be taken and holding it between the shanks, the following mantra should be recited:

14. "Om, bow to the blessing light Viṣṇu, all the gods remain in this flame which shines because of your effulgence. By your lustre and by the lustre of mantra this lamp shines. May you receive it offered with mantra for the sake of removing my *saṁsāra*, as otherwise this action of mine will be fruitless".

15. He who does this liberates all his manes.

[*Varāha said*:[1]

1-2. The person ritualistically worshipping me should, after the decoration, adorn me with *yajñopavita* of nine threads. Then the *tilaka* of sandalpaste should be put on my forehead.

3. I shall tell you of another act to be done for the good of the world, namely the uttering of the mantra for this, namely.

4. "This decoration of your face, O Vāsudeva, is done by me. This makes it more attractive. O god, snap my *saṁsāra*".

5. O Earth, by this mantra should the *tilaka* be applied in beautiful design on my face. Then taking flowers, this mantra should be uttered, namely.

6. "These flowers are for your magnanimity, O lord; make everything happy; these are created by you for that purpose, *Svāhā*".

7. After flowers, offer incense. Holding the fragrant and beautiful smoke-emitting receptacle,

8. Utter *Om Nārāyaṇāya* and then recite the mantra:

9-10. "O Keśava, your body is sweet-smelling by nature. By this smoke it is made further sweet. By the fragrance of your body make everything smell sweet. Accept this incense for my release from *saṁsāra*".

11. I shall now tell you about the offering of lamp which I accept for the welfare of my devotees.

1. This portion within brackets is given in parenthesis in the text, probably indicating that this is perhaps an interpolated part.

12. In doing the duties by me, the devotee should take a lamp with flame, hold it between the legs and utter the mantra:

13. "O lord, I bow to you Viṣṇu. All gods reside in fire. Fire shines because of your effulgence and fire is the self itself.

14. O lord, receive this bright lamp for my release from *saṁsāra*. Let not this action of mine be in vain".

15. He who offers me the lamp like this, liberates all his manes".

16. Hearing these words of lord Nārāyaṇa, Earth was wonderstruck and she asked again:

17. "I have now known about the devotees who are dedicated to your service. My mind is eager to know another matter, namely,

18. Of what material should be the vessels used in your service as to be pleasing to you".

19. At these words of Earth, the lord of the worlds said:

20. "O Earth, I shall tell you what you have sought to know, namely what vessels please me.

21. Leaving out vessels of gold, silver and bronze, what pleases me most is vessels made of copper.

22. Thus told by Nārāyaṇa, Earth devoted to *dharma* asked him again: "It appears strange to me that copper pleases you most. Why is it so to you ?"

23. Then that primordial and invincible Being, the greatest in the world, replied to Earth:

24. "O sinless Earth, listen intently to what I say about my partiality for copper,

25. Which arose seven thousand aeons ago and which is pleasing to look at.

26. O lotus-eyed one, there was a great asura named Guḍākeśa. He had a cupreous form and was absorbed in my worship.

27. I was worshipped by him for fourteen thousand years, being desirous of acquiring *dharma*.

28. I was pleased by his determination and penance, and seeing his hermitage where (later on) arose copper (I appeared there).

29. Then kneeling down, he meditated on me and seeing me in my four-armed form, he prostrated with folded hands.

30. I was immensely pleased and I spoke to him.

31. "O glorious Guḍākeśa, tell me what I may do for you. I am very much pleased with your devotion, although it is difficult to please me.

32. Ask me the boon which you desire through your thoughts, words or deeds.

33. Then with supplicant hand and pure mind, Guḍākeśa said:

34. "If you are indeed pleased with me, O lord, may I have constant devotion for you for a thousand lives.

35. (Finally) may I have death by the hurling of your disc on me.

36. Killed by the disc, may my marrow and flesh become the holy material called copper.

37. Making vessels out of it and using them in your ritualistic worship, may that be for your pleasure.

38. If you are pleased, O lord, may I have this boon".

39. I then said, "In view of your severe penance I grant you the boon you seek. May it be so as long as the world lasts. You become mine in cupreous form".

40. From then onwards Guḍākeśa was transformed into the nature of copper.

41. Therefore, O virtuous one, know that whatever is offered to me in copper vessel, gives me immense pleasure.

42. The auspicious and holy copper is dear to me. You will see it when the sun is at the zenith.[1]

43. On the Dvādaśī day of the bright half in the month of Vaiśākha, my disc will fall on you.

44. You will then reach my world." Telling thus to Guḍākeśa, I disappeared.

45. Awaiting death by the fall of the disc, he was continuing his admirable penance, thinking all the while as to when he would go to the world of Viṣṇu.

46. In due course, Dvādaśī of the bright half of the Vaiśākha month arrived, and

47. Performing the worship of Viṣṇu in due form, he implored:

---

1. The proper place of verses 41-42, which are obviously spoken to Earth is after verse 49.

48. "Let loose on me your disc glowing like fire and take away my soul quickly cutting to pieces my body".

49. Then cut by my disc, the great devotee reached me. But his flesh became copper, blood became gold and the bones became silver and other metals like zinc, tin and iron.

50. Now listen to the result of offerings made in copper vessels.

51. My real devotees should know that it is in this way that copper arose and that it pleases me.

52. The Dīkṣitas among the devotees should offer *pādya*, *arghya* etc., in this. Such is the origin of copper, such its prescription.

53. I have thus told you this. What else do you wish to ask?

Earth said:

Tell me how the Dīkṣita performs worship of Sandhyā and by what mantra.

Varāha said:

54. O Earth, listen to the mantra of Sandhyā of morning and evening.

55-57. Holding water in the palms held together and meditating on me with full devotion, the following mantra should be recited, by which one delights in my world for as many thousands of years as he uses copper vessels.

58. "All gods, Brahmā, Rudra and Indra, all in *dhyāna yoga* contemplate on Lord Vāsudeva, the source of the world, the primordial effulgence.

59. O Vāsudeva, the primordial being, bearing you in our souls, we bow to you again and again, during Sandhyā, for emancipation".

60. May the Dīkṣita worship Sandhyā with this mantra.]

CHAPTER ONE HUNDRED AND THIRTY

Expiation for eating the king's Food

Sūta said:

1. Hearing the account about *Dikṣā* from the mouth of Lord Nārāyaṇa, the goddess Earth became clear in mind and asked Him again.

Earth said:

2. "How great is the *dīkṣā* for your worship, by hearing which my mind has become very clear.

3. O the greatness of the Lord, who has established this *dīkṣā* for the four castes for their welfare !

4. But one thing lingers in my mind, O lord, and that you should be pleased to clear for the sake of devotees.

5. Formerly, you enumerated thirtytwo offences in worship. Committing such offences, how do people make expiation for them ?

6. Be pleased to tell me, O Mādhava, how this is".

7. Hearing these words of Earth, the great lord meditated for a while and then replied.

Varāha said:

8.9. "If the pure devotees dedicated to my service eat the food offered by the king, out of desire, fear or contingency, they will be tormented in hell for ten thousand years".

10. At this Earth shuddered and became struck with fear for seventeen days.

11. Then with an afflicted mind she spoke again for the good of the world:

Earth said:

12. "O lord, please hear what I have in mind. I wish to know why there is this prohibition for the king's food".

13. Hearing these words of Earth, lord Nārāyaṇa, the foremost among the knowers of *dharma*, spoke to her:

Varāha said:

14. "Listen, O fair one, to know the truth about the prohibition of the king's food for the pure devotees.

15. Although the king conducts himself with equanimity, he performs cruel actions also by the influence of Rājasa and Tāmasa qualities.

16. So the food he gives is despicable and I don't like it in the interest of upholding righteousness.

17. Listen, O Earth, to what I say further regarding the acceptability of the king's food.

18-19. After installing me with due rites and giving money

and grain to the devotees, if the food is got cooked by my own devotees, and taken after offering to me, it will not be sinful."

20. Hearing these words of Viṣṇu, the saintly Earth asked Varāha again:

Earth said:

21. O Janārdana, how can one purify oneself after taking in king's food.

Varāha said:

22. Listen, O goddess, to what you want to know, namely how people can purify themselves after eating king's food.

23. That sin can be removed by performing Cāndrāyaṇa, Taptakṛcchra and Sāntapana.

24. Then the sin will not remain, so I say. Therefore, the king's food should not be eaten by my devotees who are desirous of salvation.

CHAPTER ONE HUNDRED AND THIRTYONE

Expiation for not cleaning the Teeth

Varāha said:

1. "He who approaches me without chewing the tooth-stick[1], forfeits all merit in store by this single deed".

2. Thus told, Earth asked Him for the sake of the good of devotees.

Earth said:

3. How is it that, by a single offence, all the merit in store is annihilated ?

Varāha said:

4. Listen to the truth that I say that by a single offence, all the acquired merit becomes lost.

5. Man is impure because of the *kapha* (phlegm) and *pitta*

1. The twig like the Margosa's for cleaning the teeth.

(bile) in him and also of marrow and blood. His face is foul-smelling.

6. This impurity disappears by chewing the tooth-stick. Such purity is not got by other ācāras.

Earth said:

7. What is the atonement for one who performs the rites without chewing the tooth-stick (i.e., without cleaning the teeth).

Varāha said:

8. I shall tell you how purity can be obtained by such people.

9. *Ākāśaśayana* (sleeping in the open) for even days, purifies the people who do the rites without chewing the tooth-stick.

10. I have thus told you about the chewing of the tooth-stick and the means of purification for not using it.

11. If one does the expiation, how will he continue to have the sin ?

CHAPTER ONE HUNDRED AND THIRTYTWO

Expiation for touching Dead Body

Varāha said:

1. "O blessed one, he who touches a dead body without bathing after a sexual intercourse, remains drinking semen for fourteen thousand years".

2. Hearing this from Lord Nārāyaṇa, Earth was very sorry and she asked him:

Earth said:

3. What do you say, O lord ! This is a sad and disgustful thing. How can a man be drinking semen ?

4. This saddens me a lot.

Varāha said:

"O goddess, know this secret.

5. This is indicative of transgression, such as of man having sexual perversion in women.

6. The man who does so reaps the result of his offence.

7. There is no atonement for a deliberate offence. But I shall tell you about the atonement for the offences committed through faults of the mind.

8. Householders who are my devotees, should live on barley meal for three days, oil cake for three days and air alone for one day.

9. They then become free from sins. Those who do this in the prescribed manner are not stained by sin.

10. Thus have I told you about the atonement for one who comes to me after a sexual intercourse.

11-12. If one goes to the cremation ground disregarding the rules I have laid down, he as well as his father and grandfather become jackals and eat the dead bodies".

13. Hearing these words of Lord Hari, Earth asked again for the good of the world.

Earth said:

14. How can there be sin for those who have surrendered themselves to you ? How can it be removed even if there is any ?

Varāha said:

15. O fair one, know from me what you seek to know. I shall tell you this which removes sins.

16. Remaining on food once a day for seven days, then completely fasting for three days, and then taking *pañcagavya* removes sins.

17. I have now told you about the rules for touching the dead body. It is better that the Bhāgavatas avoid this altogether.

18. He who performs expiation in the manner suggested above, gets himself freed from all sins.

19-20. He who touches me after touching a woman in her monthly course out of lust, remains (in hell) drinking menstrual blood for one thousand years.

21. He is then born as a blind, penniless and stupid person and never realises that he is in hell.

Earth said:

22-23. Please tell me how people devoted to you can attain mokṣa even if they happen to commit some offence, and how they can get purification for the purpose.

Varāha said:

24. The person devoted to me, if he happens to touch a woman in her monthly course, shall perform penance for three days by sleeping in the open.

25. My devotee gets purified, in this manner and all sins of offence disappear from him.

26. I have thus told you about the purification after touching a woman in her courses.

27. He who enters my temple after touching a dead body, enters the womb (again and again) for thousands of years.

28. Then for ten thousand years he remains a Cāṇḍāla, then as a blind man for seven thousand years and as a frog for hundred years.

29. As a bee for three years, as a beetle for eleven years, as a snake for seven years and as a chameleon for another seven.

30. As an elephant for hundred years, as a camel for thirty-two years, a cat for nine years and a monkey for fifteen years.

31. Thus by causing offence by oneself, much sorrow is brought upon.

32. Hearing these words of Lord Hari, Earth asked with sorrow:

Earth said:

33. Why do you say, O Lord, such words which are horrifying to all men?

34. Tell me the expiation for the devotee who fails in his conduct so as to enable him to cross the barriers.

35. Hearing these words of Earth, Janārdana, the lord of the worlds, replied to her for the sake of righteous order in the world.

Varāha said:

36. My devotee who touches a dead body, shall remain taking food only once a day for fifteen days.

37. After doing like this, *pañcagavya* should be taken in.

38. Thus have I told you about the expiation to be done after touching a dead body.

39. He who performs expiation in this manner, gets cleansed of all sins and reaches my world.

CHAPTER ONE HUNDRED AND THIRTYTHREE

Expiation for passing flatus and answering calls of Nature in the Midst of worship

Varāha said:

1. He who passes flatus during my worship, gets afflicted by wind in the mind.

2. He takes birth as a bee for five years, a mouse for three years, a dog for three years and a tortoise for nine years.

3. Such is the punishment for one who does not know the *śāstra* properly.

4. Hearing these words of the lord, Earth said:

Earth said:

5. By lapses of this kind in your worship, one attains enormous sin. Please tell me the expiation in such cases.

Varāha said:

6. Listen to what I say regarding the action to be done for purification. The guilty shall spend three days and nights by fire.

7. If done like this, then no offence remains and my world is attained.

8. Thus has been told to you to remedy for offences, the faults as well as the expiations which you have sought to know.

9. O Earth, now know what happens to a man who passes motion in the midst of my worship.

10. He remains in the hell Raurava for a thousand divine years eating faeces.

11-12. I shall tell you also expiation for this. He shall lay himself in water and then in air for one day each. Then he becomes absolved of the sin.

13. Thus have I told you about the offence of passing motion during worship.

CHAPTER ONE HUNDRED AND THIRTYFOUR

Other offences during Worship

Varāha said:

1. He who neglects his duties by me, but goes about speaking of expiations,

2. Becomes a fool, O fair one, and becomes free from sin only by doing expiation himself.

3. The expiation for him is sleeping in the open for fifteen days.

4. He who approaches me wearing blue cloth, becomes a worm for hundred years.

5. I shall tell you about the nature of atonement in this case.

6. He has to perform Cāndrāyaṇa according to rules in order to get free from the sin.

7. He who touches me except in the prescribed manner becomes a fool.

8. The sandal, garland, food and prostration offered by him, I shall never receive.

9. Hearing these words of lord Nārāyaṇa, Earth asked him again out of interest in righteousness.

Earth said:

10-11. O lord, now that you speak to me about lapses in conduct, please tell me about the way *upasparśaṇa* (washing with water) is to be done.

12. I am very anxious to know this. Please enlighten me for the welfare of devotees.

Varāha said:

13. O goddess, listen to what I say in reply to what you ask. This is extremely secret.

14. Listen to the action of washing for the person who comes to me after giving up all actions in general.

15. Facing the east, the feet should be washed with water. Then three pods of mud should be applied.

16. Then the hands should be washed with seven pails of water and the feet with five pails each.

17. Then washing (all parts) with two parts should be done.

18. Afterwards water should be sipped three times and the face should be washed with the hands.

19. Then *prāṇāyāma* should be performed according to prescription for the sake of release from *saṁsāra*.

20. He who is desirous of *mokṣa* should then touch the head, ear and nose thrice.

21. After touching in this manner, water should be thrown round thrice.

22. In this manner should *upasparśaṇa* be done and that will please me.

23. For one who does like this, no sin of offence remains.

24. Hearing these words of Lord Nārāyaṇa, Earth asked in sweet words what is good for all the Bhāgavatas.

Earth said:

25. Please tell me about the torments as well as the purification of those who perform the rites without *upasparśaṇa*.

Varāha said:

26. O Earth, know in truth the secret about the way those who are guilty in my worship go.

27. He who approaches me after committing adultery, remains a worm for ten thousand and ten hundred years.

28. I shall tell you about the atonement to be done by which he gets purified.

29-30. By performing the *Mahāsāntapana* and *Taptakṛcchra* ceremonies, the Brāhmaṇas, Kṣatriyas and Vaiśyas get released from all their guilt and attain bliss.

31. I don't like the devotee who gets possessed of anger and is fickle in mind touching me.

32. I don't like the angry and possionate man. I like only those who are calm, good and pure.

33. With the senses completely under control, those who do not think of loss or gain, are free from ego and are engaged in my worship.

34. O fair one, I shall tell you another thing. Listen.

35. Even a devotee who though pure and good, approaches me with an angry mind is born a cricket and remains like that for hundred years and an eagle for hundred years.

36. A frog for three hundred years, a demon for ten years and a eunuch for six years drinking semen.

37. He is then born as a blind man for seven years, a kite for thirtytwo years, a cakravāka bird for ten years.

38. Then a moss-eater and a bird in the sky. This happens even if the offender is a Brahmin whirling in the ocean of *saṁsāra*.

Earth said:

39. O, what a rare thing have you told me ! My mind is much perturbed and I don't feel it steady.

40. I am very much afraid after hearing what you have said about what befalls the devotees (due to their lapses).

41. I am not commanding you, O lord of the worlds.

42. But I ask you for the welfare of the world, how the pure and wise devotees can be liberated.

43. Tell me the expiations for those of limited intellect and for those who are not free from desire and stupefaction.

44. (The lotus-eyed Varāha then stood in front, and my devotee Sanatkumāra said.)[1]

45. Hearing the words of Earth, the great yogi Sanatkumāra replied to her.

46. What you have asked is good and sound. The Lord in the form of the boar is the abode of all illusion.

47. O goddess, the person to whom you spoke is Lord Nārāyaṇa, the best among the knowers of *yoga* and *dharma*.

1. This is an unnecessary verse in view of the next one, and is perhaps an interpolation.

48. Hearing the words of Kumāra, Earth said: "Tell me O great Brahmin, what I ask,

49. The actions, yoga and the matters relating to soul".

50. The great Viṣṇu, the abode of all illusion, told me then as to how the angry Bhāgavata can be purified.

51. Performing the vows, he shall eat the food collected by begging in the houses, at the sixth part of the day.

52. It should be collected only from the good Bhāgavatas and from eight houses alone.

53. He who does like this gets purified of sins. So said Lord Janārdana.

54. Even the highest Brahmin, if he desires the world of Viṣṇu shall soon resort to the worship of Viṣṇu.

55. Hearing the words of Earth, the son of Brahmā told her who was keen on *dharma*.

56. O goddess, what you have said is of a secret nature. Please tell me the *dharmas* which he expounded.

Earth said:

57. Then that lotus-eyed Lord in the form of the boar holding the conch, disc and mace, spoke in words resembling thunder, for the sake of devo tees.

58. By doing these actions and observing proper conduct, O goddess, one can attain my world.

59. My worship should not be done with an angry mind or with greed or in haste, if salvation is the aim.

60. Those who worship me with full control of senses and without any trace of anger, become free from all offences and are never born again.

Varāha said:

61. O Earth, I shall tell you what happens to the man who offers forbidden flowers for me.

62. I don't accept those flowers and I don't like the persons who offer them to me.

63. Fools alone dare to offer me like this and they into the hell called Raurava,

64. And then, because of their ignorance, undergo a lot of suffering. They remain as monkeys for ten years, cats for thirteen years.

65. 'Mūka'[1] for five years, bulls for twelve years, goats for eight years, fowls for a month,

66. And buffaloes for three years. There need be no doubt about this.

67. Thus have I told you about what befalls people who offer me forbidden flowers.

Earth said:

68. O Lord, if you are pleased, tell me how your devotees doing service to you are purified by their pure mind.

Varāha said:

69. O goddess, I shall tell you what you want to know namely expiation for attaining purification.

70. For one month he should take food only once a day. For fourteen days he should adopt Vīrāsana posture. For one month after that, he should take food cooked in milk mixed with ghee during the fourth part of the day.

71. He should take barley for three days and remain on air alone for another three days.

72. He who performs like this gets freed from all sins and reaches my world.

CHAPTER ONE HUNDRED AND THIRTYFIVE

Expiation for eating goose etc.

Varāha said:

1. O fair one, listen to the expiation that is to be done for approaching me wearing red garment.

2. The red garment is equivalent to menstrual flow.

3. The man who wears red garment becomes this for fifteen years.

4. I shall tell you about the expiation by which he gets purified.

5. He should take food daily once alone for seventeen days, live on air alone for three days and on water alone for one day.

---

1. Perhaps the word is Mūṣaka meaning 'mouse'.

6. By doing this he gets freed of the sin of this offence and then becomes dear to me.

7. I have thus told you, O Earth adorned with red garment, the expiation in this matter.

8. He who touches me in darkness without a lamp, being hasty and stupefied, courts his own downfall.

9. Such a base man brings upon himself great misery.

10. "One whole life he spends as a blind man eating everything he comes across.

11. I shall tell you the expiation for this by which he becomes enabled to reach my world.

12. He should blindfold his eyes for fifteen days, eat once, alone a day for twenty days.

13. On the Dvādaśī day in any one month, he should eat only once and then take water alone.

14. Then he should eat barley cooked in cow's urine. By this expiation, he gets free from the sin.

15. Now listen to what downfall one brings for oneself by doing me service wearing black garment.

16. For five years he remains a worm in parched grain,

17. For five years an ichneumon and for ten years a tortoise.

18. Then for fourteen years he will be a pigeon and remain near where I am installed.

19. I shall tell you about the expiation for a person for the offence of wearing black garment.

20. He should take gruel for seven days and flour balls for three days, and three such balls alone for three days.

21. He who performs like this gets purified.

22. He never gets into *saṁsāra* again but reaches my world.

23. O Earth, I shall tell you the offence a devotee does if he wears unwashed cloth, although he may be otherwise pure.

24. The person clad in such a cloth returns to *saṁsāra*.

25. Such a person is born as an elephant in one life, then as a camel and afterwards as a wolf.

26. Then he is born as a jackal and then as horse. He becomes an antelope and then an ordinary deer.

27. After seven such successive lives he is born as a man again as my devotee, clever and offenceless and free from ego.

Earth said:

28. O lord, I have now known what befalls a person who wears unwashed cloth.

29. Be pleased to tell me the expiation to get rid of this offence.

Varāha said:

30. O goddess, I shall tell you about the expiation you ask for.

31. He should live on barley for three days, oil cake for three days, leaves for three days and milk for three days,

32. Rice cooked in milk for three days and air for three days.

33. In this way he can get freed from the sin of offence.

34. I shall tell you about the serious sin resulting from offering the food that is touched by dog.

35. He becomes a dog for seven lives, a jackal for seven lives, an owl for seven lives and is then born a man.

36. He then takes birth in a family of devotees, learned in the Vedas and pure-hearted.

37. Now listen to the expiation by which one crosses the ocean of *saṁsāra*.

38-39. He should live on roots for three days, fruits for three days, leaves for three days, milk for three days, curd for three days, rice cooked in milk for three days and air for three days and then take the holy bath.

40. By spending twenty one days like this, he gets freed from the offence and reaches my world.

41. O fair one, I shall tell you about what befalls a person who approaches me after eating pork.

42. He wanders in the forest as a pig for ten years and becomes a hunter for fourteen years.

43. He then becomes a rat for fourteen years and a demon for nineteen years,

44. A porcupine for eight years and a carnivorous tiger for thirty years.

45. Then he enters into *saṁsāra* and is born in a family of devotees.

46. Hearing these words of the Lord in detail, Earth said with folded hands:

47. I have now known this secret by which an eater of pork gets purified. What shall one do in order not to become an animal by offence ?

Varāha said:

48. He should live on cowdung for five days, small grains for seven days and liquids for seven days,

49. Food which is not caustic or saline for seven days and flour for three days.

50. Sesamum for seven days and milk for seven days.

51. With great forbearance and fortitude and free from ego, he should spend fortynine days in this manner.

52. He then becomes cleansed of all sins and doing service to me, goes to my world.

53. He who comes to me after eating goose-flesh, becomes a goose for fifteen years.

54. He becomes a shark for ten years and a pig for five years. Thus does one roll in *saṁsāra* after giving offence.

55. By performing this expiation, he becomes a pure devotee free from all sins and, crossing all actions, reaches my world.

56. I shall tell you the expiation for eating goose-flesh in order to get free from the sin.

57. He should live on barley for three days, air for three years, fruit for three days,

58. Sesamum for three days, and food neither caustic nor saline for three days.

59. For fifteen days in this way expiation is to be done. The offence of eating gooseflesh gets removed and he gets the liberation he desires.

CHAPTER ONE HUNDRED AND THIRTYSIX

Rules of expiation

Varāha said:

1. A man gets the sin of offence by doing service to me after touching a lamp.

2. Listen to what I say in this matter. He becomes attacked by leprosy all over the body for sixty years.

3. And this will be in the house of an outcaste.

4. After undergoing this punishment, if he happens to die in my temple, he takes birth as my devotee in a sanctified family.

5. I shall tell you the expiation for touching the lamp by which the man gets release from being an outcaste.

6. On the Dvādaśī in the bright fortnight of any month, he shall take food only in the fourth part of the day and sleep in the open.

7. Then by gifting a lamp he gets out of this sin, becomes purified and eligible to do me service.

8. Thus have I told you about the offence of touching the lamp and the way to get release from it.

9. He who touches me without bathing after going to the cremation ground commits an offence and I shall tell you what befalls him.

10. He becomes a jackal for fourteen years, an eagle for seven years wandering in the sky, in both forms eating human flesh.

11. He becomes a goblin for fourteen years. And then for thirty years, he remains eating the remains of the dead".

12. Hearing all this from Lord Nārāyaṇa, Earth said:
I have great curiosity to know why this is so.

13. The cremation ground, O lord, is praised by Rudra. How can it be otherwise when there is this holy utterance of Śiva?

14. That great god delights there holding a bright skullbone in his hand.

15. The cremation ground is dear to Rudra particularly in the night. How is it that you decry what is praised by Rudra"?

Varāha said:

16. O goddess, listen to this story which has not been fully understood even by the ascetics.

17. After accomplishing a difficult task in Tripura,[1] and killing young and old alike and beautiful women,

18. He got into the grip of sin as a consequence and was unable to move.

1. The three cities of gold, silver and iron in the sky, air and earth built for the demons by Maya and destroyed by Śiva.

19. He lost his mind, effulgence and yogic power and became discoloured.

20. He stood there in that condition surrounded by his *gaṇas*.

21. When Śiva was thought of by me, I saw him with my divine vision as completely bereft of his magical power.

22-23. Then I went there and saw the three-eyed god bereft of consciousness, knowledge and magical power. Then I asked him in a pleasing tone.

24. O Rudra, how is it that you stand here engulfed by sin. You are the creator as well as the destroyer, the source as well as manifestation.

25. You are union as well as separation, you are the repository of all and you are the sole refuge. You are the fierce god, foremost of all gods, you are Sāman and you are the various quarters.

26. Do you not know yourself surrounded by your attendant *gaṇas*. How is it that you are discoloured and swollen-eyed.

27. Tell me truly what I ask you. Contemplate on the *yoga* and *māyā* of the great Viṣṇu. I have come here for your good.

28. At these words of mine, Śiva, regained consciousness and spoke in sweet words with his eyes burning with sin.

29. Listen to the truth, O god. Who else will come to me like this other than you Nārāyaṇa, the lord of the worlds.

30. O Viṣṇu, godhood is attained by your favour.

31. I got *yoga* and *Sāṅkhya* and I have become free from affliction. By your grace I have become like the ocean full of water.

32. O Mādhava, I know you and you know me. None finds any difference between us. Brahmā too is not known as different from us.

33. All this is well, O great Viṣṇu, the repository of *māyā*.

34. Telling me like this, Śiva meditated for a while and spoke to me again:

35. "By your grace, O Viṣṇu, I destroyed Tripura (The three cities) and all the demons there.

36. But along with them I also crushed down many pregnant women, children and old men in all the ten quarters. By the sin of this action, I am not able to move.

37. I have lost all my mystic and magical powers and all my effulgence. What shall I do in this state of sin ?

38. Tell me, O Viṣṇu, what atonement I may do to purify myself and get rid of the sin".

39. I then told the regretful Rudra to take a string of skull-bones and go to Samala.

40. He then asked me to tell him what this Samala was where he was asked to go.

41. Then I told Śiva what I meant when I told him so.

42. Samala is the cremation ground which smells rotten like the sore.

43. People who have given up all desires voluntarily remain there. Taking skull-bones you too remain there.

44. Live there with great austerity for a thousand divine years and then be eating flesh to remove your sin.

45. Eat the flesh that is dear to you of those that are killed. Live there in this way along with your *gaṇas*.

46. When the thousand years are spent in Samala, go to the hermitage of sage Gautama.

47. While in Gautama's hermitage you will realise yourself and be rid of your sin by the blessing of Gautama.

48. The skull-bowl on your head full of sin will be brought down by that sage out of compassion.

49. Giving the boon to Rudra in this manner, I disappeared. Rudra wandered in the sinful cremation ground.

50. Therefore it is that the cremation ground is not liked by me, being defiled by the sin of Rudra.

51. Thus have I told you about the despicable cremation ground and the person who comes to me without purification after going there.

52. I shall now tell you about the expiation to get purified of this offence.

53. For fifteen days he shall eat only once and that in the fourth part of the day, 'sleep in the open' wearing a single cloth and seated in Kuśa grass, and in the morning should drink.

Pañcagavya.

54. He then becomes freed of all sins and reaches my world.

55. Now listen to the expiation for the offence of going to the lord after eating oil-cake.

56. He becomes an owl for two years and a tortoise for three years and then he is born a man again devoted to me.

57. I shall tell you the expiation for this by which the sin is removed and liberation from *Saṁsāra* is attained.

58. For one day he shall take barley cooked in cow's urine and in the night he shall 'sleep in the open' in Vīrāsana pose.

59. Such a person does not revert to *saṁsāra* but reaches my world.

60. He who approaches me with pork becomes a sinful dunce and brings upon himself much misery.

61. He is tormented in hell for as many thousands of years as there are hairs on my body as the boar.

62. Another effect also I shall tell you of approaching me with pork.

63. As soon as he begins to worship me, he becomes a boar.

64. I shall tell you also about another thing which befalls such a person.

65. He becomes blind and continues to reel in *saṁsāra*.

66. In the end he is born in a family of devotees, humble, cultured and effluent.

67. I shall tell you the expiation for this so as to remove the sin.

68. He shall eat fruit alone for seven days and roots alone for seven days.

69. Seven days on rice cooked in milk, seven days on butter milk and seven days on fire.[1] By this expiation he reaches my world.

70. O beautiful goddess, listen to the evil that accrues if one approaches me after drinking alcohol.

71. He remains poor for ten thousand years and then becomes purified to be my devotee again.

72. For a devotee of mine who is initiated, there is no expiation at all if he takes alcohol out of desire.

73. Listen to another thing which I tell you. One gets freed from the sin by taking in drink coloured like fire.[2]

74. He who performs expiation in this way does not incur sin and does not fall in *saṁsāra*.

75. My worshipper who eats vegetables cooked with safflower becomes a boar and is tormented in hell for fifteen years.

1. The expression is *pāvakabhojanaḥ*. What it signifies is not clear. Perhaps the word is *yavodakabhojanaḥ* which means feeding in barlay water.

2. How the evil of one drink is removed by another ts not clear.

76. Then he is born as a dog for three years and a jackal for one year.

77. Then he becomes a purified devotee and reaches my world".

78. Hearing these words, Earth asked Lord Hari:

79. O ~~great god,~~ tell me about the expiation for the sin of eating vegetables with safflower".

Varāha said:

80. He who comes to me with vegetables mixed with safflower, gets tormented in hell for ten thousand years. I shall tell you about the expiation for this.

81. For eating vegetables with safflower, the expiation is doubtless the rite called 'Cāndrāyaṇa'. For approaching me with the same, the expiation is to live on milk for twelve days.

82. He who performs such expiation gets free from that sin and reaches my world.

83. He who approaches me wearing the cloth of another without washing becomes a dunce and has to perform expiation.

84. He who touches me and serves me in that condition becomes a deer for ten years.

85. One whole life he remains foolish and irate and then becomes my devotee again.

86. I shall tell you about the expiation for this by which the devotee traverses *saṁsāra*.

87. On the Dvādaśī day in the bright half of the month of Māgha,

88. He shall stand in a pond calm and composed and thinking of me alone.

89. When the night comes to a close and the sun rises he shall take *pañcagavya* and then do service to me.

90. He who performs expiation in this way, gets free from sin and reaches my world.

91. If the devotee does not offer nine kinds of food,[1] his manes do not eat for fifteen years.

92. He who eats nine kinds of food without offering (to me), does not acquire any merit.

---

1. The expression is *navānnāni*. It may also mean 'fresh food' though the plural seems to relate to number.

93. I shall tell you about the expiation to be performed in order to get free from this sin.

94. He shall fast for three days or at least for one day and 'sleep in the open'. He gets purified on the fourth day.

95.. After doing this, when the sun rises, he may drink *pañca-gavya* which will purify him.

96. He who performs expiation in this manner, renounces everything and reaches my world.

97. He who offers me smoke of incense without offering sandal and flowers, doubtless takes birth as a goblin or demon.

98. Certainly he has to live in iron for twentyone years.

99. I shall tell you about the expiation by which he gets free from this sin.

100. On the Dvādaśī day in the bright half of any month, alternatively on the Daśamī or Ekādaśī day, he shall fast.

101. When the night ends and the sun rises, he shall drink *pañcagavya* which purifies him.

102. The manes of one who performs expiation like this get liberated.

103. He who approaches me wearing sandal, becomes a cobbler for thirteen years.

104. After that he takes birth as a boar.

105. From being the boar, he takes birth as a despicable dog and after that he becomes a man again, my devotee free from faults.

106. He gets release from *saṁsāra* and reaches my world.

107. He who performs the atonement like this, does not at all become touched by sin.

108. He who wakes me up without beating the drum, becomes deaf in one whole life.

109. I shall tell you the expiation by which the sin of not beating the drum is got rid of.

110. On the Dvādaśī day in the bright half of any month he shall 'sleep in the open' and then he becomes free from sin.

111. O Earth, he who performs expiation like this does not commit any offence and reaches my world.

112. He who eating a lot suffers indigestion and approaches me with eructations and without taking bath,

113. Becomes a dog for one life, a monkey for one life, a goat for one life, a jackal for one life,

114. A blind man for one life and then is born as a rat and is finally born in a big family as a pure and respected devotee free from faults.

115. I shall tell you about the expiation by which the devotee becomes free from sin.

116. For three days he shall live on fire, for three days on roots, for three days on rice cooked in milk, for three days on flour,

117. Three days on air, and shall 'sleep in the open' for three days.

118. At daybreak he shall clean his teeth and drink *pañca-gavya* for his purification.

119. He who performs expiation like this, does not become touched by sin and reaches my world.

120. What I have told you, O goddess, is for the (true) Brahmins. This is the greatest of all narrations.

121. It is righteousness, fame and sacred practice. It is the best of qualities and the moral of all morals.

122. He who reads this every day after rising up in the morning, liberates his manes ten generations before and ten generations after.

123. This is the healthiest of the healthy and the most auspicious of all that is auspicious. This is the gem of all gems that removes all sins.

124. The devotee who recites this with concentration of mind does not become defiled by sin even if he chances to commit an offence.

125. He who recites this after worshipping Sandhyā early in the morning, reaches my world.

126. This should not be read in the midst of the wicked or amidst incompetent disciples. This shall be imparted only to my devotees.

127. I have thus told you about the rules of expiation about which you asked me. What else do you wish to know?